DEMOCRATIC SERVICES

PLEASE RETURN

AFTER USE

GW00703130

Knowles on
Local Authority Meetings

Knowles on
Local Authority Meetings

A Manual of Law and Practice

Fifth Edition

Stephen P. Taylor

*Director of Law and Democratic Services and
Monitoring Officer, Swindon Borough Council*

and

Deborah Upton

*Assistant Director of Corporate Services and
Monitoring Officer, Medway Council*

ICSA
PUBLISHING

This fifth edition published by

ICSA Information & Training Ltd
16 Park Crescent
London W1B 1AH

First Published as *The Law and Practice of Local Authority Meetings*
1978
First (revised) edition 1987
Second edition 1993
Third edition 1999
Fourth edition 2005
Fifth edition 2008   .

© ICSA Publishing Ltd, 1978, 1987, 1993, 1999, 2005
© ICSA Information & Training Ltd, 2008

Typeset by Hands Fotoset, Woodthorpe, Nottingham and printed in
Great Britain by TJ International Ltd, Padstow, Cornwall

British Library Cataloguing in Publication Data
A catalogue record for this book is available from the British Library

ISBN13: 978 1 86072 382 7

Contents

Contents

Contents

Preface

This fifth edition of Knowles' well-established work on local authority meetings continues to acknowledge the invaluable contribution made by Raymond Knowles to this area of local authority work. Local authority law and practice have, of course, undergone many changes since this book was first published and the pace of change continues unabated. The new edition has been updated to include coverage of:

- The revised Model Code of Conduct for members
- The impact of recent case law such as *Livingstone* v. *Adjudication Panel for England*
- Interpretation and guidance on bias and predetermination
- Changes to access to information under the Freedom of Information legislation.
- Changes introduced by the Local Government and Public Involvement in Health Act 2007 (LGPIH).

We would like to express our thanks to Isabel Gillies of ICSA Publishing for her forbearance with our constantly slipping dates caused by yet further impending changes in the law which we wished to incorporate in this edition. Indeed, as this book was going to press, the Local Government and Public Involvement in Health Act 2007 was given Royal Assent on 30th October 2007. The detailed implementation of the new Act will be worked out over the coming months and in the light of the consequential Regulations. We also gratefully acknowledge help from colleagues in local government in general and would particularly like to thank Andrew Ferguson and Ian Willcox of Swindon Borough Council with whom we have developed our views on how the new legislative requirements should be interpreted and implemented. We alone, however, accept responsibility for the text and for any errors or omissions which may have escaped our notice.

The use of the words 'he' and 'she' have been used throughout the book and are, of course, interchangeable.

Stephen P. Taylor
Deborah Upton
October 2007

Publisher's acknowledgement

The publisher is grateful to the founding author of this work, Raymond Knowles, whose outstanding authorship of the first three editions has made this title the leading text in the area of local authority meetings. ICSA Information & Training would also like to thank Ben Davies for reviewing and commenting on the fourth edition of this work.

Table of Cases

Table of Cases

Table of Cases

Table of Cases

Table of Cases

Table of Cases

Table of Statutes

References are to paragraph numbers (and, where appropriate, to appendices at the back of the book) and not to pages.

Table of Statutes

Table of Statutes

Table of Statutes

Table of Statutory Instruments

References are to paragraph numbers (and, where appropriate, to appendices at the end of the book), and not to pages.

Table of Statutory Instruments

Table of Abbreviations

All Acts of Parliament occurring more than once within the text have been abbreviated subsequently: this list gives those Acts and their abbreviations. Within the text the abbreviations are followed by the Act's appropriate year/date.

Education Act	EA
Education (No. 2) Act	E(2)A
Education Reform Act	ERA
Health and Safety at Work, etc. Act	H&SWA
Highways Act	HA
Interpretation Act	IA
Local Authorities (Admission of the Press to Meetings) Act	LA(APM)A
Local Authority Social Services Act	LASSA
Local Government (Access to Information) Act	LG(AI)A
Local Government (Miscellaneous Provisions) Act	LG(MP)A
Local Government Act	LGA
Local Government and Housing Act	LG&HA
Local Government and Public Involvement in Health Act 2007	LGPIH
Local Government Finance Act	LGFA
London Government Act	LoGA
Municipal Corporations Act	MCA
Police Act	PA
Public Bodies (Admission to Meetings) Act	PB(AM)A
Representation of the People Act	RPA
Town and Country Planning Act	T&CPA
Tribunals and Inquiries Act	T&IA

Part 1
General Principles

Chapter 1
Current framework

Local government structure

1.1 This work is concerned with the law and practice relating to meetings of local authorities and associated bodies in England and of their committees and sub-committees. Though the local government system is broadly similar in Wales as to the principles which apply, there is increasing divergence from that of England in the detail as a result of the changes introduced by the Local Government (Wales) Act 1994 and the devolution of powers to the National Assembly for Wales by the Government of Wales Act 1998. The situation is somewhat different again in Scotland and substantially so in Northern Ireland, although the meetings procedures that the local authorities there follow have much in common with the practice of local authorities in England. For example, the Local Government (Scotland) Act 1973 and the Local Government (Northern Ireland) Act 1972 contain many rules similar to those in the Local Government Act 1972 (LGA 1972), which – supplemented now by Part I of the Local Government and Housing Act 1989 (LG&HA 1989) – remains the principal Act prescribing the relevant statutory provisions governing the conduct of local authority business in England. Readers in the United Kingdom outside England should, therefore, have little difficulty in applying what is said in these pages to their own perception of local differences of statutory and common law.

Administrative areas

1.2 In England – exclusive of Greater London (see 1.3) and the Isles of Scilly where there is a special council constituted by the Secretary of State[1] – the country is divided into counties and districts. The counties are either metropolitan or shire counties and within the former there are metropolitan districts and elsewhere non-metropolitan districts. Some districts are known as boroughs or cities, mostly for historical reasons. Within the shire counties particularly there are rural parishes. Wales was previously divided into counties and districts, again under the LGA 1972, but local government in the principality was completely restructured by the Local Government (Wales) Act 1994, which created 11 new counties, and 11 county boroughs each of which comprises one or more communities.

1.3 Greater London comprises the areas of the London boroughs, the City of London, and (of no real significance for local government purposes) the Inner and Middle Temples. The 12 London boroughs whose areas, together with the City, formed the former administrative county of London, are known as inner London boroughs; the remaining area of Greater London comprises outer London boroughs. A strategic Greater London Authority, comprising a directly elected executive mayor and members of the London Assembly, was created by the Greater London Authority Act 1999, resulting in a two-tier structure for the capital.

1.4 The structure of local government is often said to be predominantly two-tier because, in the greater part of the country, county and district councils operate over the same area. In the shire counties, however, it is really three-tier because of the existence of parishes and communities. In parts of England, the structure is unitary as in Wales, i.e. one local authority alone is responsible for all local government within its area. In England these are the metropolitan authorities (constituted by the LGA 1972) and the new unitary authorities (constituted under the LGA 1992) that, although district councils, are for some purposes classified as counties.

Local authorities

1.5 Local government legislation (in the LGA 1972 particularly) uses the term principal council for the local authorities in Greater London, the metropolitan areas, and the counties and boroughs and districts. Where, throughout this work, the term local authority is used it means, as in legislation, a principal council or a local council, i.e. of a parish or community, or one of the joint authorities established by the Local Government Act 1985 as a consequence of the abolition of the former Greater London Council and the former metropolitan county councils. For every parish there *must* be, and for every community there *may* be, a meeting of electors, i.e. a parish meeting or a community meeting, for purposes of discussing local affairs.[2] These meetings have power to exercise certain limited functions but are not regarded as local authorities.

1.6 The term relevant authority, introduced in the LG&HA 1989 and used in this work to identify authorities referred to in that Act, includes principal councils and some others, e.g. waste disposal authorities and a joint or special planning board constituted for a National Park.[3]

1.7 Local authorities are creatures of statute, i.e. statutory corporations (though many municipal boroughs were originally incorporated by Royal Charter), whose constitution, obligatory duties and discretionary powers are derived directly from Parliament. They are the only democratically elected bodies outside the House of Commons and exist in their own right, not as agents of central government, although, increasingly over recent years, the government has initiated and obtained statutory powers restricting the freedom of action that the authorities previously enjoyed. Local authorities are, therefore, subject to the doctrine of ultra vires (see 1.46): they can only do those things that they are compelled or permitted to do by law.[4] Most of the services that local government provides are prescribed by particular Acts of Parliament. For example, county councils and metropolitan district councils and the London boroughs have responsibilities for major functions such as education, the personal social services and for regulatory tasks in, for example, planning and consumer protection, while the district councils discharge the major services of housing, environmental health and refuse collection, among a variety of others, and make bylaws for good rule and government. The new unitary authorities, as already indicated (see 1.4), have sole or joint responsibility for all functions within their area. Shire county councils and the unitaries have close links with the police and fire services. They also have responsibilities for passenger transport and waste regulation and disposal; in metropolitan areas these services are in general provided by joint authorities. Parish and community councils have responsibility for a wide range of minor but important local services. In Wales, the distribution of services is somewhat similar. The services provided by local government change from time to time. There is, as it were, no prescribed constitutional dividing line between the functions of central government and those of local authorities: for example, responsibility for further and higher education has been transferred to independent corporations and much of that for housing is being transferred to housing associations. All local authorities act as a focus for local community action and aspirations: in other words they have a leadership and co-ordination role that goes way beyond service delivery.

Local authority meetings

Definition of 'meeting'

1.8 The definition of a meeting as 'a gathering or assembly of two or more persons for a lawful common purpose' (see *Sharp* v. *Dawes* (1876)) needs no modification in its application to local government, for one person cannot in any sense constitute a meeting.[5] A meeting implies literally the coming together of two or more people; and in the context of local government this is because there are certain legal formalities to be observed that require more than one person to be present in order that there shall be a valid and lawful decision. These legal formalities include the need for a meeting to be properly convened and constituted: see 1.33.

1.9 Not only must there be at least two people present to constitute a meeting, but there ought also to be someone presiding to regulate deliberations. These requirements (that there must be at least two persons and ordinarily someone in control) have been said to be 'axiomatic and universal'.[6] In *R.* v. *Swansea Borough Council ex parte Elitestone Ltd* (1993) it was confirmed that for a local authority meeting two members are enough. If a meeting of two is to proceed without a chairman (see 11.14) then the wish of the meeting to continue in this way should be clearly recorded – as, of course, with a larger number of members also (see 11.14). However, difficulties could arise where two members alone constitute a meeting and neither is appointed or specifically acts as chairman, because a decision could never be reached on an issue where there was an irreconcilable difference of view. Thus it may be thought that, for local government purposes, no meeting should consist of fewer than three persons: because if there are two only, the one who is chairman – and there will ordinarily be a chairman – could decide every issue as he wished by exercise of his statutory power to give a casting vote (see 7.122) in the event of an equality of votes.

1.10 The person entrusted with authority to regulate the conduct of a meeting is usually styled the chairman or chair (see 7.12) and in the case of council meetings the chairman is the chairman of the council (or the mayor in the case of those councils that have been permitted to retain their former status or assume that of one of their predecessors; or, in the case of the London boroughs, never lost that status). The ancient title of mayor, enjoyed by the chairmen of borough councils, was preserved along with some other offices of dignity by the LGA 1972, ss. 245, 246. This includes the distinctive title of Lord Mayor conferred on holders of the mayoralty in certain boroughs. The 1972 Act has been amended to provide that in those local authorities where there is an elected mayor (see 1.62), the titles of Mayor and Deputy Mayor can only be used by the elected mayor and his or her chosen deputy mayor. The statutory Guidance issued following the 2000 Act makes clear, however, that in a very few cases such as where the title of Mayor derives from a Royal Charter, this title would continue whichever form of executive were chosen. In those instances, it is for the local authority to ensure that the two mayoral titles are distinguished from each other in some way. The chairman of the council in a borough where there is an elected mayor is styled according to local preference: sometimes simply called the Chair (Hartlepool) or Civic Mayor (Doncaster); or, less obviously, called the Speaker (London Borough of Hackney) or the Civic Ambassador (London Borough of Newham).

Local authority meetings are private meetings

1.11 Generally meetings may be either public or private. A public meeting has been defined[7] as:

> 'Any meeting bona fide and lawfully held for a lawful purpose and for the furtherance or discussion of any matter of public concern, whether admission thereto be general or restricted.'

This is a wide definition. It includes any meeting in a public place[8] and any meeting on private premises[9] that the public or a section of the public are permitted to attend, whether on payment or otherwise. It might seem that local authority meetings could thus be held to be public meetings, but the public's right of admission is conferred by statute:[10] it is not a common law right: see 3.1. The fact that local authorities permitted the public to attend council and sometimes committee meetings before the law conferred upon the public a right of access did not affect the position: *Tenby Corporation* v. *Mason* (1908), where the House of Lords held that the public had no right at common law to attend a council meeting: see 3.1.

Purpose of meeting

1.12 It is always important that the purposes of a meeting should be defined at the time it is convened. We are not concerned, of course, with assemblies for social intercourse or solely for civic ceremonial (although some council meetings may embrace both incidentally), but primarily with meetings for the transaction of local authority business. In the case of all formal meetings there will be an agenda or at least a clear understanding of the terms of reference of the committee or sub-committee, working party, panel or whatever it may be.

1.13 There are other meetings, less formally structured, where the objective may be less well defined, e.g. where local authority representatives receive a deputation of electors or seek to negotiate with a trade union on some matter in dispute. In those cases the authority's representatives must understand precisely what is to be their role: they must know the parameters within which discussion is to range, and obviously the extent of their power, if any, to bind the council. Unless these things are understood beforehand (with perhaps also a plan of tactics to be adopted depending upon the trend in discussion), the meeting may well be regarded as unsatisfactory on one or other or both sides, or the local authority representatives may find they have unintentionally committed their council to an unwanted course of action.

1.14 Where one local authority joins with another or others and/or with other agencies for the discussion or co-ordination of some matter in which each is interested, the need for a clear definition of the purpose of the meeting (or, if of continuing concern, the joint committee or other body set up) is particularly important. Such a meeting or committee or body has invariably a diffuse set of objectives that are not necessarily related to one another and not immediately identifiable in terms of responsibility to one set of decision-makers.[11]

1.15 Although in most cases the objective of a meeting will be to reach decisions, this need not always be so. For example, a number of councils are experimenting with holding occasional meetings for discussion only to give members of the council the opportunity of debating, without the pressure of the need for decision-taking, such issues as crime and disorder or the local Community Strategy.

Regulation by law

1.16 The summoning, constitution and conduct of meetings (whether related to local government or not) is governed partly by statute and partly by common law. The principal statute as regards local authority meetings is the LGA 1972, complemented now by the LG&HA 1989, Part I, but there are other enactments that regulate the constitution of particular committees of local authorities. In total, however, the statutory provisions (although extremely detailed in certain respects) affect a comparatively small part of the relevant law. The standing orders (see Chapter 2) that local authorities are required or empowered to make seek to regulate matters that would otherwise fall to be dealt with in accordance with the practices and conventions recognised at common law.

Types of meeting

1.17 There are two broad categories of meetings within the sphere of local government. These can most easily, but not altogether satisfactorily, be termed formal and informal. A formal meeting is one convened in the manner prescribed by law to enable councillors (sometimes with co-opted members) to transact local authority business with the object of reaching decisions – or formulating recommendations as a basis for decisions – that are intended to commit the authority as a whole. An informal meeting is any other meeting for the consideration or transaction of business, which may or may not comprise councillors or at least comprise them exclusively. It may be a meeting convened solely for purposes of exploratory discussions between councillors and officers or between councillors and representatives of other bodies, and either is not intended to be clothed with legal formality or by its nature cannot bind the local authority.

1.18 The main general principles governing formal meetings (of the full council particularly) are outlined in the paragraphs immediately following. Formal meetings of committees, and of gatherings akin to committees, are dealt with in Chapter 9 where there is a discussion of informal meetings of the kind increasingly common in recent years.

Formal meetings

1.19 Formal meetings are those of (a) principal councils, i.e. the councils of counties and districts in England and Wales and the London boroughs; (b) the authorities created under the LGA 1985 and the LGA 1992, i.e. the statutory joint authorities, and the residuary bodies; (c) parish councils and parish meetings in England and community councils and community meetings in Wales; and (d) their committees and subcommittees. Each must be convened and constituted in the manner prescribed by statute and/or standing orders.[12] There are other meetings, not of local authorities as such, of what might be termed constituent or associated bodies, which are formal in the sense that they are required to be held by statute.

Special meetings

1.20 There are, in effect, three types of special council meeting: the annual meeting; an extraordinary meeting; and a meeting convened for a specific purpose. Each is regulated by statute in varying respects, particularly as regards the convening of meetings (see Chapter 6).

1.21 The obligation on local authorities to hold an annual meeting in every year is referred to below: see 1.23. The law also requires that certain business shall be transacted at an annual meeting, i.e. the election of a chairman or mayor particularly and the election of sheriff in those cities and boroughs that have claimed that privilege.

1.22 An extraordinary meeting of the full council is one convened otherwise than by direction of the council as a whole, i.e. either by the chairman on his own initiative or upon the requisition of a prescribed number of council members:[13] see 6.4. There is provision also for the calling of meetings of a parish or community council in similar circumstances but the term extraordinary meeting is not used. Although there was earlier provision in the LGA 1933 for such meetings the term 'extraordinary meeting' is used in the LGA 1972 for the first time to refer to meetings convened in these circumstances. An example of a council meeting convened for a specific purpose is one called to consider a proposal of a local authority to promote or oppose any local or personal Bill in Parliament.[14] Meetings of this character are dealt with in Chapter 7 (see 7.144–7.151).

1.23 Principal and parish councils are required to hold in every year an annual meeting of the full council;[15] and a parish meeting must assemble annually.[16] But a community meeting is under no such obligation. The annual meeting of a principal and a parish council must be held within the period prescribed by statute, varying according to whether it is election year.

1.24 Except in the year of election of councillors, a principal council may hold its annual meeting on such day in March, April or May as it thinks fit[17] and a parish council on such day in May as it may determine.[18] In the election year, the annual meeting of a principal council must be held 'on the eighth day after the retirement of councillors or such other day within 21 days immediately following the day of retirement as the council may fix': in the case of parish councils, on or within 14 days after the day on which the councillors elected at that election take office. The parish meeting must assemble 'on some day between March 1 and June 1 both inclusive'.

1.25 Each principal, parish and community council and parish meeting may hold in addition to the annual meeting (or any other meeting it is required to hold), such other, i.e. ordinary meetings of the full council, as it may determine.[19] It is difficult to understand why it was thought necessary to provide legislative power to do something that local authorities could surely do in any case. However, in the case of a parish council there is an obligation to hold not fewer than three meetings in addition to the annual meeting,[20] with discretion to determine the hour and days;[21] and in the case of a parish that does not have a separate parish council the parish meeting must (subject to any provision made by a grouping order) assemble at least: twice a year.[22] Some authorities fix the dates by standing orders; others determine them each year at the annual meeting.

Time of meeting

1.26 The time of meeting is not specifically prescribed by statute. In the case of principal councils the 'annual meeting . . . shall be held at such hour as the council may fix, or if no hour is so fixed at 12 noon',[23] which presumably means that, in the unlikely event of a principal council convening an annual meeting without speci-fying the time of the meeting, it would necessarily be at 12 noon but the notice might surely still be held to 'be void for uncertainty. A parish and a community council's annual meeting may, somewhat similarly, be held "at such hour as the council may fix or, if no hour is so fixed, six o'clock in the evening".[24] The proceedings at a parish or community meeting must not commence earlier than 6.00 pm.'[25]

Meetings on Sunday

1.27 There appears to be no reason in law why a local authority should not meet on a Sunday, although there may be practical and other reasons why the practice should be regarded as undesirable.[26]

Frequency of meeting

1.28 Provided a local authority holds its statutory annual meeting and observes the requirements about other meetings (see 1.25), it can decide as it wishes upon the frequency of meetings,[27] i.e. it does not necessarily need to space out equally the ordinary meetings – though it may wish to do so in order to arrange a convenient and regular committee cycle: see 10.1. The frequency of meetings will obviously be determined by the volume and incidence of business. Nicholas Ridley, when Secretary of State for the Environment, a staunch proponent of the concept of the enabling authority, envisaged a situation where a local authority might meet once a year only to let contracts for service delivery. District councils in the main meet monthly while some county councils meet quarterly, but all authorities usually dispense with meetings of the full council for the holiday period in the summer when, the expression goes, the council is 'in recess'. It is common practice for the dates of ordinary meetings to be fixed in advance at the annual meeting of a council.

Place of meeting

1.29 Meetings of a principal council must be held 'at such place, either within or without their areas as they may direct';[28] so, too, may meetings of a parish council and a community council except that the meetings must 'not be held in premises licensed for the sale of intoxicating liquor unless no other suitable room is available either free of charge or at a reasonable cost'.[29] This discriminatory prohibition against the holding of a meeting on licensed premises applies also to parish meetings, although the statute is otherwise silent as to place.

1.30 Where a local authority decides to hold a meeting outside its administrative area, it must take account of the accessibility of the venue for those entitled to be present. Thus one authority, anxious to foster its ties with a twin city across the Channel by holding a meeting there, prudently arranged for the proceedings – which were mostly of a ceremonial nature anyhow – to be confirmed at the authority's next ordinary meeting within its area in the UK.

1.31 These statutory provisions relating to place of meeting apply also to committee meetings.[30] Thus any local authority committee meeting may be held anywhere, either within or outside its area, as the council or committee may decide, except in the case of committees of a parish council or parish meeting or of a community council, which must not be held on licensed premises unless no other accommodation is available free or at reasonable cost.

1.32 Notwithstanding the above, there is an assumption throughout this work that local authority meetings will take place ordinarily at the authority's offices. Sometimes, however, particularly in the case of committees or subcommittees, a meeting will be arranged at a defined location on the highway for purposes. For instance, there maybe an inspection of a site that is the subject of a planning application. The reasons for meetings of this character are numerous. In all such instances, care must be taken to avoid obstruction of the highway, because that would constitute an offence. Highways exist for purposes of passage and anyone using a highway for some other purpose is in theory a trespasser; but so long as the meeting is not likely to interfere with the right of passage or lead to a breach of the peace, then there is no reason why a local authority should feel inhibited from arranging such a meeting. It may be thought prudent, of course, depending on circumstances, to advise people living in the vicinity of the meeting, so as to avoid unnecessary concern or speculation when they see a gathering outside their property.

1. Current framework

Requisites of a valid meeting

1.33 In order to constitute a valid meeting there must be three essentials:

- at least two persons present: but see 1.8;
- someone in the chair or a decision taken to proceed without a chairman: see 1.10; and
- a lawful common purpose: see 1.11.

In addition, in relation to local authority meetings, there must be compliance with statutory requirements and standing orders, as to the time or period within which a meeting must be held (see 1.26) and, in certain cases, as to the place of meeting. Each meeting must also be:

- properly convened, i.e. there must be public notice of the meeting and a summons sent to every person entitled to attend (see 6.2); and
- properly constituted, i.e. (i) the proper persons must be present with the appropriate person in the chair (see 7.27), and (ii) the requisite quorum of members must be present: (see 7.35).

Any irregularity in the convening, constitution or conduct of a meeting may, according to its nature (i.e. whether a council or committee or subcommittee meeting), invalidate all or part of the proceedings. But want of service of the summons will not ordinarily affect the meeting's validity and there is a presumption in law (i.e. until the contrary is proved) that, once the minutes have been drawn up and signed, the meeting was properly convened and held and the members present duly qualified; and even if there was a vacancy among the members or a defect in the election or qualification of any member, the proceedings are not thereby invalidated. This appears to be the effect of s.82 of the LGA 1972, which provides that 'the acts and proceedings of any person elected to an office under this Act and acting in that office shall, notwithstanding his disqualification or want of qualification, be as valid and effectual as if he had been qualified': see 4.2.

1.34 It follows from the previous paragraph that if a number of councillors choose to meet of their own accord – as a political group or otherwise – their informal gathering together does not constitute a meeting for the lawful transaction of business. Most local authorities are prepared to allow the use of council accommodation for informal meetings of such a character, but there have been circumstances where permission has been refused. In 1981 some 11 Labour councillors in the London Borough of Southwark were initially denied facilities by the controlling Labour group to meet in council-owned premises because the councillors had been expelled from membership of the Labour Party (after opposing the policy of the Labour caucus on the council), although the group subsequently relented. It is undoubtedly a matter for the local authority's discretion whether and when to allow the use of council-owned premises; and as (e.g. see 4.6, 9.4) a single councillor has few rights as an individual member, it may seem to follow that a number of them can claim no right by mere multiplication (although there might be some kind of right, extra-legal perhaps, in a number of councillors who wanted to meet for the purpose of framing a requisition for the calling of an extraordinary meeting of the council: see 6.4). Local authorities may think it prudent to agree a code of practice for the use of council accommodation for informal meeting purposes – governing, for example, the use for party group meetings and by individual councillors who wish to meet their constituents.

Decision-making

Determination of questions

1.35 As already indicated (see 1.15), most local authority meetings are held to reach a decision on an item or items of business: to decide a question, in the phraseology of statute.[31] This work is primarily concerned with procedural and associated matters, but it may be relevant to indicate briefly three stages in the process of decision-making: first an identification of the need for a decision; secondly, an examination of the various lawful courses of action that would lead to a solution of the need, as well as consideration and analysis of the costs and consequences; and finally, the choice of the most appropriate solution available. This process can be facilitated by careful preparation of the agenda at officer level beforehand: see 10.16. A rational or systematic approach to decision-making cannot always be pursued. There may be insufficient time to assemble and consider all the pros and cons, even if there could be perfect knowledge of all possibilities and their consequences. There is also the influence of political dogma. Much has been done, organisationally and otherwise, to improve the accountability and quality of decision-making in local government. In 1991, the then DoE issued a consultation paper on The Internal Management of Local Authorities in England to encourage debate on the issue. This debate culminated in the Local Government Act 2000 (LGA 2000), which required those local authorities with populations of 85,000 or over as at 30th June 1999 to adopt executive arrangements whereby the management of the authority is based on a separation of the executive, regulatory, scrutiny and representative roles of councillors. This Act also allowed the delegation of powers to individual members for the first time and has had a profound effect on the style and format of local authority meetings that is still being worked through. This issue is dealt with in more detail in 1.62.

Elements of a lawful decision

1.36 To be lawful a decision of a local authority, if taken by the full council or by a committee, must:

- comply with the cardinal principle of being reached by a majority of councillors present and voting at a properly constituted meeting: see 1.37;
- be one that the council is empowered or obliged to take, otherwise it is ultra vires: see 1.46;
- not offend against Wednesbury reasonableness: see 1.43; and, if taken by an officer under delegated power, it must comply with both (b) and (c) and, furthermore, come within the scope of that power (see 5.9).

12

1. Current framework

There are practical considerations, too. A decision must:

- if intended to secure action (as opposed, for example, to a resolution merely expressing the council's collective view on an issue), obviously be capable of execution or will be of no effect; and
- not purport to undo what has already been done irrevocably but it can rescind an earlier decision where this is feasible: see 1.50; and
- comply with the council's own internal processes for decision-making, and be in accordance with the council's own principles of decision-making, which are set out in the constitution of those councils operating executive arrangements (see 1.62).

A decision cannot ordinarily be impugned solely on account of the lack of qualification of a councillor,[32] though the individual member may be liable to penalty (e.g. if he votes whilst having a personal and prejudicial interest under the members' Code of Conduct). Ordinarily, too, a decision cannot be challenged because of the motive of a councillor or councillors who voted in favour of the proposition[33] or just because a councillor has not directed his mind in the meeting itself to the arguments for and against or to other relevant considerations: see *R. v. Waltham Forest London Borough Council ex parte Waltham Forest Ratepayers Association Group* (1987); see also 1.44. A decision may come within the ambit of maladministration: see 1.49.

Majority present and voting

1.37 There is a general principle governing by law the manner in which an authority shall reach a decision. This is that, save where other prescriptions apply[34] in particular circumstances:

> '... all questions coming or arising before a local authority shall be decided by a majority of the members of the authority present and voting thereon at a meeting of the authority.'[35]

1.38 This means that every decision that falls to be taken by a local authority (unless it is one that an officer or individual member, including an elected mayor, has been empowered to make) can lawfully be reached only by the full council at a properly constituted council meeting or by a committee or subcommittee acting under delegated powers, and then only upon the affirmative vote of a majority of the members present and actually voting. Thus an authority of, say, 100 members may properly be committed to a course of action at a council meeting at which no more than the prescribed quorum (see 7.35) is present (say 25 council members, which represents the quorum in the case of a principal council of that membership), of whom only three trouble to put up their hand in favour when a vote is taken and two vote against: or – a more extreme example – if one member votes in favour and no one else troubles to vote against.

General principles

1.39 Important consequences flow from this principle. It means that even where there has been extensive consultation with the public, including a local poll under s.116 of the Local Government Act 2003, or where a referendum has been held under the provisions of the LGA 2000 in relation to the operation of executive arrangements, the local authority in full council or by a committee or subcommittee (or through the agency of another local authority or a joint committee) alone can make a decision on a matter that falls to be discharged by the authority and that has not been delegated to an individual; and it must do it at a properly constituted meeting. It cannot make a decision by asking councillors by circular letter to signify through the post acceptance or rejection of a projected course of action. Nor can it do so by any informal gathering of its members: in, for example, a meeting of the majority group members of the council (see 1.34). Nor may any individual council member vote by proxy:[36] he must be present at a meeting if he wishes his vote to count. Nor at a council or committee or subcommittee meeting can an officer vote in the decision-making process; even though the council, committee or subcommittee may be discussing a matter on which it has empowered the officer to act, it is to be presumed from its discussing the matter at a meeting that the council, committee or subcommittee concerned has impliedly revoked, albeit temporarily, the act of delegation.[37] There must be a properly convened assembly of council members (in council or committee or subcommittee) so that a decision can be made in circumstances where the cut and thrust of debate and argument and counterargument can take place if members are so minded: the fact that most members may take no part in the proceedings or abstain from voting does not affect the position.

1.40 The questions to be decided are questions of every kind (except, as indicated already (see 1.37), those for which some special procedure and/or majority vote is required): the same principle applies whether the decision is concerned with major policy or administrative detail. The law does not make such distinctions but, of course, the local authority can do so by delegating to committees, subcommittees or officers, as it thinks appropriate, the power to make decisions on matters of lesser importance (see 9.80). Even before the law permitted such delegation, officers in practice operated either under extra-legal authority to act within certain defined administrative spheres or by presumption in law as agents of their authority.

Voting

1.41 Voting at every local authority meeting is ordinarily by show of hands or as otherwise prescribed in standing orders: see 7.103. This is expressly required by law in the case of parish and community councils unless standing orders otherwise provide, but no method of voting is laid down by statute in the case of principal councils (where in some cases an electronic system is used) or in the case of parish and community meetings. Every person presiding at any local authority meeting, whether of the full council, committee or subcommittee, may exercise a second or casting vote. The whole matter of voting is considered in detail in Chapter 7.

1.42 Ordinarily no account is taken by the law as to the motives of those who vote: but see 1.44. Very exceptionally, however, a decision might be set aside where it is proved that the councillors who voted in a majority for a resolution were motivated by a malicious desire to damage a third party and so committed the offence of misfeasance in public office: see the House of Lords case *Jones* v. *Swansea County Council* [1990]. Nor is there any obligation imposed by law to ensure that members only vote if present throughout a meeting and so have considered the arguments for and against a proposition. A member can come into the council chamber or committee room just as the chairman is calling for a show of hands and so cast a vote with little or no idea at all of the issue before the meeting. This is not dissimilar, of course, from what happens in the Commons.[38] Standing orders, however, often lay down that only those members present in the meeting when the proposition is put from the chair may vote. This only means present in the room and not necessarily seated, but can sometimes lead to an undignified rush after a lengthy debate. Putting the proposition means the moment when the chairman asks for those voting in favour of it. There is an important exception considered later (see 13.48): when a meeting is exercising a judicial or quasi-judicial role it would be improper for a member to cast a vote without having been present to hear the submissions beforehand.

The Wednesbury principle

1.43 There is another procedural consideration that a local authority must take into account in the course of arriving at a decision. If a decision is not to be challenged and declared of no effect on grounds of unreasonableness and therefore ultra vires (see 1.46), it must comply with what is known as the Wednesbury principle. This principle was enunciated in *Associated Provincial Picture Houses Ltd* v. *Wednesbury Corporation* [1948]. Lord Greene summarised it:

> '. . . the court is entitled to investigate the action of the local authority with a view to seeing whether it has taken into account matters which it ought not to take into account or, conversely, has refused to take into account or neglected to take into account matters which it ought to take into account. Once that question is answered in favour of the local authority, it may still be possible to say that the local authority, nevertheless, has come to a conclusion so unreasonable that no reasonable authority could ever have come to it. In such a case . . . the court can interfere. The power of the court to interfere in each case is not that of an appellate authority to override a decision of the local authority but is that of a judicial authority which is concerned, and concerned only, to see whether the local authority has contravened the law by acting in excess of the powers which Parliament has confided in it.'

The local authority's advisers clearly have a responsibility to ensure that, in reaching a decision, the council or a committee addresses its mind only to matters that it ought to take into account or does not refuse or neglect to take account of such matters and is not influenced by matters that are irrelevant. The minutes of proceedings at a meeting might usefully recite the considerations taken into account by the council, committee or subcommittee in reaching its decision, but see 12.34. The need to demonstrate that the right reasons have been taken into account in reaching decisions puts a premium on accurate and comprehensive report writing: see *R. v. Camden Borough Council ex parte Cran and Others* (1995) where McCullough J was critical of the way in which the comments of residents had been conveyed to members considering the designation of a controlled parking zone and the designation was quashed; and *Costas Georgiou* v. *Enfield London Borough and Others* (2004), where Richards J considered that the members of the planning committee were not given sufficient information to ensure the proper discharge of their functions in relation to the planning application and that the committee's decision was consequently flawed. See also: 12.32. In *R(on the application of Ware)* v. *Neath Port Talbot County Borough Council & National Grid* (2007), where erroneous advice was given by a monitoring officer to a councillor and that advice was acted upon so that the councillor did not participate in a planning decision of a local authority, the court held that any decision reached through the absence of that councillor was liable to be quashed on the grounds that it had been reached by having regard to an immaterial consideration.

1.44 In *R. v. Waltham Forest London Borough council ex parte Waltham Forest Ratepayers Action Group* (1987), the court had to consider the extent to which party-political considerations can lawfully be taken into account in decision-making. Members of the majority group on the council had discussed at a party meeting what policy should be pursued as to the setting of the rate at the forthcoming council meeting. The group agreed to support a rate increase of 62 per cent for the domestic rate and 56.6 per cent for the non-domestic rate. The group's standing orders required members of the group to refrain from voting in opposition to group decisions under penalty of the withdrawal of the party whip. A number of members who voted against this level of rate increase at the group meeting voted in favour at the council meeting at which the previously agreed amounts were passed by 31 votes to 26. A number of ratepayers sought judicial review on a variety of grounds but the Divisional Court rejected arguments to the effect (1) that the councillors had fettered their discretion by regarding themselves as bound by the terms of their election manifesto to undertake expenditure that rendered such a rate inevitable; (2) that the resolution was 'irrational' or Wednesbury unreasonable; (3) that there was no genuine or adequate consultation with representatives of commerce and industry; and (4) that six or seven councillors had voted contrary to their personal views. The Court of Appeal dismissed an appeal confined to issue (4). The court held that had the councillors in question voted for the resolution not because they were in favour of it but because their discretion had been fettered by the vote at the group meeting, then the councillors would have been in breach of their duty to make up their own minds as to what rate was appropriate. That, however, was not established on the facts. The councillors were entitled to take account of party loyalty and party policy as relevant considerations, provided they did not dominate so as to exclude other considerations. The court noted that the sanction was only withdrawal of the party whip: there was nothing to prevent a councillor who voted against the party line continuing as an independent member.

1. Current framework

Bias or predetermination

1.45 In making decisions, councillors must observe the distinction between having a closed mind to arguments that may be contrary to the rules of natural justice and therefore unlawful, and simply having a predisposition to taking a certain view. The test was set out in *Porter* v. *Magill* (2001) by Lord Hope who said that 'the question is whether the fair-minded and informed observor, having considered the facts, would conclude that there was a real possibility that the tribunal was biased'.

There have been a number of recent cases on apparent bias and closed minds. In *Mohammed Reza Ghadami* v. *Harlow District Council and Sapphire Retail Fund Ltd* (2004), a chairman of a district council planning committee had been close to developers and had conveyed to an objector the threat of compulsory purchase of his land. The court held that a fair-minded and informed observer would be led to conclude that there was a real possibility that the councillor had made up his mind in favour of the development and that he would approach the decision on the planning application with a closed mind and without impartial consideration of all the planning issues. Such apparent bias or predetermination vitiated the grant of planning permission. Also, in *Bovis Homes Ltd* v. *New Forest DC* (2002), the chairman's membership of a particular interest group would have caused a fair-minded observer to conclude that there was a real danger of bias on her part and that her presence at and participation in the relevant meeting vitiated the decision. In addition, committee members had attended the meeting with a draft resolution already prepared, which they adopted without amendment or qualification, thereby giving the impression that they had attended the meeting with closed minds. The committee's decision was quashed.

In the *Costas Georgiou* case already referred to (see 1.43), the developers' applications in their original and revised forms were considered by the local authority's conservation advisory group (CAG). The proposal was also the subject of public consultation, before the local authority's planning committee resolved to grant the consent and permission. Some members of the CAG were also members of the committee. An officers' report and revised report were prepared for the meetings of the planning committee at which decisions were due to be taken on the application. The planning committee approved the revised proposals by a majority of eight to seven. That decision was challenged on grounds that participation in the decisions by four members of the planning committee who were also members of the CAG, which supported the applications, gave rise to an appearance of bias, and that the planning committee had not been given sufficient information for the purposes of reaching the decisions and the alleged inadequacies in the information were relied on cumulatively as well as individually.

In considering the question of apparent bias, Richards J was of the view that it was necessary to look beyond pecuniary or personal interests and to consider in addition whether, from the point of view of the fair-minded and informed observer, there was a real possibility that the planning committee or some of its members were biased in the sense of approaching the decision with a closed mind and without impartial consideration of all relevant planning issues. Although the CAG's remit was to consider only the conservation implications of the applications, its conclusion was expressed in simple terms of support for the applications, without any qualification. Moreover, the support appeared to come from all those present, including three members who were also members of the planning committee. When it came to the meeting of the planning committee, nothing was said about the limited function of the CAG or about the need for those with dual membership to examine all the relevant planning issues before reaching the planning decisions. In the circumstances, the decisions were vitiated by the appearance of bias.

These cases highlight the importance of ensuring that the minutes of a meeting are clear as to the actual decision being made and record any other matters of importance. The cases also highlight the importance of members being clear as to the capacity in which they are taking part in any discussion. This is particularly crucial in 'dual-hatted' cases where they take part in various stages of the decision-making process as a member of more than one of the bodies involved. If this does occur, members must ensure that there is no conflict of interest or apparent bias.

This approach can be contrasted to that in *R. v. Hereford and Worcester County Council ex parte Wellington Parish Council* (1996) where members of the county council's gypsy liaison group who had put forward a particular location for a gypsy site voted for it in the planning committee when their application came up for consideration. Mr Justice Harrison had no doubts that such an action was proper and lawful provided that opportunity was given to all arguments to be put forward.

Members should be careful as to throwaway remarks that may be interpreted as bias or predetermination. *National Assembly for Wales* v. *Condron* (2006) concerned a planning committee's decision to allow a planning application, following a public inquiry and an inspector's report recommending granting permission. It was contended that the decision was vitiated by the appearance of bias arising out of a remark made by the chairman of the committee in a casual meeting with an objector the day before the committee meeting to the effect that he was 'going to go with the report of the inspector'. It was argued that this indicated that he had already made up his mind to accept the inspector's recommendation. The Court held that those words went no further than indicating a predisposition to follow the inspector's report and did not indicate a closed mind. It did not matter how the person to whom those words were addressed had interpreted them. The question was whether the fears expressed by the complainant were objectively justified. There was a clear distinction between a legitimate predisposition towards a particular outcome and an illegitimate predetermination of the outcome. The wider context of a chance meeting and a casual remark was also important in assessing the significance of the words used. Having regard to the terms of the inspector's report, the fact that the members of the committee had relevant training and were subject to a code of conduct, and the nature of the committee discussions, which were unusually prolonged, the Court decided that a fair-minded and informed observer would not conclude that there was a real possibility that the chairman was biased.

In the case of *R (on the application of Island Farm Development Ltd)* v. *Bridgend County Borough Council* (2006), Collins J follows a similar non-interventionist line, and confessed to some doubt as to the approach in the *Georgiou* case, when he decided that there was no apparent bias or pre-determination by the cabinet of a newly elected local authority in reaching a decision to discontinue negotiations for the sale of land, as there was no positive evidence to show that the local authority had approached the decision with a closed mind. Mr Justice Collins considered that local authority councillors were entitled to have regard to and apply policies that they believed in, particularly if those policies formed part of an election manifesto. In considering bias and predetermination, it is apparent that the courts are generally reluctant to interfere in what they consider the political process – R v. *Waltham Forest LBC ex parte Baxter* (1988) and R v. *Amber Valley DC ex parte Jackson* (1984) – instances where members have decided issues based on a political predisposition.

Decision must not be ultra vires

1.46 Although a decision may have been made in a procedurally correct manner it will be ultra vires if it is one that the local authority has no power to make. A detailed discussion of the doctrine of ultra vires would be beyond the scope of this work, but briefly it means that a local authority can lawfully do only those things that it is obliged to do by law or that it is permitted or assumed to be permitted by law to do. In the course of years, the courts have adopted a more liberal attitude to the assumed powers of a local authority – in tune, it might be said, with present-day recognition that local government is concerned with more than the mere carrying out of specific powers and duties.[39] In s.111 of LGA 1972, authorities now have power to do anything (whether or not involving expenditure, borrowing or lending money or the acquisition or disposal of any property or rights) calculated to facilitate or be conductive or incidental to the discharge of any of their functions. Local authorities and the Audit Commission have not agreed over the extent of powers conferred by s.111; and the dangers of relying on the section as a basis for exercising powers has been shown in cases involving the giving of guarantees to banks: see *Credit Suisse* v. *Allerdale Borough Council* (1994) and *Credit Suisse* v. *Waltham Forest London Borough Council* (1996). Furthermore, there is power in s.137 enabling any local authority, subject to certain restrictions (particularly the exclusion of expenditure that the authority is otherwise permitted or obliged to make), to incur expenditure not otherwise authorised. The purpose of s.137 was substantially recast by Part III of the LG&HA 1989, which makes statutory provision for economic development and discretionary expenditure by local authorities. There appears to be no need for an authority to pass a resolution specifically invoking s.137, although it may be prudent to do so. It is generally no bad thing for a local authority to indicate the legal power or duty under which it is proposing to take action. The LGA 2000 also introduced a power of well-being (see 1.85), which is intended to extend the powers of local authorities to promote or improve the economic, social and environmental well-being of their areas.[40]

'Blanket' resolutions on policy

1.47 One other matter relating to the effectiveness of a decision needs to be touched upon here. It is in order – indeed, there is much to commend the practice – for a local authority to pass a resolution setting out its general policy on any issue in order to ensure consistency in decision-making. But whatever rules or guidelines on policy the authority may establish in this way, the general principle (though there is an exception: see 1.48) is that a local authority must not so rigidly apply them that it precludes proper consideration of the merits or otherwise of individual questions that arise for decision within the general policy or guidelines. See, for example, among cases on fettering discretion in self-created rules of policy: *R. v. Port of London Authority ex parte Kynoch* (1919); and *R. v. Bexley London Borough Council ex parte Jones* (1994) compared with *R. v. Southwark London Borough Council ex parte Udu* (1995).

1.48 There is, however, at least one instance where the law permits the passing of a rigid blanket resolution. The Lotteries and Amusement Act 1976, sch.3, para.2, and the Gaming Act 1968, sch.9, para.3, concerned with the licensing of permits for commercial provision of amusements with prizes and permits for gaming machines, expressly allow policy resolutions by the local authority declaring, for example, that it will not issue or renew any permits in respect of premises of a specified class. It is evident, however, that the court will interpret the statutory rules strictly: see *R. v. Herrod ex parte Leeds City District Council* [1976] and *Walker v. Leeds City Council* (1976).

Maladministration

1.49 A further factor to be mentioned in relation to decision-making is the possibility of a local authority being declared guilty of maladministration by a local government ombudsman. The term ombudsman, not used in the statute, comes from the Swedish and means people's defender. Under the LGA 1974, Part III as amended,[41] it is open to an aggrieved individual to take a complaint of maladministration, direct or through a councillor, against a local authority (but not a parish or community council or a parish or community meeting), a police authority, or one of the authority's committees, to a local commissioner of either the Commission for Local Administration in England or the Commission for Local Administration in Wales, as the case may be. The Act does not define maladministration (it is for the ombudsman to decide whether maladministration has occurred) but it refers, for example, to the way in which an authority's decision has been made.[42] It covers administrative action or inaction based on or influenced by improper considerations or conduct (e.g. arbitrariness, malice or bias, including unfair discrimination), neglect, unjustified delay, incompetence, failure to observe relevant rules or procedures, failure to take relevant considerations into account, failure to establish or review procedures when there is a duty or obligation to do so, and the use of faulty systems. There are certain matters expressly excluded from the ombudsman's jurisdiction and he has no power to compel a local authority to redress or compensate anyone whose interests have been prejudiced through maladministration; but clearly opprobrium attaches to any authority that does not at least ensure that steps are taken to avoid in future the reason for maladministration.

Variation of decisions

1.50 Decisions once made may, so far as practicable and lawful, be subsequently varied or rescinded although standing orders ordinarily seek to limit the frequency of change in this respect: see 2.13. Clearly it would be impracticable for an authority, to purport to rescind a resolution upon which action has been taken that could not be undone; and unlawful to purport to rescind a resolution so as to disadvantage a third party who has properly relied on the decision unless, of course, the law permits the revocation or amendment of the decision when compensation may be payable. As to the position regarding committee and subcommittee decisions: see 11.38 et seq.

When does a resolution become effective?

1.51 In most instances the decision of a local authority takes effect immediately the resolution is properly passed unless there is provision in the council's constitution that a certain number of days must elapse before a decision can be acted upon to allow it to be 'called in' or referred back to the decision-maker either by a specified number of members, or by an overview and scrutiny committee, depending upon the precise arrangements adopted by the particular local authority concerned. In certain circumstances, however, a decision cannot be acted upon until specific formalities have been observed; bylaws made by an authority are of no validity until confirmed by the confirming body;[43] a decision to sell land is ineffective until the formal deed has been executed; and in some cases a decision does not take effect until formal notification has been served upon those affected by it, e.g. a decision to dismiss an employee, or a decision granting planning permission: see 1.52.

1.52 There have been several cases on whether resolution or notification amounts to a grant of planning permission: see *Slough Estates* v. *Slough Borough Council* (1969). In *R.* v. *West Oxfordshire District Council ex parte C. H. Pearce Homes Ltd* [1986] however, the issue was clearly decided, Woolf J said:

> 'Suffice it to say that even in the absence of authority I would, from my examination of the [planning] code, find a clear indication that it is the notification which amounts to the grant, and that where the notification is proceeded by a resolution of the authority that resolution should be regarded as a resolution that planning permission should be granted and that the resolution is intended to be implemented by the notification which amounts to the grant. Accordingly, until there has been notification, an applicant for planning permission has not received permission.'

This distinction between the resolution and the administrative act that gives the resolution full effect is important for several reasons. The local authority can change its mind after the resolution and before formal notification to revoke its decision. In *R.* v. *Yeovil Borough Council ex parte Trustees of Elim Pentecostal Church* (1972) there was a change of heart by the planning authority, which had previously resolved to grant planning permission, and the applicant's application for an order of mandamus requiring the council to issue planning permission was refused. Thus, of course, compensation for any revocation of planning permission cannot arise until after formal notification of the decision.

General principles

1.53 While it is important that, as a general rule, where a decision is to take effect on a certain future date, the resolution should specifically include that date, the resolution may not necessarily be defective if it does not, provided that the local authority's intention is clear, e.g. in the minutes as distinct from the resolution itself. In *Sheffield City Council* v. *Graingers Wines Ltd* (1977), it was held that there had been sufficient compliance with statute even though a resolution under s.17 of the General Rate Act 1967 (relating to the rating of unoccupied property) did not in its terms state when the resolution was to take effect and despite provision in s.17(2), as amended by the LGA 1972, s.15(1), that:

> 'the day to be specified in a resolution under subs. (1) of this section shall be ... the first day of a rate period for that area beginning after the date on which the resolution is passed.'

The Court of Appeal considered this was a serious omission but, while the trial judge held that it was fatal, the Court of Appeal took the view that, in the circumstances of the case, it was not: neither justice nor common sense required the court to isolate the resolution from its context to 'make that violent extraction of the kernel from the nut in which it shelters'.

Continuing validity of resolution

1.54 As a general rule there is no need for a local authority to pass a new resolution to replace one passed under legislation that, though repealed, is re-enacted to similar effect. For example, a resolution to apply the provisions of s.19 of the Local Government (Miscellaneous Provisions) Act 1982 (which concerned the registration of food hawkers and premises) is of continuing effect by virtue of the Interpretation Act 1978, ss.16 and 17, despite the repeal of s.19 of the 1982 Act and its re-enactment in Pt IV of the Food Act 1984.

1.55 The IA 1978 provides in s.16 that where an Act repeals an enactment the repeal does not, unless the contrary intention appears, affect the previous operation of the enactment repealed or anything done thereunder; and s.17 provides that where an Act is repealed, with or without modification, then unless the contrary intention appears, any reference in any other enactment to the Act repealed is to be constructed as a reference to the re-enacted provisions.

Inaccurate notification of a decision

1.56 What if an officer of the local authority misinterprets the terms of a decision to a third party or provides an inaccurate notification of the decision? Is the authority bound by its decision as minuted or by the officer's notification of its terms? A discussion of the concept of estoppel is outside the scope of this book but, so far as planning is concerned, this view of Michael Albery QC[44] is of interest:

'It is submitted . . . that where planning permission is granted or refused by a corporate body, the grant or refusal is constituted by the appropriate resolution of that body or of its delegated committee. On the other hand, the applicant is entitled to assume that notice of such decision received from the officer of such body entrusted with the conduct of such matters correctly represents the decision. He is not bound to call for a minute of the resolution in order to check such accuracy. If the applicant acts, as will usually happen, to his detriment on the faith of such notice, and perhaps even if he does not, the planning authority will be estopped from denying the accuracy of such notice. This estoppel will ensure for the benefit of the applicant's successors in title, in that for conveyancing purposes the notice can be treated as conveying the terms of the permission. But an applicant who has reason to suspect that the notice is less favourable to him than the resolution of which it purports to give notice is entitled to obtain copies of and to rely on the resolution itself, but not of course the application or surrounding correspondence unless these are incorporated into the resolution by reference.'

Conduct of local authority business

Traditional dispatch of council business

1.57 For many years, the traditional way in which local authorities conducted their business was through 'the appropriate channels', which meant that:

'Each matter – often irrespective of character or importance – that arises for consideration from an external source (a complaint from an individual if it cannot be dealt with at officer level or a petition from a group of aggrieved electors, representations from a local pressure group, the circulars and directions and guidance that issue forth from government departments) is ordinarily routed by way of a departmental head to the appropriate committee for consideration and subsequent report to the council sitting in full assembly and then back to the departmental head for any necessary executive action. So, too, projects which originate internally (proposals, for example, formulated by departmental heads of their own initiative or, increasingly, projects formulated by the political group which controls the local authority): these follow through the same channels.'[45]

This basic procedure, still discernible in almost every authority, has become modified over the years. There has been less propensity to 'put things to committee', individual officers and members have been entrusted with delegated powers, committee procedures have been streamlined and, more recently because of the impact of party politics, members concentrate their attention on policy issues. Increasingly local authorities have sought to improve the quality of their decision-making processes and the new executive structures are directed towards that end. These are described in more detail later on in this book: see 1.62.

Party organisation

1.58 The political organisation and greater political intensity of local government in recent years have had a profound effect on the conduct of local authority business – something that the law has recognised: particularly in the LG&HA 1989, which makes provision for political balance in the membership of a local authority to be translated into committees and subcommittees: see 9.53 et seq. There have been other changes: councillors are more assertive now than formerly, though this may only be true to a limited extent, but policy issues arise for consideration more often nowadays from the initiative of councillors through the majority party group than from officers. After a local election, members of the political party that has secured the largest number of seats will 'form an administration' to run the authority politically, decide who to appoint as committee chairs, and significantly discuss and often virtually make the more important decisions in group meetings. Control of the authority means that the group decisions can be carried through the formal meetings procedure and translated lawfully into effective action. Members of minority parties will also hold group meetings and, either in concert or separately, will provide a focus of 'opposition' in the council chamber if not in committees. Where an election has resulted in a hung – or balanced – council, then the parties may seek to arrive at some accommodation between themselves. One party group will form an administration with the support, tacit or otherwise, of another; committee chairs may in these circumstances be reduced to merely presiding over committee meetings, with a political spokesman who in practice receives the pre-committee briefing that in other circumstances would be provided by officers to committee chairs. There is no one pattern of political organisation common to all hung councils. Sometimes the committee chairs rotate on a meeting-by-meeting basis between the groups. In other authorities a chair is appointed each time the committee meets. Effective member control is sometimes operated through a representative panel of group spokesmen who meet informally before meetings for a pre-committee briefing. Devices such as these prove helpful to officers in seeking inter-party views and act as a sounding board for the chief executive's management team. As to party group meetings: see 5.34.

Official reports

1.59 The ways in which local authorities conduct their business, i.e. through the traditional processes of democratic machinery, have been the subject of several important inquiries over the past quarter-century or so. The 1960s saw publication of the twin reports of Maud on The Management of Local Government and Mallaby on

1. Current framework

Staffing of Local Government. Later, prior to the reorganisation of local government outside Greater London in the 1970s, there was the Bains report on *The New Local Authorities: Management and Structure* and the complementary Patterson report *The New Scottish Local Authorities: Organisation and Management Structures*. Then the Widdicombe report: *The Conduct of Local Authority Business in 1986*. These reports were concerned with wider issues than those that relate to local authority meetings, but many of their observations, conclusions and recommendations impinge on the decision-making process. Finally Nolan, in its Third Report of the Committee on Standards in Public Life (July 1997, Cm. 3702), looked at a number of issues relating to the subject matter of this work.

Audit Commission

1.60 Mention needs also to be made of the Audit Commission. It was established under the Local Government Finance Act 1982, and now operates under the Audit Commission Act 1998, with responsibility for the external audit of local authorities and certain other bodies through the district audit service and for undertaking studies for improving the economy, efficiency, and effectiveness of local government services. The commission has issued a number of reports that relate to the local authority decision-making process and the committee system that are referred to as appropriate throughout the text of this work.

Under s.99 of the Local Government Act 2003, the commission also has an explicit duty to produce a report 'from time to time' that categorises each authority in England according to how it has performed in exercising its functions. It does this under what is currently known as the Comprehensive Performance Assessment framework. The duty to categorise does not apply in Wales where the National Assembly and the commission are working on the Wales Programme for Improvement with its emphasis on self-assessment. In 2009, the English methodology will change again and a new Comprehensive Area Assessment framework will be developed, but it is likely that the categorisation of authorities will continue in some form.

The importance of the categorisation is seen from s.100 of the 2003 Act, which lists the powers that may be exercised by reference to the categorisation. The Secretary of State may make provision regulating, forbidding or requiring the taking of certain actions in relation to companies under the control of, or subject to the influence of, local authorities under s.70 of the Local Government and Housing Act 1989; specify performance indicators and standards to be met by best value authorities, the period within which an authority is to conduct a best value review, and matters that an authority must include in a best value performance plan all under the Local Government Act 1999; modify enactments and confer new powers on best value authorities in relation to the exercise of their functions under s.16 of the Local Government Act 1999 or s.5 of the Local Government Act 2000; prohibit local authorities from exercising their general power of well-being in relation to a particular activity under s.3 of the 2000 Act; modify enactments concerning plans or strategy under s.6 of the 2000 Act; make provision reforming law which imposes burdens under s.1 of the Regulatory Reform Act 2001; and exercise powers in the

General principles

2003 Act relating to trading, and fixed penalty receipts for litter and dog fouling offences. The Secretary of State may, by order, add to or amend those powers.

Committee system

1.61 For obvious reasons, the full council could not possibly deal with the totality of business that falls to be discharged by a local authority. Hence, because the law has compelled authorities to appoint certain committees, and the volume and pressure of business has in any event made it unavoidable, authorities conduct their business through committees. The committee system has immense advantages and has served local government well; but it has disadvantages also, and the expansion of local authority business and the demands for more effective and efficient administration have in recent years highlighted the weaknesses of the committee system, particularly its fragmentation of an authority's organisation. Accordingly, Part II of the 2000 Act has introduced a complete new system of executive arrangements for all but the smaller shire districts. In the following sections, the role of full council and the different executive models are outlined.

Executive arrangements under the Local Government Act 2000

1.62 Under Part II of the 2000 Act, a local authority with a population of at least 85,000 as at 30 June 1999 must operate one of three models of executive arrangements. These are an elected mayor and cabinet; a leader and cabinet; or an elected mayor and council manager. The intention behind the models is to separate clearly the executive from the other functions of the council in order to increase the efficiency, transparency and accountability of local authorities. In addition, local councils can delegate decision-making to individual councillors for the first time. In this way, decisions can be taken more quickly and efficiently; the individuals who make decisions should be more easily identifiable; those individuals will be publicly accountable and their actions subject to regular scrutiny; and councillors will have more time to represent their communities because they will not be spending as much time in committee meetings.

Those authorities that did not have a population of at least 85,000 as at 30 June 1999 must make alternative arrangements (sometimes called the fourth option), which need not involve a separate executive but should nevertheless provide for review and scrutiny of the discharge of the executive function: see 1.64. Currently, it is understood that there are 73 shire councils operating in this way.

Also, for the first time, every local authority must prepare, publicise and keep up to date a written constitution that sets out its governance arrangements. These arrangements go far beyond what is covered by its standing orders and include setting out the roles of councillors and officers; the function and terms of reference of full council, the cabinet and various other council bodies; the principles of decision-making; and also incorporate various codes and protocols in the constitution. The Secretary of State has issued a model modular constitution and statutory guidance to which local authorities must have regard when implementing Part II of the 2000 Act.

1. Current framework

The role of council

1.63 Under the Local Authorities (Functions and Responsibilities) (England) Regulations 2000 (SI 2000/2853), the full council must set the budgetary and policy framework of the authority within which the executive will operate. Specifically, the Regulations require full council to adopt or approve specified plans and strategies of the local authority; adopt or approve the budget and any plan or strategy for the control of the authority's borrowing or capital expenditure; determine the scheme of members' allowances; and authorise applications to the Secretary of State for the transfer of housing land. Examples of plans or strategies to be approved or adopted by full council are the Best Value Performance Plan, the Community Strategy, the Development Plan, the Local Transport Plan, the Children's Services Plan, and the Education Development Plan.

The executive arrangements models

Elected mayor and cabinet

1.64 At present there are 12 authorities with the elected mayor and cabinet model. These are Bedford, Doncaster, Hartlepool, Mansfield, Middlesbrough, North Tyneside, Torbay and Watford, together with the Greater London Authority and the London Boroughs of Hackney, Lewisham and Newham. This model can only be adopted at present following a referendum although the LGPIH Act 2007 will allow Councils to adopt the Mayoral Model following consultation with their committees, but without the need for a referendum. To September 2007, there have been 36 local referendums. A referendum can be demanded by 5 per cent of the electors of the authority by way of a petition. Under this model, an elected mayor must appoint between two and nine members of the authority to be members of the executive (i.e. a cabinet). The elected mayor provides the political leadership; proposes the policy framework and budget to the full council; and takes executive decisions within the policy framework. The cabinet implements the policy framework under the political guidance of the elected mayor and takes such decisions as a group or as individuals as may be delegated to them by the elected mayor. The Council approves the constitution; agrees the policy framework and the budget; and makes certain appointments.

Leader and cabinet

1.65 This is by far the most common form of executive arrangement under the 2000 Act, and it has been adopted by some 315 authorities in England. Under this model, the executive leader is elected (or removed) by the full council. It is for each local authority to set out in its executive arrangements how the appointment of the cabinet should work. Broadly, this will be either where the cabinet is appointed by the executive leader who also determines the scheme of delegations (strong leader model), or where the cabinet is appointed by the full council, which also determines the delegations. In both cases, the cabinet must consist of between three and ten councillors (including the leader). The division of responsibilities between the leader, the council and the cabinet is much the same as for the elected mayor and cabinet model above with the leader exercising similar powers to the elected mayor in the strong leader model. The LGPIH Act 2007 is intended to strengthen this model further by phasing in from 2009 to 2011, a requirement for councils to choose between a directly elected mayor for a four-year term, and an indirectly elected leader with a four-year term.

Elected mayor and council manager

1.66 The third of the three forms of executive arrangements set in the 2000 Act is the elected mayor and council manager form, which, like the elected mayor and cabinet model, can only be adopted following a referendum. To date, only one authority (Stoke-on-Trent) has adopted this form of executive in which the executive consists of the elected mayor and the council manager only. The council manager is appointed by and responsible to the council as a whole. The principle behind this form of executive is to achieve a clear separation between policy development by the elected mayor and council, and implementation of policy by the council manager having regard to any political steer from the elected mayor. In this model, the elected mayor provides political leadership and proposes the policy framework and budget to council. The council manager is responsible for appointing all other officers and, under the guidance of the elected mayor, develops and proposes the budget, develops and proposes details of the policy framework, and implements policy and secures service delivery.

Executive functions

1.67 Detailed regulations have been made[46] setting out those functions that cannot be an executive responsibility (e.g. determination of the council's policy framework and budget, together with regulatory matters such as town and country planning; licensing; elections; bylaws and standing orders); those functions that may be the responsibility of the executive (local choice functions, which need to be set out in the council's constitution); and those functions that are to be the responsibility of the executive (the default position). The council's constitution should be checked in case of any doubt as to whether a matter can be dealt with by the executive or whether it should be referred to a regulatory committee or to full council itself.

Key decisions and the forward plan

1.68 From time to time, an executive will be called upon to make key decisions. These are defined in regulations made under the 2000 Act as those decisions likely to either result in significant expenditure or savings having regard to the budget for the service or function to which the decision relates, or which are likely to be significant in its effect on communities living or working in an area comprising two or more wards or divisions in the local authority's area. Some authorities have set more detailed criteria and financial limits in their constitutions as to what makes a decision 'significant'. In order to ensure that the public is aware as to what key decisions are to be taken, and when they are to be discussed, the 2000 Act requires the executive leader, mayor or council manager to prepare a Forward Plan of key decisions likely to be taken over a four-month period. This is published by the local authority at least 14 days before the plan comes into effect. It is then updated on a monthly basis and a new Forward Plan published at least 14 days before it comes into effect.

Role of councillors not on the executive

1.69 In all three models set out above (see 1.62), the role of the councillors who are not on the executive is to assist the executive in policy development, propose new policy to the executive or the council, represent their electorate, and review and scrutinise policy and executive decisions.

Overview and scrutiny arrangements

1.70 Executive arrangements must also provide for the appointment for one or more overview and scrutiny committees. Sometimes these are called panels or commissions to distinguish them from the regulatory committees. In the statutory Guidance, the Secretary of State has advised that these overview and scrutiny committees should meet frequently and be 'cross-cutting' rather than service based. The committees must have the power to review or scrutinise decisions taken by the executive or any other part of the council, and make reports to the council or to the executive. They can also report on any matters that affect the authority's area or its inhabitants. Their role includes both developing and reviewing policy and holding the executive to account.

1.71 These committees are politically balanced, which ensures that a political party with an overall majority on the council and hence forming the administration of the council also has control of the overview and scrutiny committees. Where there is a majority administration, there is a logical inconsistency between providing that these committees should hold the executive to account and ensuring that they are controlled by members of the same party as the executive. Accordingly, whilst acknowledging that this is a matter for local political groups, the statutory Guidance recommends that whipping is incompatible with overview and scrutiny, and should therefore not take place.

Regulatory committees

1.72 A local authority must also maintain a number of regulatory and other committees to deal with functions such as the determination of applications for planning permission that cannot be dealt with by the executive. Further, there are also committees that must be set up under powers other than in the 1972 Act: such as a licensing committee, which a local authority is required to establish under the Licensing Act 2003.

General principles

The ethical framework

1.73 The law relating to the conduct of members was completely changed by the 2000 Act and a new ethical framework introduced based on the General Principles set out in the Relevant Authorities (General Principles) Order 2001. These are categorised in the Order as selflessness, honesty and integrity, objectivity, account-ability, openness, personal judgment, respect for others, duty to uphold the law, stewardship and leadership. These apply to the conduct of members and co-opted members when they are acting as members of the authority, including in meetings of the authority, except that honesty and integrity and duty to uphold the law apply on all occasions.

1.74 In order to give the General Principles some teeth, and to ensure that members would be subject to sanction should they not observe them, each authority is obliged to adopt a local Code of Conduct for members based on a model Code of Conduct issued by the Secretary of State. The current model Code is contained in the Local Authorities (Model Code of Conduct) Order 2007 (SI 2007/1159) which was made on 2nd April 2007 and applies to the different types of authorities, including principal councils, parish councils, National Park authorities and police authorities. Although the model code does not quote from the General Principles, it is consistent with them, and the Standards Board for England has recommended that the General Principles be included as a preamble to the local Code adopted by each authority.

The Code of Conduct

1.75 The Code (see Appendix 2) is written as if addressed to a member individually ('This Code applies to **you** as a member of an authority') and sets out General Obligations on each individual member. The Code states that a member must:

- Treat others with respect.
- Ensure that the Council's resources are not used improperly for political purposes.
- Have regard to the Local Authority Code of Publicity made under the Local Government Act 1986.
- Have regard to relevant advice from the Monitoring Officer and the Chief Finance Officer when reaching decisions (optional for parish councils).
- Give reasons for decisions.

Conversely, under the Code the member must not:

- Do anything which would cause their authority to breach any of the equality enactments.
- Bully any person.
- Intimidate anyone involved in investigations or proceedings relating to an allegation of failure to comply with the Code.
- Do anything to compromise the impartiality of those who work for and on behalf of the authority.
- Disclose confidential information except in specified circumstances.

1. Current framework

- Prevent another person from gaining access to information to which that person is entitled by law.
- Conduct himself in a manner that could reasonably bring his office or the authority into disrepute.
- Use his position as a member improperly to confer on or secure for himself or any other person an advantage or disadvantage.

The Standards Board has issued Guidance on the Code (see Appendix 3), which is available on their website and which goes through the various provisions of the Code and sets out how the Standards Boards considers the requirements of the Code should be interpreted. For example, it expands on what is meant by bullying and makes the point that bullying behaviour should be contrasted with the legitimate challenges which a member can make in challenging policy or scrutinizing performance.

So far as confidentiality is concerned, the Code permits disclosure of confidential information in specified circumstances including where this is reasonable and in the public interest, and where the disclosure is made in good faith and in compliance with the reasonable requirements of the authority. The Guidance issued by the Standards Board goes through the various elements. In considering what reasonable requirements can be imposed by a local authority, the Guidance explains that a member should comply with the authority's policies or protocols on such matters as whistle-blowing and states that concerns should be first raised through the proper channels before disclosure. It may be that when local authorities consider what requirements to lay down in relation to the 'public interest test', they apply the same criteria as are used in relation to the release of committee papers and to Freedom of Information Act requests. It could also be helpful if members were required to contact the Monitoring Officer for advice before they released confidential information.

The General Obligations set out in the Code apply to the conduct of members and co-opted members when they are acting as members of the authority, including in meetings of the authority. The Code intends that the requirements not to intimidate, not to bring the office or authority into disrepute, and not to improperly use the position as a member to secure an advantage, should apply at any other time where that conduct constitutes a criminal offence for which the member has been convicted.

In the case of *Ken Livingstone* v. *Adjudication Panel for England* (2006), however, it was decided by Collins J. that s.52 of LGA 2000 only enabled the Code to apply to activities of a member when performing the functions of his office. In that case the Mayor of London had been confronted by a newspaper reporter after leaving a reception at City Hall. A brief interchange had taken place during which the Mayor had made offensive remarks and had compared the reporter, who he knew to be Jewish, to a concentration camp guard. As the Mayor was not 'performing his functions' on that occasion, the Code did not apply to those comments despite the clear intention set out in the Code. Collins J. made the obvious point that the Code can go no further in what it regulates than the Act permits. The wording of the current Code that it applies 'at any other time' in relation to specific matters is, therefore, clearly limited in its effect. It will not extend to conduct beyond that which is properly to be regarded as falling within the phrase 'in performing his functions' as a member.

General principles

It is clear from the *Livingstone* case that unlawful conduct of itself is not necessarily covered and so, for example, a councillor who shoplifts or is guilty of drunken driving will not be caught by the Code if the offence had nothing to do with his position as a councillor.

In order to partially reinstate the pre-*Livingstone* position, the Government has included provisions in the Local Government and Public Involvement in Health Act 2007, to extend the ambit of the Code so that it is not limited to actions taken only in an official capacity provided that such conduct would constitute a criminal offence.

Personal and prejudicial interests

1.76 The Code also introduces the concepts of personal interests (see 4.35) and prejudicial interests (see 4.38). If a member has a personal interest in a matter under discussion at a meeting of the authority such that a decision upon it might reasonably be regarded as affecting to a greater extent than the majority of other council tax payers, ratepayers or inhabitants of the electoral division or ward, or parish if not warded, the well-being or financial position of himself, a member of his family, or any person with whom he has a close personal association, then the nature and existence of the interest should disclosed at the start of that discussion unless the exceptions set out in the Code apply.

If the member with a personal interest also has a prejudicial interest such that it is one that a member of the public with knowledge of the relevant facts would reasonably regard as so significant that it is likely to prejudice the member's judgment of the public interest, then the member must withdraw from the room where the meeting is being held.

The Code does provide, however, that a member does not have a prejudicial interest where:

- the matter under discussion does not affect the financial position of the member or those in relation to whom the member may have a personal interest;
- the matter does not relate to the determining of any approval, consent, licence, permission or registration in relation to the member or those in respect of whom the member may have a personal interest; or
- the matter relates to specific exceptions such as housing, school meals, school transport and travel expenses, statutory sick pay, members allowances, indemnities, ceremonial honours, or setting the council tax.

Perhaps the most significant exemption is where the matter under discussion does not affect the financial position of the member or any person or body in whom the member has a financial interest. This is, in effect, reviving the old 'pecuniary interest' test so that if there is no pecuniary or financial interest, then the member does not have a prejudicial interest to declare unless the matter relates to a licensing or regulatory matter affecting the member or those in relation to whom the member may have a personal interest.

Prior to withdrawing, a member with a prejudicial interest may make representations, answer questions, or give evidence at a meeting open to the public, provided that the public are also allowed to attend the meeting for the same purpose, whether under a statutory right or otherwise. This does allow members with a prejudicial interest to influence the decision and the Code does not distinguish between those members who belong to special interest groups, or who were elected on a particular issue, and those members who would personally gain financially from exercising that right and concern has been raised at the failure to make such a distinction.

A further provision of the Code is that Cabinet members will have a prejudicial interest in any business before an Overview and Scrutiny Committee that relates to a cabinet or executive decision in which they were involved. On that basis, they would not be able to be held to account by the committee. This provision of the Code, however, is overridden by s.21(13) of the LGA 2000 which enables an Overview and Scrutiny Committee to require an executive member to attend a meeting of the committee to answer questions so this overrides any code provision which might prevent this happening.

1.77 The Code also requires members to maintain a Register of Interests, which is held by the Monitoring Officer of the authority. Details of 'sensitive information' that could create a serious risk of violence or intimidation need not be disclosed at meetings or registered, provided the Monitoring Officer agrees. The Code further requires a member to register with the Monitoring Officer as a personal interest, the interests of any person from whom the member has received a gift or hospitality of at least £25. It will be interesting to see how this operates but so far as disclosure of personal interests at meetings is concerned, it is important to appreciate that the member is only obliged to declare a personal interest where he is aware, or ought reasonably to be aware, of the existence of the personal interest.

The Standards Board for England

1.78 In England, the ethical framework established by the 2000 Act is enforced at national level by the Standards Board for England. In discharging its function, the Standards Board must have regard to the need to promote and maintain high standards of conduct by members and co-opted members of relevant authorities as defined in the Act. It must receive complaints of breaches of the Code of Conduct by members and must appoint ethical standards officers to investigate complaints that the board considers serious enough for investigation. Ethical Standards Officers may then investigate, or refer the less serious cases to the local Monitoring Officer for investigation. If the Ethical Standards Officers have investigated and found a breach of the Code to have taken place for which some penalty should be awarded, then they may refer serious breaches to the Adjudication Panel for England for adjudication by a case tribunal, which has a range of sanctions available and may suspend a member for up to one year, or disqualify him from holding office for up to five years.[47] Less serious breaches may be referred for sentence to a local Standards Committee, which has a variety of sanctions but may suspend the member for up to three months. In addition, the Standards Board may also issue guidance on the conduct of members. To that end it regularly issues bulletins and advice. The Standards Board's website is a useful resource in that respect.

The Standards Board has come under criticism for the way in which it operates and for the backlog that built up in relation to the number of complaints it receives. The number of complaints has, however, reduced and the Board received 3,549 allegations between 1st April 2006 and 31st March 2007 compared to 3,836 during the same period in 2005/06. In addition, the Board has also dealt with the backlog by increasingly referring matters for local investigation. For the period 1st April 2006 to 31st March 2007, ethical standards officers referred 347 cases for local investigation – equivalent to 55% of all cases referred for investigation. It is anticipated that an increasing number of complaints will be referred by ethical Standards Officers to local Monitoring Officers for investigation, which will further improve the backlog but could have severe resource implications for some authorities. In addition, the provision for local filtering in the Local Government and Public Involvement in Health Act 2007 (see 1.89) will have further resource implications for local authorities and their standards committees. It is intended to introduce the new arrangements from April 2008.

Local Standards Committees

1.79 At local level, each relevant authority has the obligation to establish a Standards Committee that has the statutory duty to promote and maintain high standards of conduct by members and co-opted members of the authority and assist them in observing the authority's Code of Conduct. In addition, the Standards Committee is responsible for advising the authority on the adoption or revision of its Code of Conduct; monitoring the operation of the code; and advising, training, or arranging to train members and co-opted members on matters relating to the Code of Conduct. The Standards Committee also has the function of granting dispensations in appropriate circumstances. Some authorities give the Standards Committee a wider remit to cover such issues as whistle-blowing and complaints procedures. Standards Committees are discussed further in Chapter 13.

The modernisation agenda and community leadership

1.80 Central government's modernisation programme is an overall strategy designed to promote democratic renewal by ensuring that local authorities are accountable, open and responsive to local needs. To that end, the Local Government Acts of 1999 and 2000 have been structured to ensure that:

- the councils' political decision-making processes are efficient, transparent and accountable;
- there is continuous improvement in the efficiency and quality of the services for which they are responsible;
- they actively engage the community in local decisions; and
- they have the necessary powers to work with others to promote or improve the economic, social and environmental well-being of their areas.

The changes to the political decision-making processes have been looked at in 1.62 above. We can now turn to continuous improvement, community engagement and the well-being powers.

1. Current framework

Continuous improvement

1.81 Under the Local Government Act 1999, best value authorities are required to make arrangements to secure continuous improvement in the way in which they exercise their functions, having regard to a combination of economy, efficiency and effectiveness. The duty is subject to an obligation to consult with representative groups of stakeholders. Continuous improvement is driven in a variety of ways including the preparation of Best Value Performance Plans and by carrying out Best Value Reviews.

1.82 The Best Value Performance Plan is the main document by which a local authority is judged in terms of best value and links with the council's overall performance management framework. The Council's external auditor reports on the Performance Plan and failure to comply with the statutory requirements could, in extreme cases, leave the council open to statutory intervention by the Secretary of State.

Community engagement

1.83 The principle of community engagement is of fundamental importance to the modernisation agenda introduced by the 2000 Act. Councillors are the elected leaders of their communities and in order to ensure that they actively engage the community in local decisions there are a number of instances where local authorities are statutorily required to consult with the community. For example, these range from deciding on the form of executive arrangement already mentioned and setting the annual budget to consulting on the development plan or other specific statutory consultation processes.

1.84 However, the 2000 Act introduces a duty to prepare a Community Strategy and to consult widely on it. The Community Strategy is intended to establish a long-term vision for the area, taking into account wider regional and national visions for better quality of life. One of the key bodies involved in this exercise will be the local strategic partnership. This is a voluntary body made up of representatives from the public and voluntary sector. It need not necessarily be chaired by a councillor, but the council is an important component of the partnership. The performance of the local strategic partnership is subject to council scrutiny to monitor the achievements of the council and other accountable partners in the activities that they have promised to deliver as well as monitoring progress against long-term outcomes.

Well-being power

1.85 Local government has no powers of general competence. Instead, a local authority has specific statutory powers in relation to the carrying out of its various functions, together with a general power, introduced by s.2 of the LGA 2000, to do anything that it considers likely to achieve the promotion or improvement of the economic, social or environmental well-being of its area. The link with community engagement is that the power must be exercised having regard to the community strategy.[48]

1.86 However, the well-being power has limitations put on it such that it doesn't override any prohibition, restriction or limitation on the powers of a local authority set out in other legislation.[49] Neither does it apply to community, parish or local councils. The well-being power cannot be used to raise money (whether by precepts, borrowing or otherwise) and is subject to the control and guidance of the Secretary of State. Accordingly, the use of the well-being power has been relatively infrequent to date, despite the encouragement in the statutory Guidance that the powers should be the first resort of local authorities seeking to achieve improvements in the well-being of their areas. This may change with the implementation of ss.93-97 of the Local Government Act 2003 on charging and trading.

What next?

1.87 In July 2004, the government published a document entitled *The Future of Local Government – Developing a 10-year Vision*. Its aim is to create sustainable communities that will improve the local delivery of services, increase public engagement in the decisions that affect them, and lead to better outcomes for people and places.

1.88 In January 2005, the government developed this theme further in *Sustainable Communities: People, Places and Prosperity*, which sets out a five-year strategy outlining the governance arrangements for delivering sustainable communities. At the same time, two papers entitled *Vibrant Local Leadership* and *Why Neighbourhoods Matter* were issued that form part of the 10-year vision for local government already mentioned in 1.87.

1.89 These documents set out the government's intention to devolve power to a neighbourhood level in order to revitalise neighbourhoods, strengthen local leadership and increase regional prosperity to create places in which people want to live and work. They emphasise the importance of local government delivering excellent services and leading and enabling community empowerment, and propose to give opportunities for all communities to have more control over their own neighbourhoods through a proposed Neighbourhood Charter, which might include the ability for communities to own their own assets (e.g. playgrounds or community centres). There could also be more delegation of budgets by local authorities, which could include a small community fund held by councillors who would act as 'mini-mayors' in their wards. This would give them a clear leadership role and enable them to make a difference to their neighbourhoods. The documents also set out the government's wish to develop a new approach to create more directly elected mayors in the larger cities with increased powers to transform those cities.

In 2006, these themes were developed into the White Paper *Strong and Prosperous Communities* which proposed a community call for action, and opportunities for local asset management, together with a revised duty requiring authorities to involve local people. It also proposed the introduction of Local Area Agreements which would formally set out local priorities. These proposals, and others relating to the ethical framework, are set out in the Local Government and Public Involvement in Health Act 2007 which was given Royal Assent on 30th October 2007.

In essence, the Act proposes that:

- The Code of Conduct requirements will not be limited to Members acting in their official capacity (cf *Ken Livingstone* v. *Adjudication Panel for England*). Members will have to sign a new declaration. The change will be retrospective but not retroactive.

- Complaints of breaches of the Code of Conduct will be made to local Standards Committees instead of the Standards Board for England unless the Standards Board intervenes ('local filtering'). The Standards Committee can refer it to the Monitoring Officer or the Standards Board for England or decide to take no action. The complainant will have the right to require the Standards Committee to review its decision.
- The Standards Board for England's general powers will be broadened. It will be able to require authorities to send them periodic returns about complaints and casework and about the functions of the Standards Committee and Monitoring Officer.
- Standards Committees will have to be chaired by an independent member.
- Regulations may provide for the creation of joint Standards Committees.
- Standards Committees will decide appeals about the inclusion of a post on the list of politically restricted posts.

A further development is that a Green Paper, *The Governance of Britain*, was published in July 2007. The Green Paper takes a broad overview of constitutional issues, and makes some substantial suggestions of national significance. It describes a tripartite relationship between government, parliament, and local communities. It emphasises the need to enable people to become active citizens, and makes a commitment to devolve power directly to people. It is proposed to consult on the following topics:

- extending the right of people to intervene with their elected representatives through community rights to call for action;
- duties to consult on major decisions through mechanisms such as citizens juries;
- powers of redress to scrutinise and improve the delivery of local services;
- powers to ballot on spending decisions.

Describing *Strong and Prosperous Communities* as a first step, the Green Paper proposes a number of other ways to strengthen the ability of citizens to influence local decisions and hold service providers to account. It proposes:

- A formal petitioning system, that would require authorities to consider and investigate petitions from local communities, and guarantee petitioners and the wider community a response on the issues which have been raised.
- The possibility of a new provision for local communities to apply for devolved or delegated budgets to fund projects which will benefit the local community.
- The provision of regular and accessible real-time data on local services, and other options for citizens to contribute to services in the area and ensure that service providers feel more accountable to them.
- Support for members of the public who undertake governance and scrutiny responsibilities.

The Green Paper refers to representative democracy, and the necessity for citizens to understand the different roles and responsibilities of central and local government. In what is intended to be a mark of confidence in local government, it is proposed that the Secretary of State for Communities and Local Government will work with the Local Government Association to establish a concordat between central and local government. It is intended that 'this will establish for the first time an agreement on the rights and responsibilities of local government, including its responsibilities to provide effective leadership of the local area and to empower local communities where possible'.

1.90 The leadership role of local authorities and councillors is a recurrent theme of the government's vision for local government. This theme will be developed further over the next few years, and further changes can be expected to be made to the governance arrangements of local authorities.

Notes

1 LGA 1972, s.265.
2 Ibid., ss.9, 27.
3 LG&HA 1989, s.21.
4 For a comprehensive list of local authority functions see *Cross on Local Government Law*, 8th edn. Appendices A and B (1991): and *The Functions of Local Authorities in England* (1992), HMSO.
5 The few exceptional cases where one person can constitute a meeting (e.g. as under the Companies Act, which provides that 'one member of the company present in person or by proxy shall be deemed to constitute a meeting') have no application to local government.
6 Sebag Shaw and Dennis Smith, *The Law of Meetings* (1947).
7 Law of Libel Amendment Act 1888, s.4.
8 A 'public place' is any highway, public park or garden, any sea beach and any public bridge, road, lane, footway, square, court, alley or passage, whether a thoroughfare or not, and includes any open space to which, for the time being, the public have or are permitted to have access, whether on payment or otherwise: Public Order Act 1936. s.9(1).
9 'Private premises' are defined as 'premises to which the public have access (whether on payment or otherwise)' only by permission of the owner, occupier or lessee of the premises': ibid.
10 LGA 1972, ss.100A, 100E, added by LG(AI)A 1985, as regards principal councils: see generally Chapter 3.
11 For a discussion of the problems inherent in multi-organisations (outside the scope of this work) see: R. J. P. Harris and D. J. Scott, *Perspectives on Multi-Organizational Design 8 Local Government Studies 31*.
12 See generally LGA 1972, s.99, and sch.12; and LoGA 1963, s.1.
13 LGA 1972, sch.12, paras.3, 9, 25.
14 Ibid., s.239.
15 Ibid., sch.12, paras.1, 7, 23.
16 Ibid., para.14.
17 Ibid., sch.12, para.l(2)(b).
18 Ibid., sch.12, para.7(2).
19 Ibid., paras.2, 8 and 24.
20 Ibid., para.8.
21 Ibid., para.8(2).
22 Ibid., para.14(3).
23 Ibid., para.1(4).
24 Ibid., paras.7(3), 23(3).

1. Current framework

25 Ibid., paras.14(4), 32(1).

26 An opinion to the contrary appeared in the *Justice of the Peace and Local Government Review* of 21st September 1963, but no grounds for the opinion were advanced.

27 LGA 1972, sch.12, paras.2(1), 8(1), 24(1).

28 Ibid., paras.10(1), 26(1).

29 Ibid., paras.10(1), 26(1).

30 Ibid., s.99 applies the provisions of sch.12 to committees and subcommittees.

31 Ibid., sch.12, Pt VI, para.39(1).

32 Ibid., s.82, but the position may be different where the council is acting in a quasijudicial capacity.

33 A decision could be set aside if the council were guilty of the rarely invoked offence of misfeasance in public office because councillors voted with the object of maliciously damaging a third party: see 1.42.

34 For example, a majority of the whole number of council members is required for a resolution to promote or oppose a Bill: LGA 1972, s.239, and see 7.144.

35 LGA 1972, sch.12, para.39.

36 A proxy is a person appointed by someone to act and vote for him at a meeting. The term is also applied to the instrument by which such person is appointed. There is no common law right to vote by proxy (*Harben* v. *Phillips* (1883) and no statutory right conferred in respect of local authority meetings.

37 A local authority or committee that has arranged for the discharge of any of its functions by a committee, subcommittee, or officer, or other local authority, is not precluded from exercising those functions: LGA 1972, s.101 (4); see 9.83.

38 House of Commons standing order No.37 provides that an MP can vote in a division without having heard the question put, i.e. there is no need even to know what is being voted on!

39 Local government is more than the sum of the particular services provided. It is an essential part of English democratic government.' Report of the Royal Commission on Local Government in England (1969), Cmnd 4040, p. 146, – a sentiment endorsed by the Widdicombe Committee in its interim report (see 1.58).

40 LGA 2000, s.2.

41 LGA 1988, s.29 and sch.3, and LG&HA 1989, ss.22–28.

42 'If circumstances are not properly reported or if facts are omitted from a report to a committee the authority itself might be found guilty of maladministration in its decision-making. The ombudsman may find maladministration if serious complaints are not reported to the appropriate committee. Promises made by the authority and not fulfilled may result in a finding of maladministration. Procrastination and even, perhaps, undue haste may also produce an adverse finding by the ombudsman. These issues have now to be kept very much in the forefront of the mind of those who write reports and draft minutes.' R. G. Brooke, 'Modern Approach to Committee Practice' (1979) 143 *Local Government Review* 3.

43 Bylaws for good rule and government are made by simple resolution of the local authority, but the bylaws must be 'made under the common seal of the authority' and do not have effect until confirmed by the appropriate confirming authority: LGA 1972, s.236(3).

44 (1974) 90 *Law Quarterly Review* 351, 360; and see 'The Legal Effects of Statements by Planning Officers', ibid. in which it is quoted. See also *Southend-on-Sea Corporation* v. *Hodgson (Wickford) Ltd* (1961); and *Lever Finance Ltd* v. *Westminster (City) London Borough Council* (1971); discussed in S. H. Bailey, C. A. Cross and J. F. Garner, *Cases and Materials in Administrative Law* (1977), p.259.

45 See Raymond Knowles, *Effective Management in Local Government* (1980), p.6.

46 The Local Authorities (Functions and Responsibilities) (England) Regulations 2000 (SI 2000/2853).

47 The current decisions of the Adjudication Panel indicate that simple refusal to comply with the requirement to register interests will normally result in a disqualification for one

year. A failure to withdraw for a prejudicial interest is likely to result in a suspension or disqualification for one year – less if no personal gain or loss, and more if there was personal gain or if the councillor had actually been advised of the interest. Serious criminal action will usually lead to disqualification for an extended period (e.g. physical assault on a traffic warden has resulted in a one-year disqualification). Bullying or abuse of officers or members of the public is also likely to result in disqualification rather than suspension (e.g. instances of racism have resulted in disqualification for 18 months and three years; and accusations of political bias and abuse of a council's solicitor have resulted in a three-year disqualification).

48 LGA 2000, s.4.
49 Ibid., s.3.

Chapter 2
Standing orders

Statutory provisions

Discretion and obligation

2.1 All local authorities have statutory power to make discretionary standing orders if they choose, under the LGA 1972:

- for the regulation of council proceedings and business; and
- regarding the quorum, proceedings and place of meeting of their committees and subcommittees.

But 'relevant authorities' must incorporate certain mandatory standing orders into their constitution with respect to staff and regulating certain aspects of their proceedings and business, and for contracting purposes: see 2.4–2.5.

Model standing orders

2.2 A model set of standing orders for the guidance of local authorities in regulating their proceedings and business was issued by the former Ministry of Housing and Local Government in 1963 and reprinted in 1973. Although the model is out of date in many respects – it is based on the LGA 1933, long ago repealed – the standing orders of most local authorities today are still largely based on this model. The National Association of Local Councils (NALC) revised its model standing orders for parish and town councils in 2003, but there has been no revision of the model set for principal authorities. Those of the model standing orders still relevant and basically useful are reproduced throughout this work and referred to as, e.g. old model standing order. As to standing orders that the law compels local authorities to adopt and observe (mandatory standing orders), see 2.4.

2.3 In 1995, the Association of District Secretaries (now the Association of Council Secretaries and Solicitors) published a set of draft Standing Orders, written in plain English, for the guidance of local authorities in devising their own standing orders to meet local circumstances and local methods of working. Again, these have not been revised since the LGA 2000.

Mandatory standing orders

2.4 The Widdicombe Committee (see 1.59) had recommended that local authorities should be statutorily required to include in their standing orders a number of matters of a procedural character. It favoured also the codification of conventions and established practices: see 2.24. Following the coming into force of the LG&HA1989, which gave effect to several of Widdicombe's proposals, the DoE set up a working party of local government officers and civil servants, to prepare a new model set of standing orders and to distinguish between those that were core and mandatory, i.e. not revocable, alterable or suspendable by authorities other than in prescribed circumstances, and those that were non-mandatory, free to be adopted, revoked, amended or suspended or not as an authority wished – as, indeed, was and is currently still the position of discretionary standing orders made under the 1972 Act: see 2.2.

The working party dutifully produced a set of draft standing orders that, for some four years, were the subject of consultation and inconclusive discussion. What emerged – apart from mandatory standing orders as to staff: see 13.34 – were no more than two procedural core standing orders of comparative triviality: see 2.5. However, several of the standing orders drafted by the working party are reproduced in this book and are referred to in each case as 'one of the draft core standing orders' to distinguish it from an 'old model standing order': see 2.2.

2.5 Various Statutory Instruments have, since the LG&HA 1989, required local authorities to make or modify standing orders so that they include the provisions set out in the regulations or provisions.

The Local Authorities (Standing Orders) Regulations 1993 accordingly came into force on 1st April 1993. The regulations in reg.2 and sch.1 and reg.3 relate to the appointment of chief officers and prescribe a procedure for investigation by an independent person where misconduct by the head of the paid service has been alleged, a procedure that impinges on hearings of appeals against disciplinary action: see 13.54. It is in reg.4 and sch.2 that standing orders are required to be made in relation to the recording of votes and the signing of minutes of an extraordinary meeting.

2.6 Following the LGA 2000, the Local Authorities (Standing Orders) (England) Regulations 2001 came into force on 7th November 2001. These make amendments to the 1993 Regulations, and provide that an authority must make standing orders with relation to staff (Part IV sch.1), regulation of its proceedings (sch.2) and disciplinary action against the Head of Paid Service, Chief Finance Officer and Monitoring Officer (sch.3).

In addition, the Local Authorities (Executive Arrangements)(Modification of Enactments and Further Provisions)(England) Order 2001 provides that standing orders made under s.8 LG&HA 1989 be amended to include political assistants (reg.5), and specifies the provisions that are to be included in standing orders with regard to contracts, including the procedure to be followed.

Common law applies where there are no standing orders

2.7 In the absence of standing orders, either discretionary or mandatory, governing a local authority's procedures then, except so far as statutory provisions may apply, common law rules must be followed. In other words, common law applies wherever standing orders are silent on a particular point.

2. Standing orders

If an authority does not make standing orders affecting its proceedings (or if two or more authorities appointing a joint committee do not make standing orders governing the joint committee), or if the standing orders made in either case do not cover such matters, then the Executive, committees (or joint committee) or subcommittee of either may themselves determine the quorum, proceedings and place of meeting. In determining its own quorum, proceedings and place of meeting, however, the committee, joint committee or subcommittee should – on the analogy of *Picea Holdings v. London Rent Assessment Board* (1971) – follow the practice of the parent local authority or authorities. At common law if no quorum is fixed, all acts of a committee must be done in the presence of all members of the committee (*Re The Liverpool Household Stores Association Ltd* (1890)), but in local government this is clearly overridden by the statutory provision that all questions coming before the local authority must be decided by a majority of those present and voting at a properly constituted meeting (LGA 1972, sch.12, para.39, as applied to committees by s.99).

Variation and revocation

2.8 A local authority may vary or revoke or, within certain restraints, suspend its discretionary standing orders, i.e. those made under the general enabling power of the 1972 Act. A relevant authority cannot, however, vary or revoke or suspend mandatory standing orders. As standing orders, whether discretionary or mandatory, are made by simple resolution of the authority (subject to requisite notice of intention: see 2.18), so, too, may the variation or revocation of discretionary standing orders. Where a discretionary standing order has been revoked the resolution effecting the revocation may itself be rescinded, in which case the original standing order becomes again operative: *Weir v. Fermanagh County Council* (1913).

2.9 Some authorities stipulate that standing orders shall be altered or rescinded only upon the recommendation of the standards or other committee with responsibility for making recommendations for the review of standing orders, while others require that a certain period of prior notice shall be given before formal amendment. In *R. v. Flintshire County Council, ex parte Armstrong-Braun* (2001), the Council made a standing order preventing any one councillor from putting a matter on the agenda for discussion at a council meeting without being seconded by another council member. One of the arguments for judicial review was that a councillor who was not a member of a party or group would be excluded if he could not get the support of other councillors. As part of his judgment, Schieman LJ found that the Council had not fully considered the democratic implications of their alterations to standing orders.

Suspension

2.10 Although there is no specific power enabling an authority to suspend its discretionary standing orders, i.e. to decide, by resolution that for a special purpose or for a period of time one or other of its standing orders shall be of no effect, there is general acknowledgement that this can properly be done. Old model standing order no. 40, for example, provides:

> '(1) Subject to paragraph (2) of this standing order, any standing orders may be suspended so far as regards any business at the meeting where its suspension is moved.
> (2) A motion to suspend standing orders shall not be moved without notice . . . unless there shall be present at least [one half of the whole number of the] members of the council.'

The suspension must be by resolution: it cannot be implied (*R. v. Hereford Corporation ex parte Harrower and Others* (1970); and see 2.13). Despite the terms of the model standing order, Widdicombe expressed this view:

> 'We think it undesirable that procedural rules should be capable of change in mid-meeting by suspension of standing orders. Some safeguards are required. We are not convinced that . . . the model standing orders. . . are of themselves sufficient, and propose that standing orders should not be capable of suspension or amendment without advance notice of motion except on the vote of two-thirds of the membership of the council. All standing orders should be statutorily required to include such a limitation.'

A two-thirds majority would need a change in the law because a local authority needs only a majority of those present and voting at a meeting to reach a decision. In *R. v. Teddington UDC* (1928) a standing order requiring a two-thirds majority to rescind a resolution was held ultra vires.

Validity

2.11 Local authorities could quite properly make standing orders without express statutory power or obligation to do so: every constituted body has an inherent right to regulate its own proceedings, though necessarily within the law. The fact that standing orders are made under statutory power and authority does not give them the force of law (but see 2.15): they are not bylaws, nor can they impose penalties; and if they purport to override or are in conflict with the law they are ultra vires: see *R. v. Teddington UDC*, above. Even a standing order that goes beyond what the law strictly requires may be ultra vires, e.g. a standing order that requires a councillor to refrain from speaking rather than simply declaring and not voting when in arrears with council tax payments. In other words, where a statute deals specifically with a subject matter, standing orders cannot lawfully go further; but where this is not so the local authority is free to apply a standing order to the subject matter (see 9.47, where *R. v. Newham London Borough Council ex parte Haggerty* (1986) is discussed, in which it was held that as there is no statutory framework for the eligibility of councillors for committee membership, it is open to an authority by standing orders to establish its own criteria for membership provided they are not irrational.

2. Standing orders

The question of validity was considered at length in *R. v. Flintshire County Council, ex parte Armstrong-Braun* (2001) (see 2.9) and it was held that, in principle, a standing order could be quashed as falling outside the policy of the LGA 1972.

Compliance and enforceability

2.12 There is authority for the view that a local authority is bound to observe its discretionary standing orders (see *R. v. Woolwich Borough Council* (1922)). In *R. v. Hereford Corporation ex parte Harrower & Others* (1970) at p. 1427, Lord Parker CJ said:

'It is quite clear that there is a statutory duty on the local authority to comply with standing orders as they exist at the time and if those standing orders have not been suspended then there is a duty to comply with them.'

This case was concerned with standing orders in respect of contracts and not in regard to the regulation of internal domestic business.

However, in *R. v. Rushmoor Borough Council ex parte Crawford* (1981) the court made an order of certiorari to quash a decision of the majority Conservative group on the council suspending all Labour opposition councillors from committee membership because the decision to do so contravened the council's standing orders. In *R. v. Educational Services Committee of Bradford City Metropolitan Council ex parte Professional Association of Teachers* (1986), the Court held that a resolution passed by the committee to rescind a previous decision of the council to afford recognition to the applicant trade union was ultra vires for lack of compliance with standing orders.

2.13 In *Hereford*, above, the local authority had suspended its standing orders by implication. The council had decided, quite openly, to invite tenders for the installation of central heating in certain flats from only the local electricity and gas boards and the National Coal Board, but omitted to suspend its standing orders that provided for open competitive and not select tendering. The court held that although the council could properly suspend its standing orders it could do this only by formal resolution of the council and not by implication. It also emerged from this case that if an authority acts contrary to its standing orders, the ratepayers have sufficient legal right to enable them to seek an order of mandamus against the authority.

2.14 The effective power of a local authority to enforce compliance with standing orders upon its individual council members is limited. It would therefore be unwise for an authority to make a standing order that could be flouted with impunity. As an example, the banning of smoking at meetings might well be held to be unreasonable and therefore unlawful for the council to order a member out of a council meeting who persisted in smoking in defiance of a standing order prohibiting it, because he has a lawful right to be present subject to temporary exclusion for disorderly conduct. It is at least open to doubt whether smoking in contravention of a standing order could be classed as disorderly conduct. However, a local authority could properly ban smoking in that part of the council chamber or committee room allocated to the public.

Whether it would be appropriate to do so if councillors themselves persisted in smoking would need to be considered, perhaps under the principles governing the conduct of members, laid down by the Secretary of State.[1] The position as regards officers is quite different: compliance with standing orders can be an express or implied part of their employment contract, and breach of standing orders could be dealt with as a disciplinary matter.

2.15 Where a local authority is in breach of a mandatory standing order, if the breach is so fundamental that the substance of a statutory requirement has not been complied with, any decision affected by the breach may be void and, in principle, susceptible to judicial review. Breach of standing orders is likely to be significant in the context of maladministration (see 1.49) and unquestionably breach by an authority of its own internal procedures and of mandatory standing orders, will be regarded as failing in an administrative as well as probably a legal context. *Haggerty*, above, shows that the courts will use compliance with standing orders as a measure of the validity of a council's action.

2.16 Most political groups recognise that the discipline of internal procedural rules is necessary, and are therefore disposed towards persuading their members to keep in line. However, in the event of difficulties with members who continually disregard standing orders, discussing the issues with the political group leaders may be a good a starting point.

Procedural considerations

Formal making of standing orders

2.17 Standing orders are made by simple resolution by the full Council as regards standing orders that apply to the authority's proceedings and business generally; or by the executive or a committee or subcommittee where the council itself has not made standing orders relating to its committees and the committee or subcommittee wishes formally to regulate committee or subcommittee proceedings. Standing orders made by a committee or subcommittee cannot override the standing orders of the local authority: see 2.7. The form that standing orders take is dealt with below: see 2.27.

2.18 Although there are no special formalities for making standing orders (there is no approval of a confirmatory body to be sought), the democratic implications of the standing orders should be explained. The general law affecting the convening of a council meeting requires notice to be given of the intention to make standing orders in the summons to the council meeting at which the motion is to be put. An authority can decide that, before any amendment of standing order comes into force, it is confirmed by a subsequent meeting. A simple majority is necessary: *R. v. Teddington UDC*, above, and see 2.10.

2.19 In practice, the standing orders will be drafted by officers to meet the wishes and needs of the local authority, and may first need to be approved by the standards committee or other committee set up for this purpose, and submitted by recommendation to the full Council for approval. Mandatory standing orders do not necessarily need to follow the precise wording of the requisite regulations: they can be 'of like effect'.

2. Standing orders

Amendment of standing orders

2.20 Where the standing orders themselves prescribe the procedure for amendment, the procedure should be followed (see 2.9) provided it does not purport to override the law. Mandatory standing orders can presumably be amended, to such limited extent as may be necessary to correct any ambiguity or other misstatement, provided they remain 'of like effect'.

Periodical review

2.21 Each local authority should undertake a regular review of its discretionary standing orders, annually or at some other predetermined interval of time, as part of the Monitoring Officer's review of the Constitution. It is unlikely that major changes will be needed in those that deal with the rules of debate, but it may be necessary to take account of changes in the law and organisational structure during the past year, and any practical procedural difficulties that have arisen that could be helped by amending or modifying standing orders.

Supply to members

2.22 Councillors (and co-opted, i.e. non-voting, members, too) must be provided with an up-to-date copy of standing orders. Old model standing order no. 41 is to the following effect:

> 'A printed copy of these standing orders, and of such statutory provisions as regulate the proceedings and business of the council shall be given to each member of the council by the town clerk/clerk of the council upon delivery to him of the member's declaration of acceptance of office on the member's being first elected to the council.'

It is common practice to provide members with a copy of the Constitution, including, standing orders, as part of the members' information pack that many authorities produce.

Content

What should be included

2.23 What is included in discretionary standing orders is entirely a matter for determination by each local authority, although enforcement is a necessary consideration: see 2.14. The main purpose is to provide for the better regulation of proceedings but most authorities now incorporate staffing and financial regulations and a variety of provisions relating to the corporate structure and organisation of the authority into their Constitution. However, there are often well-established practices or conventions governing the conduct of local authority business that are not incorporated in formal standing orders: see 2.24.

Conventions

2.24 Widdicombe said, '. . . it saw an important role for local conventions in dealing with those matters where the need is for clear rules but which are not sufficiently susceptible to legal definition to lend themselves to standing orders and on which there is too great a variety of local circumstances for national codes of conduct to be appropriate.' It recommended that each local authority should draw up and make publicly available a list of the conventions it observes in relation, for example, to the following:

- the basis on which committee places are apportioned among councillors (now governed by LG&HA 1989, s.15: see 9.44);
- channels for councillors' contact with officers;
- the relationship between committee chairmen and chief officers;
- responsibility for agenda;
- the rights of councillors to obtain information and advice from officers;
- any arrangements for informal working groups or regular briefing meetings with officers that are not formally constituted as committees of the council;
- attendance of officers at party groups;
- the allocation of support services to councillors; and
- the status of any staff attached to the political groups or individual councillors.

Widdicombe did not believe that conventions should necessarily be given the force of law.

The danger of giving them a statutory status would be that the conventions would be over cautious and avoid some of the more problematic relationships. Even without statutory status, the local government ombudsman would generally take such conventions into account in deciding whether maladministration had occurred. See 2.15.

2.25 There are advantages in having conventions in a single document, and some or all of the above are often incorporated into the Constitution of a council.

2.26 It has also become customary for hung, or balanced, councils to produce conventions to govern the handling of business where there is no overall political control or even any council leader. Among items commonly covered are: dealing with business between meetings; procedure on equality of votes and use of the casting vote; briefing meetings; and the use of delegated powers of officers. These questions will vary from council to council depending on the approach adopted.

Form

2.27 Standing orders should be easy to understand though often they are not for a variety of reasons. Sometimes, because they are couched in the words of a statute or, in a misguided attempt to secure precision, the wording is so difficult that an

2. Standing orders

authority has to produce an explanatory note for the convenience of council members to show the intention. A useful tool for the convenience of members is a summary of the standing orders or the use of a flowchart.

2.28 Standing orders should be bound together with covers of suitable size so that they may be referred to easily at meetings. The date when the standing orders were made or last reviewed should be shown together with the date when they became effective; and in the case of a loose-leaf system (which makes for easier updating) there should be an indication of the date when each standing order was approved. The orders should be grouped in a logical sequence, and – a recommendation made in the model standing orders – it is a convenient practice for appropriate extracts from statutes to be printed in a distinctive typeface, such as italics, at the head of each standing order. Mandatory standing orders might be treated similarly.

Note

1   Relevant Authorities (General Principles) Order 2001 (SI 2001/1401).

Chapter 3
Admission of press and public

Introduction

Origin of right of admission

3.1 The right of members of the public to attend local authority meetings has been acquired gradually over the years. At the beginning of the century, council meetings were regarded at common law as private meetings, even though the local authority in full assembly was transacting public business. The local authority's entitlement to exclude the public, and press representatives, from their meetings was affirmed in *Tenby Corporation* v. *Mason* (1908), which arose out of the Tenby authority's refusal to allow a local newspaper reporter to attend council meetings after, it was alleged by the council, the reporter had produced seriously inaccurate reports of the proceedings. As a result of the court judgment, Parliament passed the Local Authorities (Admission of the Press to Meetings) Act 1908 (LA(APM)A 1908), which gave a right to 'duly accredited representatives of the press' to be admitted to council meetings, but in s.5 provided that 'nothing in this Act shall be construed so as to prohibit a local authority from admitting the public to its meetings'. Even earlier it had been held in *Purcell* v. *Sowler* (1877) that at common law an authority might expressly or impliedly consent to the attendance of non-members at its meetings, so council meetings were open meetings only so far as the local authority thought fit to allow the public to attend.

3.2 It was nearly 50 years later, in the Public Bodies (Admission to Meetings) Act 1960 (PB(AM)A 1960), that the public was accorded a specific right to be admitted to the meetings of local authorities and certain other bodies to which it applied. Then in the reorganisation of local government in the 1970s, the LGA 1972 extended that right to permit the public to attend meetings of local authority committees. A major development occurred when the Local Government (Access to Information) Act 1985 (LG(AI)A 1985), which applies only to principal councils (see 1.5), extended this right of admission to subcommittees from 1st April 1986 by additions to the 1972 Act, and made detailed provisions obliging those authorities to supply the public with agenda and reports in advance of all meetings, again by adding new provisions to the 1972 Act. As to what constitutes a committee or subcommittee, see 9.6.

Admission of the public

General principle

3.3 Every principal council and its committee and subcommittee meetings must now be open to the public, except when the public is excluded – as it must be – because

3. Admission of press and public

confidential information (see 3.10) might otherwise be disclosed during an item of business or – as it may be – if information within one of the statutorily specified categories of exempt information (see 3.11) might be disclosed. The general principle underlying the 1985 Act is that meetings should in general be open to the public, including the press. Widdicombe, however, suggested some restriction according with its view that purely deliberative committees (including, significantly, the policy and resources committee) that do not make decisions could comprise councillors of one party only. It said:[1]

'What concerns us about the 1985 Act is that it applies equally to committees that have no decision-taking powers but are purely deliberative. We think that this is misconceived, and that the same distinction between decision-taking and deliberative committees should be made with regard to access to information as with regard to committee membership. It is a simple reality, which no legislation can alter, that politicians will develop policy options in confidence before presenting the final choice for public decision. We do not think this unreasonable. If the law prevents them from conducting such discussions in private in formal committees, then they will conduct them less formally elsewhere. We have heard that some local authorities have been creating new informal mechanisms expressly to avoid the effects of the 1985 Act. It is unsatisfactory to force policy deliberation out of the formal committee system into groupings of indeterminate status. It is also unnecessary. No decision can be taken by a local authority without it eventually being referred to a decision-taking committee or the council, where there will be full public access to the meeting and the documentation. Given this basic safeguard, we can see no benefit in applying the Act also to deliberative committees. We would not in any way wish to discourage individual local authorities from opening deliberative committees to the public and press if that is appropriate to their particular circumstances, but do not believe that they should be required by law to do so.'

3.4 So far as those councils with executive arrangements are concerned, however, the LGA 2000 provides that, subject to regulations made by the Secretary of State, it is for a local authority executive to decide which of its meetings, and which of the meetings of any committee of an executive, are to be open to the public and which of those meetings are to be held in private (see 6.41). The Local Authorities (Executive Arrangements) (Access to Information) (England) Regulations 2000 make clear that although the making of a key decision by the executive must take place in public, as must a discussion on a matter included on the Forward Plan and on which a decision is likely to be made within 28 days of the meeting, there is no general requirement for the executive to hold meetings in public. For example, meetings that are convened for the sole purpose of an officer briefing members, such as cabinet briefing meetings, need not be open to the public.

General principles

Meetings open to the public

3.5 With the exception of meetings of a local authority executive as referred to in para.3.4, the meetings required to be open to the public and press are those of principal councils as defined in the 1972 Act, of the authorities established by the LGA 1985, and of certain other authorities[2] and of the committees and sub-committees of all such authorities. Parish and community councils remain subject, as regards the admission of the public to meetings, to the provisions of the PB(AM)A 1960 as extended by the LGA 1972, s.100.[3] This means that parish and community councils and their committee meetings must be open to the public unless by resolution excluded from the whole or part of any meeting 'whenever publicity would be prejudicial to the public interest by reason of the confidential nature of the business to be transacted or for other special reasons stated in the resolution and arising from the 'nature of the business or of the proceedings'. The National Association of Local Councils (NALC) has recommended that the spirit and letter of the 1972 legislation should be accepted at parish and community council meetings.

3.6 Some Councils have developed innovative ideas to increase public participation and to increase the entitlement of the public to attend committee meetings. Some local authorities now have a public question time at cabinet or committee meetings and, for example, applicants or objectors to planning applications are increasingly permitted to attend and address planning committee meetings.[4] Some councils limit such participation to residents of that local authority's area. Commonly, where members of the public are allowed to speak, there is a time limit for public participation in a general question time of around 15 minutes. Also, how long an individual is allowed to speak is usually limited to, say, five minutes. Wherever possible, groups or individuals are encouraged to nominate one representative, who can be a councillor (even if they have a prejudicial interest (provided they leave once they have spoken)), to speak on behalf of all. Advance notice of appearance is usually requested to be given to the council so that officers can brief members on the facts and, in the case of a planning matter, on the relevant planning issues, and provide proper advice on how to respond. Once the committee begins its decision-making discussion on a particular application the public are not permitted to speak again. The advantages to such participation are that it does enable the public to make direct representations to the decision-making body and ensures that all members are aware of the issues involved. There are recognised disadvantages, however, in that the process can be time-consuming in relation to contentious matters; objectors can be inarticulate or verbose, even unreasonable and unpleasant particularly if, having taken the time and trouble to attend, the decision is not one that they are seeking; and, inevitably, this does make meetings longer. It is good practice for the chairman to ask any subsequent objectors if they have anything new to add, to ensure that the committee do not have to sit through a number of objectors all making the same point.

3.7 It is also common for local authorities to allow local electors or other members of the public, under procedures set out in standing orders, to ask questions at council meetings: see 7.47. As to the submission of petitions or the hearing of deputations at council meetings: see 7.45 et seq.

3.8 In order to increase access to those members of the public who are not able to attend the meeting, there are also a number of councils who allow the radio or television to broadcast meetings that are of particular public interest, and some councils now broadcast their own meetings via the Internet.

Notice of meetings

3.9 Public notice must be given of meetings of a principal council and its committees and subcommittees,[5] and copies of the agenda and accompanying reports must be made available to the public: otherwise the transaction of business is prohibited (see more particularly Chapter 6). These requirements, arising out of the LG(AI)A 1985, are of particular significance in the case of committee and subcommittee meetings because there is elsewhere already an obligation upon local authorities to give public notice of council meetings. Separate arrangements relate to meetings of an authority's executive (see 3.4).

Closed meetings

3.10 The transaction of business likely to involve disclosure of confidential information that requires principal local authorities to exclude the public means:[6]

- information furnished to the council by a Government department upon terms, however expressed, which forbid the disclosure of the information to the public; and
- information the disclosure of which to the public is prohibited by or under any enactment or by the order of a court.

In either case, the reference to the obligation of confidence is to be construed accordingly. Because there is a statutory requirement upon the local authority or a committee or subcommittee to exclude the public in these circumstances, the generally accepted view is that there may be no need for a resolution to that effect to be passed beforehand: it is sufficient for the chairman to ask the public to withdraw so that confidential information can be dealt with.

3.11 Local authorities may by resolution[7] – they have discretion in the matter[8] – close meetings if it is likely that otherwise information within one of the specified categories of exempt information would be disclosed. These categories[9] of exempt information cover such matters as information relating to an individual, financial and business affairs of people or companies, action likely to lead to a prosecution, and legal privilege. The Secretary of State has power to amend the list.[10] It was revised with effect from 1st March 2006 (SI 2006/87). The 2006 Order substitutes a new Sch.12A for the previous Sch.12A, Parts 1 to 3 of which apply in relation to principal councils in England. In Part 1 of the new Sch.12A, some of the descriptions of information listed in Part 1 of the previous Sch.2A are replaced by simpler and clearer descriptions. Similarly, in Part 2 of the new Sch.12A, some of the previous qualifications are replaced by a public interest test under which information can be considered exempt if and so long, as in all the circumstances of the case, the public interest in maintaining the exemption outweighs the public interest in disclosing the information. There is no statutory definition of what constitites the 'public interest' but in March 2007 the Information Commissioner issued an updated Freedom of Information Act Awareness Guidance Note No 3 which sets out relevant factors to be considered. Consequential amendments are also made to ss 100F (additional rights of access to documents for members of principal councils) and 100I.

3.12 So far as Standards Committees are concerned, the Relevant Authorities (Standards Committee) (Amendment) Regulations 2006 (SI 2006/87) provide that information falling within any of the categories in Sch.12A of the 1972 Act, together with a further three categories of information set out in the Regulations, may be exempt in relation to a meeting of a Standards Committee or subcommittee. The additional three categories set out in the Regulations cover such matters as the personal circumstances of any person, and the deliberations of a Standards Committee in reaching a finding on a referred matter.

3.13 resolution for the foregoing purpose of excluding the public on the grounds that exempt information would otherwise be disclosed must:

- identify the proceedings, or part of the proceedings, to which it applies; and
- state the description, in terms of Sch.12A to the LGA 1972, of the exempt information giving rise to the exclusion of the public. Where such a resolution is passed the, local authority may lawfully exclude[12] the public during the proceedings to which the resolution applies (see 3.11).

3.14 A procedural difficulty can arise where a committee is conducting quasi-judicial business that is not concerned with an item of exempt information and, having heard the representations, wishes to consider its decision in private. The committee may find it difficult to find a reason for excluding the public but it would seem reasonable – although in the final resort only the courts can decide – for all the proceedings to be conducted in public session until the parties have concluded their statements when the chairman should say, or words to like effect: 'We will now retire to consider the representations that have been made and will reassemble shortly to announce our decision.' In other words, there would be no resolution to exclude the press and public. It was precisely in order to remove such a possibility of challenge to the courts that a specific power was given to the Standards Committee to decide that the public could be excluded from its deliberations in designated circumstances (see 3.10). In the case of hearings under the Licensing Act 2003, this has been dealt with in a different way by expressly providing in the Licensing Act (Hearings) Regulations 2005 that the licensing authority may exclude the public from all or part of a hearing where it considers that the public interest in so doing outweighs the public interest in the hearing, or that part of the hearing, taking place in public. It is important, therefore, that the statutory authority under which the committee is acting is checked to see if there is any specific power applicable to exclude the public, if it is likely that a committee will be seeking to exclude the public from all or part of its proceedings,

3. Admission of press and public

Exclusion must be reasonable

3.15 Local authorities may well regard it as important that the spirit of the law should be observed and that their proceedings should be as open as practicable. In any case, an authority must act reasonably when exercising its discretion to exclude the public from a meeting and must justify its action by reference to the statutory list of items of exempt information (see 3.11). An authority clearly cannot by subterfuge exclude the public in circumstances where it is required to admit it, e.g. by failure to give requisite notice of the meeting or by deciding to meet in a place that is manifestly inadequate to accommodate members of the public (see 3.17). In *Stoop* v. *Kensington and Chelsea London Borough Council and Another* (1991), in an application for judicial review of a decision of the council, it was held that where a local authority committee votes to refuse planning permission and then adjourns into private session to receive advice from its solicitor about the chances of successfully resisting an appeal and the likelihood of an award of costs against the authority in the event of the appeal being successful: (a) the solicitor's advice is exempt information within the meaning of the 1972 Act, Sch.12A, and therefore the committee is entitled to receive it in private; and (b) the requirement of fairness in decision-making does not require that an objector to the grant of planning permission should be given an opportunity to make further representations between the committee's receipt of that advice and its decision to change its mind and grant planning permission. Moreover, the applicant himself did not have a right to remain in the meeting when the public was excluded.

Who are the public?

3.16 The right of admission to local authority meetings applies to the public generally,[13] i.e. it is not restricted to council tax payers or electors or local residents alone, except in the case of a panel meeting or a community meeting.[14]

Adequacy of accommodation

3.17 There are obviously practical limits to the right of the public to be admitted. How much space is set aside is a matter for the local authority's discretion. During the passage of what was to become the PB(AM)A 1960 it was said that:[15]

> '. . . the duty imposed on a local authority . . . will be to choose a room big enough to take some members of the public and some reporters. It will not have to provide accommodation for an unlimited number of each . . . The usual way in which any body whose deliberations are open to the public complies with its obligations is by providing reasonable but limited accommodation for members of the public and then allocating it on the basis of first come, first served.'

3.18 If a local authority or committee or subcommittee decides to meet in a very small room and then says in effect 'We cannot have the public in because there is no room', it would be acting in bad faith; and in such an event, the Lord Chief Justice said in *R. v. Liverpool City Council ex parte Liverpool Taxi Fleet Operators' Association* (1975), the authority would not be beyond the long arm of their Lordships' court. It would seem, therefore, that where a council or committee or subcommittee is to discuss a matter in which it knows there is considerable public interest, it must either provide more accommodation for the public than is ordinarily available or at least ensure that the accommodation is no less than that ordinarily available.

3.19 On occasions, some local authorities change the normal venue for a committee meeting if it is known that a particular matter is likely to generate a large public attendance. For example, one council moved its planning committee meeting to a local theatre when considering a major planning application affecting a significant part of the borough.

Admission of Press representatives

Substantially same rights as public

3.20 Representatives of the press enjoy no rights of admission to local authority meetings greater than those conferred upon the public[16] except that an authority is required, as far as practicable, to provide 'duly accredited representatives of newspapers' with reasonable facilities (see 3.21). The term duly accredited representatives of newspapers is not defined in the LGA 1972 (nor in the LG(AI)A 1985 which amended it), but 'newspaper' includes: (a) a news agency that systematically carries on the business of selling and supplying reports of information to newspapers; and (b) any organisation that is systematically engaged in collecting news (i) for sound or television broadcasts; or (ii) for programmes to be included in a cable programme service that is or does not require to be licensed.

Facilities for the press

3.21 While a meeting is required to be open to the public, duly accredited representatives of newspapers attending the meeting for the purpose of reporting the proceedings for those newspapers must, as far as practicable, be afforded reasonable facilities for taking their report and, unless the meeting is held in premises not belonging to the council or not on the telephone, for telephoning the report at their own expense.[17] Principal authorities must, on request and on payment of postage or other necessary charges for transmission, supply for the benefit of any newspaper:

- a copy of the agenda for a meeting and accompanying reports;
- such further statements or particulars, if any, as are necessary to indicate the nature of the items included in the agenda; and
- if the proper officer thinks fit in the case of any item, copies of any other documents supplied to members of the council in connection with the item.[18]

It is permitted to be make a charge for transmission, not a charge for the documents themselves.

3. Admission of press and public

Photography, live broadcasts and tape recordings

3.22 It is expressly provided that:[19]

> 'nothing ... shall require a principal council to permit the taking of photographs of any proceedings, or the use of any means to enable persons not present to see or hear any proceedings (whether at the time or later), or the making of any oral report on any proceedings as they take place.'

This, it is submitted, does not refer only to press or similar representatives: it means that a principal council could deny a councillor or a member of the public the right.[20] There is thus no express prohibition and local authorities often now allow, for example, TV cameras and radio reporters to be present at meetings on special occasions – so long as there is no adverse effect on the conduct of proceedings (see 3.24).

Other considerations

Qualified privilege of documents provided

3.23 Where any accessible document for a local authority meeting:

- is supplied to, or open to inspection by, a member of the public; or
- is supplied for the benefit of any newspaper,

the publication thereby of any defamatory matter contained in the document is privileged unless the publication is proved to be made with malice. Care should always be taken with items such as motions set down for debate in council particularly when sensitive subjects that may refer to the actions of individual members are being dealt with.

Exclusion of public and press in event of disorder

3.24 The statutory obligation upon principal councils to admit the public and the press to their meetings is 'without prejudice to any power of exclusion to suppress or prevent disorderly conduct or other misbehaviour at a meeting' (and see 7.130 et seq. where the whole question of disorderly conduct at meetings is considered).

3.25 If the chairman of a meeting thinks it desirable or necessary to adjourn the meeting because of disorder among the public present (see 7.135) the council, committee or subcommittee cannot afterwards resume proceedings with the public still debarred from admission on the assumption that readmission would again lead to disorder, because this would be a contravention of the public's right of admission. But those persons, whether individuals or a group, could properly be excluded if persisting in disorder when business proceeded.

General principles

3.26 There appears to be no right for the press or public upon readmission, or at the end of the meeting, to be told what business was transacted in their absence,[21] although the chairman might think it appropriate to outline what has been decided.

Standing orders

3.27 There is no provision in the existing model standing orders or mandatory standing orders in respect of the admission or exclusion of the public from local authority meetings,[22] but there is no reason why standing orders should not be made regulating, within the law, local arrangements.

3.28 It is not uncommon for local authorities to include in standing orders pro forma motions that may be moved without notice, e.g. motions to exclude the public and the press. Thus in the case of a principal council when exempt information is to be considered:

> 'That under s. 100A(4) of the Local Government Act 1972, the public be excluded from the meeting for the following item(s) of business on the grounds that it (they) involve(s) the likely disclosure of exempt information as defined in paragraph(s) . . . (respectively) of Part 1 of schedule 12A of the Act.'

Or, in the case of, say, a parish or community council:

> 'That the public be excluded from this meeting during consideration of . . . as publicity would be prejudicial to the public interest because of the confidential nature of the business to be transacted.'

Practical considerations

3.29 The legislation regarding admission of the public to to meetings has created a different way of working for some councils, including an increased number of officer/member working groups, member seminars, and briefing meetings. Transacting some business in public can be inhibiting for members and, inevitably in some instances, council members are prone to indulge in party political debate for the benefit of the press, rather than to address their minds meaningfully to the business before the meeting.

Access to information

Extended access to documents

3.30 The LG(AI)A 1985 considerably extended the right of the public (and the press) to inspect the documents of principal local authorities and of their committees and

3. Admission of press and public

subcommittees,[23] and conferred on councillors, as members of those authorities, a statutory right of access to council papers.[24] The rights of the public in this respect are mentioned briefly here because in many ways the rights are closely identified with the right of access to local authority meetings: indeed, in R. v. *Hackney London Borough Council ex parte Gamper* (1985) (see 4.11), it was said that for councillors with a 'need to know' there is no logical distinction between access to documents and attendance at meetings. Public access to documents (agenda and reports) prior to a meeting is dealt with at 6.26 et seq. as regards council meetings and at 10.7 as regards committees; and to other documents (minutes and background papers) at 8.38 as regards council meetings and at 12.60 in respect of committees. The statutory right of councillors in this connection is discussed in Chapter 4. The introduction of the Freedom of Information Act 2000, and its full implementation on 1 January 2005 in relation to access to information held by local authorities, has further extended the range of information and documentation able to be accessed by the press and the public, and this issue is given more detailed consideration in paras. 3.34–3.38.

Duty to publish other information

3.31 Each principal council is also required to publish the following information and to keep it available for public inspection:[25]

- a register giving the name and address of every councillor and the ward or division represented, and the name and address of every member of each committee and subcommittee;
- a list specifying the powers exercisable by officers under delegated authority, and the title of the officer where the power is exercisable for a period of more than six months;
- a document summarising the rights that the law confers[26] upon members of the public to attend local authority meetings and council, committee and sub-committee meetings, and to inspect and copy and be furnished with documents; and
- a register of interests of members and co-opted members.[27]

Recent developments

Review of past practice

3.32 The Policy Studies Institute carried out a research project during 1995 to evaluate the first 10 years of the operation of the LG(AI)A 1985. The result, published in its report *Public Access to Information,* in general complimented local government on the manner in which authorities had applied the legislation and had in many cases gone beyond it. The report contained recommendations and a list of suggested 'best practices' as follows:

- publicity: more active steps to publicise rights including special leaflets;
- awareness: use of targeted publicity for the press and training for members;

General principles

- background papers: listing on committee papers with contact numbers;
- committee papers: seven days' advance notice wherever possible and available at local centres;
- documents: official jargon should be avoided and use of plain English encouraged;
- exempt information: minimal use encouraged to enable policy matters to be discussed in public;
- agenda: public items should be taken first;
- venues: larger accommodation should be used when necessary; and
- charging: charges should be kept as low as possible.

Good practice

3.33 Also in 1995, the then local authority associations circulated a 'good practice note', *Open Government*. It recommended that each local authority should draw up a policy on access to information by the public, assisted by the advice contained in the note, which also set out an updated, but not comprehensive, list of statutory provisions providing access rights for the public. In 2000, the model council constitution issued by the Secretary of State included a section on access to information and this has been adapted by each council to provide a summary of how information can be accessed in terms of its own decision-making structure.

Freedom of Information Act 2000

3.34 The Freedom of Information Act 2000 provides a general right of access to recorded information held by public authorities. It is intended to promote a culture of openness and accountability within the public sector by providing a right of access to information held by it. These rights are also to help promote public involvement in the decision-making process by allowing the public access to relevant information, and facilitate better understanding of how public authorities carry out their duties, make their decisions and spend public money.

3.35 The general right of access to information, however, is subject to exemptions. There are 23 categories of exemptions, some of which are absolute and others that are not. If an absolute exemption applies, then the local authority need not disclose the information. Although some absolute exemptions relate to obvious matters of secrecy, such as the intelligence services or information whose disclosure is positively prohibited by law, most of the absolute exemptions are designed to carve out from disclosure under the Act information whose availability is governed by some more specialised set of rules, and that may be accessible to the applicant by other means. For example, personal data of which the applicant is the data subject will be dealt with under the Data Protection Act 1998, disclosure of information that is subject to a duty of confidence at common law will be governed by common law principles, and disclosure of information in court documents is a matter for the rules of the court concerned. In these cases, the exemption is made absolute not to place it beyond the public gaze, but to prevent a potentially uncomfortable interaction between two specialised and potentially incompatible regimes for its disclosure.

3. Admission of press and public

3.36 If a non-absolute exemption applies, then information is only exempt from disclosure if in all the circumstances of the case, the public interest in maintaining the exemption outweighs the public interest in disclosing the information. Examples of such exemptions are law enforcement, audit functions or where it is argued by the local authority that disclosure would prejudice the effective conduct of public affairs. In the latter case, such an exemption would only apply if this was the reasonable opinion of a qualified person who, so far as local authorities are concerned, must be the monitoring officer or, in his absence, the chief executive.

3.37 The Information Commissioner is the enforcing authority for the FOI Act 2000 and various Guidance has been issued to assist local authorities in implementation. With regard to Councillors, the Information Commissioner decided that a local authority had to release details of those telephone calls a councillor had claimed for in his expenses, although the phone numbers could be redacted (Case Ref: FS50074146).

The Information Commissioner recently decided a case in respect of the quorum needed for a licensing sub-committee, when the Council sat with a quorum of two but refused to provide a copy of its legal advice (Case ref: FS50098767). The local authority relied on the S41 exemption as they claimed the information was provided in confidence, as it was part of legal advice obtained by another public authority and shared 'in confidence'. As the S41 exemption is an absolute one, there was no need for the Information Commissioner to consider whether the public interest test applied, and a different decision may well have been reached if he had had to decide whether the public interest test had been correctly applied.

Notes

1 Widdicombe Report, para.5.63.
2 This means, in addition to the principal councils listed at 1.5: a joint authority, a joint board or joint committee if a body corporate discharging the functions of two or more principal councils, a police authority which is a body corporate, and a combined fire authority (LGA 1972, s.100J, added by LG(AI)A 1985), and joint consultative committees with health authorities: LG(AI)A (Extension) Act 1986.
3 So, too, do the council of the Isles of Scilly and joint boards or joint committees that discharge functions of any of these bodies (or of any of these bodies and of a principal council or a new authority established under the LGA 1985): LG(AI)A 1985, s.4 and sch.2, para.4(2).
4 See 'Permitting the public to speak at planning committees' by Alec Samuels: an experiment by Southampton City Council: (1993) 162 *Local Government Review* 161.
5 LGA 1972, s.100A(6), added by LG(AI)A 1985.
6 Ibid. s.100A(3), added by LG(AI)A 1985.
7 Ibid. s.100A(4).
8 In exercising this discretion, an authority should bear in mind the underlying principle of open government and thus exclude the public only if satisfied it is right to do so, having regard to the information to be disclosed.
9 LGA 1972, sch.12A.
10 Ibid. s.100I(2).
11 Under the PB(AM)A 1960, s.1(2), which previously applied to all local authorities but no longer to principal councils, the power to exclude the press and public was very widely drawn in general terms (see 3.5). When the Bill was before the Commons on 5th February 1960, Margaret Thatcher, one of the sponsors of the Bill, said it had been found impossible

General principles

to draft a clause that would cover all individual cases where the public should be excluded. The 1985 Act sought to overcome that 'impossibility' but it is interesting now to see how closely the terms of the exempt information follow what Mrs Thatcher, now Baroness Thatcher, said in the Commons in 1960: 'There are two prongs to this clause. Publicity would be prejudicial for two main groups of reasons. The first group is where the matters under discussion are of a confidential nature. They may relate to personal circumstances of individual electors. They may relate to a confidential communication from a Government department asking local authorities for their opinion on a subject which the minister would not like to be discussed in open session until he is a good deal further on and has received the views of local authorities. There is another group of subjects which perhaps could not be strictly termed confidential but where it would be clearly prejudicial to the public interest to discuss them in open session. They may relate to staff matters, to legal proceedings, to contracts, the discussion of which tender to accept and other such matters. On this prong the press has to be excluded for a special reason which would need to be stated in the resolution for exclusion. Where the matter is confidential it would not need to be specified further in the resolution for exclusion. Where it was for a special reason, that reason would need to be specified in broad general terms in the resolution for exclusion.'

12 LGA 1972, s.100A(5), added by LG(AI)A 1985.
13 The point was made by Sir Jocelyn Simon, Solicitor-General, during the passage of the Bill through Parliament: House of Commons Official Report, col. 162: 30th March 1960.
14 LGA 1972, ss.13(1), 32(1).
15 By the Solicitor-General: House of Commons Official Report, cols. 119–20; 30th March 1960. Note, too, the words 'so far as practicable' in LGA 1972, s.100(1).
16 During the passage of the Public Bodies (Admission to Meetings) Bill through Parliament, the Solicitor-General made it clear in the Commons on 30th March 1960 that the press should not be admitted at the expense of the public, nor vice versa. At an earlier occasion, Henry Brooke, the then Minister of Housing and Local Government, said: 'If the public gallery is full, that does not entitle members of the public to occupy the seats set aside for the press, not would it be proper if members of the press attended . . . in enormous numbers, to say that only reporters could come in and that provision could not be made for the public.'
17 LGA 1972, s.100A(6)(c), added by LG(AI)A 1985.
18 Ibid. s.100B(7), added by LG(AI)A 1985.
19 Ibid. s.100A(7).
20 See B. E. H. Cotter. 'The Admission of Press and Public to Meetings of Local Authorities' (1974) 138 *Local Government Review* 174.
21 A view expressed at 137 JPN 153 but, of course, the public can always inspect the minutes of the meeting.
22 But the old model standing order no. 11 was to this effect: 'If any question arises at a meeting of the council (or of a committee thereof to which the Public Bodies (Admission to Meetings) Act 1960 applies by virtue of section 2(1)) as to the appointment, promotion, dismissal, salary, superannuation or conditions of service, or as to the conduct of any person employed by the council, such question shall not be the subject of discussion until the council or committee, as the case may be, has decided whether or not the power of exclusion of the public under section 1(2) of the Public Bodies (Admission to Meetings) Act 1960 shall be exercised.'
23 Access to documents of a limited range of other local authorities, i.e. parish and community councils, the council of the Isles of Scilly and joint boards or joint committees which discharge functions of any of these bodies (or of any of these bodies and a principal council) is still governed by the LGA 1972, s.228 as amended, and is thus exercisable by electors and not members of the public generally.
24 LGA 1972, s.100F, added by LG(AI)A 1985. The rights are in addition to any common law or other rights. Widdicombe suggested that these rights should all be contained in statute with no reliance on common law: Widdicombe Report. para.5.71. A council constitution will include a section on rights of access to information.

3. Admission of press and public

25 LGA 1972, s.100G, added by the LG(AI)A 1985, and amended by the LG&HA 1989, s.194 and sch.l.

26 This means not only the rights conferred by Pt VA and Pt XI of the LGA 1972 but under 'such other enactments as the Secretary of State by order specifies': and the Local Government (Inspection of Documents) (Summary of Rights) Order 1986 specifies for this purpose the several enactments listed in the schedule to the Order. See also: Appendix 1 of a good practice note, *Open Government* (1995), published by the then local authority associations.

27 LGA 2000, s.81 requires the monitoring officer to establish and maintain such a register. The register must be available for inspection by the public at an office of the authority at all reasonable hours. Once the register is established, the council should publish in one or more local newspapers a notice stating the availability of copies of the register and where it may be inspected. This requirement applies to all relevant authorities, including parish councils.

Chapter 4
Local authority membership

Election of councillors

General considerations

4.1 Members of a local authority are those persons who have been elected in accordance with the statutory rules relating to local elections[1] to serve for the requisite term of office in a representative capacity on one of the authorities referred to earlier (see 1.5): indeed, sometimes on more than one, for a person may be a member both of the county council and of a district council, or of the district and parish. When submitting himself for nomination for election and, if elected, then throughout his membership, the person must be of full age and a British subject and possess certain qualifications linking him with the area of the authority.[2] In addition, he must be free from a number of disqualifications.[3] So long as a councillor remains qualified he cannot be removed from office, though he may resign voluntarily at any time. The whole process of election and the detailed rules relating to qualification and disqualification are for the most part matters outside the scope of this work.

4.2 Some reference needs to be made in general terms, however, to the position of persons who may act as councillors though strictly disqualified from office and of the consequences of their attendance at meetings of the council and committees and sub-committees. In this respect s.82 of the LGA 1972 is important; it provides that:

> The acts and proceedings of any person elected to an office under this Act and acting in that office shall, notwithstanding his disqualification, be as valid and effective as if he had been qualified.

'Office' means the office of councillor or chairman or vice-chairman of the council or elected mayor or executive leader but not membership or the chairmanship or vice-chairmanship of a committee or sub-committee, none of which is of itself an 'office' within the Act. Nevertheless, there is a presumption elsewhere in the Act, in Sch.12, para. 41(3), applied to committees and subcommittees by s.99, that a local authority meeting has been properly constituted:

> Until the contrary is proved, a local authority meeting whose minutes have been made and signed in accordance with this paragraph shall be deemed to have been duly convened and held, and all the members present at the meeting shall be deemed to have been qualified.

4.3 The vacation of office by councillors who do not secure re-election and the coming into office of new councillors can pose administrative and procedural difficulties for local authorities. Standing orders as a rule should provide for the transitional period between the day of election and the annual meeting and the appointment of newly constituted committees (see Chapter 9). Most authorities avoid holding meetings during this period but sometimes, of course, urgent business demands that decisions must be made by councillors. The normal practice that appointments to committees are made for the council year, i.e. until the start of the next annual meeting, is necessarily conditioned by the rule that persons not re-elected at the end of their term of office cease to be councillors 'on the fourth day after the ordinary day of election' and that newly elected councillors 'shall come into office on the day on which their predecessors retire'.[4] This can cause difficulties in the payment of members' allowances – this means that councillors not re-elected may lawfully attend meetings of committees and sub-committees and meetings of outside bodies on which they represent the council on the second and third day after the date of election.[5] A councillor not re-elected may, as committee chairman, for example, properly act as such during this period. But a newly elected councillor cannot in practice attend to any council business until the annual meeting following his election, when committee membership is decided, and in any case cannot act as a councillor until he has made a declaration of acceptance of office. On this basis, he is also not able to receive payment by way of members' allowances. Under the Local Government Act 2000, s.52(2), the form of declaration of acceptance of office under this section may include an undertaking by the declarant that in performing his functions he will observe the authority's code of conduct for the time being under s.51 of the 2000 Act. The Local Elections (Declaration of Acceptance of Office) Order 2001 (SI 2001/3491) sets out the form of declaration.

As to the National Code of Local Government Conduct (see 4.7 and Appendix 3).

Rights, duties and obligations

Introduction

4.4 It is appropriate to consider briefly the rights, duties and obligations assumed by councillors following election because these are significant in relation to local authority meetings. If, for example, councillors en bloc ceased to attend meetings then the business of the local authority could not continue for very long: how long would depend upon a number of factors. Supposing the members failed to attend the first meeting of the council after their election so that the council's annual meeting could not take place: the council would not be properly constituted because it would not have a chairman.[6] On the other hand, if the members met at the annual meeting, elected a chairman, conducted such other business as the law required and passed resolutions delegating considerable executive power to officers[7] it is conceivable that the authority could function effectively and legally for some time: until no doubt some specific act required the council's formal resolution. In the absolute extremity, i.e. if through the failure of members to attend meetings it became impossible for local government to be carried on, the Government would invoke the default powers available.[8]

General principles

4.5 Widdicombe[9] divided 'the various activities that councillors undertake' into four main areas:

- activities directly related to council business, that is, attending meetings of the council and its committees and sub-committees; preparation for such meetings; meetings with council officials; travelling to and from council meetings; membership of committees;
- meetings with organisations or bodies on which councillors represent the council;
- attendance at party meetings in relation to council activities;
- meetings with the public including dealing with electors' problems, surgeries and pressure groups; attending public consultation meetings.

This suggests – as indeed is the case[10] – that most of the time which councillors spend on council activities (on average 74 hours a month) is on council, executive and committee meetings or in related preparation and travel (on average 46 hours): by contrast 13 hours a month were spent on constituency-related matters and five hours on party group meetings.

Rights and duties generally

4.6 A councillor when elected to office possesses certain rights conferred by law, e.g. is entitled to attend council meetings without hindrance; and if he can show a 'need to know' in relation to a particular item of business, can claim a common law right to attend the meeting of the committee or sub-committee concerned (see 4.12). He has otherwise only a limited right as an individual councillor (see 4.71).

The councillor also assumes certain other obligations on gaining office, e.g. he undertakes in his declaration on acceptance of office to fulfil the duties as councillor to the best of his judgment and ability (see 4.3) and undertakes to observe his authority's code of conduct (SI 2001/3941) (see 4.7) and may conceivably have some personal responsibility for breach of the code of conduct (see 4.49); but does not incur any general legal duty to attend to his voluntarily imposed tasks, e.g. he is not bound to attend meetings, although it could be argued in making the declaration of acceptance of office a councillor undertakes to discharge his duties, and there are instances (see 7.117) where liability may be incurred if he fails to attend a meeting which he ought to attend. If, however, a councillor neglects to attend meetings over a prescribed period he forfeits the office of councillor (see 4.82). A councillor's common law right to information – now clarified and given statutory backing – is discussed below (see 4.14 et seq).

National code of conduct

4.7 Section 31 of the Local Government and Housing Act 1989 enabled the Secretary of State to issue a National Code of Local Government Conduct. However, this was repealed by s.107 of the Local Government Act 2000, from a date to be appointed. The Local Government Act 2000 provides for the Secretary of State or the National Assembly for Wales to specify by order a model code of conduct which must be adopted by local authorities, and members and co-opted members must undertake to observe the code of conduct in the performance of their functions.

Right to attend meetings

4.8 A councillor has an absolute right throughout his term of office to attend every council meeting of the local authority to which he has been elected. Nowhere is this right expressly stated but an authority would be acting unlawfully if it sought to exclude a member from a meeting of the full Council, e.g. either by failing to summon him to the meeting or by denying him admission; even the exclusion of a councillor for disorderly conduct or other misbehaviour can only be for a strictly limited period: (see 7.132). But a parish or community councillor, if not on the electoral roll for the parish or community concerned, has no right to attend and take part in the proceedings of a parish or community meeting. This arises because a person, though not on the electoral register, is qualified to be a parish or community councillor if, for example, he lives outside the parish or community but within three miles of it. The National Association of Local Councils regards this as an absurdity because it means, for example, that a councillor who may have taken a leading part in a parish or community council's decision has no right to explain or defend it at an electors' meeting (although he may be invited to attend and address the electors present), nor may he vote. The law does, however, permit a parish or community council chairman to take part in the proceedings and he must preside if present; and although he cannot vote with the body of electors, he has a casting vote.

4.9 Where, however, a member:

- ceases to be qualified for membership of the authority; or
- becomes disqualified for membership of the authority; or
- ceases to be a member of the authority by reason of failure to attend the meetings (see 4.94);

and the authority has, where necessary, declared the member's office to be vacant, the authority could properly deny him admission as a member – though he could, of course, attend as a member of the public.

4.10 The right of a councillor to attend committee meetings is, however, a qualified one. In the first place a councillor need not serve on any committee at all: he cannot be appointed to a committee if unwilling to serve (see *R* v. *Sunderland Corporation* (1911), where it was held that a person who is appointed to serve on a committee may lawfully resign against the will of the council); nor can he dispute the council's decision if it does not appoint him to any committee or, having appointed him, deprives him of committee membership (*Manton* v. *Brighton Corporation* (1951), although the council must be scrupulous in observing its standing orders in this respect: *R* v. *Rushmoor Borough Council ex parte Crawford* (1981) and see 2.13). So long as he remains a member of a committee, he is entitled to attend all the committee's meetings for the duration of his local authority membership. As to a councillor's right to attend meetings of committees/cabinet to which he has not been appointed, e.g. where he claims a 'need to know' (see 4.16).

General principles

4.11 A councillor who has not been appointed to a particular committee can claim a right to attend a meeting of the committee, but not to vote, if able to show a 'need to know'. This appears to be a result of *R* v. *Hackney London Borough Council ex parte Gamper* (1985),[12] where the court applied the principle enunciated in *City of Birmingham District Council* v. *O and another* (1983) (see 4.17) which related to a councillor's entitlement to information. It has always been open to a local authority (in circumstances usually prescribed by standing orders) to permit a councillor to attend meetings of committees of which he is not a member, but prior to the *Gamper* case it was thought that no councillor could claim a right to attend – except in so far as he could be present in the public gallery as a member of the public. In *Hackney*, however, the court took the view that there was really no logical distinction between access to documents and access to meetings, i.e. the common law was the same if access was necessary in order to enable the councillor to perform his duties as a councillor. The court also decided that members of parent committees had an automatic right to attend all of that committee's subcommittees.

Right with others to call meetings

4.12 A councillor has no right, as an individual member, to demand a meeting of the full Council. He can, however, join with others in requisitioning a council meeting (see 6.4). Any right he may possess of calling a meeting of a committee is dependent on standing orders.

Access to information

4.13 It has long been recognised that a councillor has a common law right to be provided with or to inspect council documents which it is reasonably necessary for him to see in order to carry out his duties as a councillor. That common law right has now been restated in important respects (see 4.15 et seq); and in 1986, for the first time, the councillor, if a member of a principal council, was given a statutory right of access to prescribed categories of document (see 4.14). A councillor has always, of course, been able to exercise the same power of inspection of documents that members of the public or electors possess (see 3.26).

4.14 A councillor's statutory right of access to documents is provided by s.100F of the LGA 1972, added by the LG(AI)A 1985, which came into effect on 1st April 1986. This provides that 'any document which is in the possession or under the control of a principal council and contains material relating to any business to be transacted at a meeting of the council or a committee or sub-committee' must be open to inspection by any member of the principal council. This means that a councillor's statutory right of access is limited to documents concerned with business about to be transacted at a meeting. A member cannot, for example, demand to see a document which relates to business not yet due to come before a meeting; and it is submitted that if he wishes to delve into a matter which has been dealt with in the past he must resort to the right of access available to the public generally or to his common law entitlement (see 4.15). Indeed, it is expressly stated that the statutory rights are in addition to any other rights which a councillor might have. Section 22 of the LGA 2000 provides that the

4. Local authority membership

Secretary of State may make regulations in respect of access to information, and the Local Authorities (Executive Arrangements) (Access to Information) (England) Regulations 2000 came into force on 9th January 2001. These regulations give additional rights to allow any member of a local authority to inspect any document which contains material relating to any business to be transacted at a public meeting. In the event of a private meeting, they provide that any member can inspect the documentation when the meeting concludes. They also allow any member to inspect documentation following an executive decision being made by a member, or key decision by an officer. This right does not extend to documents which contain exempt information (see 3.35).

4.15 A councillor's common law right of access to council documents is dependent (and always has been though not expressed in precisely the same terms) upon a 'need to know' in order to enable him properly to perform his duties as a councillor: *R v. Barnes Borough Council ex parte Conlan* (1938). But it has never been an absolute right. Humphrey J said in *Barnes* it could not extend to all documents 'since in the case of a large local authority it would be an impossible burden to become acquainted with all the council's business'. And there is no right to 'a roving commission to go and examine the books or documents of a corporation'. Mere curiosity or desire to see and inspect documents is not sufficient (see *R v. Southwold Corporation* (1907)). Nor can a councillor properly exercise the right for some indirect motive, e.g. to assist someone in litigation with the council (see *R v. Hampstead Borough Council* (1917)).

4.16 In the case of *R v. Hackney London Borough Council, ex parte Gamper* (1985) the applicant was a councillor on the respondent council, and was also a member of the council's public services and housing committees, and chairman of a housing services sub-committee. The council created three new sub-committees of the public services committee, two of which were responsible for looking after the direct labour organisations (DLO) employed by the council. The applicant, in his capacity as a member of the parent committee and of the housing services sub-committee, requested access to certain documents and meetings of the DLO sub-committees. The council refused him access to the documents and to the meetings. He applied for an order to quash the council's decision.

The court decided that the principle that a council member had a right of access to committee documents provided he could show that he had a 'need to know' and that where he was a member of the committee in question he would generally be assumed to have such a need to know, were equally applicable to sub-committee documents. The council should have considered whether the applicant had a need to know in respect of the confidential documents; and since the council had merely considered whether the documents were confidential, and not whether the councillor had a need to know, the council's decision was quashed. It was also held that, even if the council had considered the applicant's individual need to know, its decision to refuse the applicant access to the documents was a decision which no reasonable council could have reached if properly directed in law. Furthermore, there was no logical distinction between access to documents and attendance at meetings and therefore since, on the facts, the applicant needed to attend the meetings of the DLO sub-committees in order to perform his duties properly as a member of the council, the council's decision would be quashed.

General principles

4.17 This followed the decision taken by the House of Lords in *City of Birmingham District Council* v. *O and another* (1983). In that case a member of the city council's housing committee had asked to see the papers of the social services committee concerning the adoption proceedings of a child in the council's care. The councillor, as a member of the housing committee, had become aware that the prospective adoptive parents had a bad record of rent arrears and that the husband had previously served a prison sentence, and the councillor believed that to allow the adoption proceedings to continue could constitute a serious error of judgement by the social services committee. The councillor's request for access to the social services committee's papers was not opposed by the council but by the prospective adoptive parents, who sought judicial intervention through an order of prohibition to prevent disclosure. The House of Lords held that the general principle was that a councillor was entitled by virtue of his office to have access to all written material in the possession of the council provided he had good reason for such access, and that a councillor ex hypothesi normally had good reason for such access to all written material in the possession of a committee of which he was a member and, second, that a councillor had no automatic right of access to material in the possession of a committee of which he was not a member. In the case of information in the possession of a committee of which he was not a member, a councillor had to demonstrate a need to know such information in order to be able to carry out duties as a councillor properly. This decision was ultimately a decision for the council itself, although the council was entitled expressly or impliedly to delegate this function. Applying those principles, there were undoubtedly grounds for questioning the wisdom of the proposed adoption, and the council itself would ultimately be responsible if the adoption should prove unsuccessful. It was therefore not unreasonable for the council to permit the councillor to have access, in confidence, to the files of the council's social services department relating to the child and the applicants. The position was not altered by the fact that the council had delegated its functions in relation to adoption to the social services committee, because the council itself had a residual responsibility for the committee's actions and an obligation, in appropriate circumstances, to exercise some degree of control over the committee. (See 1.43 as to the *Wednesbury* principle.)

4.18 In *R* v. *Clerk to Lancashire Police Committee ex parte Hook* (1980), the question arose as to whether a councillor elected after a highly confidential report had been considered and acted upon had a right to see the document to enable him to perform his duties as a councillor. The Court of Appeal (Lord Denning MR dissenting) upheld the decision of the divisional court refusing to grant an order directing the clerk of the police authority to provide an unabridged copy of the report to the new councillor. The report was the result of an inquiry conducted by the chief constable of Hampshire. It disclosed serious shortcomings in the Lancashire police force and leading counsel had advised the police authority that, as the report contained defamatory statements, publication might endanger the privilege that would otherwise attach to it and that the safest course would be to refuse new members access to it. The report was leaked, however, and a police officer was awarded substantial damages for libel. The new councillor in good faith sought through the courts to compel the clerk to supply him with an unabridged copy of the report.

4. Local authority membership

Waller LJ, citing *Stuart* v. *Bell* and *Adam* v. *Ward* (1917), held that the committee had not decided on improper advice and said the final decision must in the last resort be that of the committee, which could take into consideration possible adverse effects on innocent people of allowing the inspection of documents. It was not reasonably necessary for the new councillor to have access to matters not disclosed to enable him to carry out his duties: he was not concerned with the daily management of the police force. Lord Denning dissented. He said the new councillor simply wanted to be better informed at any subsequent consideration of the matter. A member has a right to see all a committee's documents, and this included a new member.

4.19 This area can present difficulties when faced with requests by members to see file papers and confidential reports. However, the above cases make it clear that an officer faced with a request is required to satisfy himself that the member is entitled to the information. The crucial questions are these: is it necessary for the member to see that particular document or paper to get the information he is seeking; and are the duties he is seeking to carry out those which he has 'as a councillor'; are they, in other words, consistent with his responsibilities as an elected member of the council in question? These can be difficult questions to answer – and a difficult position for the member to understand. Because of this, it is good practice for there to be a written code and for any necessary appeals machinery to be set up in advance.

4.20 An anomaly was created by the Local Government (Access to Information) Act 1985, whereby councillors are entitled to inspect documents containing certain categories of exempt information (i.e. information not open to the public) even though they may have a financial interest in the matter. The effect is that, for example, councillors may inspect the tenders of firms for council contracts even where they are proposing to tender in a private capacity. This is clearly wrong, as councillors should never be entitled to inspect documents in which they have a financial interest, unless they are open to the public. This would however constitute a breach of the Code of Conduct, whereby a member must not use his position to gain an advantage for himself or others.

Obligations generally

4.21 The obligations of a councillor at a meeting are the same whether the meeting is that of the full council or a committee or sub-committee. He must avoid doing anything which might encourage a charge of maladministration against the council and is expected:

- to comply with standing orders;
- to behave in an orderly manner;
- to refrain from taking part in the consideration or discussion and voting on any contract or other matter in which he has a prejudicial interest or in respect of which he is otherwise prohibited from voting;
- to observe the law.

General principles

Compliance with standing orders

4.22 If a councillor fails to comply with standing orders he should be:

- called to order by the person presiding, if the omission to comply is a breach of the order of debate at a meeting;
- interviewed by the chairman of the council, or the leader, and asked to comply if the offending member is in breach of some other standing order.

If a councillor behaves in a disorderly manner at a meeting the chairman can, with the consent of the meeting, order him to leave temporarily; and in an extreme case of persistent disregard the council could show its displeasure by depriving the member of all committee membership (see 7.132). It could not properly, however, deny him a right to be present at any committee or sub-committee meeting if he can show a 'need to know' (see 4.11); and it is probable that the council could not impose its will on a political group which insisted on appointing a particular member to a committee under the proportionality regulations (see 9.53). A councillor may however be bringing his office into disrepute by his behaviour, which is a breach of the code of conduct.

Confidentiality of council papers

4.23 Councillors are expected to treat as confidential all papers which they receive in the course of council business unless made public by law or by the authority's express or implied consent. The revised model code of conduct provides that a member must not:

(a) disclose information given to him in confidence by anyone, or information acquired by him which he believes, or ought reasonably to be aware, is of a confidential nature, except where –
   (i) you have the consent of a person authorised to give it;
   (ii) you are required by law to do so;
   (iii) the disclosure is made to a third party for the purpose of obtaining professional advice provided that the third party agrees not to disclose the information to any other person; or
   (iv) the disclosure is –
      (aa) reasonable and in the public interest; and
      (bb) made in good faith and in compliance with the reasonable requirements of the authority; or
(b) prevent another person from gaining access to information to which that person is entitled by law.

This wording has altered from the model code issued in 2001, and is in line with the Freedom of Information Act 2000. It does however give members flexibility under (a)(iv) above to decide what is in the public interest, and may lead to challenges in respect of members 'leaking' information.

4.24 All reports made or minutes kept by any committee or cabinet shall, as soon as the committee has concluded action on the matter to which such reports or minutes relate, be open for the inspection of any member of the council.

Payment of allowances

4.25 An entirely different system of allowances for councillors was introduced under s.18 of the LG&HA 1989 with these three purposes in mind:

- to give each council greater freedom, within an overall ceiling on remuneration, to adopt a system of allowances suited to its own circumstances;
- to end the apparent incentive to multiply the number of days on which councillors undertake approved duties; and
- to restrict the ability of councils to pay allowances in respect of party political activities.

Certain former allowances under the LGA 1972 were retained, i.e. those relating to the reimbursement of travelling and subsistence allowances incurred on 'approved duty'. The Local Government Act 2000 additionally introduced new categories for members, and the current position, set out in the Local Authorities (Members Allowances) Regulations 2003 (SI 1021/2003) which came into effect on 1st May 2003 briefly summarised, is as follows:

- special responsibility allowance, for leader, deputy leader, cabinet members and chairmen of committees, and leaders of political groups;
- basic allowance;
- attendance allowance;
- dependant carers allowance;
- conference attendance allowance;
- co-optees allowance;
- travelling and subsistence allowances.

4.26 Entitlement to special responsibility, basic and attendance allowances depends on a scheme made by each principal authority concerned.

4.27 Allowances payable under the LG&HA 1989[13] must be in accordance with a scheme made by the principal councils concerned. The scheme must provide for payment of a basic allowance of the same amount to each member and special responsibility allowances which need not be the same and fall into one or more categories specified, i.e. acting as leader or deputy leader of a political group; presiding at meetings; representing the authority at meetings of, or arranged by, any body; membership of a committee or sub-committee that meets with exceptional frequency or for exceptionally long periods; acting as spokesman for a political group on a committee or sub-committee; and other activities requiring at least the same time and effort as any of the foregoing[14] and may provide for attendance allowances payable in respect of the performance of such duties as are specified in the scheme and fall into one of the categories set out in the regulations, i.e. attendance at meetings of the authority or any of its committees or sub-committees or any other body to which the authority makes an appointment or nomination; at other meetings authorised by the authority, one of its committees or subcommittees, or a joint committee (but not private political group meetings); at meetings of local authority associations.

Recent reviews of allowances carried out by independent panels set up for the purpose have suggested reductions, and in some cases abolition, of attendance allowances. The use of such panels was encouraged by the local authority associations which issued guidance to chief executives in 1995.

4.28 A member of a parish or community council who is a councillor is entitled to receive an attendance allowance of such reasonable amount, not exceeding the prescribed amount, as the council may determine for the performance of any approved duty.[15] Alternatively such a member may opt instead to receive a financial loss allowance, not exceeding the prescribed amount, in respect of any loss of earnings necessarily suffered, or any additional expenses (other than travelling or subsistence) necessarily suffered or incurred in performance of the approved duty. But payment may not be made under these provisions to parish or community councillors in respect of duties performed within the parish or community or grouped parish or community.

4.29 Councillors are also entitled to travelling and subsistence allowances in respect of expenditure necessarily incurred in the performance of approved duties.[16] Except for parish and community councillors, travelling expenses are payable in respect of all approved duty, whether within or outside the area of the authority, and with no minimum distance; and a subsistence allowance is payable to a member where the expenditure on subsistence is necessarily incurred by him. For parish and community councillors, travelling expenses and subsistence allowances are not payable unless the duty lies outside the parish or community or grouped parish or community. An authority may pay allowances to any member attending a conference or meeting held inside or outside the United Kingdom for the purposes of discussing matters which in its opinion relate to the interests of the area or its inhabitants but this does not extend to conferences or meetings convened by a commercial or political organisation. All these allowances are payable to members of a number of other prescribed bodies. Maximum rates for certain allowances are specified or prescribed by regulations. An authority has power to defray travelling and other expenses reasonably incurred by or on behalf of any members in making official and courtesy visits, inside or outside the United Kingdom, on behalf of the council and in the reception and entertainment of distinguished persons visiting its area.

4.30 Under the Police and Magistrates' Courts Act 1994 (now the Police Act 1996), a new scheme of allowances was introduced for councillors and independent members of police authorities based on an hourly rate within prescribed maxima. Rates for attending conferences convened by one or more police authorities or by an association of police authorities continue to be governed by the regulations affecting local authorities as a whole.

Duty to disclose pecuniary and non-pecuniary interests

4.31 Probably the most important obligation imposed upon a councillor by law is that which requires him to disclose any pecuniary interest in a matter which is before a meeting at which he is present and to refrain from participating in the discussion thereon and from voting. The provisions of s.94 of the LGA 1972 provided that if a member of a local authority had any pecuniary interest, direct or indirect, in any contract, proposed contract or other matter, and is present at a meeting of the local authority at which the contract or other matter is the subject of consideration, he should at the meeting and as soon as practicable after its commencement disclose the fact and shall not take part in the consideration or discussion of the contract or other matter or vote on any question with respect to it. This section is prospectively repealed by the LGA 2000 from a date to be appointed, presumably because the model code of conduct now covers this area satisfactorily.

Declarations of interest

4.32 The statutory regime governing declarations of interests was sharply criticised by the Nolan Committee. It recommended that all pecuniary and non-pecuniary interests should be treated together; that they should be registered and declared where members were 'likely to be influenced' in their consideration of the issue; and that members should withdraw where there was a real danger of bias: in other words where the member was affected more than the generality of people by the decision being taken. Nolan took the view that the existing statutory position was difficult to understand and even more difficult to comply with.

4.33 Following on from the Nolan recommendations, the LGA 2000 gave power to the Secretary of State to issue and revise a model code of conduct in respect of local authorities. The Local Authorities (Model Code of Conduct) (England) Order 2001 (SI 3575/2001) came into force on 27th November 2001 and set out a model code of conduct for both those authorities operating executive arrangements and those who operate alternative arrangements. The model code of conduct was revised by Local Authorities (Model Code of Conduct) Order 2007, SI 2007/1159. The provisions of the model code set out in the Schedules are mandatory, and every local authority had to adopt the code of conduct for members and co-opted members.

4.34 The code of conduct may also incorporate any optional provisions of that model code and may include other provisions which are consistent with it. As soon as reasonably practicable after adopting or revising a code of conduct under this provision, a relevant authority must:

- ensure that copies of the code or revised code of conduct are available at an office of the authority for inspection by members of the public at all reasonable hours;
- publish in one or more newspapers circulating in its area a notice which (a) states that it has adopted or revised a code of conduct; (b) states that copies of the code or revised code are available at an office of the authority for inspection by members of the public at such times as may be specified in the notice; (c) and specifies the address of that office; and
- send a copy of the code or revised code, in the case of a relevant authority in England or a police authority in Wales, to the Standards Board for England, and in the case of a relevant authority in Wales, to the Commission for Local Administration in Wales.

General principles

A relevant authority may publicise its adoption or revision of a code of conduct in any other manner that it considers appropriate.

4.35 A councillor must declare his interest either at the start of a meeting or prior to the item on the agenda in which the interest arises. Some local authorities have a practice of having agenda items at the beginning for members to give notice of their interests. Interests are then recorded in the minutes, and the minute book itself then suffices as a record of particular declarations so made.

Personal interests

4.36 Members need to declare any personal interests that they have in matters to be discussed at meetings, before the matter is discussed or as soon as they become aware of it. Personal interests are defined by the Standards Board as: 'a matter that affects the well being or financial position of the member, their relatives or their friends more than it would affect other people in the authority's area.' Members are advised to look at how any decision reached in a meeting would affect:

- You and their jobs and businesses.
- You and their employers, firms that you or they are a partner of, and companies in which you or they are directors of corporate bodies in which you or they have a 'beneficial interest' in a type of share with a face value (as shown on the share certificate) of more than £5000.

In addition, members also have to consider organisations in which they or their friends or family hold positions of general control or management, including companies, charities, lobbying groups and trade unions.

4.37 Personal interests, and the nature of them, must be declared (i.e. 'I declare a personal interest as I am employed by xxxx'), even when it is shown in the register of members interests. Personal interests can also be those which would negatively affect, as well as those which would benefit, a member.

Having declared a personal interest, a member can stay in the room and vote unless his interest is also prejudicial.

Prejudicial Interests

4.38 The Standards Board advises members that 'you must ask yourself whether a member of the public who knows the relevant facts would think that your personal interest was so significant that it would prejudice your judgment of the public interest'. Members who declare a personal and prejudicial interest must take no part in the debate and must leave the room.

4.39 Members also have prejudicial interests when sitting on overview and scrutiny committees which are checking a decision made by another committee on which the member sits. A member can however attend an overview and scrutiny committee to give evidence or answer questions (see 1.76).

The revised code of conduct has sought to clear up the area of members who are appointed to external bodies by the council, or who hold positions in their own right (see 1.76).

Standards committee dispensations

4.40 The Secretary of State is no longer empowered under s.97 LGA 1972 to remove a disability imposed on members – this was prospectively repealed by the LGA2000. Members can now apply for a dispensation to their own standards committee. The circumstances in which a dispensation can be obtained are set out in reg. 3 of the Relevant Authorities (Standards Committee) (Dispensation) Regulations 2002 (SI 2002/339). A dispensation can be obtained in two distinct circumstances:

- when at least 50% of those entitled to participate are prevented from doing so by a prejudicial interest, or
- when the political balance of a decision making body is upset.

4.41 Dispensations must not be granted as a matter of course, as the Standards Committee must be satisfied in the light of all the circumstances of the case that it is appropriate to grant a dispensation. They can only be obtained by written application to the Standards Committee, and the power to grant a dispensation cannot be delegated either to individual members of the Standards Committee or to officers.

4.42 The Standards Committee can grant dispensations for an occasion or occasions. In addition, they can grant a dispensation for members to remain in the room but not vote. Regulation 3(2)(a) effectively allows a Standards Committee to grant a dispensation for a period of up to four years. The Standards Committee needs to be satisfied that the criteria for granting a dispensation would be met for the whole period, however the Standards Board for England considers that such circumstances will be rare. Dispensations are not available to individual members of the executive to allow them to exercise delegated decision making, and alternative arrangements must be made by the authority if this arises, e.g. the decision could be taken by the cabinet or delegated to an officer instead.

4.43 The Standards Board for England strongly recommends that members relying on a dispensation in order to participate in consideration of a matter in which they have a prejudicial interest, state this publicly at the same time as they declare the existence of the nature of the interest.

4.44 The Monitoring Officer must ensure that the existence, duration and nature of a dispensation is recorded in writing and such record is kept with the Register of Interests. It is also useful for the committee clerk to know what dispensations are in existence to prevent embarrassment or difficulty when questions are raised by other members.

Personal liability

4.45 Responsibility for decisions made in council or committee meetings is, politically at least, a collective responsibility: the responsibility is that indivisibly of the members as a whole and the decision made is taken in the name of the local authority (see 5.13 as to the immunity of councillors (and officers) in this respect). There are, however, circumstances in which a council member incurs personal liability at law, for example for breach of the code of conduct.

4.46 A mandatory standing order entitles a councillor to require that his vote against a motion shall be recorded in the minutes (see 8.25) and this may well save him from unjustified personal liability. If, however, the minutes do not disclose who voted for and against a proposition it is open to a member to prove that he voted against. Thus in *Attorney-General* v. *Tottenham Local Board* (1872) a member who proved he had opposed a scheme was held not liable personally for illegal expenditure even though he was present when the payment was authorised.

4.47 It has always been the function of an authority's advisers to alert members to any possible illegality of a course which the council or committee wishes to pursue. Where an authority persists in pursuing what the officers believe may be an unlawful course of action the officers should do what they properly can to protect the interests of the authority and its individual members. In *R.* v. *Browne* (1907) and *Davies* v. *Cowperthwaite* (1938) it was held that it was not necessarily misconduct for a councillor to ignore the advice of the town clerk if the councillor honestly believed the advice to be erroneous; but this view now needs to be related to the duties of the monitoring officer and the chief finance officer, and the action which the law requires to be taken by the local authority on their report (see 4.49 and 13.14). In addition, the model code of conduct provides that members should have regard to the advice of the monitoring officer and chief finance officer. Because expenditure on items which are lawful in themselves can be so excessive and unreasonable in amount as to render the expenditure unlawful, the committee clerk should ensure that the grounds for the decision and the reasoning are fully recorded; and it may be useful to include a phrase to this effect:

> '... and the council/committee therefore considered it reasonable in all the circumstances [to take the action decided upon]'.

Monitoring officer

4.48 Relevant local authorities have a duty[17] to designate one of their officers, to be known as 'the monitoring officer', who cannot be the head of paid service nor the (s.151) finance officer. The Monitoring Officer is responsible under s.5A(2) LGHA1989 for preparing a report if she considers that any proposal, decision or omission, in the course of the discharge of functions of the relevant authority, by or on behalf of the relevant authority's executive, constitutes, has given rise to or is likely to or would give rise to any of following:

- a contravention by the authority, by any committee, or sub-committee of the authority, by any person holding any office or employment under the authority or by any such joint committee of any enactment or rule of law *or of any code of practice made or approved by or under any enactment*; or

- any such maladministration or injustice as is mentioned in Part III of the Local Government Act 1974 (Local Commissioners) or Part II of the Local Government (Scotland) Act 1975 (which makes corresponding provision for Scotland); or
- a matter which the Public Services Ombudsman for Wales would be entitled to investigate under the Public Services Ombudsman (Wales) Act 2005,

to prepare a report to the authority with respect to that proposal, decision or omission. Where the authority are operating executive arrangements, the monitoring officer shall not make a report in respect of any proposal, decision or omission unless it is a proposal, decision or omission made otherwise than by or on behalf of the relevant authority's executive.

4.49 The monitoring officer must consult so far as practicable with the head of paid service and the chief finance officer when preparing a report, and as soon as practicable after a report has been prepared she must arrange for a copy of it to be sent to each member of the authority and, where the authority has a mayor and council manager executive, the council manager: s.5A(5).

4.50 The council's executive must consider any report by the monitoring officer (or deputy) at a meeting held not more than 21 days after copies of the report are first sent to members of the executive; and to ensure that no step is taken for giving effect to any proposal or decision to which such a report relates at any time while the implementation of the proposal or decision is suspended in consequence of the report: LG&HA 1989, s.5A(6) (s.5A as added). As soon as practicable after the executive has finished considering the monitoring officers report, it must itself prepare a report which specifies what action (if any) the executive has taken in response to the monitoring officer's report; what action (if any) the executive proposes to take in response to that report and when it proposes to take that action; and the reasons for taking the action specified in the executive's report or, as the case may be, for taking no action: s.5A(8) (s.5A as added). As soon as practicable after the executive has prepared that report it must arrange for a copy of it to be sent to each member of the authority and the authority's monitoring officer.

Responsibility for maladministration

4.51 The view has been expressed that 'the acts of individual members ... may become the subject of maladministration':[18]

> A commitment entered into by a member of the council, particularly if he has been held out by the council as having authority, e.g. by a public surgery advertised by the council, could well give rise to a finding of maladministration if the obligation is not honoured. The failure of one committee member to disclose a non-financial interest, as defined by the code of conduct, might constitute maladministration by the local authority itself.

4.52 Widdicombe proposed that breach of the National Code of Local Government Conduct should be prima facie maladministration so far as the code comes within the ombudsman's ambit,[19] and indeed the ombudsman may make a finding of mal-administration by the council in such circumstances.

4.53 In addition, the exercise of a local authority power in order to obtain an election advantage ('gerrymandering') is unlawful and any person responsible for the formulation and implementation of such a policy is liable for any resulting loss incurred by the relevant local authority: *Porter* v. *Magill* (2001).

Co-option

General power of co-option

4.54 Local authorities have long been able to include within the membership of their committees persons who are not elected members of the appointing authority. The position now is that the general effect of the power to co-opt in the LGA 1972, 102(3), has been modified by the LG&HA 1989, s.13, by defining, in somewhat complex terms, the two categories of voting and non-voting members of a committee, sub-committee or joint committee.

4.55 Thus local authorities have a general power[20] to co-opt persons from outside their membership to any committee, other than a committee for regulating or controlling finance, appointed under the enabling power of the 1972 Act to set up committees.[21] The provisions as to co-option do not apply to statutory committees (see 9.23) where the constitution of the particular committee and the duty or power to co-opt are regulated by the enactment concerned. The power to co-op rests with the council in full assembly and not with committees;[22] although the selection of persons to serve as co-opted members is usually left to the committees. There is no power to co-opt to the full council.[23]

4.56 Co-opted persons appointed under the general enabling power must not be disqualified from membership of the appointing authority[24] but do not need to be positively qualified to be a councillor of the authority. The law is silent as to the qualification of persons for co-option. In practice local authorities which, for example, invite voluntary bodies to appoint a representative to serve on a committee as a co-opted member do not ask (although presumably they could do) whether the representative is of full age or a British subject or fulfils the requirements as to residential qualifications. The former restriction on the number of co-opted members to not more than one-third of the membership of a committee no longer applies.[25] Although persons holding politically restricted posts are prohibited from membership of a local authority, this prohibition does not appear to affect co-option on to committees.

Rights and obligations

4.57 A co-opted member of a committee has, in general, no voting rights (but see 4.55); nor does he possess any rights or privileges in respect of any other committee of the council, nor may he attend council meetings (other than in his capacity, of course, as a member of the public). A co-opted member is, however, under the same obligations as members of the council which appoints him: he must observe the council's standing orders and, most importantly, must comply with the statutory rules relating to disclosure of pecuniary interests (see 4.31). Co-opted members are entitled to travelling and subsistence allowances on the same basis as councillors[26] but not to an attendance allowance, although a financial loss allowance is payable in lieu.

4.58 The general rule now is that, with some exceptions, co-opted members have no voting rights.[27] The exceptions cover co-opted members of a number of specified committees and their sub-committees, including sea fisheries, superannuation, National Parks, and education appeal committees, advisory committees and other committees exercising functions prescribed by regulations.[28] Functions so prescribed include land management, the promotion of tourism, the management of a festival (in the case of a county council), functions under, inter alia, the HA 1980 or the Local Authority Social Services Act 1970 discharged by a committee comprising county and district members. Other than in the case of advisory committees and other cases prescribed by regulations,[29] to be a voting member of a sub-committee a co-opted member must also be a member of the local authority; in addition the Secretary of State may approve arrangements for co-opted members of education committees and sub-committees representing persons who appoint foundation governors of voluntary schools to be voting members.

Co-opted member as committee chairman

4.59 In the past it was acknowledged that a co-opted member of a committee could be elected as its chairman, although it was recognised there were disadvantages. Even in the different circumstances of today a committee could, if so minded, elect a co-opted member as its chairman but, except when the business before the committee was business on which the co-opted member was entitled to vote, he could not otherwise exercise the power of a person presiding to give a second or casting vote. A co-opted member cannot fulfil the full tasks of a chairman in any case: he could not as such attend council meetings and pilot his committee's proposals through the full assembly, nor answer questions put to him there, nor indeed represent the committee on other committees. A councillor vice-chairman could conceivably deputise for a co-opted member chairman in such circumstances; and there is the somewhat analogous situation where the chairman of a police authority is a magistrate or an independent member (see Chapter 9).

Removal of co-opted member

4.60 It would seem that a local authority can always remove from committee membership any person whom it has co-opted to a committee on the analogy of *Manton v. Brighton Corporation*: (see 4.10). As it has power to remove a council member from one of its own committees (or a joint committee to which it is a party), then it must be presumed to have similar power over a co-opted member. This view is reinforced by the decision in R v. *Peak Planning Board ex parte Jackson* (1976), in which a distinction is made between nomination and appointment. If the outside body upon whose nomination the person has been co-opted notifies the local authority that it wishes to replace its nominee then, always assuming that the co-opted person has not become disqualified, the local authority alone can determine whether to accede to the nominating body's request.

Representation on other local authorities and public bodies

General considerations

4.61 Local authorities are often invited, and in some instances have a right, to be represented on other bodies, both statutory and voluntary, i.e. other than those to which the rules relating to political balance apply (as to which, see 9.53), although, of course, where the numbers of representatives allow, there is no reason why an authority, should not appoint on the basis of political proportionality. The role to be exercised by the representatives on these other bodies depends upon the terms of their appointment. Any conflict of interest that might arise as between the aims and objectives of the council and those of the other body could have severe repercussions for members – or, indeed, officers. In *Burgoïne and Cooke* v. *London Borough of Waltham Forest and McWhirr* (1996) the court held that officers representing the council on an outside body were unable to take advantage of an indemnity given by the council, thus rendering them personally vulnerable when the outside body went into liquidation. This position has now changed as a result of the Local Authorities (Indemnities for Members and Officers) Order 2004 (see 4.71). In addition, members have to bear in mind whether they need to declare a personal and prejudicial interest when discussing matters that relate to outside bodies to which they are appointed (see 4.38).

4.62 It is good practice for the local authority to know the terms of reference of each body to which a member (or officer) is appointed, and whether that body carries indemnity insurance in respect of the member (or officer). Indeed, some insurance companies require the authority to show that they have managed the risk by vetting activities and maintaining accurate records

4.63 The appointment or nomination of representatives on other bodies is ordinarily reserved to the full council, unless they are executive appointments, and dealt with at the annual meeting. Old model standing order no. 16 regulates the voting on appointments in this manner:

> Where there are more than two persons nominated for any position to be filled by the council, and of the votes given there is not a majority in favour of one person, the name of the person having the least number of votes shall be struck off the list and a fresh vote shall be taken, and so on until a majority of votes is given in favour of one person.

Nomination or appointment?

4.64 It is a matter dependent upon the circumstances of each particular case whether the representative is an appointee or a nominee. In all cases of co-option, the

4. Local authority membership

submission of a person's name is mere nomination and it is the local authority on whose committee the person is to serve that makes the actual appointment. In such a case the nominating body cannot recall the nominee or revoke the appointment: his continuation in office is solely for the appointing local authority to decide. In other cases where the local authority or other body itself appoints its representatives on another local authority or other public body, the local authority can always revoke the appointment and substitute another representative at any time.

Defamatory statements in council and committee

General principle

4.65 Statements in council and committee meetings are subject to the general principles of law relating to defamation[30] that is to say, a person who makes a defamatory statement (one exposing a person to hatred, ridicule or contempt, or which causes him to be shunned or avoided, or which has a tendency to injure him in his office, profession or trade) commits a tort and is liable for the consequences which flow from such an act.

Privilege

4.66 It is a general defence in an action for defamation for the defendant to show that the statement was made on a privileged occasion. There are two kinds of privileged occasion: absolute and qualified. Local authorities do not enjoy absolute privilege even when acting judicially (see *Royal Aquarium and Summer and Winter Gardens Society* v. *Parkinson* (1892)). Where the privilege is absolute – as in certain judicial and Parliamentary proceedings – it is a complete defence to an action for defamation.

4.67 Qualified privilege attaches to: 'an occasion where the person who makes a communication has an interest or a duty, legal, social or moral, to make it to the person to whom it is made, and the person to whom it is so made has a corresponding interest or duty to receive it.'

4.68 Qualified privilege will attach to statements made in council, cabinet and committee. Where pleaded in an action for defamation the author of the defamatory statement must prove (a) a duty to make the statement, and (b) an interest on the part of the recipient to receive it: but the plaintiff may still succeed if able to prove malice on the defendant's part because an essential feature of qualified privilege is the absence of malice. Reckless disregard as to whether what is said is true or not will also destroy qualified privilege. It was held in *Horrocks* v. *Lowe* (1972), affirmed by the House of Lords [1975] that where an alderman honestly believed in the truth of his assertions but had no reasonable grounds or was hasty in jumping to conclusions or was irrational or prejudiced, this did not destroy his privilege. Lord Denning said:

It is of the first importance that the members of a local authority should be able to speak their minds freely on a matter of interest in the locality. So long as they honestly believe what they say to be true, they are not to be made liable for defamation. They may be prejudiced and unreasonable. They may not get their facts right. They may give much offence to others. But so long as they are honest, they go clear. No councillor should be hampered in his criticisms by fear of an action for slander. He is not to be forever looking over his shoulder to see if what he says is defamatory. He must be allowed to give his point of view, even if it is hotly disputed by others. This is essential to free discussion.

In *Royal Aquarium and Summer and Winter Garden Society* v. *Parkinson*, supra, Lord Esher MR described a statement made by a county councillor at a meeting to which privilege attached as made by one 'utterly regardless of the truth, or of any personal injury he might be inflicting, perfectly reckless whether what he was saying was true or false'.

4.69 It seems probable, though not free from doubt, that informal meetings on council business are not occasions to which qualified privilege attaches such as, for example, a party group meeting, and meetings of officers. The position as regards working parties is also uncertain, but there would seem to be greater prospect of being able to show the identity of interest between the giver and receiver of information that is necessary to support a defence of qualified privilege. Working parties are now so much an accepted part of the machinery of local Government that the principles set out by Lord Denning, in *Horrocks* v. *Lowe* supra, are likely to apply. Whatever the status of the meeting, the defence of qualified privilege would not, of course, extend to remarks made once the chairman had closed proceedings.

4.70 The Standards Board have taken the view in some cases that remarks made by one councillor to another in cabinet/committee are part of the political 'cut and thrust' and do not in themselves necessarily bring a councillor into disrepute.

4.71 The Local Authorities (Indemnities for Members and Officers) Order 2004 states that an indemnity cannot be provided to an officer or a member in respect of any claim to delegation that they may wish to make against another, but an indemnity may be given in respect of any claim brought against them.

Other defences

4.72 There are certain other defences. Justification can be pleaded if the words are true and justification provides a complete answer. It is also a good defence to show that what was said was fair comment on a matter of public interest, honestly believed to be true, relevant and not inspired by malicious motive, and that the statements of fact on which the comment was based were materially true.[31] Fair and accurate reports of meetings of local authorities and their committees are privileged unless the publication is proved to be made with malice.

Committee chairmanship

4.73 The most significant change in a councillor's role, from the viewpoint of the law and practice of local authority meetings, is upon becoming mayor/chairman of the council or a committee chairman; although politically he may regard leadership of the council as of paramount importance.[32] The duties and responsibilities of a council chairman or mayor are discussed later, our concern here is to examine the role as chairman of a committee. There are, of course, other political offices apart from that of leader: each party will ordinarily appoint a number of whips.

Differing conceptions

4.74 The role adopted by a committee chairman is influenced partly by his own conception of what it should be both in committee and outside the committee room and by the degree of authority ordinarily bestowed upon the chairmanship by local custom. Nowhere today does a committee chairman restrict himself solely to presiding at meetings of his committee and to acting as spokesperson at council meetings. Even within a narrow concept of his role, varying attitudes are adopted: some members see their task as chairman as a mere interpreter of the committee's collective will; but others think it proper that they should influence and guide the committee in the decisions it makes. Where it is the authority's practice to re-elect the same committee chairman year after year as long as he is willing to serve, there is greater likelihood of his becoming the shaper rather than the interpreter of the committee's views,.

4.75 The choice of committee chairmen lies in the gift of the majority party on the council but in some authorities the parties arrive at an understanding to share the chairmanships in rough proportion to their strength on the council – although very often the minority party will not allow any of its members to accept a committee chairmanship so as not to jeopardise its opposition role and clear itself of any responsibility in the application of the policy of the dominant group.

4.76 The principle of rotating or shared chairmanship has gained much credence with the development of hung, or balanced, councils in recent years. Such authorities where no one party has overall control produces great problems for chairmen in committee and conventions often need to be formulated in order to allow business to proceed. There is nothing inherently unlawful in having chairmen change from meeting to meeting. In such cases the first item of each agenda will be 'Appointment of chairman for the meeting'. When operating a system of this kind it is important to be clear as to the extent of the chairman's powers and the length of time he will hold office: is it purely for the duration of the meeting at which he is elected or does he hold office until the next such appointment is made – presumably at the next meeting? Either course of action can be taken but it must be clear at the time of the appointment. When the chairman's authority ceases at the end of the meeting it is usual to have a convention that the various group spokespersons for each committee will be given authority to be consulted on action required between meetings.

4.77 Another difficult question is whether a meeting can proceed if no chairman has been appointed at all. There may be no nominations or an equality of votes for rival candidates. Legal opinion is divided on whether the meeting can properly proceed but probably on balance it can do provided the meeting itself passes a resolution to that effect. At common law a committee meeting can control its own proceedings, subject to compliance with standing orders, so if it expresses a clear wish to proceed then there seems no reason why it cannot do so. In such circumstances the clerk will simply call-over the agenda items, ensuring that there is a resolution passed to decide any issues and proceed to the next item while taking care not to play any part in the debate itself. A pragmatic solution such as this, to keep business flowing, is not to be commended and every effort should be made to appoint a chairman for every meeting. In so far as council meetings are concerned there must be someone presiding (see 1.9).

Chairman's action

4.78 In practice a committee chairman is invested with considerable power and influence. But the authority with which he is endowed and the power he exercises are based on convention: 'probably', it was once said, 'the only example in local government of a convention analogous to the constitutional convention'. The practice of chairman's action – now largely fallen into disuse since it was challenged in the courts (see 4.79) – began as a convenient arrangement whereby officers in circumstances of urgency between meetings sought authority from the committee chairman before taking this, that, or some other course of action. It avoided delay and was a convenient, workable arrangement which facilitated the dispatch of business but rested solely on mutual trust and confidence and good faith. It was purportedly clothed with legality by ensuring that, at the next ensuing meeting of the committee, the chairman's action was confirmed. Strictly speaking, an individual council member could not be empowered to make decisions because it was and still is unlawful for an individual councillor to be given delegated authority since this would be outside the powers conferred by statute, in respect of committees. This position is different in respect of executive functions as a result of the LGA 2000, which allows delegation of decision making to individual members of the executive (see 9.4).

4.79 The practice of chairman's action was examined judicially in *R* v. *Secretary of State for the Environment ex parte Hillingdon London Borough Council* (1986).[33] That case put one question beyond doubt (indeed there was probably little doubt anyhow) but left at least another unsettled. The question settled is that there can be no valid delegation to an individual councillor because s.101 of the LGA 1972, while it permits delegation to a committee, sub-committee, officer or another local authority, does not empower a committee chairman to act alone – even if purportedly comprising a committee of one (see next paragraph). It is open to doubt, however, whether the Hillingdon case wholly outlawed the chairman's action.

4.80 *Hillingdon* was decided on circumstances that may not ordinarily arise. The local authority had sought judicial review of the Secretary of State's refusal to determine appeals against enforcement notices issued by the council on the authority alone of its planning committee chairman. The council had purportedly clothed the chairman with delegated powers to give 'instructions regarding the institution or defence of legal proceedings or the representation of the council in any matters referred to him by the director of law and administration and expressly to make decisions on a number of matters including enforcement procedure under the Town and Country Planning Act'. In other words, the chairman was not merely as a matter of administrative practice required to be consulted in circumstances of urgency and to

4. Local authority membership

approve a course of action which an officer wished to take, but was purportedly empowered to make decisions on a continuing basis in a specific sphere of the local authority's functions. Furthermore, the council had sought to justify its standing orders provision on the argument that it had fixed at one the membership of a committee to which it had delegated decision-making powers. The standing orders did not provide for ratification of the committee chairman's action and in the particular circumstances which gave rise to the court proceedings there had been no ratification.

4.81 What then, are the implications of *Hillingdon* on the practice of chairman's action? It could be argued that the judgment does not rule out chairman's action provided its operation is well regulated and any decision made by a committee chairman is subsequently confirmed by resolution of the council or committee or subcommittee with delegated powers. Woolf J in *Hillingdon* said:

> There may be difficulties in overcoming the problem by a duly authorised committee ... ratifying the ultra vires action of the chairman retrospectively. As to this, I need to express no conclusive view because there was no ratification in this case.

4.82 That there was no ratification in *Hillingdon* is understandable. On the authority's contention that the delegation was lawful it followed logically that there was no requirement for confirmation because any decision, properly made under valid delegated authority, becomes effective from the time it is made. That said, however, there is authority for the view that there can be no effective ratification of action which is in itself unlawful. As to that, in relation to chairman's action, the law remains unclear and, as Widdicombe has pointed out, 'unsatisfactory' (see 4.89).

4.83 It may be that, so long as a committee chairman is not asked to make a decision which affects or prejudices third-party interests, it is not unlawful for officers to continue to seek a committee chairman's concurrence with a projected course of action in circumstances of urgency, where it would be impracticable within the time available to call together the full committee or sub-committee. The court in Hillingdon appears to have recognised that this might be perfectly lawful within limits. Referring to *R* v. *Brent Health Authority ex parte Francis* (1985) (in which the chairman of the health authority had made a decision about the exclusion of the public from its meetings), Woolf J said:

> In this case ... urgent action was subsequently ratified by the authority when the meeting was held ... However, this decision related to the internal procedures of the authority and I can see a very real distinction between a chairman acting alone in exercising this sort of function in relation to its own proceedings and a chairman purporting to take a decision which legislation such as the Town and Country Planning Act requires to be taken by the authority before enforcement proceedings are commenced.

4.84 Difficulties of the kind discussed here can be overcome, as the learned judge in Hillingdon himself observed, by delegating the necessary authority to an officer:

> I ... accept that it would be difficult to fault a procedure where the decisions are taken by a fully authorised officer pursuant to s.101 in consultation with the elected chairman ... this would be a simple way of dealing with these urgent matters which could not go before an elected committee or subcommittee but for which it is undesirable for a single officer to take sole responsibility ...

4.85 This is not the position in respect of executive functions; the LGA 2000 s. 15(2) provides that decision-making may be delegated to an individual member of the cabinet, as well as to officers. However, where an individual member intends to make a key decision, the rules in respect of access to information apply (SI 2000/3272) and any report in respect of the decision to be taken must be made public for at least five clear days (subject to the usual rules as to exempt information, see 12.20). In addition, a copy of the report should be supplied to the relevant overview and scrutiny chairman, or where there is no chairman to every member of the committee. In addition, there are requirements for the recording of decisions taken by individual cabinet members (see 12.20)

As to delegation to an officer, a local authority can in certain circumstances be bound by the act of an officer within his ostensible authority but beyond the scope of his delegated authority.

There could well be contentious matters or issues of political sensitivity where a local authority would be reluctant to allow an officer complete freedom to act, though willing to make the delegation conditional upon consultation with the appropriate councillor. It is important that consultation alone is envisaged and not prior approval, for that would be indistinguishable from purportedly conferring delegated authority upon an individual member.

4.86 The importance of getting both the form and the procedure of delegation right was shown in *Fraser* v. *Secretary of State for the Environment and the Royal Borough of Kensington and Chelsea* (1987). This, again, was an enforcement notice case but here the action had been taken by an officer acting under the council's standing orders which required him to obtain 'the written approval of the mayor or the chairman of the appropriate committee or sub-committee with delegated powers'. The director of planning and transportation drafted a letter which was sent to the chairman of the planning committee for approval. A discussion then took place on the telephone after which the director signed the letter. Mr Justice Nolan, as he then was, considered this to be a valid exercise of the discretion vested in the officer concerned, who had clearly made up his mind before discussing the matter with the chairman: the action came within the phrase 'in consultation with' used by the judge in *Hillingdon* (see 4.79).

4.87 These circumstances can be contrasted with those in *R* v. *Port Talbot Borough Council ex parte Jones* (1988). Here the action under review was the allocation of a council house and the housing officer, Mr Hale, made it clear in evidence that without pressure from the chairman of the housing committee, Mr Lewis, he would not have

4. Local authority membership

allocated it as he did. Mr Justice Nolan found this to be the wrong side of the line in terms of legality –

> The discretion to allocate the house ... could only lawfully be delegated to Mr Hale. In the light of his affidavit, to describe the decision as made by him as the authorised delegate of the council would be a travesty of the facts.

4.88 In view of the foregoing, involvement of the chairman in action between meetings should be carefully controlled and clearly understood. At the most, allowing a chairman to take decisions should be confined to those situations where no third-party rights are infringed either generally or particularly. This effectively means that only internal arrangements and administrative detail within the authority itself can safely be left in the hands of an individual member. Indeed given the fairly generous guidelines approved in *Kensington and Chelsea* (see 4.86) there is little need for a chairman to be asked to act alone. Legally there is no reason why an officer who has delegated powers which are exercisable 'in consultation' with one or more members cannot change his mind in the event of disagreement with the member or members concerned. The central fact must always be that the decision itself is made by the officer, and care must be taken to ensure that politically sensitive issues, such as in *Port Talbot* (see 4.87) are not left to be dealt with under delegated powers.

4.89 It is hardly surprising that Widdicombe took the view that the position as regards chairman's action is 'unsatisfactory'[34] and sought to devise a solution which 'is consistent with the corporate framework of local government and at the same time is consistent with sensible administrative practice'. It concluded:

> We believe ... that the law should allow the possibility of delegation of decisions to chairmen themselves ... Such delegation should not be at large: it should not become a device for avoiding decision-taking by committees, nor a means of chairmen adopting a ministerial style of administration. The legislation should set clear limits on the scope of delegation to chairmen. It should be permissible only where a decision is required because of urgency. In other circumstances the legislation should state that any decision of the chairman is unlawful, irrespective of whether the council or committee purport to ratify it retro-spectively. This should remove the legal doubt about ratification ... The chief executive either directly or by delegation to one of his chief officers, should be required to agree in each case that the matter is urgent before any decision can be taken ... We propose furthermore that the decision taken under delegated powers should be reported to the next meeting of the committee or sub-committee in question, that the provisions introduced by the Local Government (Access to Information) Act 1985 should apply to the report and other documents on which the decision is based, and that the chairman should not be able to take a decision where he or she has a pecuniary interest in the matter.

General principles

Widdicombe's proposals were only adopted in respect of executive functions.

Implied authority

4.90 It must be apparent from all that has been said in the foregoing paragraphs that a committee chairman must be careful not to overreach his implied authority. If the scope of that authority is codified there is less risk.

It is generally recognised, but again only as a convention, that a committee chairman may, by virtue of his office, make suggestions – even, perhaps, in exceptional circumstances, give directions – to an officer. It is also recognised that, by virtue of his chairmanship, he may enjoy a certain limited freedom of access to property under the control of his committee on the assumption that he is doing what the committee would direct him to do. But legally a committee chairman, like any other individual council member, has no power or authority other than that expressly conferred upon him by resolution and thus can only properly give orders through a decision made at a properly constituted meeting.

Failure to attend meetings

Statutory provisions

4.91 The law expressly provides that where a council member fails throughout a period of six consecutive months from the date of his last attendance to attend any meeting of the authority then, subject to certain exceptions, he ceases to be a member of the authority unless the failure was due to some reason approved before the expiry of that period. The authority's approval, it is submitted, if not limited in time (and most authorities in giving approval will specify both the reason to which the approval relates and the period for which it will run), lasts until it ceases to have effect because the councillor has resumed attendance, or the reason to which the approval relates no longer applies, or the councillor's term of office has ended. Under the LGA 2000 s.107 any period during which a member is suspended or partially suspended (i.e. for standards issues) is disregarded for the purpose of calculating the period of six consecutive months and, therefore a period during which a member fails to attend meetings which are immediately before, and another such period that falls immediately after, a period of suspension or partial suspension is treated as consecutive.

4.92 Attendance as a member at a meeting of any committee or sub-committee, or at a meeting of any joint committee, joint board or other body by which for the time being any of the functions of the authority are being discharged, or which was appointed to advise the authority on any matter relating to the discharge of those functions, and attendance as representative of the authority at a meeting of any body of persons, is deemed to be attendance at a meeting of the authority. It does not matter how informal the meeting as long as an attendance is recorded.

4.93 Attendance is generously defined. Does, however, the attendance of a councillor as a non-member of a committee or sub-committee in exercise of any right to do so conferred either by standing orders or on the basis of a 'need to know' (see 4.11) count as attendance for the foregoing purpose? This question has not come before the courts but it is likely that the court would probably tend towards favouring preservation of a councillor's qualification rather than otherwise: certainly if the councillor was entitled to an attendance allowance on the particular occasion concerned, it would be difficult to argue that his attendance did not count.

4.94 A member of any branch of the naval, military or air forces when employed during war or any emergency on any naval, military or air force service, and a person whose employment in the service of the Queen in connection with war or any emergency is such as, in the opinion of the Secretary for the Environment, to entitle him to relief from disqualification on account of absence, does not cease to be a member of the authority by reason only of a failure to attend meetings of the authority if the failure is due to that employment.[35]

Practical considerations

4.95 There is some argument as to whether it is an officer's duty to alert a councillor to risk of forfeiture of office because of failure to attend meetings. Sooner or later the authority's attention will need to be directed to the position and it would be an act of courtesy on the officer's part to warn the member concerned of the near approach of the expiry of the six months' period. But ought an officer to assume that a member is going to default? It may be that a member, instead of being grateful for the kindly warning, would take exception to what he might regard as precipitate action on the officer's part. And just when should the matter be reported to the council? No later than the member is approached? That hardly seems appropriate, for no question can yet arise of disqualification. Does the authority need to be informed at all unless and until the member defaults and so disqualifies himself? These questions suggest that there should be a locally acceptable code of practice which can be put into effect automatically.

4.96 An authority cannot retrospectively approve an excuse for failure to attend meetings after the six months' period has expired. This was thought permissible formerly because s.63 of the 1933 Act did not contain the words 'before the expiry of that period' – provided the authority acted before declaring the office vacant. If a member once loses his office through failure to attend for the six months' period, the disqualification cannot be overcome by his subsequently resuming attendance (see *R. v. Hunton ex parte Hodgson* (1911)). Nevertheless, the office becomes vacant only when the authority declares it to be vacant[36] which the authority must do and a casual vacancy arises.[37]

Political group meetings – Their increasing importance

4.97 There has been earlier reference to the significant politicisation of local authorities over the past several years and the consequent removal of effective decision-making to majority group councillors meeting away from public gaze in the party group. This means that many important decisions on policy are first made by the majority group of a local authority and afterwards translated into effective and lawful action through the formal cabinet system. It was said (prior to the LGA 2000):[38]

> The effect ... has been most marked. With decisions settled by a political process beforehand, the purpose of the committee has changed from one of decision-making to a debating forum where the minority parties and the public can be informed of the decisions of the majority party. The opposition can use the meetings to challenge the policies of the majority party and to seek information from officers. The recommendations before committees will be defended politically by the chairmen and other members and not by officers, whose role will be confined to presentation and interpretation of the facts and the submission of professional judgments.

This is however still a common criticism in most instances, and there appears to be a perception that the cabinet system 'rubber-stamps' decisions that are taken beforehand. Minority group councillors also hold group meetings to organise, if they can, a cohesive approach in opposition to the majority group policies.

4.98 Political group meetings are not local authority meetings and are thus in a sense outside the scope of this book for several reasons (but see 4.101 et seq.). The decisions taken in group meetings cannot bind the authority; strictly speaking, no officer can be called upon to attend and/or advise such meetings; and in practice they are often wholly informal in character and the decisions, even when not disputed (as frequently they are), cannot bind any of the party members.

4.99 It is common practice for members of each political party on the local authority to hold a group meeting before each council meeting to discuss business on the council meeting agenda, decide upon the party line to be pursued on at least the more important items, and apportion out responsibility for speaking in support or opposition as the case may be. The efficiency and effectiveness with which party business is conducted 'behind the scenes' appears to depend, first, upon the strength of the particular party within the authority (a party with an overwhelming majority tends not to be over-meticulous in its organisation; but where the parties are narrowly balanced each plans its, tactics with considerable care); and, secondly, upon the personal qualities of the party whips and other party officials.

4.100 The proprieties ought to be and generally are observed. The activities of the party groups are restricted to determining the course of action to be taken at formal meetings of the authority: no group, even when composed of all the council members of the majority party on the council, can by decision in the group meeting legally bind the local authority. Where, however, members of the majority party on a particular committee or sub-committee decide to defer action pending discussion 'in another place' there is always the possibility, inadvertently rather than by design, that officers may find themselves under pressure to take action following a political decision in a group meeting or, more rarely (but it can happen), for officers to be asked to take account of the views of the majority group rather than, say, the appropriate committee chairman. Officers must, of course, act with tact and discretion in such circumstances: they must be realistic and recognise that the leader individually or the group collectively has or can secure the support of the majority of councillors, but at the same time the officers must require compliance with due formality and insist – in

4. Local authority membership

practice invariably through the chief executive – that any political decision so made shall be properly reported to and confirmed by the appropriate committee/cabinet or the council and therefore taken legally.

Regularisation of party control

4.101 Widdicombe addressed itself to political activity of this character. Its recommendation for pro rata representation on committees was substantially implemented by the LG&HA 1989, s.15 and this, it believed, would 'help remove any sense that such groups are somehow improper or alien to local government' – a point made to it in written evidence:

> It has been said that the political parties should also do more themselves to remove any sense of mystery surrounding party groups. particularly where they are discussing issues which will come before the council or its committees for decision. It should be noted, however, that the Freedom of Information Act 2000 does not extend to political group meetings.

4.102 Widdicombe expressed the view:

- that there needs to be greater openness about groups and their proceedings so that unnecessary suspicions are avoided: party groups should not meet in a hole-and-corner atmosphere;
- that the formulation of decisions in party groups outside the formal local government system should not be allowed to undermine the statutory safeguards that apply within the system; and
- that there should be adequate access to the advice of officers so that the policy of the majority group does not become predetermined without full knowledge of the facts and law.

On this last point Widdicombe said that officers' terms and conditions of service should be amended so that no special inhibition is placed on the attendance of officers at party groups (see 5.30).

4.103 It is impossible here to recite in full all that Widdicombe had to say about the incursion and operation of party politics in local government. In summary, however, it proposed that the national political parties (and local parties and groups) should take steps:

- to ensure that party groups keep a publicly available list of those attending their meetings;
- to ensure observance of their model standing orders in so far as they limit the number of non-councillors attending meetings of party groups, preclude non-councillors from voting at such meetings and prevent non-councillors from determining the policy to be followed by the party group on matters before the council for decision;

- to debar from attendance at party group meetings persons disqualified from council membership following surcharge proceedings by the auditor;
- to ensure that the National Code of Local Government Conduct is implemented in respect of conflicts of interests arising at meetings of party groups and to amend their model standing orders accordingly.

Group meetings not 'committees'

4.104 The distinction between group meetings and formal meetings of the local authority and its committees and sub-committees is important. Usually this is clear but not always. Thus in *R* v. *Hyndburn Borough Council* (1985)[39] a decision of a group leaders' meeting (comprising the leader and deputy leader of the Conservative Group and the leader and deputy leader of the Labour Group on a local authority) not to allow SDP/Alliance Group councillors to attend was held to be lawful on the grounds that the meetings, designed for purposes of informal consultation between the political parties and chief officers, formed no part of the formal committee machinery of the council: 'Any decision which it was felt goes beyond this category, whether as a matter of political prudence or to avoid any doubts about legalities, is referred to committee for ratification', acknowledged Woolf J.

4.105 Political group meetings of the kind discussed here, because they are not local authority meetings, are not obliged to be open to the public and nor are they subject to the provisions of the Freedom of Information Act 2000.

Footnotes

1 Widdicombe, paras.7.15–7.30, recommended a simplification of the electoral system to provide for single-member wards or divisions and a uniform period of office of four years. This proposal was not pursued at the time but it may be that the Government will look at the electoral arrangements for councillors as part of its review of the internal management of local authorities.

2 In *Parker* v. *Yeo* (1992), it was held that the town or county hall could be a councillor's 'principal or only place of work' for the purposes of qualification for election. This decision has been criticised and Labour Party headquarters advise its candidates not to rely on it.

3 Disqualifications now include employment in a politically restricted post in any local authority in the country: LG&HA 1989, s.1.

4 LGA 1972, s.26(1) and (7)(b).

5 Unless a contrary intention appears, a provision of an Act comes into force at the beginning of the day in question (see IA 1978, s.4(a)). Thus a person not re-elected at an election held on a Thursday goes out of office at the moment after midnight on the Monday following. i.e. at the start of the fourth day after the Thursday, and must cease to act as a councillor not later than during the Sunday.

6 Section 2, LGA 1972, provides that for every county and every district there shall be a council consisting of a chairman and councillors; s.3 provides that the chairman of a principal council shall be elected annually; and s.4 that the chairman's election shall be the first business transacted at the annual meeting of a principal council.

7 A local authority may properly arrange for the discharge of its functions by an officer: LGA 1972, s.101 (see 5.9).

8 The power of the central government to act in default is related to particular statutory functions. There is no legislative power to replace the local authority in its entirety.

9 *Widdicombe Research Volume II: The Local Government Councillor*, p. 41.

4. Local authority membership

10 The figures quoted are from *Widdicombe Research Volume II: The Local Government Councillor*, ch.5, and relate to a survey in 1985.

11 LGA 1972, s.79.

12 See also *R v. Sheffield City Council ex parte Chadwick* (1985) and *R v. Hyndburn Borough Council ex parte Strak* (1985). All three cases had been brought by Alliance councillors who had been excluded from committees.

13 s.18 and Local Authorities (Members' Allowances) Regulations 1991, 1993 and 1995.

14 1991 Regulations, reg.9(1).

15 LGA 1972, ss.173–178, as amended.

16 All these allowances are payable under the LGA 1972, as amended, and regulated by the Local Authorities (Members' Allowances) Regulations 1991 1993, and 1995.

17 R. G. Brooke and R. Greenwood, '*The Procedures of the Local Commissioners*' (1978) 4 *Local Government Studies* 13.

18 Widdicombe Report, para.6.19.

19 Widdicombe Report, para.5.99.

20 LGA 1972, s.102(3).

21 Ibid. s.102(1).

22 Committees cannot determine their own constitution but a committee can be empowered by the council to decide whomsoever to appoint to fill co-opted places.

23 The aldermanic system, abolished long ago, whereby persons could be brought in from outside the council's membership, was, in effect, a system of co-option.

24 LGA 1972, s.104(1).

25 This restriction was removed by the LG&HA 1989, s.13(8).

26 Ibid. s.173 (4).

27 LG&HA 1989, s.13, which prescribes the basic division into voting and non-voting coopted persons.

28 Local Government (Committees and Political Groups) Regulations 1990, as amended, and the Parish and Community Councils (Committees) Regulations 1990: see Appendix E.

29 Ibid.; and the Parish and Community Councils (Committees) Regulations 1990.

30 See, e.g., *Clark & Lindsell on Torts*.

31 Defamation Act 1952, s.7.

32 See s.19.

33 The practice was also examined – and the view was the same – in *R v. Secretary of State for Education and Science ex parte Birmingham District Council and Another:* (1984).

34 Widdicombe Report, para.5.74.

35 LGA 1972, s.85(3).

36 LGA 1972, s.86.

37 Ibid. s.87(1).

38 See R. G. Brooke, 'Modern Approach to Committee Practice' (1979) 143 *Local Government Review* 3.

39 Unreported but see (1986) 150 *Local Government Review* 57.

Chapter 5
The role of officers

Introduction

The local government service

5.1 Each local authority separately and independently appoints and employs staff for the discharge of its functions[1]: white-collar (officers) and blue-collar employees (manual workers), now on 'single-status' terms and conditions settled locally but incorporating common core conditions negotiated at national level through collective bargaining by local authority and trade union representatives. Local authority employees collectively comprise the local government service,[2] which is a concept rather than a clearly defined entity, i.e. it is unlike the civil service, which represents identifiable and integrated central government employment in the service of the Crown, but it ensures interchangeability of employees between local authorities and continuity of service for several purposes. The concern in this work is, however, with those officers associated in one way or another with the local government decision-making process in meetings. This means the chief executive in particular in advising on and giving effect to policy; the secretary or director of administration who, with the committee staff, has administrative responsibility for the mechanics of the decision-making process including the servicing of committees; and the departmental chief officers who, as members of the chief executive's management team, also have a role in policy advice and an operational role in service delivery (in many cases nowadays overseeing services contracted out under outsourcing arrangements) and in the public protection and regulatory services (see 1.7). As to the head of the paid service, the monitoring officer, proper officer: see respectively 13.49, 4.49, 5.15; and as to the role of officers in quasi-judicial proceedings: see 13.17.

5.2 Authorities, other than parish or community councils, have power to appoint assistants for political groups on the council subject to stringent conditions and safeguards.[3] These political assistants are the only local government officers who are able to be appointed having regard to their political activities or affiliations. A political group cannot have more than one political assistant and the number of political assistants is limited to three in each council. There are strict rules set out in s.9 of the LG&HA1989 on how a political group qualifies for a political assistant. The pay and political activities of a political assistant, once appointed, are restricted by statutory regulation. The political assistant's purpose is to provide assistance, in the discharge of any of their functions as members of a relevant authority, to the members of any political group to which members of the authority belong. As the political assistants have much contact with the leadership and membership of their group, it can often be useful for the secretariat to liaise with them on the various

5. The role of officers

operational matters that need to be arranged, or matters of policy clarified, with the political groups. The role and remuneration of the political assistants has recently been consulted on by the Office of the Deputy Prime Minister which has led to an increase in their maximum annual remuneration to £34,896.

Member–officer relationship

Officer role

5.3 The traditional approach to decision-making meant that the role of officers in the past was limited to the giving of professional advice and procedural guidance although, in the one-time 'secrecy' of committee deliberations, officers could exercise considerable influence up to the point at which a decision was made. Indeed, it was often said that the officers were the non-voting partners in the conduct of local authority business. How effective in practice this input from officers was depended largely on the relationship between councillors and their chief officers; but where, as was not uncommon, there was real partnership in the sense of mutual trust and confidence, the influence of officers often meant that councillors accepted – sometimes perhaps too unquestioningly – what the officers proposed.

5.4 Important changes have taken place in comparatively recent times. The more significant is that local authorities now have express statutory power to delegate decision-making to officers (see 4.17) on the same terms and subject to the same limitations as in the case of delegation to committees and subcommittees. Another is that the practical effect of opening committees and subcommittees to the public (see Chapter 3) has meant that – as formerly and still so in the case of meetings of the full council – officers are more inhibited in making a contribution to member deliberations. On the other hand, it could be argued that the present-day role of the chief executive as the council's principal policy adviser enables him to take a larger share in decision-making at top level in his contact with the leader of the council; indeed, and this has been a particularly significant change; the chief executive's role now is to give executive effect to the political aspirations of the majority group.

5.5 The difficulty in setting out clearly the relationship between members and officers has been the cause of friction in many local authorities in recent times. Increased political emphasis in the functioning of local government has often led to senior officers becoming identified with one or other political groups and this inevitably raises problems when political control changes. In an attempt to cure this s.7(2) of the LG&HA 1989 required all appointments of officers to be made on merit (see 13.34). More recently, the Nolan Committee recommended that every local authority should have a written code or protocol that would govern the relationship between members and officers. This approach has been repeated in the Local Government Act 2000: Guidance to English Local Authorities issued by the Secretary of State, which states that local authorities should develop appropriate conventions setting out the roles, responsibilities and rights of officers and members and establishing the key principles governing officer/member relationships. A model Protocol for Member/Officer relations issued by the Association of Council Secretaries and Solicitors has been adopted by a number of authorities.

General principles

5.6 Despite the changes of recent years and the uncertainties that have arisen, one thing remains clear: officers owe a duty both in legal and managerial terms to the council as a corporate whole, which overrides allegiance to whichever group, political or otherwise, is in control of the authority. This approach has been endorsed in the 2000 Act Guidance, which confirms that in relation to those authorities operating executive arrangements, officers should be responsible for day-to-day managerial and operational decisions within the local authority and should provide support both to the executive and all councillors in their several roles. Moreover, the Guidance emphasises that it is a key principle that all officers are employed by and accountable to the local authority as a whole.

5.7 However, relationships have had to take account of the political climate and the sensitivity demanded; and legislative changes have been introduced to strengthen the perceptions of political neutrality. The emphasis on management, particularly since Maud, has been reflected in the change of titles from town clerk and clerk of the council to chief executive, and with the 1970s reorganisation there emerged the new post of secretary, whose job embraces committee administration and much of the subject matter of this work, hived off from the chief executive. Legislation has defined statutory duties entrusted to officers already in post by the device of designation: the LGA 1972 requires authorities to designate one of their officers as the 'proper officer' (see 5.15) with duties covering many of the responsibilities relevant to this work; and the LG&HA 1989 extended the practice by requiring authorities to designate one of its officers (in practice it was usually the chief executive) as head of the council's paid service with specific duties in relation to the council's workforce; and in particular to designate another as monitoring officer charged with the duty of alerting councillors to risk of illegality or impropriety (see 4.49).

Responsibility for committee work

5.8 Formerly, the business of summoning members to meetings, the preparation of agenda and its despatch, and the subsequent compiling of the minutes of proceedings were virtually everywhere the responsibility of the town clerk or clerk of the council. Nowhere were the duties of this officer prescribed by statute, at least in respect of committee work, although certain statutes laid down specific tasks upon the holder of the office. The duty of undertaking committee work was set out in the officer's contract of employment and generally regulated by standing orders. Since reorganisation, however, and the emergence of the office of chief executive with duties differing substantially from those of the former clerk, greater variations exist between authorities in the distribution of top-level duties. It was Bains's view that 'the head of the central administrative department is rather analogous to the secretary of a company' and it thus adopted the title secretary for that officer. An authority's committee work is now more often than not entrusted to the county, borough or district secretary (sometimes designated the county, borough or district solicitor, particularly where there is responsibility for legal work), director of administration or equivalent. It is this officer who, whatever the designation of the job, generally discharges the statutory responsibilities imposed upon the proper officer.[4]

5. The role of officers

5.9 It may be thought important as a general principle that the task of convening committee meetings and particularly of minuting proceedings should be wholly centralised. There are patent disadvantages in any practice that allows some committee work to be performed by or within the department of a chief officer charged with the service for which the committee is responsible. Thus it was once common in local education authorities for education committee work to be discharged within the education department because of the particular character of the service and elsewhere for personnel, formerly establishment, committee work, to be under the control of the establishment/personnel officer on the grounds that there was a high degree of confidentiality in the proceedings. These attitudes have been re-emphasised in recent years with the development of internal markets within local authorities, with the associated requirement to identify and charge for support costs. The moving of committee servicing in-house by departments has sometimes been seen as an easy way of saving costs, but the disadvantages usually outweigh any narrow financial savings. There are the practical management issues of ensuring quality control across the whole of the council's committee servicing arrangements and ensuring a consistent standard approach, and (particularly in the smaller authorities) of providing back-up if officers are away. There also remains the potential risk that officers with a professional or sectional interest in a committee's proceedings might consciously or unconsciously allow this interest to affect their recording of proceedings. Those whose responsibility it is to service committees should do so impartially and that impartiality may be thought more likely to exist and be seen to exist where committee work is wholly independent of sectional interests. See also as regards agenda control: 10.18; and as to what should be included or excluded from minutes: 12.17.

Delegation to officers

5.10 The delegation of functions to an officer may be either to an individual officer by name or, preferably, to a post-holder (see 3.31 as to the obligation of the local authority to publicise officer delegations of more than six months' duration). The effect of delegation to an officer is that the act of the officer becomes the act of the local authority: see *Battelley* v. *Finsbury Borough Council* (1958). Delegation in this sense means conferring authority on an officer to make decisions within the parameters of the delegation arrangements; hence the officer cannot pass on the decision-making authority to a subordinate, for otherwise the dictum *delegatus non potest delegare* would be infringed. It is evident, however, that the courts will not ordinarily upset a decision taken by a subordinate officer in the name of the chief officer to whom power has been delegated, particularly where what has been done was an administrative act. See a range of cases including *Provident Mutual Life Assurance Associates* v. *Derby City Council* (1981); and *R.* v. *Southwark London Borough Council ex parte Bannerman and Others* (1990).

5.11 A distinction needs to be made, however, between real delegation, which connotes the exercise of discretion, and mere executive tasks that officers can perform without formal delegation.[5] The delegation must not be fettered in such a way that, in effect, the decision in a particular instance is really made by an individual councillor; as explained earlier (see 4.86), this would be unlawful. Action taken under delegated

99

powers does not have to be confirmed: it is immediately effective. Local authorities will, however, as a rule require officers to report what they have done under delegated power.

Can there be delegation to a group of officers?

5.12 The statutory provisions governing the carrying out of functions by officers clearly refer to 'an officer';[6] and although the general rule of interpretation is that 'words in the singular include the plural and words in the plural include the singular', it is submitted that delegation is not permissible to a group of officers. The matter is a practical one rather than one of legality. An individual can be made accountable for what he does under delegated authority, but if a group of officers were collectively entrusted with the discharge of functions, both the powers so delegated and accountability would be diffused. Who in officer group decisions of this kind would decide what course to pursue if there was disagreement? If the decision were to be settled by majority vote, this would undermine the position of the chief executive in his management team. In practice, a committee minute or delegation requiring a number of officers to be involved in the exercise of a delegated power is likely to authorise a chief officer to exercise the delegation in consultation with one or more colleagues.

Liability of officers

Immunity from personal liability

5.13 Local authorities, as corporate bodies, are separate and distinct from the persons who comprise an authority for the time being; and this means that individual councillors are not personally liable for the consequences of what is done in good faith and lawfully by the local authority. The position of officers, as servants of the corporate authority, is somewhat different but statutory provisions provide immunity against personal liability for both members and officers. The Local Government (Miscellaneous Provisions) Act 1976, s.39, extends to local authorities in the execution of their statutory powers and duties the following provisions of the Public Health Act 1875, s.265:

> 'No matter or thing done, and no contract entered into by any local authority . . . and no matter or thing done by any member . . . or by any officer of such authority or other person whomsoever acting under the direction of such authority shall if the matter or other thing were done or the contract were entered into bona fide for the purposes of executing this Act subject them or any of them personally to any action liability or claim or demand whatsoever; and any expense incurred by any such authority member or officer or other person acting as last aforesaid shall be borne and repaid out of the fund or rate applicable by such authority to the general purposes of this Act.'

5. The role of officers

This immunity does not extend to protect individuals from action by an auditor; and see 5.15 as to the personal liability of officers as representatives of their employing authority.

Carrying out unlawful decisions

5.14 When officers, in advising members, find themselves called upon to implement decisions that are legally questionable, they need to act with care to avoid liability to audit sanctions and possible civil or criminal action. When a decision is challengeable on grounds of unreasonable exercise of the council's discretion, the officers can act to implement the decision without fear, because such decisions are legal until successfully challenged: see *Associated Provincial Picture Houses Ltd* v. *Wednesbury Corporation* (1948). However, where the decision is palpably unlawful then an officer acting on it would be liable in the same way as councillors themselves. See *R.* v. *Saunders* (1845) and *Attorney-General* v. *De Winton* (1906), where the court held that a treasurer asked to make an illegal payment should disobey.

Indemnity of officers acting as council representatives

5.15 An officer who becomes liable to surcharge or damages as the result of carrying out an unlawful decision can only rely on any indemnity given by the council. The limitation on this was graphically shown in *Burgoïne and Cooke* v. *Waltham Borough Council and McWhirr* (1996), where action taken on behalf of an outside body on which the officers concerned represented the council was not covered by the specific terms of the indemnity given. Thus officers carrying out the decisions of committees should be alert to any illegality and should examine the basis of any appointment to any outside body on which they sit as council representatives, including the precise wording of any indemnity given to them either by specific committee resolution or under any contractual obligation.

5.16 The situation relating to indemnities has been clarified further over recent years and the courts have confirmed that an indemnity can be granted by virtue of ss.112 and 111 of the 1972 Act both to defend and to instigate proceedings in appropriate cases. In *R.* v. *DPP ex parte Duckenfield* (2000), the South Yorkshire Police Authority was able to pay the costs of an officer prosecuted following the Hillsborough disaster. In *R.* v. *Westminster City Council ex parte UMPO* (2000), the court upheld the legality of an indemnity granted by the council to councillors and officers involved in the homes for votes issue as being within the scope of s.111 of the 1972 Act. In that instance, the indemnity was conditional on their being exonerated from any misconduct. Finally, in *R.* v. *Bedford BC ex parte Comninos* (2003), Sullivan J held that s.111 empowered a local authority to indemnify officers for their legal costs when instigating libel proceedings arising out of their conduct of an election.

5.17 The position on indemnities further changed in November 2004 when the Local Authorities (Indemnities for Members and Officers) Order 2004 came into force. The powers under those Regulations are in addition to the existing powers that local authorities already have, including those under s.111 of the 1972 Act. The Regulations make it clear that that an indemnity may be provided by means of insuring its officers and members. Under the Regulations, a council (including principal councils and parish councils) can indemnify an officer or member in relation to any action that is authorised by the council or the exercise of any function at the request of, with the approval of, or for the purpose of the authority. The Regulations also allow an indemnity to be given where when exercising the function in question, the officer or member does so in a capacity other than that of officer or member. This would permit an indemnity, for example, to cover the case where the officer or member acts as the director of a company at the request of his authority, and thus is acting in his capacity as a director. The council can also provide an indemnity where the action complained of is outside the powers of the council, or of the officer or member, provided that the action was taken under a reasonable belief that it was within those powers.

5.18 Where an indemnity has been given or insurance provided under the Regulations in relation to criminal proceedings against a member or officer, or a breach of the members' Code of Conduct, the terms of the indemnity must require the local authority or insurer to be reimbursed should there be a criminal conviction or a finding that there has been a breach of the members' Code of Conduct.

Except for the limited circumstances set out in 5.18 (above), indemnities cannot be given under the Regulations in relation to criminal acts or intentional wrongdoing, fraud, recklessness, or in relation to the bringing of (but not the defence of) any action in defamation. Accordingly, in the circumstances outlined in *Comninos* (see 5.16), the authority would not be able to rely on the new powers set out in the Regulations but would have to rely on its s.111 powers.

Proper officer

Appointment by designation

5.19 A proper officer must be appointed by every local authority. s.270(3) of the LGA 1972 provides that:

> 'Any reference in this Act to a proper officer and any reference which by virtue of this Act is to be construed as such a reference shall, in relation to any purpose and any local authority or other body or any area, be construed as a reference to an officer appointed for that purpose by that body or for that area, as the case may be.'

The choice of proper officer is entirely at the discretion of the local authority and obviously depends upon local circumstances. It would be prudent for an authority to appoint another officer to act as such in the event of his incapacity in a vacancy in the office.

5.20 The term 'proper officer' is peculiar to local government. It is a phrase used to identify a person designated as being responsible for a particular function or range of functions. Thus it is used in a variety of contexts, e.g. as the officer responsible for administering the local registration scheme for births, marriages and deaths, and in connection with committees as the officer responsible for summoning, clerking and minuting the meetings.

Committee officers

Committee clerks

5.21 The officers primarily concerned with committee practice are those who were at one time always termed committee clerks: and we use this term as a matter of convenience though it is now somewhat outdated and might misleadingly imply an officer of lesser status than that increasingly accorded. All will be concerned with the preparation of agenda and drawing up minutes and reports, and many will be entrusted with more responsible duties, such as advising the committee (either on procedural matters or acting wholly as the chief executive or secretary's representative) and taking limited or full responsibility for overseeing executive action on a committee's decisions.

5.22 The status of committee clerks depended in the past upon the ability of individual officers and the inclination or disinclination of the former town clerk/clerk of the council to entrust them with effective tasks. Often, too, the role of committee clerks has varied according to the size of the authority and the extent to which their work has been dominated by legal rather than administrative considerations. Thus, for example, Herbert Morrison felt able to say of the one-time largest local authority:[7]

'There is an important officer attached to committees called the committee clerk ... These men are of high standing, and they have substantial salaries. They are the eyes and ears of the chief officers concerned.'

Flatteringly, too, in a manual published some years ago under the auspices of the former Society of Clerks of Urban District Councils:

'The perfect committee clerk requires to possess the foresight of Old Moore, the accuracy of an adding machine; the judgment of Solomon; the patience of job; the memory of an elephant; the coolness and tact of a high ranking diplomat; and the literary skill of Bernard Shaw!'[8]

5.23 The committee clerk is no longer a relatively junior officer – sometimes no more than a minuting clerk – with predominantly clerical duties whose principal accomplishment was that of an efficient shorthand writer, with the ability to draft 'agendas, minutes and reports in a clear, well-written, grammatically correct style'. There has been a notable improvement of status in the case of most authorities, particularly the larger ones, encouraged, it is suspected, not only by the difficulty nowadays in retaining on committee work officers of requisite ability but also by the trend towards requiring legal representation at some committees or overview and scrutiny commissions only when legal issues arise. Posts have been accorded better designations (committee officer, committee administrator, committee manager, even assistant town clerk or assistant chief executive) and entrusted with real responsibility for handling the work of a major committee or a group of related smaller ones.

5.24 Committee work has always been a good grounding for advancement on the administrative side of local government. But career prospects in the past were restricted and at best the able committee clerk could expect to aspire to an administrative post of assistant town clerk, embracing responsibility also for general office management of the clerk's department, election work and members' business. With the emergence of a better understanding of the importance of the administrative and managerial side of local authority work, new avenues of promotion opened up for the able administrator. In the first place there was establishment (now personnel) work, to which was added a wide range of management services and techniques (work study, network analysis, project co-ordination and corporate planning); this has meant that committee work has become comparatively less attractive than formerly for the able generalist, who now sees better prospects in these other directions.

5.25 Today, as already indicated (see 5.8), responsibility for committees often rests with the county (or borough or district) secretary or director of administration, who has inherited most of the duties of clerkship relinquished by the chief executive without departmental ties. This may in some cases mean that the ablest committee clerks can aspire to the post of secretary, but those appointments are still frequently held by lawyers who have responsibility also for legal work.

Training

5.26 Little attention was given in the past to the training of staff for committee work. Most attained their knowledge and expertise by practical experience on the job and thus competence depended on the environment in which committee staff worked. Deserving of special mention, however, are the courses in committee administration run for many years by what is now the South West Regional Assembly. Held usually over a period of a week on a residential basis, they still represent the main systematic instruction geared to the practical needs of students of varying levels of experience.

5.27 The late Sir George Mallaby advocated the abolition of committee clerks as such. He wanted career committee clerks replaced by people drawn from every department in the authority and seconded for this particular service for a two-year stint. The constant roulement of these young officers from their own departments to what is in effect the authority's secretariat and then back to their own departments would widen the horizons of the officers themselves:

'In time it would also disseminate throughout all ranks of the authority a knowledge and awareness of the multitude and complexity of its problems.'

5. The role of officers

Qualifications

5.28 Local authorities, in advertising committee clerk posts, rarely specify any particular qualifications but increasingly ask for education to degree standard. In the past, the public service stream examinations of the Institute of Chartered Secretaries and Administrators have provided the recognised professional qualification for administrative staff in local government, but these have now been discontinued. Interestingly, there has been a recent attempt to introduce suitable National Vocational Qualifications for committee administration and it is hoped that this will prove successful.

Officers at meetings

General

5.29 Officers are not, of course, part of the membership of the local authority;[9] and so they cannot be a party to the decisions made in the full assembly or in committee or subcommittee, even though, outside the council chamber or committee room they may well be invested with delegated power (see 5.10) enabling them to make decisions of sometimes greater significance than those made by members collectively in council or committee. Nevertheless, officers do participate in discussion at committee and subcommittee meetings and may influence the decisions made by reason of the facts that they lay before the members or of the advice that they tender. In many authorities the relationship between members and officers is one of mutual trust and confidence, and in these cases the officers act virtually as non-voting partners in the business of local government. In other words, the officers join in the debate whenever they think fit, speak more than once if need be, sway members deliberately towards one course of action rather than another until the point when a decision is about to be made, when they must hold their silence – and, of course, accept unquestionably the decision when it is made, whether it is to their liking or not.

Council meetings

5.30 At council meetings, however, it is the tradition that officers shall not speak unless, exceptionally, any one of them may be called upon to do so. The chief executive may have announcements to make and either he or the secretary will be responsible for advising the chairman, and occasionally even the full council on procedure but it is seemly that in the full assembly the councillors should be seen to be the decision-makers.

Committees

5.31 If it is acceptable locally that an officer may join freely in discussion in committee, the officer should be scrupulous in ensuring, particularly if wishing to influence the council members to take the course he favours, that all the relevant facts are before the committee including the pros and cons of alternative courses of action. Where an officer's report is not comprehensive enough to cover all the issues, the committee runs the risk of having its decision declared invalid, as in *R. v. Isle of Wight ex p O'Keefe* (1990). The officer must take care, too, not to dominate the committee so as to virtually impose his will upon the members, particularly nowadays with members of the public present, and if he finds in the course of debate that the majority of members are against him he must not then press his view unduly.[10]

5.32 If, on the other hand, officers are discouraged from speaking at meetings then they must rely on the written material prepared for the committee. There are times, however, when it is the duty of an officer to speak out even if forbidden to do so. No officer should sit silently by and allow his committee to embark on a course of action that is ultra vires or may have consequences that the members have clearly overlooked. As has been said elsewhere:[11]

'It is often a matter of judgment, not easy to exercise in practice, when discursive discussion in committee takes an unexpected turn, whether the officer should speak or hold his tongue. He must be careful to distinguish between, for example, errors of fact and errors of judgment. The officer ought to stand up – and persist in standing up and speaking even if ordered to sit down – if he sees his committee about to make a decision of consequence on a misunderstanding of fact. To remain silent would be a gross dereliction of duty. But it may be wise for him to remain unmoved and unspeaking if the committee in full possession of the facts is about to make a decision which is wayward, capricious, imprudent or manifestly wrong.'

Of course, this must now be read in the light of a specific legal duty imposed upon the monitoring officer (and a somewhat analogous duty on the chief finance officer) to report in writing on proposals or courses of action likely to involve breach of the law.

5.33 It needs to be borne in mind that some officers will not be regular participants in committee business: many 'back-room boys' may attend only very exceptionally, perhaps merely to listen to discussion on a particular issue (when they might conveniently sit in the seats reserved for the public) or to advise on a matter that they have been handling personally or to support their chief officer if detailed information is asked for. For such officers committee attendance will be an unusual experience and they may need to be briefed to ensure they understand the conventions of committee procedure, know where to sit, when to speak (and whether to stand or remain seated when speaking), when to leave and so on. Such briefings should be part of the routine of pre-committee work. There is, however, much to commend the practice of some local authorities in arranging periodical training sessions (for no more than a day or half a day) to advise officers who may not be regular committee attenders on committee procedure and practice.

Attendance at party groups

5.34 The ability of officers to act as effective advisers to councillors will in some local

5. The role of officers

authorities depend on whether they attend, or are prepared to attend, meetings of the party groups. Widdicombe's research showed that attendance was the exception rather than the rule, possibly because of this specific clause often found in officers' terms and conditions of service:

> 'The officer should not be called upon to advise any political group of the employing authority either as to the work of the groups or as to the work of the authority, neither shall he or she be required to attend any meetings of any political group.'

In the case of chief executives, chief and deputy chief officers there is this additional sentence:

> 'This shall be without prejudice to any arrangements to the contrary which may be made in agreement with the officer and which includes adequate safeguards to preserve the political neutrality of the officer in relation to the affairs of the council.'

Widdicombe felt that this makes unnecessarily heavy weather of the subject. It recommended that no special inhibition should be placed on attendance at party groups subject to the following safeguards:

- all requests for attendance should be addressed to the chief executive who should decide which officers should attend; and
- the chief executive should notify the other parties and offer a similar facility.

These safeguards, it was said, should be included in the list of conventions that Widdicombe recommended that all local authorities should prepare, and, later in 1997, repeated in the protocol advocated by the Nolan Committee (see 1.59). In addition, it is suggested that where there are non-councillors present at party group meetings, the officer should be specifically informed of this in order to ensure that confidentiality is not breached.

Notes

1 As to the power of employing the generality of local authority employees: see LGA 1972, s.112(1). Certain other categories of staff are employed under specific legislation.
2 There are several books on the local government service including various encyclopedic loose-leaf works.
3 LG&HA 1989, s.9.
4 Bains Report, para.7.34.
5 There are several cases where the courts have considered the implications of, for example, unauthorised action by an officer: *Warwick Rural District Council* v. *Miller-Mead* (1962),

where it was held that a local authority can regularise the action by subsequent ratification, *Lever Finance Ltd* v. *Westminster (City) London Borough Council* (1971), where it was held that an authority may be bound by the doctrine of estoppel when it is not prepared to ratify what has been done by an officer. In Lever, Lord Denning MR said at p.231: 'An applicant cannot himself know, of course, whether such a delegation has taken place: that is a matter for the "indoor management" of the planning authority. It depends on the internal resolutions which it has made. Any person dealing with it is entitled to assume that all necessary resolutions have been passed.' Now, of course, an applicant could inspect the authority's statutory list of delegations to officers: LGA 1972, s.100G(2); and see 3.2.

6 LGA 1972, s.101(1).
7 Herbert Morrison, *How Greater London is Governed* (1932).
8 *The Clerk of the Council and his Department* (1951).
9 For this reason it is not good practice to include the names of officers among those recorded as present at a council, committee or subcommittee meeting. Nevertheless, a record might usefully be made that a named officer, having declared an interest, withdrew from the meeting, and must necessarily be made where an officer – where charged with a specific duty to report, as, for example, in the case of the monitoring officer, or otherwise – has advised the meeting that a projected course of action is unlawful.
10 When an officer is speaking in council or committee he must take care to ensure that he can be heard and understood by everyone in the room. Roland Freeman in *Becoming a Councillor* (2nd edn, 1975), p.85, tells the story of a new member of a small district council who rose somewhat nervously after a meeting had been in progress for an hour to say, 'On a point of order, I can't hear what the clerk is saying and could he possibly speak up a little.' As the new councillor sat down an older member leant across to him and said, 'I'm so glad you did that. I haven't heard a word he's said for the past seven and a half years!'
11 Raymond Knowles, *Effective Management in Local Government*.

Part 2
Council Meetings

Chapter 6
Preliminaries

Notice and summons

Essential prerequisites

6.1 There are two essential preliminaries to the holding of a council meeting, i.e. the meeting in full assembly of a principal, parish or community council, and usually called full Council. These are the giving of notice and the service of a summons: the former is a public intimation, published in prescribed manner, to the community at large, not merely to local government electors; the latter is directed privately to the council members who are entitled to attend. Notice is general while the summons is individual.

6.2 If there is failure to comply with statutory requirements as to notice and summons then the meeting itself may not be properly convened and the business transacted of no effect: see more particularly 6.20. In certain circumstances the notice, and in every case the summons, must specify the business to be transacted. In this sense the agenda (a term not used in any of the statutes regulating local authority meetings until introduced by the LG(AI)A 1985: see 6.21) may be said to be part of the notice and summons. In the case of parish and community meetings the obligation at law is to give public notice only.[1]

Initiation of a meeting

6.3 As indicated earlier (see 1.19) a council meeting will be held:

- as directed by statute, e.g. the annual meeting;
- in accordance with the timetable of meetings fixed by the council, usually at the annual meeting, i.e. the cycle of ordinary meetings;
- for a special purpose required by statute or on the decision of the council; or
- upon the requisition of the chairman or the prescribed number of members, i.e. an extraordinary meeting.

Requisitioned meetings

6.4 It is expressly provided that if the chairman of a principal, parish or community council refuses to call an extraordinary meeting after a requisition for that purpose, signed by five members (in the case of a principal council: three in the case of a joint authority or two in the case of a parish or community council), has been presented to him; or if, without so refusing, the chairman does not call the meeting within seven days after the requisition has been presented, then, in the case of a principal council any five members (or in the case of a joint authority any three members and parish or community council any two members) may on that refusal or on the expiration of the seven days, as the case may be, themselves call an extraordinary meeting of the council forthwith. For a suggested standing order: see 6.13; and as to the subsequent withdrawal of a councillor who signed the requisition: see 6.18. There is provision also for the calling of parish and community meetings in similar circumstances, but the term extraordinary is not used. The NALC model standing orders do not cover this area, however.

What is meant by 'presented'?

6.5 The use of the word 'presented' in the statute suggests an act more formal than, say, serving the requisition by post or other method of delivery, and it may be that the requisition should be handed personally to the chairman by one of the signatories to the requisition. If, of course, the chairman cannot be contacted because of absence from the area and is thus unable to receive the requisition, it may be, strictly, that the requisition should be handed physically to the vice-chairman, who is empowered generally to act in the absence of the chairman, but it is submitted that the presenter must make reasonable attempts to present the requisition to the chairman before going to the vice-chairman. Compliance with the requirement to present the requisition is important because if an extraordinary meeting was called on the false claim that the chairman had refused or had neglected to call the meeting, the extraordinary meeting subsequently called by individual councillors might be held invalid.

What is meant by 'call a meeting'?

6.6 The obligation on the chairman to call an extraordinary meeting in the foregoing circumstances is to ensure that the notice and summons to the meeting are given within the prescribed seven days. It does not mean that the meeting itself must take place within that period (*Mallon* v. *Armstrong* (1982)). The requisition could ask that the meeting be held on a particular date but the chairman has discretion and is not bound to comply with such a request. Upon the chairman's refusal or neglect, the extraordinary meeting called by the prescribed number of members – these do not necessarily have to be the members who signed the requisition – can be held whenever the members themselves determine: there is no time limit. In exercising discretion as to date, the chairman ought not to delay unduly in calling the meeting.

Notice

6.7 In the case of every meeting of the full Council, public notice must be given:

- three clear days at least before a meeting of a principal council (and of its committees and subcommittees: see 10.7 et seq.) and published at the council's offices; or, if the meeting is convened at shorter notice, then at the time it is convened; or

6. Preliminaries

- three clear days at least before a meeting of a parish or community council 'fixed in some conspicuous place'[2] in the parish or the community as the case may be; or
- not less than seven clear days beforehand (fourteen days in certain cases) in the case of a parish or community meeting by posting the notice in some place or places in the parish or the community as the case may be.

Although there is no statutory requirement to such effect, the notice at least of an ordinary or annual meeting is often signed by the chief executive[3] or the chairman: as to who signs in the case of an extraordinary meeting see 6.11. Public notice must be given:

- by posting the notice in some conspicuous place or places within the area of the local authority; and
- in such other manner, if any, as appears to the authority to be desirable for giving publicity to the notice.

6.8 The LGA 2000 (s.98) amended the LGA1972, by the addition of a provision allowing the Secretary of State by Order to amend the three clear days set out in Sch. 12 para.4 to such greater number of days as he may specify. The Local Authorities (Access to Meetings and Documents) (Period of Notice) (England) Order 2002 came into force on 1st October 2002, and amended the period of three clear days to five clear days in relation to England, in relation to principal councils.

'Clear days' has long been interpreted in practice, on the basis of a ruling in *R. v. Herefordshire Justices* (1820), as meaning weekdays excluding the day a document becomes available and the day on which the meeting is held. This decision was supported in *R. v. Swansea City Council ex parte Elitestone Ltd* (1993). More specifically the period means five periods of 24 hours running from midnight to midnight and should not include Saturdays or Sundays (unless in its application to the inspection of agenda and reports council offices are open on those days (see 6.27).

6.9 There is an assumption in s.100A(6) LGA1972 (added by the LG(AI)1985) that the power exists for the summoning of a principal council on less than five clear days' notice and provision is made for notices to be posted (and agenda to be deposited) in these circumstances. The only power to call meetings, and the formalities to be complied with, is in the LGA 1972 and this makes no mention of less than five clear days. In view of the doubtful legal basis for giving less than the five clear days' notice it would seem prudent that meetings of the full council should only be called in these circumstances in truly exceptional cases, if at all.

6.10 The notice of an ordinary meeting of a principal, parish or community council and of a parish or community meeting may take any form so long as it includes the time and place of the intended meeting. The notice must be reasonable and effective with sufficient information to enable an interested person to attend: thus the time must be precise as to date and time and the place of meeting clearly described. The notice must be prominently displayed, even in the case of a principal council where the requirement is merely to publish the notice at the council's offices rather than in some conspicuous place: it should, therefore, be displayed near the main entrance to the council's offices (and, if there is more than one town or county hall or council offices in the area the notice should, it is suggested, be displayed at each); in the other cases the notice should be conspicuously displayed on official notice boards throughout the parish or community.

6.11 The statutory requirements as to notice are contained in two places in the LGA 1972: first, in Sch.12 as originally enacted, and secondly in s.100A(6), which was added by the LG(AI)A 1985. Additional notice is required of meetings at which resolutions are to be considered to promote or oppose a Bill in Parliament (see 7.150).

Extraordinary meetings

6.12 In the case of an extraordinary meeting of a principal or parish or community council there are two additional requirements as to form. In addition to the time and place, the notice must specify the business proposed to be transacted at the meeting, and must be signed by the members of the council who have called the meeting. This can be in general terms so long as the purpose of the business is fairly indicated (see 6.29). In any case the requirement that an agenda and accompanying reports must be open to public inspection (see 6.26 et seq.) reduces the need for the business to be spelt out in detail in the notice. If the chairman of the council calls a meeting of a principal, parish or community council, it is not clear whether he should sign the notice; but in the case of a parish or community meeting the notice must be signed by the person or persons convening the meeting.[4]

6.13 One of the draft core standing orders put forward by the working party (see 2.3) related to extraordinary meetings of the council in these terms:

'0–1 The chairman of the council may at any time call an extraordinary meeting of the council.

2 If the office of chairman is vacant, or if the chairman is unable to act for any reason, the vice-chairman of the council may at any time call an extraordinary meeting of the council.

3 If the offices of chairman and vice-chairman are both vacant, or if both the chairman and the vice-chairman are unable to act for any reason:

a) the leader of the council (if any), or

b) any two members of the panel appointed under paragraph (7) below may at any time call an extraordinary meeting.

4 The appropriate number of members of the council may call an extraordinary meeting of the council if a requisition for such a meeting signed by the appropriate number of members of the council has been presented to the chairman of the council, and either he/she has refused to call a meeting or, without him/her so refusing, no extraordinary meeting has been called within seven days of the presentation of the requisition.

5 The appropriate number of members of the council is:

a) in any circumstances, the number of members who then form a quorum of the council; or

b) in relation to any item of business where any political group have required that the provisions of standing order 0 (opposition priority business) should be applied to an item of business, and the question on that item of business has not been put to the vote, or has been put to the vote as a result of a resolution under standing order 0 (allocation of time), standing order 00 (termination of meeting) or standing order 00 (closure motions), at least five.

Variation:

In subparagraph (b), the number specified may be increased to a number greater than five but not greater than one-tenth of the whole number of members of the council.

6   Any requisition under paragraph 4 may be presented to the chairman by being left for him/her with the proper officer.

7   At, or as soon as possible after, the annual meeting of the council, the council shall appoint a panel of at least four members of the council for the purposes of paragraph 3.

8   Where any person or persons decides to call an extraordinary meeting of the council, he/she shall signify to the proper officer that he/she has done so, the business to be transacted and the date and time for which the meeting is called. The proper officer shall thereupon ensure that the notices and summonses required by paragraph 4(2) of Schedule 12 to the 1972 Act are published and sent.

9   Any extraordinary meeting of the council which may be called shall be held at [place] or such other place as the chairman of the council may appoint.

10   No extraordinary meeting shall be called unless it is proposed to transact at the meeting business which, in accordance with the relevant enactments and these standing orders, may be transacted at that meeting.

Variation:

Either paragraph 3(a) or paragraphs 3(b) and 7 or all three passages may be omitted.'

It must be noted, however, that the draft standing orders preceded the LGA2000. In the case of a council operating executive arrangements, a member of the executive cannot be chosen to act in the place of the chairman or vice-chairman's absence at a meeting (LGA1972 Sch.12 Part I para.5(5)). There must therefore be doubt as to whether it is appropriate for the leader of the council to call an extraordinary general meeting at which he cannot preside.

Summons generally

6.14 A summons to attend a council meeting must be sent to every member of the principal, parish or community council as the case may be:

*   at least five clear days beforehand (three in the case of a parish council – see 6.8 above);
*   specifying the business to be transacted at the meeting;
*   signed by the proper officer of the council (see 6.16); and
*   left at or sent by post to the usual place of residence of the member, and, of course, giving date, time and place of meeting.

This means that the document sent to councillors should strictly be phrased literally in the manner of a summons, e.g. 'You are hereby summoned to attend a meeting . . .' or words to like effect. There is no similar statutory obligation to summon members to attend executive, committee or subcommittee meetings (see 10.8). These statutory requirements apply whatever the type of meeting concerned: ordinary, annual or extraordinary or one called for a special purpose, e.g. to consider the promotion of a private bill in parliament. There is no statutory requirement for members to be sent an agenda, but in practice this will form part of the summons. Delivery can be either personally by hand or by post; if the latter, then first class post should be used wherever possible and timetables will usually make this necessary. Members of principal councils may give notice to the proper officer of their wish for the summons to be sent to an address specified in their notice rather than their normal residence; any such notice should be in writing and the effect is to make delivery to the specified address a valid service of the summons (see 3.9).

6.15 There is no obligation to summon individual electors to a parish or community meeting; those entitled to attend must rely on the public notice. It may be thought appropriate to notify individually parish or community councillors as the case may be. The chairman of a parish or community council is specifically entitled to attend a parish or community council as the case may be (or, where a grouping order is in force, for any meeting of the parishes or communities within the group), whether or not he is an elector for the parish or community, and it may be that he should be individually notified.

Signature on the summons

6.16 As indicated above (see 6.14), a summons must be signed by the proper officer, i.e. the officer appointed for that purpose by the local authority, and, strictly, any document bearing the signature of an officer not so appointed will be invalid (see *West Ham Corporation* v. *Benabo* (1934), and other cases that concern notices under the Housing Acts). But a signature purporting to be that of the proper officer may be a facsimile. There may seem in practice little need for anyone to sign on behalf of the proper officer, but it may be that such a summons would not be effectively challenged under the analogy of *Tennant* v. *London County Council* (1957), where it was held that this was permissible in respect of the authentication of the documents under s.184 of the LoGA 1939.

6.17 There may be some instances where, for historical or other reason, the summons will be signed by an officer not needing to do so as the proper officer.

Member's withdrawal from requisition

6.18 What is the position if a councillor, having signed a requisition for an extraordinary meeting (see 6.4), indicates before the summons is issued that he wishes to withdraw his signature? Does this invalidate the requisition? Where a course of action is prescribed by statute, those who exercise an entitlement to initiate that action cannot withdraw. The steps laid down should be started the moment the requisition is presented and thereafter not stopped by anything that may intervene before the issue of the summons (and certainly not between the summons and the holding of the meeting because under common law a meeting once convened cannot properly be postponed: see 6.39.)

6.19 Of course the statutory provisions do envisage that the chairman of the council might refuse or neglect to call a meeting following the requisition, notwithstanding the clear duty to call it (see 6.6). It therefore seems reasonable to assume that if before the summons is issued a councillor who has signed the requisition withdraws, with the result that fewer than the number of councillors prescribed are, in effect, left seeking the meeting, the chairman will probably be judged to have acted reasonably if he refuses to call the meeting. There is the fallback position whereby a similar number, who do not need to be the same councillors, can call the meeting themselves.

Want of service

6.20 At common law, failure to serve a summons upon everyone entitled to attend a corporate assembly invalidates the meeting.[5] However, so far as a meeting of a principal, parish or community council is concerned, there is express statutory provision to this important effect, i.e. that: 'want of service of any . . . summons . . . on any member of the . . . council concerned shall not affect the validity of the meeting.'

Nevertheless, care should be taken to ensure there is no defect of service. The courts could be expected to construe this provision strictly and want of service on a substantial number of councillors or wilful failure or neglect to summon members could affect the validity of the meeting. It is recognised as good practice that any request from a member that he does not wish to receive a summons over a specified period (because, for example, of his absence overseas on holiday or business) should be ignored, although of course the reasons for this should be explained to the councillor. A record should be kept of the service of the summons to support evidence that the law has been complied with.

If a member of a principal council gives notice in writing to the proper officer that he wants any summonses to attend meetings of the council to be sent to him at some address specified in the notice, other than his place of residence, any summons addressed to him and left at, or sent by post to, that address shall be deemed sufficient service of the summons: see LGA 1972, Sch.12, Pt I, para. 4(3).

Council meeting agenda

Business must be specified

6.21 The agenda for a meeting is the list of items of business to be transacted. There has always been a statutory prohibition against the transaction of business not on an agenda in the case of principal councils, although the statutory provisions were at one time differently worded in this respect for no apparent reason: 'a strange discrepancy' Vaisey J called it in *Ayles* v. *Romsey and Stockbridge RDC* (1944). The position is now clear beyond doubt.

6.22 The prohibition against the transaction of business not specified in the agenda is now reinforced by the following provision in s.100B(4) of the LGA 1972, which was added by the LG(AI)A 1985:

> 'An item of business may not be considered at a meeting of a principal council unless either:
> a) a copy of the agenda including the item (or a copy of the item) is open to inspection by members of the public . . . for at least five clear days before the meeting or, where the meeting is convened at shorter notice, from the time the meeting is convened; or
> b) by reason of special circumstances, which shall be specified in the minutes, the chairman of the meeting is of the opinion that the item should be considered as a matter of urgency.'

The obligation to make the agenda available for public inspection is dealt with below (see 6.26 et seq.). The power conferred upon the chairman of the meeting represents an unusual, if not unique, statutory provision and it raises the question whether it remains wholly wrong, as it was until recently, to include in any council agenda a concluding item: Any other business. It may be that, at least in the case of committee meetings, it would not be improper now to provide for any other business that the chairman decides is urgent. The discretion given to the chairman probably could not be challenged, though presumably it might, if the chairman exercised this power on so regular a basis that the justification becomes suspect.[6]

Urgent business

6.23 The power enabling the chairman of a meeting to permit the transaction of urgent business (see 6.22) confers power with statutory authority on an individual member. The way in which this is handled in committees and subcommittees is dealt with in Part Three of this book: in particular in 9.90; but the problem arises as to whether urgent business of any kind is appropriate, or indeed lawful, at meetings of the full council.

6.24 A number of problems associated with the LG(AI)A 1985 stem from the failure to repeal or amend provisions in the LGA 1972, which are completely incompatible. Calling meetings at less than five clear days is one example of the resulting confusion (see 6.9); urgent business at council meetings is another. The LGA 1972 in para.4(5) of Sch.12 provides:

> 'Except in the case of business required by or under this or any other Act to be transacted at the annual meeting of a principal council and other business brought before that meeting as a matter of urgency in accordance with the council's standing orders, no business shall be transacted at a meeting of the council other than that specified in the summons.'

6. Preliminaries

The literal interpretation of this paragraph means that urgent business can only be considered at the annual meeting of a council, and then only if the authority's standing orders allow for it. The effect of the 1985 Act is to restrict this still further by requiring the chairman to be of the opinion that the business is urgent before it can be considered (see 6.23). It does not extend the facility to consider urgent business to ordinary or extraordinary meetings of the council. Placing an item such as 'To consider such other business as the chairman considers urgent' does not satisfy the requirement that the business should be specified. The only exception to this would be where business required by law to be done was inadvertently omitted from an agenda. In these circumstances it would be permissible to deal with the business even though not specified on the agenda.

Urgent business at adjourned meeting

6.25 Nothing can be transacted at an adjourned meeting except the unfinished business of the original meeting (see 6.39). Urgent business could properly be dealt with if the chairman considers it urgent under the statutory discretion accorded to him but only if the adjourned meeting is the annual meeting of the council and provision for dealing with urgent business is included in standing orders.

Public access to agenda

6.26 There is an obligation upon principal authorities, but not others, to make copies of the agenda for a meeting and copies of any report for the meeting open to inspection by members of the public for five clear days before the date of the meeting except that:

- where the meeting is convened at shorter notice then the documents must be open to inspection from the time the meeting is convened; and
- where an item is added to an agenda afterwards, copies of any report relating to the item must be available for inspection from the time the item is added to the agenda.

Regulations (SI 2002/715) came into force on 1st October 2002, which required the three clear day period set out in ss. 100A to 100K LGA1972 to be amended to five clear days in respect of England.

6.27 The precise terms of the statutory obligation require agenda and reports to be open for inspection at the offices of the council for at least five clear days. The phrase 'offices of the council' would appear not to cover premises such as libraries unless they form part of the council's administrative headquarters. The meaning of 'clear days' has already been discussed (see 6.8) and in this context should not include a Saturday or Sunday unless the offices happen to be open on those days and inspection is possible. It is also laid down that there is no obligation to make documents available for public inspection before copies have been made available to members, although the precise effect of this proviso is unclear. Unless these requirements have been complied with, the business concerned cannot lawfully be dealt with at the meeting:

the judge in *Swansea* (see 6.8) had no doubt that the strict statutory requirements had to be complied with in every case, even in the absence of proof of damage by a third party.

6.28 There may be excluded from the copies of reports the whole or any part that relates only to items during that, in the opinion of the proper officer, the meeting is not likely to be open to the public. In such cases the copy report or the relevant part of it must be marked 'Not for publication' and a statement put on the report indicating, in the prescribed terms, the item of exempt information by virtue of which the council is likely to exclude the public during the item to which the report relates. The proper officer should act reasonably, i.e. take careful account of the circumstances, in forming his opinion. If the business is, in fact, dealt with in open session, the relevant papers should be handed out to the press representatives and the public present at the meeting.

With what detail should business be specified?

6.29 It is not necessary that the items for consideration at a meeting should be set out in absolute detail so long as the business is fairly stated. This means that those who are summoned to the meeting or are entitled to be present can judge whether the business warrants their attendance or not: it is especially important that the business to be transacted should be specifically stated if it is important and not merely a matter of routine or common occurrence and where the meeting has been specially convened. For example, in *R. v. The Corporation of Dublin* (1911), a special meeting of the corporation was summoned on a requisition of seven ratepayers to consider the question of unemployment in the city and ways and means of alleviating it. At the meeting a resolution was passed authorising the city treasurer to arrange payment of £10,000 on useful works for the alleviation of unemployment. It was held that the notice of the meeting was insufficient to enable the meeting to pass such a resolution. In a later case, *Longfield Parish Council v. Wright* (1918), Peterson J said:

> 'It may be that a very important question is going to be considered at the meeting; it may be on the other hand that the only business is purely formal, paying some tradesman or something of that description. In the one case the members would attend in force and in the other case it was a mere matter of form, the members would not attend beyond the necessary quorum. Accordingly, the notice convening the meeting should contain sufficient description of the important business which the meeting is to transact, and the meeting cannot in ordinary circumstances go outside the business mentioned in that notice.'

6.30 The position as regards oral reporting by officers or of indicating that a report will be laid on the table is more appropriately dealt with in Chapter 10.

6.31 It is not sufficient to include an item on the agenda that, for example, says in effect, 'To receive the report of . . . committee', unless the report itself is circulated to

6. Preliminaries

councillors and made available for public inspection for the five clear days preceding the meeting; nor an item, 'The chief executive will report', unless the subject matter and the purport of the oral report are fairly summarised on the agenda.

Defamatory matter in documents

6.32 There is statutory protection as regards defamatory matter in published documents that are required to be accessible to members of the public. It is expressly provided by s.100H(5) of the 1972 Act that where any such document:

- is supplied to, or open to inspection by, a member of the public; or
- is supplied for the benefit of any newspaper under s.100B(7),

the publication thereby of any defamatory matter contained in the document is privileged unless the publication is proved to be made with malice.

Regulation of order of business

6.33 The agenda will not only specify the business to be transacted but will also determine the order in which that business is dealt with at the meeting. Usually this order, so far as it is not determined by statute, will be prescribed in standing orders, and the standing orders will invariably provide that the council may on grounds of urgency, possibly of convenience, vary that order on particular occasions. A lengthy draft core standing order suggested by the working party (see 2.4) for the regulation of business at council meetings was in these terms:

'0–1 Unless the council otherwise order in accordance with paragraph 3, the order of business at every meeting of the council shall be:
   a) in the absence of the chairman and vice-chairman, to choose a member of the council to preside;
   b) at the annual meeting, and at any other meeting which is the first after the office of chairman shall have become vacant, to elect a chairman;
   c) at the annual meeting, and at any other meeting which is the first after the office of vice-chairman shall have become vacant, to appoint a vice-chairman;
   d) except where the minutes of all earlier meetings of the council have already been signed as a correct record or, in accordance with standing order 00, any unsigned minutes are to stand over until the next suitable meeting, to approve as a correct record the minutes of the last meeting of the council, and of any earlier meeting of which the minutes have not been so approved, and for the person presiding to sign them;
   e) to receive communications from the person presiding;
   f) where the meeting has been summoned by members under standing order 0, to consider the business specified in the summons;
   g) where a meeting has been summoned to consider:
      i) a change of the name of the area of the authority under section 74 of the 1972 Act,

ii) a change in the name of the authority under section 144 of the 1989 Act,

iii) the promotion or opposition of a bill under section 239 of the 1972 Act,

iv) the presentation of a petition to The Queen praying for the grant of a charter under section 245 of the 1972 Act, or

v) the grant of the title of honorary alderman or the admission of an honorary freeman under section 249 of the 1972 Act,

vi) a report from the chief financial officer under section 114 of the Local Government Finance Act 1988,

vii) a report of the monitoring officer under section 5 of the 1989 Act, to consider the business for which the meeting has been summoned;

h) where the meeting is the last ordinary meeting before 2nd April in any year, and where the council have not set an amount for their [council tax] for the ensuing financial year, to consider the setting of such an amount;

i) to receive petitions from members of the council; or from local government electors for the area of the authority;

j) the asking and answering of questions under standing order OO;

k) to consider items of business, if any, which were on the agenda of the last meeting of the council and which were not disposed of or did not lapse;

l) to receive and consider reports, minutes and recommendations of committees in the order prescribed under paragraph (2);

m) to consider motions of which notice has been submitted by members of the council in accordance with standing order O in the order in which they are recorded as having been received;

n) to consider other business, if any, specified in the summons for the meeting.

Variations:

1 For London boroughs, replace item (a) with: "(a) in the absence of the mayor, to decide whether the deputy mayor (if present) shall preside, and if not, to choose a member to preside;".

2 For London boroughs, omit item (c).

3 For authorities outside Wales, omit subparagraph (ii) of item (g).

4 For authorities other than councils of cities and boroughs, omit the reference to the admission of honorary freemen in subparagraph (v) of item (g).

5 For county councils, replace item (h) with: "(h) where the meeting is the last ordinary meeting before 1 March in any year, and where the council has not yet resolved to issue a precept for the ensuing financial year, to consider the issuing of a precept;".

6 Item (i) will require amendment if a variation in standing order OO is adopted. The items of business under item (1) in the last paragraph shall be considered in the order in which they are listed in the agenda for the meeting, and that order shall be in accordance with arrangements determined from time to time by the council.

Variations:

Replace "in accordance with arrangements determined from time to time by the council" with either: "determined by the chairman of the council" or "determined by the proper officer after consultation, so far as practicable, with the leaders of the political groups".

6. Preliminaries

3) The order of business in paragraph (1) may be varied by
   a) direction of the person presiding, made with the unanimous consent of the members present, but not so as to alter the order of items (a) to (g); or
   b) a resolution of the council, [moved, seconded and put without comment] but not so as to alter the order of items (a) to (g), or to override the provisions of standing order 0.

4) If the person presiding decides that an item of business not included in the agenda for the meeting sent with the summons for the meeting may be taken for reasons of urgency, that item shall, subject to any direction or resolution under paragraph (3), be taken at the end of the other items of business.'

6.34 There is other business dealt with at the annual meeting, i.e. invariably to appoint committees for the ensuing year and, where the authority is divided into different political groups, provision will be made to review their representation on committees and on other bodies.[7] There may also be an item to receive a report on the appointment of leader of the council and leader of the opposition, chief whip and opposition chief whip and their deputies. As to the allocation of time to the several items of business: see 7.34.

Notification of questions

6.35 Although questions proposed to be asked by members are not usually specified in the agenda, there have to be arrangements to ensure that prior notice is given in order that answers can be prepared in advance of the meeting. Old model standing order no.8(2) is to the following effect in this respect:

'A member of the council may:
a) if . . . clear days' notice in writing has been given to the town clerk/clerk of the council ask the chairman/mayor or the chairman of any committee any questions on any matter in relation to which the council have powers or duties or which affects the . . .
b) With the permission of the mayor/chairman, put to him or the chairman of any committee any question relating to urgent business, of which such notice has not been given; but a copy of any such question shall, if possible, be delivered to the town clerk/clerk of the council not later than . . . o'clock in the morning of the day of the meeting.'

Question time at council meetings is dealt with in at 7.41 et seq.
6.36 As in practice officers will provide the leader of the council or committee chairman, as the case may be, with the basic facts and material for answering questions, it is probably better that members should not seek the aid of officers in drawing up their questions. Otherwise there is a danger that officer may consciously or unconsciously frame questions to enable the leader or a committee chairman in answering to score a point or evade the issue. Questions are not always asked to elicit

information: many are put merely as a device to make a political point. Those asked of executive members are more likely to relate to the local authority's functions than any put to the leader of the council, but the comments on relevance in the case of original motions apply equally to questions.

Postponement and adjournment

Postponement

6.37 It is doubtful whether a council meeting, once convened, may properly be postponed in any circumstances: see *Smith* v. *Paringa Mines Ltd* (1906), in which it was held in a company case that the postponement of a general meeting of share-holders was inoperative without special power to postpone being given by the regulations governing the meeting and therefore resolutions passed at a gathering of shareholders held in pursuance of the notice were valid and effective. It is unquestionably bad practice to cancel or abandon or postpone any meeting once it has been validly convened, and unlawful in any case to purport to postpone an annual council meeting to a date outside the prescribed statutory period for its convention. If circumstances make it impossible for the meeting to be held as convened (for example, the last minute destruction of the council chamber or other meeting place), the proper course would seem to be to hold the meeting as nearly as possible in accordance with the notice and summons and then adjourn it. The purported postponement of a meeting is to be distinguished from failure to make a meeting see (6.38).

Failure to make a meeting

6.38 Until a quorum is present no council meeting can commence. In practice it is usual to wait a reasonable time to allow latecomers to assemble but, strictly, if a quorum does not exist at the time fixed for the commencement of the meeting, the meeting fails and those present are not competent to resolve upon its adjournment. It is therefore desirable (though in practice rare) for there to be a standing order to the effect that if a quorum is not present within, say, half an hour from the time appointed for the meeting, it shall stand adjourned. Alternatively, the meeting must be reconvened.

Effect of adjournment on convention

6.39 An adjourned meeting is part of the original meeting that it continues (*Scalding* v. *Lorant* (1851)). It is not essential for notice of an adjourned meeting to be given (*Kerr* v. *Wilkie* (1860)), but there is advantage in doing so. Nothing can be transacted at the adjourned meeting except the unfinished business of the original meeting (*R.* v. *Grimshaw* (1847)). Nevertheless, of course, there is nothing to stop a local authority from convening a separate meeting of the council to take place on the same day as the adjourned meeting – logically after the end of the adjourned meeting rather than before it – to conduct new business.

6.40 Because the rules of debate continue to apply to an adjourned meeting (see 6.39), a careful note needs to be kept of the names of members who have spoken already in a particular debate since under standing orders those members may not be entitled to speak again. This could cause considerable difficulty in adjourned budget meetings where the adjournment may come midway through the debate rather than at the end of a particular item of business. In such circumstances it is advisable to supply members with a note of the proceedings so far, who has spoken, and the procedure to be followed at the adjourned meeting.

Meetings of the executive

6.41 Meetings of the executive are to be held in public or private under s.22 LGA 2000, and subject to regulations made, it is for the executive to decide which meetings are to be public and which are to be private. The Local Authorities (Executive Arrangements) (Access to Information) (England) Regulations 2000 (SI 2000/3272) make provisions relating to public access to meetings. Where the leader, mayor or council manager (as appropriate) considers that:

- a key decision will be made; and/or
- a decision is likely to be made within 28 days on a matter that is contained within the Forward Plan, or is the subject of notice given under reg.15 is likely to be discussed; and
- an officer who is not a political adviser, assistant or council manager will be present at the discussion (reg.7),

the meeting will be held in public.

Under reg.15, if it is impracticable for a key decision to be included on the Forward Plan the proper officer must inform the chairman of the relevant overview and scrutiny committee that the executive wish to make a decision about the particular matter. If there is no chairman, then each and every member must be informed. The decision cannot be taken until five days have elapsed since the written notice given to the chairman or members was made publicly available. In practice, this notice can take the form of an item on the agenda of the executive meeting, subject to an authority's individual standing orders.. For matters of special urgency, see 6.48.

For the purposes of the Regulations, an officer briefing meeting for members is not to be treated as a meeting (SI 2002/716).

Exclusion of the public

6.42 The public may be excluded from any part of an executive meeting:

- where it is likely that confidential information would be disclosed in breach of confidence;
- where it is likely that exempt information (as defined in Sch.12A LGA1972) would be disclosed;

- where it is likely that the advice of a political adviser or assistant would be disclosed; and
- where a lawful power is used to exclude a member or the public in order to maintain order or prevent misbehaviour at the meeting.

The regulations set out that a resolution must be passed under (2) and (3) above, but in practice it is advisable to pass a resolution for all of the above circumstances.

Public access to agenda

6.43 There is an obligation to make copies of the agenda for a meeting and copies of any report for the meeting open to inspection by members of the public when they are made available to the executive or decision making body, for five clear days before the date of the meeting, except that:

- where the meeting is convened at shorter notice then the documents must be open to inspection from the time the meeting is convened; and
- where an item is added to an agenda afterwards, copies of any report relating to the item must be available for inspection from the time the item is added to the agenda.

This is very similar to the obligations under the LGA 1972; see 6.7 for a discussion of clear days and council offices.

6.44 Regulations(SI 2002/716) came into force on 1st October 2002 that required the three clear days period set out in SI 2000/3272 be amended to five clear days in respect of England. The provisions for full council were brought into line on the same day (see 6.4).

6.45 There may be excluded from the copies of reports the whole or any part that relates only to items during which, in the opinion of the proper officer, the meeting is not likely to be open to the public. In such cases the copy report or the relevant part of it must be marked 'Not for publication' and a statement put on the report indicating, in the prescribed terms, the item of exempt information (LGA 1972, Sch. 12A) by virtue of which the council is likely to exclude the public during the item to which the report relates. However, unlike the provisions for council meetings, the report can also be private if it contains confidential information or the advice of a political adviser or assistant, and this should be marked on the report in the same way (reg.1 1). The proper officer should act reasonably, i.e. take careful account of the circumstances, in forming his opinion. If the business is, in fact, dealt with in open session the relevant papers should be handed out to the press representatives and the public present at the meeting.

6.46 A list of any background papers should be included in every report, and at least one copy must be available for inspection by members of the public at the council offices (reg.6). Copies must be provided, if required, and the regulations provide that a reasonable fee can be charged for this. However, it would seem that a request could be made under the FOIA, and under that Act the Council would not be able to charge (unless of course it met the statutory limits).

6.47 The refusal or obstruction of access to the agenda and reports may be treated as an offence under reg.23, for which a fine at level 1 can be imposed on summary conviction. There is no equivalent provision in the LGA1972 in respect of council agendas and reports.

Urgent business

6.48 Unlike full council, the legislation provides that urgent business may be dealt with by the executive, provided certain criteria are fulfilled. If the business to be dealt with is a key decision, then agreement that the decision is urgent and cannot reasonably be deferred needs to obtained from the chairman of the relevant Overview and Scrutiny Committee or, if there is no such person, the chairman of the authority, or, if there is no such person, the vice-chairman of the local authority (reg.16 SI 2000/3272).

6.49 A quarterly report of urgent executive decisions should be made to the full council (reg.20).

Additional rights of access for members

6.50 In addition to the usual 'need to know' principles set out in 4.6, any member of a local authority has a right to inspect the agenda and reports of executive meetings.

6.51 Members are also entitled to inspect any document that relates to business transacted at a private meeting, or any decision made by an individual member with delegated authority, or any key decision made by an officer with delegated authority, at the end of the meeting or after the decision has been taken, as appropriate (reg. 17). However, this does not apply where this would involve the disclosure of exempt information within certain categories (Sch.12A LGA1972 paras.1, 2, 4, 5 and 7) or the advice of a political adviser.

In practice, this provision of inspection can be satisfied by making agendas and reports available at the council offices; they do not have to be sent to each member.

Notes

1 LGA 1972, Sch.12, paras.15(2), 30(2).
2 What is a conspicuous place is a question of fact: *West Hero Corporation* v. *Thomas* (1908).
3 The 'proper officer' could sign the notice under s.234 of the 1972 Act; and thereunder 'signature' includes a facsimile of a signature by whatever process reproduced. As to the proper officer: see 5.18.
4 LGA 1972, Sch.12: Pt III, para.15(2); Pt V, para.30(2). See also as to public notice of a parish meeting: s.233(2).
5 *Kynaston* v. *Shrewsbury Corporation* (1736); *sub nom. R* v. *Shrewsbury Corporation*, Lee *temp.* Hard 147; *Smyth* v. *Varley* (1849); even though dispensed with by a particular member: *R.* v. *Langhorn* (1836); see also *Staple of England (Mayor, etc. of Merchants of)* v. *Bank of England* (1887).
6 It may be thought prudent for the chairman's consent to the transaction of urgent busi-ness to be put into writing and signed with the reason why the business is regarded by the chairman as urgent. There is nothing to stop the chairman consulting whomsoever he wishes in arriving at his decision.
7 Although this may be done 'as soon as practicable after the meeting': LG&HA 1989, s.15.

Chapter 7

Conduct

General character of proceedings

Introduction

7.1 Proceedings and the business transacted at a meeting of a principal, parish or community council, i.e. of the full council, must:

- take place in public except to the extent that the public is required to be excluded; (i) in the case of a principal council either during an item of business whenever it is likely that confidential information (see 3.3) would be disclosed in breach of the obligation of confidence or by resolution whenever there would otherwise be disclosure of exempt information (see 3.11); (ii) in the case of any other authority when the council by resolution excludes the public because publicity would be prejudicial to the public interest (see 3.28);
- follow any order prescribed by statute and standing orders or as set out in the agenda: the order of business is regulated by statute only in the case of the annual meeting of a principal council which pre scribes that the election of chairman must be the first item (see 6.33);
- have been set out in the notice where the meeting has been convened by councillors (see 6.2) and in every case in the summons and in the case of principal councils in the agenda and accompanying reports (see 6.22): the transaction of business that is outside the scope of a notice convening a meeting will not render the whole meeting irregular: *Re British Sugar Refining Co.* (1857); and
- be intra vires, i.e. within the scope of the authority's powers and duties. In practice, local authorities sometimes pass resolutions on matters over which they have no jurisdiction but in which the local community may have an interest. There is no reason why they should not do so, but a resolution to act in defiance of the law is clearly ultra vires.

In addition, the meeting itself must be properly constituted, i.e. it must have been lawfully convened by public notice and individual summons to councillors entitled to attend (see 6.7 and 6.14), the proper person must be in the chair (see 7.13), and a quorum must be present (see 7.35).

Insignia

7.2 The mayor in the case of a borough will wear the robes and chain of office at a council meeting, and the chairman in other cases a badge of office. Robes may also be

7. Conduct

worn by the deputy mayor, and ex-mayor's badges by councillors who have held the mayoralty; but in comparatively few boroughs now do councillors wear robes. Most important of the insignia at council meetings is the mace, which is the emblem of power and dignity of the mayor and the symbol of authority. All boroughs, except new boroughs created under the LGA 1972 and unitaries under the LGA 1992, have at least one mace and many have two or more; and in every case the mace (or maces) is (or are) carried by the mace-bearer into the council chamber proceeding the mayor and placed in position horizontally before the mayor (with the crown to the right or in the more important direction) to remain there while the council is in session, and then carried in procession in front of the mayor on leaving. The deputy mayor, when acting on the mayor's behalf at council meetings (but no one else), is entitled to have the mace precede him.

Opening ceremony

7.3 Most local authorities open proceedings in the full assembly with a modicum of ceremony, adding to the dignity of council proceedings. In the case of a borough it is usual, after council members have assembled, for the mayor and chief executive (preceded by the mace-bearer) to enter the council chamber in procession; and for the members and public to stand on their entry either as a matter of course or upon the announcement of the mace-bearer: 'Ladies and gentlemen: Be upstanding for His Worship the Mayor'. In many instances the meeting is closed in somewhat similar manner.

Prayers

7.4 In some authorities it is the custom for proceedings to begin with prayers. Where the practice is followed prayers are usually led by the mayor or chairman's chaplain (ordinarily an honorary post to which an appointment is made personally by the mayor or chairman) or in some cases by local preachers or as custom may dictate. A number of authorities have a standard council prayer specifically drafted for the purpose, often by representatives of local churches.

Business generally

7.5 The nature of the proceedings will vary according to the purpose of the meeting. Thus an annual meeting, apart from essential business (such as the election of a chairman and the appointment of committees for the ensuing year), is largely of a ceremonial character (particularly in the case of mayor-making); and an extra-ordinary meeting will be concerned as a rule with one item of business alone. Ordinary meetings will follow a fairly uniform pattern and the greater part of the business will be the consideration of committee/cabinet reports. So long, however, as an authority observes statutory requirements and does not violate the common law rules governing meetings procedure (including its own standing orders), the conduct of proceedings is for each authority to decide.

7.6 Business is ordinarily conducted in a formal manner and this means that for the greater part discussion takes place upon a motion before the assembly. It is a convention that officers do not participate in any way (although the chief executive or monitoring officer may be called upon to advise on procedure or he or any other chief officer may exceptionally be invited to speak: but see 5.30). This means, as a general rule, that the officers' influence over proceedings and the efficient and effective dispatch of business is limited to preparatory work beforehand, i.e. in the preparation of council papers, the careful briefing of the chairman and the leader of the council, portfolio holders and committee chairmen, the stage-managing of procedure, and attention to the several matters relating to the physical conditions of the council chamber or other accommodation in which the meeting is to be held (e.g. see 10.52).

7.7 There is no reason in law why officers should not be invited to participate in council meetings just as they do in committee or cabinet: it is usually a matter of convention and practicality. With very large meetings it can be difficult to control proceedings where there is constant reference to officers whose views are then interpreted by members for purposes of the debate. On balance, therefore, it is better to restrict discussion to members themselves, particularly since in many authorities – certainly the larger ones – items will already have been discussed by the cabinet and/or in committees. However, it is important to ensure that decisions are not taken based on incorrect or misunderstood facts; and if this possibility arises then officers should be given the opportunity to correct them or provide an accurate interpretation.

Confirmation of minutes

7.8 The confirmation of the minutes of the previous meeting is always placed as an early item on the agenda (see more particularly 6.33). Old model standing order no.9 is to this effect:

'1 The mayor/chairman shall put the question that the minutes of the meeting of the council held on the . . . day of . . . be approved as a correct record.

2 No discussion shall take place upon the minutes, except upon their accuracy, and any question of their accuracy shall be raised by motion. If no such question is raised, or if it is raised then as soon as it has been disposed of, the mayor/chairman shall sign the minutes.'

7.9 The minutes of an extraordinary meeting of the council (see 6.12) can be confirmed at the next following ordinary meeting. One of the mandatory standing orders[1] is to this effect:

'Where in relation to any meeting of the authority the next such meeting is a meeting called under paragraph 3 (extraordinary meetings) or schedule 12 to the Local Government Act 1972, the next following meeting of the authority (being a meeting called otherwise than under that paragraph) shall be treated as a suitable meeting for the purposes of paragraph 41(1) and (2) (signing of minutes) of that schedule.'[2]

---

7. Conduct

Behaviour of members

7.10 Although there are some forms of behaviour that are not expected of members present at a council meeting, e.g. conduct that is so disorderly as to interrupt business (as to which see 7.132), there are no widely accepted conventions otherwise governing councillors' behaviour (although often members are expected to make obeisance to the chair when entering or leaving the council chamber and to stand when addressing the chair) and few other instances where behaviour is regulated by standing orders. One reason for this may be that it would be difficult to secure compliance, because in the final resort there is no power to exclude a councillor – probably not even temporarily (see 7.130) – from a council meeting at which he is lawfully entitled to be present.

7.11 The standing orders of the House of Commons do contain several restrictions on the conduct of Members of Parliament in the House and the Speaker is endowed with formidable authority to secure compliance. MPs are required to keep in their places and not rove around the chamber; they must not read any book, newspaper or letter in their places except in connection with the business of the House; they are not permitted to wear decorations or uniforms and it is the custom for Members to wear jackets and ties; they may not smoke during any of the proceedings of the House, nor may refreshments be brought into or consumed in the chamber. It may seem strange, in view of the noisy behaviour often heard when proceedings in the Commons are broadcast, that members are expected to maintain silence or converse only in undertones, that members must not disturb a member who is speaking by hissing or interruption and that cries of 'Shame!' are strongly condemned. The Lords is directed by standing orders to maintain dignity and order. It may be thought that a council standing order to similar effect might be of advantage and there is no reason why an authority should not introduce one if it so wished.

Addressing the chair

7.12 Councillors should be expected (and standing orders will often so provide) to stand when speaking at a council meeting and always to address the chair. Whether the term Sir or Chairman or Mr Mayor is employed is a matter of local custom (but Mr Mayor can never properly be shortened to Mayor). The manner of addressing a woman chairman varies. The form most favoured appears to vary from between Chairman and Madam Chairman and often Madam rather than Sir. Shortly after the Sex Discrimination Act 1975 came into effect the term Chairperson was favoured in some quarters but has not been widely adopted, if at all. The practice has grown up in some local authorities of referring to a committee chairman as Chair: some councillors in occupying the chair object, however, to being addressed as a piece of furniture!

The chairman

Election of chairman of the council

7.13 The chairman of a principal, parish or community council must be elected annually from among the councillors and the election must be the first business transacted at the council's annual meeting. It was decided in *R. v. McGowan* (1840) that any business carried out before the election of the chairman – in that case the election of aldermen – was void, but the election of the chairman was valid: see also *R. v. Parkyns* (1828). Anyone so elected cannot act in the office until the prescribed declaration of acceptance of the office has been made, which usually follows on immediately after the election.

Procedure on election

7.14 No procedure for the election is prescribed by statute and it is rare for standing orders to do so. In practice, councillors often agree upon a nominee beforehand (in the majority party group where the authority is run on party political lines with or without informal agreement with minority parties) so that at the annual meeting there is usually only one nomination proposed and seconded: a prior arrangement of this kind enables someone other than the nominee to preside at his election (see 7.21). However, where more than one nomination is made various methods can be adopted to determine the chairman: a direct vote is convenient where there are only two nominees; or an elimination vote can be used where there is a larger number (which does not often occur), a succession of votes being taken, on each of which the nominee receiving the fewest votes is excluded from the next vote. If more than one nomination is anticipated there is virtue in making the appointment by ballot, and standing orders normally provide for this.

7.15 Voting at the election proceeds in the normal way, i.e. the election is decided by a majority of the councillors present and voting (but see 7.111). The person presiding at the meeting must give a casting vote in the case of an equality of votes;[3] but where the person presiding only remains a member because of the saving provisions for chairman and vice-chairman, he is not entitled to any other vote.[4] Most authorities try to avoid contested elections for the chairmanship, particularly in the case of boroughs where mayor-making is regarded as an important civic and ceremonial event and lack of unanimity is hardly conducive to the dignity of the occasion. One authority claims to have avoided the repetition of an earlier disaster where the chairman-elect failed to be elected to the annoyance of the majority group and the embarrassment of relatives who were present to see him installed: it holds what is in effect a 'shadow' annual meeting, which recommends a nominee for election and although there still remains the possibility of unexpected challenge this has not occurred.

Failure to elect

7.16 If a council fails to elect a chairman the council is not properly constituted[5] and (except in the case of the chairmanship of a parish or community council or meeting) the High Court may direct the election to be held at a time fixed by the Court. Despite the mandatory terms of the law as to election annually it would not seem improper for a council to elect a chairman pro tem but, the term of office should be clearly stated.

7. Conduct

Proper officer role if necessary

7.17 The following draft core standing order was suggested by the working party (see 2.4) to apply in circumstances where exceptionally it may be necessary for an officer to assist in securing someone in the chair:

> '0–1 Any power of the chairman of the council in relation to the conduct of a meeting of the council may be exercised by the person presiding at the meeting.
>
> 2 If it is necessary to choose a member of the council to preside in the absence of the chairman and vice-chairman, the proper officer shall call on a member of the council to move that a member of the council to be named by that member shall take the chair.
>
> 3 If discussion arises, the proper officer shall exercise the powers of the person presiding to regulate that discussion, and to maintain order at the meeting.
>
> 4 The motion, and any amendments, shall be put to the meeting in accordance with standing order 00 (voting on appointments).'

Adjournment of election

7.18 A council may for a specific reason wish to adjourn the election for a short period, either until later in the proceedings (because, perhaps, of the absence of a particular councillor who is a candidate or of the proposer of a candidate) or to a later meeting (e.g. for political reasons). It would seem, on a strict interpretation of the terms of the statute, that this cannot be done: the election must be the first item of business (see 7.13). It may be, however, that an adjournment of the meeting could meet the circumstances although other difficulties might thereby be created.

7.19 On the other hand, it is arguable that the law does not require that someone shall necessarily be elected but only that the first business shall be the election. Therefore, so long as the question of election is considered as the first item of business, the decision on that consideration could be to adjourn the election. This is probably not a persuasive argument: indeed, the fact that the person presiding at the election is compelled to give a second or casting vote in the event of an equality of votes (see 7.15) seems additional support for the view that parliament's intention was that the election must take place so that the council can be properly constituted.

Election of disqualified councillor

7.20 If the person elected as chairman is disqualified from being a councillor it would seem that the election is nevertheless valid by the terms of s.82 of the LGA 1972, which provides that:

> 'The acts and proceedings of any person elected to an office under this Act and acting in that office shall, notwithstanding his disqualification or want of qualification, be as valid and effectual as if he had been qualified.'

In *Forrester* v. *Norton* (1911), it was held that since the election of the councillor had not been challenged by an election petition, he was a councillor de facto whose election as chairman was rendered valid by s.73 of the Municipal Corporations Act 1882 (now s.82 of the 1972 Act). This would not extend, it is submitted, to validate the election to the chairmanship of a person who is not de facto or lawfully a councillor.

Presiding at one's own election

7.21 It is well established that a person who presides at an election is disqualified from being a candidate. In *R.* v. *Owens* (1858), the mayor of a borough had presided over the election of councillors and, as returning officer, had returned himself as one of the persons elected; the validity of this election was successfully impeached. Local practice, no matter how long established, cannot justify disregard of this rule: see *R.* v. *Reynolds* (1896).

Vacation of chair before election

7.22 However, if an outgoing chairman wishes to be re-elected he can provide a substitute to perform his functions temporarily (see *R.* v. *White* (1867)). This in practice is what is ordinarily done, though it means that a person must be proposed as a candidate before the election. If, while presiding, his name is put forward as a candidate, he cannot then vacate the chair because the proposal made while he occupies the chair would be void. It means also that an outgoing chairman wishing to be re-elected must not preside and further must not be in the meeting[6] because if he is present he must preside (see 7.27).

Failure to give notice of election

7.23 There is authority for the view that the election of a chairman at a meeting for which notice has not been given is invalid. In *R.* v. *Langborn* (1836), in an action impeaching the validity of a mayoral election, the jury found that one of the burgesses (all of whom were entitled to vote) had not been served with a notice of the meeting at which the mayor was elected, and it was held that he was not duly elected. The statutory provision that stipulates that want of service of a summons on any member shall not affect the validity of a meeting of a principal, parish or community council would seem to avoid challenge on these grounds. It might be, however, that the election of a chairman of a parish or community meeting would be held invalid if the requisite notices of such a meeting were not given.

Vice-chairman

Appointment

7.24 A principal council must[7] and a parish and community council may[8] appoint a member of the council to be vice-chairman of the council. The LGA 1972 follows the wording of the former 1933 Act and refers to the appointment and not the election of a vice-chairman, but the difference in term is of no significance. The vice-chairman, unless he resigns or becomes disqualified, holds office until immediately after the election of a chairman at the next annual meeting.[9] During that time he continues to be a member of the council notwithstanding the statutory provisions relating to the retirement of councillors.[10] Where a parish or community council decides always to have a vice-chairman it may be convenient to adopt old model standing order no.2, which is to the effect that 'The council shall at the annual meeting appoint a vice-chairman.'

7.25 What has been said earlier about the procedure for the election of a chairman applies equally to the appointment of a vice-chairman (see 7.13).

Powers

7.26 Subject to standing orders anything authorised or required to be done by, to or before the chairman may be done by, to or before the vice-chairman.[11] Standing orders can place such restrictions upon the vice-chairman's powers as the council thinks appropriate, except that it would not be lawful for standing orders to prohibit the vice-chairman from presiding at a meeting of the full council in the absence of the chairman because the law expressly requires him if present to take the chair (see 7.28). Old model standing order no.3 is to the following effect:

> 'Any power or duty of the mayor/chairman in relation to the conduct of a meeting may be exercised by the person presiding at the meeting.'

Who presides?

Principal councils

7.27 The chairman of the council (or the mayor) if present at a meeting of the full assembly of a principal council must preside. If, for any reason, he vacates the chair, he must leave the meeting (as to whether he need leave the council chamber altogether: see 4.37) so as not to contravene this specific statutory direction that he must preside if present. In *Re Wolverhampton Borough Council's Aldermanic Election* (1961), which concerned an election of aldermen for which the mayor was a candidate, the mayor vacated the chair just before the council proceeded to the election of aldermen but he delivered a voting paper and remained in the council chamber. Glyn-Jones J said:

> 'In my opinion it was Parliament's intention that at a meeting of the council the mayor's place, and his only place, should be in the chair. Seated in the mayoral chair he can exercise all his one and indivisible functions . . . When he is not in the mayoral chair . . . then, since his functions are one and indivisible, he has lost his right to exercise any of them so far as taking part in the meeting is concerned.'

7.28 If the chairman is absent from the meeting then:[12]

- except in Greater London, the vice-chairman of the council if present must preside; or
- in the case of a London borough council, the deputy mayor, if at that time he remains a councillor and is chosen for that purpose, must preside, unless the authority is operating executive arrangements that involve a mayor and cabinet executive or a mayor and council manager executive;

if:

- in the case of a principal council outside Greater London both the chairman and vice-chairman of the council are absent from a meeting of the council, another member of the council chosen by the members of the council present must preside. However, a member of the executive of a principal council may not be chosen; or
- in the case of a London borough council the mayor and deputy mayor are so absent or the deputy mayor being present is not chosen another member of the council chosen by the members of the council present must preside unless the authority is operating executive arrangements that involve a mayor and cabinet executive or a mayor and council manager executive.

Parish and community councils

7.29 The chairman of the council must preside at a meeting of a parish council or a community council as the case may be if present at the meeting.[13] If the chairman is absent from the meeting, the vice-chairman, if present, must preside.[14] If both the chairman and the vice-chairman are absent from the meeting, then such councillor as the members of the council present shall choose must preside.[15]

Parish and community meetings

7.30 In a parish having a separate parish council, the chairman of the parish council, if present, must preside at a parish meeting; and if he is absent the vice-chairman, if any, must, if present, preside. In a parish that does not have a separate parish council, the chairman chosen for the year in question must, if present, preside. If the chairman and the vice-chairman of the parish council or the chairman of the parish meeting, as the case may be, is absent from an assembly of the parish meeting, the parish meeting may appoint a person to take the chair and that person has, for the purposes of that meeting, the powers and authority of the chairman. In a community for which there is a community council, the chairman of the council, if present, must preside at the community meeting (LGA 1972, Sch.12).

In any other case a community meeting must appoint a person to be chairman at that meeting (LGA 1972, Sch.12, para.33(1)).

7. Conduct

Powers and duties of person presiding

Generally

7.31 Upon taking the chair at a meeting the chairman (or whoever may be presiding) becomes invested with authority to regulate and control proceedings for the purposes of the meeting. The powers and duties of the chairman are not prescribed by statute (except in certain limited respects: he has conferred upon him, for example, the power to give a second or casting vote in the case of an equality of votes (see 7.120)), but derive from standing orders and common law. He collects his authority from the meeting.

7.32 So long as the chairman acts bona fide and remains in the chair he has a virtually absolute rule. Admittedly the full council could by majority decision dislodge the person presiding (see *Booth* v. *Arnold* (1895)), but not if he is the chairman of the council or the vice-chairman of the council, because the duly elected chairman of a principal or parish or community council remains in office until he resigns of his own accord, or becomes disqualified, and if present at a council meeting must preside, as must a vice-chairman if present in the absence of the chairman. While acting in good faith the chairman's decisions, even if not strictly correct, will be upheld by the court, provided no substantial injustice has arisen as a result. It strengthens a chairman's position if a local authority adopts a standing order on the lines of old model standing order no.42, which is to this effect:

> 'The ruling of the mayor/chairman as to the construction or application of any of these standing orders, or as to any proceedings of the council, shall not be challenged at any meeting of the council.'

If, however, the chairman acts improperly or mala fide his decisions are not binding, and in a proper case the court will intervene. The proper course for anyone who considers that a ruling of a chairman is erroneous is to seek an order of the court compelling the chairman to convene a fresh meeting: the court will not ordinarily interfere unless the complaint of irregularity comes from a representative majority of the meeting, but if a specific individual right is infringed action could be taken by the party aggrieved.

Specific functions

7.33 From judicial decisions there has emerged a widely recognised catalogue of powers and duties of a chairman. Thus it is the duty of the chairman and his function (see *National Dwellings Society* v. *Sykes* (1894)): to preserve order, and to take care that the proceedings are conducted in a proper manner, and that the sense of the meeting is properly ascertained with regard to any question which is properly before the meeting.

More specifically it is the chairman's responsibility:

- to determine that the meeting is properly constituted and that a quorum is present;
- to inform himself as to the business and objects of the meeting;
- to preserve order in the conduct of those present;
- to confine discussion within the scope of the meeting and reasonable limits to time;
- to decide whether proposed motions and amendments are in order;
- to formulate for discussion and decision questions that have been moved for the consideration of the meeting;
- to decide points of order and other incidental questions that require a decision at the time (see *Re Indian Zoedone Co.* (1884));
- to ascertain the sense of the meeting by:
  - putting relevant questions to the meeting and taking a vote thereon (and if so minded giving a casting vote);
  - declaring the result; and
  - causing a ballot to be taken if duly demanded;
- to approve the draft of the minutes or other record of proceedings;
- to adjourn the meeting when circumstances justify or require that course;
- to declare the meeting closed when its business has been completed.

The chairman's responsibility under (j) to adjourn the meeting must not be taken to mean that the power of adjournment vests solely in the chairman. A chairman cannot adjourn a meeting without the consent, express or implied, of those present. There could be implied consent in exceptional circumstances when, for example, a member may have collapsed and died in the course of proceedings. The right of adjournment is vested in the assembly but in practice, of course, only the person presiding can declare the assembly's decision to adjourn. As to the effect of an improper adjournment by a chairman (see 7.83).

Allocation of time

7.34 Although it is in general the responsibility of the person presiding to ensure the orderly and efficient despatch of business and so to conduct proceedings that a requisite amount of time is allotted to the several items of business, those present can properly seek to influence the progress of business. The standing orders working party (see 2.4) proposed a core standing order in these terms:

'00–1 A member of the council may move, without comment, that the time of any meeting of the council shall be allocated between the items of business to be considered.

2 If an item of business is to be considered as opposition priority business, such a motion shall not be accepted until such an item of business has been concluded.

3 The person presiding may refuse to accept the motion if he/she is of the opinion that the business before the meeting is being conducted with sufficient speed or if such a motion has been rejected earlier in the same meeting.

4 If the motion is accepted, it shall be seconded and put to the vote without amendment.

7. Conduct

5 When the council resolve, on a motion under this standing order, that the time of the meeting shall be allocated among the items of business to be considered,

   a) no points of order may be raised except by the person presiding;

   b) no closure motion under standing order OO (13) shall be moved;

   c) the questions necessary to dispose of the item under consideration when the resolution is adopted shall be put without further discussion (except as specified below) not later than [fifteen] minutes (or such other period as shall be specified in the motion) after the resolution is adopted;

   d) the questions necessary to dispose of each following item of business shall be put without further discussion not later than [fifteen] minutes (or such longer period as is specified in the motion) after consideration of the item is started, provided that the mover of any motion put at the expiry of any such period shall be permitted to reply for not more than [three] minutes before the motion is put to the vote.'

Quorum

General considerations

7.35 A quorum is the minimum number of members whose presence is necessary at a meeting for the valid transaction of business. In the absence of special custom or particular regulation, by statute or otherwise, a majority of the members of a body must be present at a duly convened assembly in order that an effective meeting should exist (*Mayor, Constables and Company of Merchants of the Staple of England* v. *Governor and Company of the Bank of England* (1887). In the case of local authorities, a quorum is prescribed by statute for meetings of a principal, parish and community council but not for meetings of committees and subcommittees (LGA 1972, Sch.12, paras.6, 12, 18). (See 11.16.)

7.36 If a quorum is not present at a council meeting any business transacted is, generally speaking, invalid. The mere fortuitous assembly of the requisite minimum number of councillors can never constitute a meeting for the purpose of transacting valid business because there must be an intention to meet known to all members entitled to attend, i.e. there are, as already indicated, statutory formalities in regard to notice and summons which must be observed before a meeting may properly be held (see 1.33).

Statutory regulation

7.37 Subject to what is said below in 7.39, no business may be transacted at a meeting of:

- a principal council unless at least one-quarter of the whole number of members of the council are present (LGA 1972, Sch.12, para.6); or
- a parish or community council unless at least one-third of the whole number of members of the council are present but in no case is the quorum to be less than three (LGA 1972, Sch.12, paras.12, 28).

Council meetings

Calculation of quorum

7.38 The quorum is ordinarily calculated in relation to 'the whole number of members of the council'; and this means the total number of seats: *Newhaven Local Board* v. *Newhaven School Board* (1885). If, however, more than one-third of the members of the authority become disqualified at the same time, then – until the number of members in office is increased to not less than two-thirds of the whole number of members of the authority, i.e. seats – the quorum must be determined by reference to the number of members remaining qualified instead of by reference to the whole number of members. This provision is intended to meet the situation where a considerable number of members, i.e. more than one-third, are disqualified. If seats are vacant for other reasons, e.g. by reason of death or resignation, then these can be taken into account in calculating the total number of members. Members who have died or resigned clearly must not be counted with members who are disqualified.

Duration of quorum

7.39 Is it necessary, once a meeting has commenced with the requisite quorum present for that quorum to be present throughout the meeting or at least present at the time a vote is taken? This can indeed pose a difficulty with the increasing length of meetings and the trend towards informality. The legal position appears to vary between company meetings, parliamentary business and council meetings. There seems to be a widespread perception that the local government position is similar to the parliamentary one, i.e. that proceedings should continue until attention is drawn to the absence of a quorum. While this may be a reasonable and practical course to adopt, particularly during lengthy debates, the legal position is clear and somewhat different: any business transacted at a council meeting in the absence of a quorum is invalid. So care should be taken to ensure that the requisite number of members is present whenever a decision is taken.

7.40 A draft core standing order put forward by the working party (see 2.4) is set out below:

'0–1 If, during any meeting of the council, the person presiding, after causing the number of members present to be counted, declares that there is not a quorum present, the meeting shall stand adjourned for fifteen minutes.

2 If, after fifteen minutes, the person presiding, after again causing the number of members present to be counted, declares that there is still no quorum present, the meeting shall end.

3 Notwithstanding any provision in these standing orders that notices of questions or motions shall lapse, the consideration of all business which is on the agenda of a meeting brought to an end under the previous paragraph and which has not been completed before the meeting is brought to an end shall be postponed to the next meeting of the council, whether ordinary or extraordinary.'

Some authorities provide, somewhat similarly, in a standing order to this effect, for a short interval to elapse between the formal recognition that a quorum is not present and the decision to end the meeting:

'If the chairman finds that a quorum is wanting, the bell shall be rung for three minutes. If a quorum is then wanting, the meeting shall end and the remaining business carried forward.'

Question time

Types of question

7.41 Many local authorities devote an allotted time to questions at every council meeting. Widdicombe attached importance to question time 'as a means by which minority parties and "backbench" councillors may not only obtain information but also call the majority party to account'. There are, therefore, in effect two types of question: the spontaneous question, which may be asked at any time without notice; and the deliberate question, which, because of its character and the need usually for some research or verification of facts before an answer can be prepared, requires advance written notice. Questions are not, as a rule, set out in the agenda, though many authorities record both questions and answers in council minutes.

Spontaneous questions

7.42 Old model standing order no. 8 provides, in part, that:

'A member of the council may ask the chairman of a committee any question upon an item of the report of a committee when that item is under consideration by the council.'

In some authorities, portfolio holders now also make a report to the full council and this standing order should be amended accordingly. Whether or not the committee chairman/portfolio holder answers will depend upon the question. If necessary, the chairman can always ask the member concerned to give notice or offer to provide the answer later.

Deliberate questions

7.43 The standing orders working party suggested a core standing order regulating questions at council meetings in these terms:

'00–1 Subject to paragraph (2) if a member of the council wishes to ask a question at a meeting of the council of:
a) the chairman of the council;
b) the leader of the council (if any);
c) the person appointed or chosen to preside in any committee;

141

    d) a member of the council appointed by the authority to any joint authority or joint board of which the authority is a constituent authority; or

    e) a member of the council who is, as a result of action taken by or on behalf of the authority, a member or director of any company,

s/he shall give notice in writing to the proper officer of the question at least [seven] days before the meeting at which the question is to be asked.

2 No member shall give notice of more than one question for any meeting.

3 A list of the questions of which notice has been given shall be circulated to members of the council at, or before, the meeting at which they are to be asked.

4 If the person presiding at a meeting of the council considers that, by reason of special circumstances, it is desirable that a question shall be asked at a meeting of the council although due notice of the question has not been given, and if he/she is satisfied that as much notice as is possible has been given to the person of whom it is to be asked, he/she may permit the question to be asked.

5 Every question shall be put and answered without discussion, but the person to whom the question has been put may decline to answer it. If the person presiding permits, the member asking a question may ask one relevant supplementary question which shall be put and answered without discussion.

6 An answer to a question may be given by the person to whom it is addressed or by a person on his/her behalf, and may take the form of:

    a) an oral answer;

    b) a reference to information contained in some publication;

    c) a written answer, which shall be circulated to members of the council at the latest with the summons for the next meeting of the council.

7 No question shall be asked more than [twenty] minutes after the council has entered on the item of business under which questions are to be asked.

8 If notice of a question has been given, and that question is not for any reason asked orally, and unless the member who gave notice of it withdraws the question or the member to whom it is addressed refuses to answer, the question shall be given a written answer in the same way as under paragraph 6(c).

9 If a member wishes to ask a question of an officer or other person who is, as a result of action taken by or on behalf of the authority a member or director of a company, he/she shall give notice of the question in the same way as for a question to a person mentioned in paragraph 1. Unless the member giving notice withdraws it or the person to whom it is addressed refuses to answer, the question shall be given a written answer in the same way as under paragraph 6(c).

10 Every question shall be relevant to some matter in relation to which the authority have functions, or which affects the area of the authority, or part of it, or the inhabitants of that area, or some of them.'

7.44 There are many ways in which question time can be regulated. If the authority sets a time limit for question time then it might permit members to ballot for a specified number to be answered orally and the remainder dealt with by written answer, much in the manner of parliamentary procedure. It is also a matter for consideration whether a councillor's question should be answered if he is absent when the question is called or, alternatively, provision made by standing orders that:

'If a member who has submitted a question is not present when the question is called, the question may, with the consent of the council, be asked by any other member.'

Widdicombe proposed that it should be obligatory on all local authorities to provide for question time at council meetings. 'The precise form of the requirement', it said, 'would need further consideration but it should be limited to questions from councillors as opposed to questions from the public gallery', and the arrangement should provide for:

- a reasonable time limit (at least 30 minutes);
- questions to be handed to the chief executive and addressed to the leader or the chairman of the responsible committee;
- a reply to be given unless there is good reason to the contrary (e.g. confidentiality); and
- a right to at least one supplementary question, with the questioner having priority.

This substantially reflects common practice, but with the complexity and range of council activities question time can sometimes still take up a disproportionate share of time at council meetings. This can be mitigated by arranging for questions and answers to be circulated prior to or at the beginning of the meeting. Setting up a procedure for question time at committees/cabinet also helps relieve pressure on time at meetings of the full council.

Petitions and deputations

Petitions

7.45 Petitions submitted to a local authority by a body of its citizens are usually presented to the full council by one of the council members. This procedure is followed so that the council as a whole may have knowledge of the petition and the petitioners assured that it has been received by the council. Practice varies but as a rule no speech or debate is permitted on the petition that, either on the motion of the member presenting it or of the chairman or automatically under standing orders, is referred to the appropriate committee or cabinet for consideration.

Deputations

7.46 A local authority may also receive a deputation at a council meeting when the issue is thought sufficiently important to justify that course rather than refer the deputation to an appropriate committee or the cabinet. The standing orders working party (see 2.4) drafted this core standing order covering both petitions and deputations:

Council meetings

'00–1 At a meeting of the council any member of the council may present a petition, signed by persons other than members of the council, which is relevant to some matter in relation to which the authority have functions, or which affects the area of the authority, or part of it, or the inhabitants of that area, or some of them. The member presenting the petition shall satisfy himself/herself that the petition is proper to be received.

2 A member wishing to present a petition shall give notice of his/her intention to do so to the [proper officer] before the beginning of the meeting at which he/she wishes to present it.

3 The presentation of a petition shall be limited to not more than [three] minutes, and shall be confined to reading out, or summarising, the prayer of the petition, indicating the number and description of the signatories, and making such further supporting remarks relevant to the petition as the person presenting it shall think fit.

4 Petitions shall be presented in the order in which notice of them is received by the proper officer.

Variations:

1 The power to present a petition may be extended to any member of the public. The power can be extended either to local government electors for the area of the authority, or to local government electors, community charge-payers or rate-payers for the area of the authority, or to any person likely to be affected by the matter in question. The choice of how wide a definition of the public should be selected will depend on local circumstances. If this widening is wanted, paragraphs 1 and 2 should read as follows, with the appropriate adjustment of the phrase in square brackets according to the view taken on the proper definition of "the public":

- 1 At a meeting of the council any member of the council or [a local government elector for the area of the authority] may present a petition which is relevant to some matter in relation to which the authority have functions, or which affects the area of the authority, or part of it, or the inhabitants of that area, or some of them.

- 2 At least [seven] days before the meeting at which the petition is to be presented, the person wishing to present it shall give notice of his/her intention to do so to the proper officer and shall show the petition to him/her. Where the person pro posing to present the petition is not a member of the council, the notice of intention to present a petition shall not be accepted unless the proper officer has satisfied himself/herself that the petition is proper to be presented.

2 Arrangements may also be made to give members of the public the right to attend as a deputation to put their views to the council. Again different views are possible on how wide a definition of 'the public' is appropriate. If this variation is adopted, the following provisions should be added, replacing also paragraph (4) of the foregoing text:

3 Any person likely to be affected by a matter in relation to which the authority have functions, or which affects the area of the authority, or some of it, or the

144

inhabitants of that area, or some of them, may ask that a deputation should be received by a meeting of the council. Such a request shall be made to the proper officer at least [seven] days before the meeting to which it relates. The person making the request shall indicate the matter to which the request relates, the number (which shall not be more than [five]), names and addresses of the persons who will form the deputation, and the member or members of the deputation who will speak for them.]

4 On being called by the person presiding, the person or persons speaking for the deputation may make, during a period not exceeding [five] minutes, such remarks as he/she or they think fit, provided that the remarks shall relate to the matter indicated when the request was made, and that the remarks do not constitute a personal attack upon any person. The person or persons speaking for the deputation shall be heard in silence.

5 The members of the council may, during a further period not exceeding [five] minutes for each deputation, ask questions of the members of the deputation. Such questions shall be asked and answered without discussion.

6 Petitions shall be presented, and deputations received in the order in which notice of them is received by the proper officer, without making any distinction between petitions and deputations.'

Standing orders often also contain a provision for committees/cabinet to report back on petitions after a prescribed period of time, usually of six months.

Public participation

7.47 One of the old draft model standing orders prepared by the Association of Council Secretaries and Solicitors (see 2.3) was to this effect:

'The chairman [of the council] will indicate the time at which questions may be put to him by individual members of the public. If the chairman rules a question to be proper (particularly in that it refers to a matter of general concern and not the affairs of an individual named or not), the chairman may ask a member or an officer to respond. The time allowed for questions and answers shall not, without the consent of the council, exceed fifteen minutes, or in the case of one questioner, five minutes. Written questions may be entertained and written response may be used. Questions and responses shall not be matters for debate.'

Motions

Discussion out of order otherwise

7.48 Discussion and debate at a council meeting will ordinarily only be permitted on a motion properly before the full council: that is to say, any matter before the meeting for consideration must be expressed as a motion in positive terms to adopt a certain course of action or to do some act or declare a particular attitude. When passed by a majority of the members present and voting, with or without amendment, the motion becomes a resolution.

Types of motion

7.49 Motions are broadly of two types: original and procedural. The first, defined more explicitly below in the local government context, is one propounding a substantial issue for consideration and action; a procedural motion (see 7.72), sometimes called a formal motion, and which includes a dilatory motion, is one affecting matters of procedure or form. An amendment is a motion to amend the main proposition before the meeting.

Original motions

7.50 An original motion may not be moved at a council meeting unless prior notice thereof has been given so that its terms may be included in the agenda. This is necessary so as to comply with the statutory requirement that the summons to attend (and, sometimes, the notice of) the meeting must specify the business to be transacted (see 6.1). The procedure for the giving of notice and the consequential steps are usually prescribed in standing orders. Only one original motion can be before the council at any one time.

7.51 The draft core standing order prepared by the working party (2.4) on notices of motion is set out below:

'00–1 Any member of the council may give notice of not more than one motion for consideration at any meeting of the council, and may in addition give notice of a motion under paragraph (11).

2 The leader of the council (if any) may give notice of more than one motion for consideration at any meeting of the council.

3 Notice of every motion to be moved at a meeting of the council other than a motion which, under standing order 00, may be moved without notice shall be given in writing, signed by the member or the members of the council giving the notice. The notice shall state for which meeting of the council the notice is given.

4 Unless the person presiding at the meeting is of the opinion that a motion should be considered as a matter of urgency, notice of every motion of which notice is required shall be delivered to the proper officer at least [one] day before the day on which the summons must be sent to members of the council for the meeting for which the notice is given.

5 The proper officer shall not accept any notice of motion which, by reason of any enactment or any provision in these standing orders (other than paragraph (9) below), could not be considered at the meeting for which it is given.

6 The proper officer shall record the time and date at which every such notice is delivered to him. That record shall be open to the inspection of every member of the council.

7 Every motion shall be relevant to some matter in relation to which the authority

have functions, or which affects the area of the authority, or part of it, or the inhabitants of that area, or some of them.

8 A motion shall only be moved by a member by whom notice has been given, or by a member authorised by such a member.

9 Subject to paragraph (11) below, where a notice of motion has been given for any meeting, and that motion is within the terms of reference of any committee of the authority, the motion shall be deemed to have been referred by that meeting to the next meeting of the committee or committees within whose terms of reference it falls. A memorandum appended to the minutes of that meeting shall record the references that are deemed to have been so made. If any question arises as to which committee the motion is to be referred, it shall be determined by the chairman of the council.

10 Where a motion has been referred, or is deemed to have been referred, to a meeting of a committee, that committee shall consider it at their next meeting and shall either report upon the motion to the next meeting of the council, or include their views upon the motion in their next report to the council.

11 Notwithstanding paragraph (9), but subject to the provisions of the Education Act 1944 and the Local Authority Social Services Act 1970, a motion may be considered without first being referred to a committee if the council so resolve on a motion, of which notice under paragraph (1) above is required, but which shall be moved, seconded, and put without comment.

12 Where notice of a motion has been given for any meeting, and that motion is neither moved (for whatever reason) nor deemed to have been referred to a committee, the notice shall lapse, and the motion shall not be moved without further notice.'

7.52 There are in practice countless variations of the foregoing in use but the general effect is much the same in every case. What is important is that the arrangements for giving notice to the proper officer are clearly set out and well understood by members. Standing orders usually require notices to be in the hands of the proper officer at least seven working days before the date of the meeting. Arguments about when and where a notice was sent by post can be embarrassing: if possible a standing order requiring personal delivery is to be preferred.

Motions that stand referred

7.53 Where, under old model standing order no.6(4), a motion stands referred without discussion to a committee when proposed and seconded, the proposer has no right to a speech, introductory or otherwise. It is submitted that the proposer could, under standing orders, with the consent of the council and without seeking to explain the reason, alter the wording of the motion. The term without discussion means precisely that. No one may speak and there can be no discussion unless the chairman allows the motion to be dealt with at the meeting at which it is brought forward, i.e. it does not stand referred. Nor, if it stands referred, is any amendment permissible. This is because the council, in referring the motion to a committee for consideration and report, is neither accepting nor rejecting it. If a councillor wishes to make a point essential to the motion he can do so in one or both of two ways: he can ask to be allowed to attend and speak at the committee meeting at which the motion is to be considered (indeed he may be so entitled under standing orders); and he will in any case ultimately have an opportunity of participating in the debate when the committee's report comes before the full council.

Rejected notices of motion

7.54 The proper officer must consider whether the motion of which notice has been given is one that may properly be accepted. If it is and notice has been given in time, then he must proceed to place it on the agenda for the next council meeting. If he considers the terms of the motion out of order, illegal, irregular or improper, he should consult the chairman and/or the leader or take such other action as may be laid down in standing orders. In any case, if a motion is rejected the member giving notice should be so advised. A standing order covering these matters might be framed in these words:

> If notice is given of any original motion that, in the opinion of the proper officer, is out of order, illegal, irregular or improper, the proper officer shall immediately submit such notice to the chairman and it shall not be accepted and placed on the agenda without his sanction. In the event of non-acceptance, the proper officer shall so inform the member giving notice.

7.55 A motion that seeks to require the local authority to do something that it patently cannot do would be out of order and one that sought action that was ultra vires or otherwise illegal would similarly be out of order. One that was defamatory or offensive could be ruled out as improper. But a motion ought not to be rejected merely because it refers to matters that are not within the scope of the authority's powers and duties. What may be relevant for the council's consideration is a difficult question to determine. A motion protesting against the raising of railway fares, for example, may be considered relevant, in that it may affect the council's housing tenants or employees and have an impact on staff recruitment or the letting of houses. There are some topics of general interest to the local citizens on behalf of whom the council may deem itself the proper representative body to express opinion; but there are limits to this. Expressions of opinion on foreign affairs, for example, are not the concern of local government and are not appropriate for debate by a local council.

7.56 A motion that is rejected must nevertheless be recorded in the book kept for that purpose and a note made to the effect that it was rejected.

7.57 A motion may also be rejected on the grounds that it is vague and equivocal in its terms: and in such circumstances it may properly be returned to the member with an indication to that effect and need not, it is submitted, be recorded in any way until it has been resubmitted in acceptable form. Whether a motion that is ungrammatical or otherwise imperfectly expressed but whose purport is clear should be corrected by officers is a matter of judgment: if the grammatical error is a simple one it might be corrected but if the changes that ought to be made are extensive it would be wise for the officers tactfully to seek the member's prior approval before making corrections. In any event it is advisable for there to be an 'early warning system' in existence so that the form of a notice of motion can be considered by officers before being placed on the council agenda.

Debate on a motion

7.58 The meeting is not bound to pursue consideration of a motion in the form in which it is originally proposed or to come to any decision upon it at all. Original motions may be passed with or without amendment or may be thrown out, and the debate may at any time be interrupted either by the moving of a procedural (or dilatory) motion (see 7.72) or by a member raising a point of order (see 7.84).

Need a motion be seconded?

7.59 Notwithstanding that notice of motion has been duly given the motion must still be moved at the meeting. At common law it is not necessary that a motion should be seconded: in *Re Horbury Bridge Coal, Iron and Wagon Co.* (1879), James LJ said:

> 'There is no law of the land which says that a motion cannot be put without a seconder and the objection that the amendment was not seconded cannot prevail.'

In practice most local authorities require by standing orders that every motion – whether one of which notice has been given or otherwise – shall be seconded as a prerequisite to its being open to discussion. Where standing orders require a seconder and a motion is moved but not seconded, it drops as a matter of course and the next business can be proceeded with.

7.60 Old model standing order no.10 (which deals fairly comprehensively with the rules of debate at council meetings) includes the following provision:

> '1) A motion or amendment shall not be discussed unless it has been proposed and seconded, and unless notice has already been given in accordance with standing order 6 it shall, if required by the mayor/chairman, be put into writing and handed to the mayor/chairman before it is further discussed or put to the meeting.
> 2) A member when seconding a motion or amendment may, if he then declare his intention to do so, reserve his speech until a later period of the debate.'

Alteration of motion

7.61 In the course of discussion on a motion – or even before discussion commences – the proposer may wish to make an alteration that he thinks might make the motion more acceptable to members. Old model standing order no.10 provides that:

> '9 A member may with the consent of the council signified without discussion:
>
> a) alter a motion of which he has given notice; or
>
> b) with the further consent of his seconder alter a motion which he has moved if (in either case) the alteration is one which could be made as an amendment thereto.'

Withdrawal of motion

7.62 Old model standing order no. 10, giving effect to the common law rule, provides for the withdrawal of a motion in these terms:

> '10 A motion or amendment may be withdrawn by the mover with the consent of his seconder and of the council, which shall be signified without discussion, and no member may speak upon it after the mover has asked permission for its withdrawal, unless such permission shall have been refused.'

Problems can arise where a member who has given notice of motion decides at the meeting not to move it or to withdraw it, possibly because, suspecting that it will not secure the council's backing, he may not wish to see it defeated for political reasons. Should the chairman assume that the member's silence is tantamount to withdrawal of the motion? But what if the council refuses to give consent to its withdrawal? The better course probably is for the chairman to rule that the motion falls for not having been moved.

Amendments

Definition

7.63 An amendment is a formal proposal to vary the terms of a motion before the latter is adopted by the meeting. The motion in its original form, before amendment, is called 'the original motion'. The original motion, altered by the incorporation of any amendments passed, is known as the main motion or substantive motion; and this substantive motion may be further amended. If amendments fail the motion should still be referred to as the original motion: it becomes a substantive motion only if amendments have succeeded.

Motions and amendments that may be moved without notice

7.64 Some motions and amendments may be moved without notice. A relevant standing order in this respect is the following, one of the core standing orders drafted by the standing orders working party (see 2.4):

7. Conduct

00–1 The following motions may be moved without notice at any meeting at which they would be in order:

a) to elect a chairman of the council, to appoint a vice-chairman of the council, or to appoint a person to preside at the meeting at which the motion is made;

b) motions relating to the accuracy of the minutes;

c) motions under standing order 0 -(change in order of business);

d) motions extending the time limit for speeches;

e) "that the council (or committee or subcommittee) proceed to the next business";

f) "that the question be now put";

g) "that the debate be now adjourned";

h) "that the council (or committee or subcommittee) do now adjourn";

i) motions under standing order 00 (allocation of time) and standing order 00 (termination of meetings);

j) motions under standing order 0(b) (suspension of standing orders without notice);

k) motions in accordance with section 100A(2) or (4) of the 1972 Act to exclude the public from a meeting where there is likely otherwise to be disclosure of exempt or confidential information;

l) motions giving consent of the council, committee or subcommittee where it is required under these standing orders;

m) motions to refer a petition which has been presented to the council to a committee for consideration;

n) where a matter has been remitted to a committee or subcommittee, a motion to appoint a special committee or subcommittee to consider the matter.

Variations:

1 If the variant in standing order 00 is adopted, requiring a motion before disciplinary measures are taken against a member, add a new subparagraph:

o) "motions under standing order 00 (prevention of disorderly conduct) that a named member be not further heard, or do leave the meeting";

2 If the variant in standing order 00 is adopted, allowing a member with the council's consent to remain at a meeting, notwithstanding a pecuniary interest add a new subparagraph:

p) "motions inviting a member to remain under standing order 00 (pecuniary interests)".

2) On consideration of a report or a recommendation from a committee, sub-committee or officer, the adoption of the report or recommendation and any resolutions consequential upon that adoption may be moved without notice.

3) An amendment to a motion may be moved without notice, but shall be relevant to the motion. No amendment shall be moved to an amendment.

4) An amendment shall be either to refer the matter to a committee, a subcommittee or an officer for consideration (or reconsideration), to leave out words, or to insert or to add other words, but such omission, insertion or addition or words shall not have the effect of simply negativing the motion before the meeting.

5) With the consent of the meeting, signified without discussion, a member may

a) alter a motion of which he/she has given notice, or

b) with the further consent of the seconder, alter a motion which has been moved and seconded, if (in either case) the alteration is one which could be made as an amendment thereto.

6 With the consent of the seconder (if he/she is still present) and of the meeting, signified without discussion, the mover of a motion or an amendment may withdraw it. No member shall speak to such a motion or amendment after the mover has asked consent for its withdrawal, unless such consent has been refused.

7 At a meeting of the council, no motion or amendment shall be moved to rescind any resolution of the council which was passed within the preceding six months or which is to the same effect as one which has been rejected within that period: provided that such a motion may be moved if:

a) it is recommended by a committee or subcommittee; or

b) notice of such motion has been given by as many members as would constitute a quorum of the council.

8 Where the consent of the council, committee or subcommittee is required for any thing, that consent may be given either:

a) by the person presiding asking the meeting whether there are objections to the consent being given, and if no objection is raised, giving that consent; or

b) if objection is raised, or if the person presiding so chooses, by a motion moved, seconded and put to the meeting.'

Although the above, similar to many standing orders widely adopted in practice, includes as an amendment in subpara.4 a proposal to refer the subject of discussion to a committee for consideration or reconsideration, to treat this as a separate category of amendment is contrary to the rules governing amendments. The same result could be achieved by deleting/adding words from/to the motion and it might be better to leave the definition of amendment to these two courses of action. If, part only of the motion is reconsidered then an amendment would be needed, followed by a vote on the substantive motion as amended.

7.65 An amendment must not negate the motion that it seeks to alter, because the same effect can be secured by voting against the motion. It must be pertinent and relevant to the original motion, or otherwise a question may be brought before the council of which the requisite notice has not been given (see 7.51). It must also be within the scope of the meeting, for the same reason.

7.66 There are circumstances during the discussion of contentious business when the chairman may have difficulty in interpreting the rules governing amendments. For example, an amendment may be moved that, otherwise consistent with the rules outlined above, virtually displaces the original motion. It is a matter of judgment for the chairman whether such an amendment is acceptable, although in practice he will probably ask for advice from officers.. The chairman would probably be wise to allow rather than disallow amendments if thereby the sense of the meeting can finally be determined on the issue before it. After all, the purpose of the rules of debate (and of standing orders) is to help members to do what they want to do so far as it is consistent with the law.

7. Conduct

Amendments must be put to meeting

7.67 The chairman must put an amendment that has been moved (and, if standing orders so require, seconded) unless:

- it is ultra vires, i.e. it is outside the scope of the meeting or beyond the council's powers;
- it is irrelevant, where it bears no relation to the original motion or subject matter;
- it is inconsistent, where it is incompatible with a decision previously taken at the same meeting;
- it is vexatious and intended only to impede the transaction of business; or
- in bona fide exercise of his discretion as chairman he has grounds for excluding it by standing orders or resolution of the meeting itself.

An improper refusal to put an amendment will vitiate the decision to which the proposed amendment relates: *Henderson* v. *Bank of Australasia* (1890).

Series of amendments

7.68 Each amendment must be voted separately. There can be no amendments of an amendment and if notice is given of several amendments these should be taken in due succession: the chairman should examine the amendments and determine the order in which they should be put to the meeting. No amendment can be considered that is inconsistent with an amendment already adopted or that reproduces an amendment previously rejected. There are circumstances when a motion cannot be amended, e.g. in the case of a special meeting of the council to pass a resolution in specific form to meeting statutory requirements.

Order of debate

General considerations

7.69 There are various procedural matters that are often referred to collectively as the 'order of debate'. Again, it is relevant to quote the following draft of a core standing order drawn up by the standing orders working party (see 2.4):

'00-1 The rules of debate in this standing order shall apply to all meetings of the council, of any committee and of any subcommittee.

Motions and amendments

2 A motion or amendment shall not be discussed unless it has been proposed and seconded: provided that, in a committee or subcommittee which consists of five or fewer members, an amendment shall not require to be seconded.

3 When seconding a motion or amendment, a member may reserve his speech until a later period of the debate by declaring his/her intention to do so.

4 When any motion of which notice has not been given, or any amendment has

been moved and seconded, the person presiding may require that it shall be put into writing and handed to him/her before it is further discussed.

5 Only one amendment may be moved and discussed at a time. No further amendment shall be moved until the amendment under discussion has been disposed of: provided that the person presiding may permit two or more amendments to be discussed (but not voted upon) together if he/she thinks that this will facilitate the proper conduct of business.

6 If an amendment is not carried, other amendments may be moved to the original motion. If an amendment is carried, the motion as amended shall take the place of the original motion and shall become the motion upon which any further amendment may be moved.

Speeches

7 If two or more members offer to speak, the person presiding shall call on one to speak.

8 When speaking, a member shall address the person presiding.

9 A member shall direct his/her speech to the question under discussion, or to a personal explanation or a point of order under the provisions of the next paragraph.

10 A member may claim to speak on a point of order or in personal explanation, and shall be entitled to be heard forthwith. A point of order shall relate only to an alleged breach of a specified statutory provision or a specified standing order, and the way in which the member raising it considers that it has been broken. A personal explanation shall be con- fined to some material part of a former speech by him/her in the current debate which may appear to have been misunderstood.

11 The ruling of the person presiding on a point of order or on the admissibility of a personal explanation shall not be open to discussion except on a motion of which due notice has been given.

Ancillary motions

12 When a motion is under debate, no other motion shall be moved except the following:
   a) to amend the motion;
   b) a closure motion under the next paragraph;
   c) a motion under standing order 00 (prevention of disorder);
   d) a motion under section 100A(2) or (4) of the 1972 Act (exclusion of the public).

13 The following closure motions shall be permitted during discussion of another motion ("the original motion"). They shall be moved, seconded and put without discussion. If the motion is moved and seconded, then the person presiding shall proceed as follows:
   a) "that the meeting proceed to the next business":
      The person presiding shall permit the mover of the original motion to reply, and shall then put to the vote the motion to proceed to the next business; if that motion is carried, the original motion shall lapse;
   b) "that the question be now put":

7. Conduct

If the person presiding is of the opinion that the matter before the meeting has been insufficiently discussed, he/she may refuse to accept the motion; if he/she accepts the motion, he/she shall put to the vote forthwith the motion that the question be now put; if this is carried, he/she shall permit the mover of the original motion (at meetings of the council) any right of reply to which he/she is entitled under standing order (OO)(5) and (at meetings of committees or subcommittees) a right to reply for not more than three minutes, and shall then put that motion to the vote:

c) "that the debate be now adjourned" and

d) "that the meeting do now adjourn":

If the person presiding is of the opinion that the matter before the meeting has been sufficiently discussed, he/she may refuse to accept either of these motions, and instead put the motion that the question be now put; if he/she is of the opinion that the matter has not been sufficiently discussed and cannot reasonably be sufficiently discussed on that occasion, he/she shall put the adjournment motion to the vote without giving the mover of the original motion a right of reply on that occasion; the original motion or remaining business shall then stand over as uncompleted business until the next meeting of the council, committee or subcommittee, as the case may be.'

7.70 A further draft core standing order put forward related to the rules of debate at council meetings to this effect:

'OO–1 When speaking, a member shall stand.

  2 While a member is speaking, the other members shall remain seated, unless rising to a point of order or in personal explanation.

  3 Whenever the person presiding rises during a debate, a member then standing shall resume his/her seat, and the council shall be silent.

  4 Except with the consent of the council, signified without comment, the mover of a motion shall not speak for more than [10] minutes and no other speaker shall speak for more than [5] minutes. For the purposes of this paragraph a person who moves an amendment is not moving a motion, and the length of time allotted to the mover of a motion does not include any time permitted under a right of reply.

  5 A member who has spoken on any motion shall not speak again while it is the subject of debate, except:

    a) to speak once on an amendment moved by another member;

    b) if the motion has been amended since he/she last spoke, to move a further amendment;

    c) if his/her first speech was on an amendment moved by another member, to speak on the main issue, whether or not the amendment to which he/she spoke was carried;

    d) in exercise of a right of reply under the next paragraph of this standing order or under standing order OO(13) [set out in 7.69];

    e) on a point of order or by way of personal explanation under standing order OO(a) [set out in 7.69].

  6 The mover of a motion has a right of reply at the close of the debate on the motion,

immediately before it is put to the vote. If an amendment is moved, the mover of the original motion shall have a right of reply at the close of the debate on the amendment but shall not otherwise speak on the amendment. The mover of an amendment shall have no right of reply to the debate on that amendment.'

As to content of speeches: see next paragraph; and as to points or order: see 7.84.

Content of speeches

7.71 The power vested in a chairman by common law to regulate the conduct of a meeting (see 7.33) and to preserve order (see 7.130) may be assumed to include power to direct a councillor to cease making unseemly remarks in the course of a speech. It could be helpful, however, if there is a standing order to such effect:

> The chairman shall check a member for irrelevance, tedious repetition, failure to address the chair, unbecoming language, or reflections of a personal character on another member. If the member disregards the chairman, the chairman may order him to end his speech and, if he considers it necessary, following a resolution of the council or on his own initiative, order his removal from the meeting.

When a standing order in these or like terms applies and a councillor makes a defamatory statement unchecked, the chairman would not appear to incur liability for allowing the defamatory statement because:

- until the statement is made the chairman could hardly be expected to anticipate it; and
- even if checked or unchecked further defamatory statements are made by a councillor, the act of defamation is a personal liability upon the defamer.

As to defamatory statements: see 4.66.

Procedural motions

7.72 Procedural or formal motions are designed to close the debate, either by forcing an immediate vote on the motion or amendment before the meeting or by postponing a decision on the motion or amendment: hence they are sometimes termed: closure, as in old model standing order no. 7 (see 7.62); dilatory, this being best used to describe a motion that obstructs or frustrates the transaction of business; or interruptive motions. They cannot be moved by anyone who has moved or seconded or spoken on the original motion being debated, and no person may intervene in discussion on a particular motion by moving more than one formal motion.
7.73 The procedural motions include:

(a) the motion to proceed to next business;
(b) the motion 'that the question be now put';
(c) the motion to adjourn the debate;
(d) the motion to adjourn the meeting;

referred to in old model standing order no.7 and a variety of suspensive motions, i.e. those that suspend debate, including the motion 'that the question lie on the table' but, most particularly within the local government context, the motion 'that the matter be referred back to committee'.

The previous question

7.74 The previous question may be moved – usually in the form 'That the council proceed to the next business' or 'That the motion be not now put'; or, simply, 'I move the previous question' – by any member who has not spoken on the original motion and provided no one else is speaking at the time. It derives its name from the fact that it proposes an independent issue that must be decided previously to the main issue. If properly seconded it may be discussed but cannot be amended; and if carried the original question is removed from the scope of the meeting and can only be revived by a motion at a subsequent meeting. However, if the motion is lost then the implication is that the meeting desires the substantive question to be put to the vote forthwith and thus further discussion cannot be permitted. The mover of the previous question has no right of comment on the reply of the mover of the original motion.

'That the question be now put'

7.75 This motion, which is a form of closure, must be voted upon without debate after it has been moved and seconded, unless the chairman refuses to accept it on the grounds that the matter before the meeting has been insufficiently discussed. If carried, the main question must be put immediately after the mover of the original motion has been given his right of reply. If the matter under discussion is an amendment the closure affects only that amendment.

7.76 There is nothing to prevent the chairman himself applying the closure, with the consent of the meeting, if he is of opinion that the views of the minority have been reasonably heard (*Wall* v. *Exchange & Northern Assets Corporation* (1981)). This he can do simply by calling on the mover of the motion to reply to the debate.

Adjournment of debate

7.77 This motion, which may seek to delay discussion on the question before the meeting either for a specified time or indefinitely, may be moved by any member other than the mover or seconder of the main question or the mover or seconder of any amendment or formal motion in reference to it. No amendment is possible except as regards the period of suspension or the time to which discussion is to be postponed or the place to which adjournment is proposed. If the motion is not explicit as to this, then, depending on standing orders, the discussion on the main question will be resumed at the next ordinary meeting of the council. Such a standing order may be to this effect:

> 'When a motion that the debate be now adjourned is carried the discussion shall be resumed at the next meeting of the council, when the member who moved its adjournment shall be entitled to speak first.'

If the motion is rejected, a second motion for adjournment may be moved during the same meeting after the lapse of a reasonable time or such period as may be prescribed in standing orders.

Adjournment of meeting

7.78 A motion to adjourn the meeting (a suspensive motion) is a more drastic proposition than any of the procedural motions so far considered, for it operates if carried to bring about a suspension of the entire proceedings either for a particular period or indefinitely. An adjournment may be:

- sine die, i.e. for an unspecified period of indefinite duration; or
- for an unspecified period not exceeding a given maximum; or
- until a date specified, or for a fixed interval of time; or
- to another place; or
- for a given time and to a named place.

There is no statutory power to adjourn a council meeting but at common law an assembly is deemed to be invested with the power to adjourn its proceedings of its own volition (*Stoughton* v. *Reynolds* (1737)).

7.79 It seems that, even where certain matters must be transacted on a particular day, a local authority has an implied power to adjourn so as to enable business that could not be finished for lack of time on the day fixed to be brought to its conclusion (*Rex* v. *Carmarthen Corpn.* (1813)); and this inherent power exists also where it is not possible to transact the whole of the business for which a meeting has been called (*Kerr* v. *Wilkie* (1860)).

7.80 The motion to adjourn may be proposed at the close of any speech but cannot be moved by a person who has already spoken on the question then before the meeting or who has moved or seconded an amendment or formal motion in relation to it. When moved and seconded the motion creates an independent question for the immediate consideration of the meeting, and discussion on the substantive question (and on the previous question if it has been moved) must give way to the motion to adjourn the meeting.

7.81 Discussion on the motion is governed by the ordinary rules of debate (except in so far as they may be altered by standing orders) but:

- the mover has no right of reply nor has the owner of the original motion;

- no amendment is permissible other than alteration of the time or place of adjournment (or both); and
- subject to standing orders the motion to adjourn may be renewed after the lapse of a reasonable time in the course of the same meeting.

Standing orders sometimes limit the effect of the motion, for example: when a motion 'that the council do now adjourn' is carried, the council, before adjourning, may take the remaining business on the agenda that is unopposed, and the question under debate, if any, shall stand adjourned to the next meeting.

In cases where such a standing order applies, the chairman after the motion has been carried should seek the view of the meeting as to the unopposed business.

Adjournment by chairman

7.82 The power of adjournment vests in the full assembly: it arises from 'the common right, which is in the whole assembly, where all are upon an equal foot' (*Stoughton v. Reynolds* (1736)). This means that only in exceptional circumstances, e.g. in the case of persistent disorder, can the chairman order an adjournment (see 7.131).

7.83 If a chairman illegally declares a meeting to be adjourned, e.g. in circumstances where it is patently not the wish of the majority of those present, then after the chairman has left the members may elect someone to preside over the transaction of the remainder of the business, and their act and the business transacted are valid (*R. v. Doris* (1908)). In *National Dwellings Society* v. *Sykes*, above, Chitty J said:

> '. . . in my opinion, the power which has been contended for is not within the scope of the authority of the chairman: namely, to stop the meeting at his own will and pleasure. The meeting is called for the particular purposes . . . According to the constitution . . . a certain officer has to preside. He presides with reference to the business which is then to be transacted. In my opinion, he cannot say, after that business has been opened, "I will have no more to do with it; I will not let this meeting proceed; I will stop it; I declare the meeting dissolved and I leave the chair." In my opinion, that is not within his power. The meeting by itself can resolve to go on with the business which the other chairman forgetful of his duty or violating his duty, has tried to stop because the proceedings have taken a turn which he himself does not like.'

What if the chairman of the council, who must preside if present at the council meeting (see 7.27), having improperly declared the meeting adjourned, remains in the council chamber? If he does remain he cannot be deemed to be 'in the meeting' and the council could elect someone else to preside (see 7.22).

Points of order

7.84 A point of order is an objection submitted to the chairman for decision claiming some irregularity in the constitution or conduct of the meeting. The more usual irregularities include:

- the use of irrelevant or improper language;
- that a quorum is not present;
- that an amendment is a simple negative of the motion before the meeting;
- that the motion is ultra vires or not within the scope of the notice given;
- that no question is before the meeting, e.g. where a motion has not been seconded (if this is required by standing orders);
- any non-compliance with standing orders.

7.85 A member may raise a point of order at any time without notice. It must, however, be raised immediately the alleged irregularity or impropriety becomes apparent. The member who is speaking must stop, sit down and allow the chairman to make a decision; and the chairman's decision is conclusive and final. Ordinarily no debate is permitted on a point of order; but some authorities do allow a short discussion of the point raised, but this does encourage others to express views as to whether the point of order should or should not be upheld and that is a decision better left for the chairman.

7.86 A point of order relates to procedure. It is not concerned with the arguments or the principles or the political views put forward in debate or with the truth or falsehood, correctness or incorrectness of statements made in the course of debate. A difference of opinion is not a point of order. Nor may a member making a point of order abuse it by making a speech.

7.87 When a point of order is raised, it is a common occurrence for the member raising it not to specify the standing order or rule of debate alleged to have been infringed. The chairman should be rigorous in asking for this information since a 'point of order' is often used to clothe a simple disagreement and give the member a second opportunity to speak when not entitled to do so. Thus a useful standing order is as follows:

> 'On any member indicating a desire to raise a point of order s/he shall state at the outset the standing order or rule of debate considered to have been infringed. Every point of order shall be decided by the chairman before the debate proceeds and his/her decision shall be final and cannot be discussed.'

Personal explanation

7.88 A member may find that he has made a misstatement that is being quoted by a later speaker or that the latter has misunderstood or misquoted him. In such circumstances the member is allowed to rise on a point of explanation and to interrupt the speaker for a few moments while he (the member) makes the desired correction. This prevents the speaker developing his argument on wrong facts or

7. Conduct

figures or a misunderstanding and so wasting the time of the meeting. The concession is one that should be carefully controlled by the chairman to avoid misuse similar to that which afflicts points of order.

Consideration of committee reports

General approach

7.89 The consideration of committee/cabinet reports is ordinarily the main item of business of the full council. These reports – whose style will depend upon local practice –

- record matters dealt with by committees under delegated powers and submitted to the council for information; and
- submit recommendations for the council's approval with or without amendment or rejection or reference back.

It is the practice of some local authorities to require the submission of the full minutes of committees, or an edited version or a selection of those minutes containing recommendations for the council's consideration. This gives rise to procedural problems because the minutes of committee proceedings are a record of business already transacted and thus cannot be altered in the full assembly. For this, and other persuasive reasons discussed later (see 12.40), most authorities make use of the report system, which requires committees to submit a report of their proceedings, with any necessary recommendations, instead of the minutes.

Procedure

7.90 The practice in dealing with committee/cabinet business (whether submitted by way of reports or minutes) varies between authorities. Some prescribe by standing orders the order in which each report will be taken. Others may vary the order from meeting to meeting if an alteration is thought likely to facilitate the transaction of business. Some consider and debate as the meeting thinks appropriate each report in turn. Others require the chairman to call-over all the reports first to ascertain which items are agreed and which may be opposed. If any member raises objection to any item, that paragraph is put aside to be dealt with after all unopposed committee business has been disposed of.

Reception of reports

7.91 Although some local authorities regard a reference to a portfolio holder or committee's report on the agenda as sufficient presentation, in which case the chairman calls over the report paragraph by paragraph, most first require each committee chairman or portfolio holder in turn (or someone on his behalf in each case) when invited so to do by the chairman to bring the report formally before the council for consideration by moving 'that the report of the . . . committee be received'.

The motion is regarded as a procedural one, not requiring a seconder and one not to be debated. Indeed, if the motion were voted upon and rejected the effect would be that the report had not been received, which, it has been said, is absurd since the council has already had it and debated it! In any case if a report is not received, what happens to it? It cannot dissolve into the air! To avoid such a nonsense arising, standing orders can make provision to the effect that:

> 'No amendment to the motion for the reception of a report shall be in order, except that consideration of the report be postponed or that the report be referred back to the committee for further consideration.'

Motion 'that the report be received'

7.92 The motion 'that the report be received' is wholly appropriate and can be resolved upon in those terms where the whole of the report records action taken in pursuance of delegated powers or otherwise contains no recommendations calling for action by the council. The use of the word 'received' indicates that the council has had the report before it but does not necessarily approve or disapprove it. There are variants, useful in distinguishing the 'reception' of the report for procedural purposes and its 'reception' in another sense: thus the motion could be 'that the report be accepted' or 'that the report be noted'. As to the minuting of the consideration of committee reports: see 8.10.

Amendments by leave of the council

7.93 If the committee chairman, or someone on his behalf, wishes to make an amendment to the report (which, strictly, may only be done with the leave of the council) or proposes to speak himself in explanation or elaboration of a particular paragraph in the report, it is usual for an indication to that effect to be given in moving the reception of the report. Thus the committee chairman may say 'I move the reception of the report and' – as the case may be – 'with the leave of the council wish to make a correction on paragraph . . .' or 'I would like to say something on paragraph . . .'. The committee chairman will then make his correction or statement when the paragraph concerned is called from the chair.

Adoption of report

7.94 Where a committee report contains recommendations on which there is no dissent, the motion at the conclusion of the call-over of the report, moved either by the committee chairman or the chairman of the meeting, is to the effect 'that the report be approved and adopted' or, alternatively, 'that the report and the recommendations contained therein be approved'. If any recommendation is amended in the course of the report's consideration then the motion at the conclusion of the call-over is to the effect 'that the report, as amended, be approved and adopted'.

Dealing paragraph by paragraph

7.95 Where committee reports are not too lengthy it may be thought preferable to dispense with the formal moving of the whole report and simply deal paragraph by paragraph with each report. This removes the need for the procedural motion (see 7.91). Each paragraph is moved and seconded in the usual way and each paragraph is then open for discussion and possible amendment. Authorities that prefer this practice believe it avoids confusion.

Reference back

7.96 It is in order, upon the reception of a report or later in the course of debate, for a motion (not an amendment, for the motion for reception is procedural only) to be moved 'that the report be referred back to the committee/cabinet' either 'for further information' or 'for further consideration' or with an instruction that some specified action be taken. Additional, there can be a reference back to a particular paragraph of a report.

Withdrawal of report

7.97 Alternatively, the committee/cabinet chairman might decide, with the leave of the council, to withdraw a report or a paragraph within that report, either in the light of the debate that has taken place or because circumstances have arisen since the committee's meeting that make such a course desirable. The withdrawal of a report or one of its paragraphs should be regarded as exceptional. It may be a tactical move politically to avoid defeat on a proposal of importance but, as a general rule, proceedings placed before the full council with the object patently of being acted upon should not ordinarily be withdrawn.

Regulation by standing orders

7.98 The particular procedure favoured by a local authority in dealing with reports at a council meeting should be laid down in standing orders.

Rescission of resolutions

Not at meeting at which passed

7.99 It is a widely accepted rule and a matter of common sense that a resolution cannot be rescinded at the meeting at which it is passed or adopted, even though all present are prepared to consent to such a proposition. Different considerations might apply in the case of a committee meeting (see 11.38).

If passed at earlier meeting

7.100 A resolution passed at one meeting may be rescinded at a subsequent meeting provided there are no practical obstacles, e.g. where action taken under the original resolution would make its rescission a nullity or the rights of third parties who have acted on the earlier decision need to be taken into account and safeguarded. A proposal to rescind a resolution must be treated as an original motion (see *Mayer* v. *Burslem Local Board*, above) unless it arises out of a committee report. Local authorities normally make provision in standing orders to control the rescission of resolutions (and to restrict the frequency with which unsuccessful motions can be revived). Old model standing order no.14 is to this effect:

> 'No motion to rescind any resolution passed within the preceding six months, and no motion or amendment to the same effect as one which has been rejected within the preceding six months, shall be proposed unless the notice thereof given in pursuance of standing order . . . bears the names of at least . . . members of the council. When any such motion or amendment has been disposed of by the council, it shall not be open to any member to propose a similar motion within a further period of six months.'

provided that this standing order shall not apply to motions moved in pursuance of a recommendation of a committee.

7.101 The kind of decisions that can be rescinded are, generally speaking, those that have determined the authority's policy or that otherwise are of continuing effect. There is a category of decisions that can be rescinded only in special circumstances – revoked is a more appropriate term – which includes, for example, the revocation of planning permission with consequent liability to pay compensation.

Rescission of a rescission

7.102 Where a resolution is rescinded and later the rescinding resolution is itself rescinded then, in the absence of any clear indication to contrary effect, the original resolution is revived (see *Weir* v. *Fermanagh County Council* (1913): but it is bad practice to leave in doubt, or leave to be implied, the true intention of a decision). As a general rule, the purported rescission of a resolution is of no effect if executive action has been taken under the original resolution and the intention is to invalidate what has properly been done under such resolution.

Voting

General considerations

7.103 As indicated earlier (see 1.37), in all ordinary instances questions coming or arising before a local authority are required to be decided by a majority of the members present and voting thereon at a properly constituted meeting of the authority.[16] In the case of principal councils the method of voting is not prescribed by statute; in the case of parish and community councils the voting is by show of hands unless standing orders otherwise provide,[17] and any member may 'on requisition' require that the voting shall be recorded so as to show whether each member present and voting gave a vote for or against the question.[18] In the case of parish and community meetings a question is similarly decided as a rule by show of hands in the first instance (although the statute does not expressly so stipulate), and the decision of the person presiding as to the result of the voting is final 'unless a poll is demanded'.[19]

7.104 The following draft core standing order was proposed by the standing orders working party (see 2.4) on which the mandatory standing order specified in the next paragraph impinges:

'00–1 Except where a requisition is made under the next paragraph, the method of voting at meetings of the council, committees and subcommittees shall be by show of hands.

2 If a requisition is made by the specified number of members, the voting on any question shall be recorded so as to show whether each member present gave his vote for or against that question or abstained from voting.

3 The specified number of members is:
   a) one-fifth of the members entitled to vote at the meeting; or
   b) where the council is divided into political groups, in the case of a meeting of the council, such number as is equal to the number of members of the second largest political group, and, in the case of a meeting of a committee or subcommittee, the number of seats on that body allocated to the second largest political group among the members of the council, whichever is the less.

Variation: A smaller number than that specified may be adopted.

4 If a vote is taken by show of hands, any member who is present when the vote was taken may require that his/her vote or abstention shall be recorded in the minutes by notifying forthwith the proper officer of his/her wish.

5 Where a vote is required on a motion to appoint or elect a member of the council to a position to be filled by the authority, and there are two or more members nominated for that position, the names of all those nominated shall be put to the meeting in alphabetical order of surname. Those entitled to vote shall each vote for only one person. If there is not a majority of those voting in favour of one person, the name of the person having the least number of votes shall be struck off the list and a fresh vote shall be taken, and so on until a majority of votes is given in favour of one person.'

7.105 A mandatory standing order[20] relating to the recording of votes is set out below:

'1 Where immediately after a vote is taken at a meeting of a relevant body any member of that body so requires, there shall be recorded in the minutes of the proceedings of that meeting whether that person cast his vote for the question or against the question or whether he abstained from voting.

2 In this paragraph "relevant body" means the authority, a committee or subcommittee of the authority or a relevant joint committee or subcommittee of such a committee.'

The importance of this entitlement for the individual councillor is discussed later (see 7.115). Members who are present and do not vote may, in certain circumstances, be regarded as having acquiesced in the decision taken (see 7.115). There are instances, however, in which a member may well wish his abstention to be recorded: where, for example, the motion to the effect that a council employee be reprimanded and the individual member feels he cannot vote against it because he regards the reprimand as being wholly inadequate and does not want his vote to be recorded against the only sanction likely, and so leave a false impression on the record.

Meaning of 'present and voting'

7.106 Members present at a meeting who do not vote or are prohibited from voting on the particular question before the meeting are nevertheless present for purposes of forming the necessary quorum; and a bare majority of those who in fact vote is sufficient to pass a resolution even if that number is less than the quorum. If, however, members under a disability are excluded from the meeting by standing orders or themselves voluntarily leave the council chamber until the particular matter is disposed of, they are not 'present'; as would be the case with a member who has declared himself disabled from taking part, but who has not actually been excluded, or voluntarily left.

Who may vote

7.107 Council members at a council meeting, if 'present' in the sense just referred to, i.e. are under no legal disability from voting, are entitled to vote. It has been held that persons who are de facto councillors may vote until such time as they are in fact unseated: *Holden* v. *Southwark Corpn* (1921).

7.108 What if a member who is clearly under a disability persists in speaking and voting? As indicated above, such a member is probably technically not present and therefore the chairman of the meeting would be justified in refusing to count his vote 'for the "vote" has been cast illegally and . . . can be said not to be a vote at all'. As to a vote cast by a councillor having an interest in an issue of a quasijudicial character (see 11.33).

7.109 The position is more difficult where the member concerned, thought to be under a disability, e.g. having a prejudicial interest), has chosen not to declare it and takes part in the debate and votes. In these circumstances it is, perhaps, better for the vote to be counted since the only person who can decide whether a disability of this kind exists is the member himself. A further difficulty that can arise from these circumstances is the possibility that the decision itself might be challengeable as illegal, certainly if it depended on the vote of the member who was subsequently shown to have a disabling interest. Any chairman finding himself faced with this situation would be well advised to persuade the meeting to adjourn for a short period so that the question could be discussed with the member concerned.

Methods of voting

7.110 Despite differences in the words of the statute most local authorities proceed by taking most votes by show of hands and the chairman will ordinarily make his decision on the evidence of the show of hands without taking a count. There is no reason, however (at least in the case of principal councils) why a vote should not be taken in some other way, e.g. by voice or by conduct (such as nodding the head): and it is well established that there can be an implied vote in favour by silent assent. However, this is not good practice. Where an interested person was present at a meeting at which a resolution was carried unanimously and so entered on the minutes and the defendant did not dissent or abstain from voting though he did not expressly indicate assent, it was held that he had voted for the resolution: *Everett v. Griffiths* (1924) (see also 7.115).

7.111 In some authorities, electronic voting systems have been installed in order to expedite the taking of votes, but these would not be permissible in the case of parish and community meetings. There are circumstances where it is impracticable to reach what might be termed a fairly representative decision by simple majority vote, e.g. in the case of the election of persons to various offices where there are several nominations, or in the selection of an individual from a shortlist of candidates for a staff appointment when the interviewing panel cannot agree. Local authorities as a rule adopt some kind of balloting system that provides for the choice of nominee who secures the greatest number of individual votes, but this can be an imperfect mechanism because it can produce a perverse result, e.g. the choice may fall on someone with fewer votes than the aggregate of votes for other candidates. Old model standing order no. 16 referred to earlier makes this provision:

'Where there are more than two persons nominated for any position to be filled by the council, and of the votes given there is not a majority in favour of one person, the name of the person having the least number of votes shall be struck off the list and a fresh vote shall be taken, and so on until a majority of votes is given in favour of one person.'

7.112 Some local authorities have experimented with the single transferable vote system[21] in circumstances where there are more nominees than places available, e.g. on the election of the mayor, committee chairmen and vice-chairmen, and in choosing councillors to serve 'on committees, subcommittees, and as representatives on outside bodies'. A standing order that has been used by one such authority provides:

'If the number of nominations exceeds the number of vacancies there shall be a secret ballot of the members present at the meeting in which each member of the council shall vote for as many candidates as there are vacancies to be filled. Vacancies shall thereupon be filled using the single transferable vote system. Any ballot shall be conducted by the secretary whose return shall be final and conclusive.'

Council meetings

The Electoral Reform Society (whose principal object is to promote the adoption of proportional representation for elections in the British Isles and elsewhere) states:

'In some cases, a party can win more votes, but fewer seats, than its opponents. Where one party dominates a local council there is a danger that issues will not be fully discussed and proposals will not be effectively scrutinised. If we had a proportional voting system, a party's share of seats would reflect its relative popularity with the voters. If no party had an absolute majority of votes in an election, no party should have a majority of seats. Parties should be forced to work together to reach agreements acceptable to a wider range of voters.'

Challenge to chairman's ruling

7.113 Any challenge to a chairman's ruling, including his decision on a vote on a show of hands, must be made promptly at the time (*Anthony* v. *Seger* (1789)). A show of hands, convenient though it is at both council and committee meetings, is 'only a rude and imperfect declaration of . . . sentiments'. Where it is believed that the chairman's declaration of the result of a show of hands is in error the proper course is for the meeting to call for the voting to be determined more accurately in some such manner as described in the foregoing paragraphs. In *Cornwall* v. *Woods* (1846), the court refused to upset a decision of a meeting of parishioners at which a rate was fixed because, if the chairman was in error, the correct procedure should have been to call for a division or a poll.

Taking a poll

7.114 Exceptionally, in the case of parish and community meetings there is provision in law for the taking of a poll in certain circumstances (LGA 1972, Sch.12, paras.18–34). A poll may be demanded before the conclusion of a meeting on any question arising and must be taken if the person presiding consents or the poll is demanded by not less than 10, or one-third, of the electors present at the meeting, whichever is the less. A poll so demanded is a poll of the local government electors and is conducted substantially as for the election of parish or community councillors as the case may be.

Abstention

7.115 It may be convenient here to discuss more fully a point referred to earlier. There is a presumption that councillors who merely abstain from voting assent to the resolution and where no formal vote is taken all those present are presumed to have assented, and this is important in determining personal liability for surcharge. Without this presumption there would be endless argument over whether an individual should or should not be held liable who did not actively vote against unlawful expenditure. Nevertheless, other evidence of opposition may suffice for exemption from personal surcharge. A record of abstentions from voting has the added advantage of accounting for all members present at the time the vote was taken.

7.116 The principles involved are drawn from common law, mostly in cases which concern appeals against surcharge by the district auditor. If a councillor votes against a proposal and his vote is not recorded in the minutes, other evidence may protect him: see *Attorney-General* v. *Tottenham Local Board* (1872). In the classic case of *Roberts* v. *Hopwood* (1925), four councillors who had initially been surcharged were able to show to the satisfaction of the court that they dissented from the motion to incur unlawful expenditure; and in another case, *Rothnie* v. *Dearne UDC* (1951), Devlin J said:

> 'No one should suppose that the mere failure to vote against an illegal resolution necessarily entails the consequences which have followed in this case.'

The principle that abstention may amount to acquiescence is at least partly based on the duty that a councillor undertakes in making his declaration of acceptance of office (see *Asher* v. *Secretary of State* (1974); and as to acceptance of office: see 4.3).

7.117 What if a councillor absents himself from a meeting knowing that a proposal to incur unlawful expenditure is to be put forward at the meeting? Is the member not in breach of his duty? Regard must be had to all the surrounding circumstances. An absentee for good reason is not likely to incur personal liability; but inability to attend a meeting at which a matter is finally decided does not absolve a councillor from doing what he can to oppose the illegality. An eminent former district auditor and inspector of audit has said this of an unreported case (*Barnes* v. *District Auditor for No. 11 District* (1976)) in which Watkins J declared that liability could arise 'by either action or inaction'.

Special consideration was given to the position of certain individual members. Two members of the old council had not been present at council meetings at which resolutions had been passed authorising expenditure held to be illegal. They had been present at earlier committee meetings when the proposals had been discussed and officers had advised of their illegality. The district auditor found that they were aware that the proposals were to be considered by the council at the meetings from which they were absent, and that they knew or ought to have known that the proposals were illegal. He held that they were therefore under a duty to attend the council meetings and to oppose the proposals or, if they were unable to attend the council meetings, to take such steps as they would to make known their opposition. Since they failed in this duty he held that they shared responsibility for authorising or incurring the expenditure and also that loss was caused by their negligence and misconduct.

One person, one vote

7.118 The practice of voting by show of hands means that each person present at a meeting must, in order to vote, put up one hand only and so exercise one vote. It is, in any case, a common law rule that every person voting at a meeting is reckoned as one vote (*Rex* v. *Rector of Birmingham* (1837) pp.259, 260); that each voter is accorded one vote unless there exists, in some form, a specific provision to the contract (*Re Horbury Bridge Coal, Iron & Wagon Co.* (1879)), as in the case, of course, of a chairman's second or casting vote (see 11.37).

7.119 The principle of one person one vote means that on each issue on which a vote is taken a person may vote once only, either for or against. A person cannot properly vote both for and against even though this could be said to have the same effect as an abstention because the vote for and the vote against cancel each other out; nor even, it would seem, to correct an error made in voting in the first place (see 7.128) or to suggest by the record that a quorum was present when it was not.[22]

No authoritative decision exists as to whether an error on the part of a voter in giving his vote can be corrected. When the result has been declared the voting is regarded as closed: before the declaration the chairman could presumably exercise a discretion to allow a voter to correct an error.

Chairman's casting vote

7.120 Although at common law the person presiding at a meeting has no casting vote, the chairman of every local authority meeting has a second or casting vote that may be exercised where there is an equality of votes.

7.121 There are differing opinions as to what precisely is meant by the term a second or casting vote. It has been argued that it means that whoever presides may only vote to avoid a deadlock on an equality of votes if he has already exercised his right to vote as a councillor. The preferred view, and the one generally accepted, is that the true intention of the statute is that the person presiding may vote to avoid a deadlock no matter how it arises, i.e. whether he had already voted or not. Cave J said in *Nell* v. *Longbotton* (1984):

> 'The justification of a second or casting vote, as it is called, is the creature of the statute law introduced for the purpose of avoiding the deadlock which would otherwise enure.'

Thus the position therefore seems to be as follows: if there is an equality of votes, whether or not the voting includes a vote by the chairman, the chairman may 'break the deadlock' by then using the casting vote. If the chairman does not elect to use his second or casting vote in this way the proposition falls to the ground, i.e. it is not carried. In the case of a controversial question or in other instances where an affirmative vote is not required as a matter of urgency, the chairman may choose not to exercise his second or casting vote on the grounds (though he is not bound to explain his action) that in his impartial capacity as chairman he ought not to determine an issue on which opinion is equally divided or where the matter can be raised again at a later date. Of course a chairman may not regard his role as impartial where he had been put into the chair by the ruling group's control of the vote or where there is a hung council; and this was so in recent cases before the courts (see 7.123).

7.122 Examples may help clarify what a chairman may or may not do. Suppose, after a motion has been moved and seconded and the chairman asks those present to signify, first those in favour and three members so signify, and then those against and three members so signify, the chairman may use his casting vote. If, however, when the proposition has been put, three members, including the chairman, vote in favour and three members vote against, the chairman may use his second vote in favour. The preferred opinion seems to be (although there is some doubt as to whether it could be sustained) that the chairman cannot withhold his ordinary vote and then purport to give two votes when it is evident how the voting is going, i.e. he cannot properly say when there are, for example, two votes for and three against a proposition: 'I'm in favour of the motion so it's a tie and I'll use my casting and second vote to carry the motion.' He can however, give a contingent casting vote in certain circumstances (see 7.124).

7.123 In the late 1980s, the Lord Mayor of Bradford's use of his second or casting vote in a hung council in favour of his own party's policies was challenged before the courts. The Lord Mayor had consistently used his second or casting vote to secure the passage through the council of proposals of his fellow councillors which in a hung situation might not otherwise have secured approval. In *R. v. Bradford Metropolitan City Council ex parte Wilson* (1989), the Divisional Court held that the purpose of a chairman's second or casting vote was to break deadlocks that would otherwise arise in view of the lack of such a vote at common law. If a chairman always used that vote in such a way as to preserve the status quo, the effect would be to maintain the deadlock rather than break it. The court decided not to interfere in such a case as this, where the Lord Mayor had used his second or casting vote honestly and according to his own perception of what was best in the public interest. In *R. v. Bradford Metropolitan City Council ex parte Corris* (1989), the Court of Appeal took a similar view when upholding a refusal to grant judicial review in respect of another instance where the Lord Mayor's second or casting vote had again been used in favour of the implementation of his own party's policies. The court said it did not think that the power to give a second or casting vote was fettered by any implied restriction that it should be exercised without regard to any party political considerations, nor by an inter-party agreement on the rotation of the lord mayoralty that it would not be used politically.

Contingent casting vote

7.124 A casting vote may be given contingently in circumstances where the chairman has good reason for believing that one of the votes cast may be invalid. Thus in *Bland* v. *Buchanan* (1901), both petitioner and respondent were candidates for the office of mayor of a borough. The mayor in office presided at the election. Sixteen votes, including the mayor's first vote, were cast for the respondent and 15 for the petitioner. The mayor, with good reason for believing that one of the votes cast for the respondent might be impeached, purported to give a casting vote for the respondent. The casting vote was held valid in these circumstances.

7.125 The extent to which the above principle can be stretched appears uncertain.

In *Bland*, above, the mayor was simply reinforcing a decision that a majority of councillors had supported. The more interesting question is whether a contingent casting vote could be used to reverse a decision that had been dependent upon a vote that was subsequently impeached. The principle appears to be the same, but the implications suggest that a contingent vote in these circumstances should be used only in exceptional circumstances, e.g. where a decision of the council is required to comply with a timetable.

The moment of decision

7.126 We have considered earlier when a resolution becomes effective (see 1.51). But when, precisely, does a meeting commit itself to a decision on a vote? Suppose, after a show of hands on a motion but before a requisition, i.e. a recording of the vote, is demanded (either under standing orders or, in the case of a parish or community council, under statutory provisions), a late-arriving member turns up and demands to be included in the voting. Is this permissible or is the requisition a clarification of the voting already under way, i.e. merely machinery for ascertaining accurately what the sense of the meeting was on the discussion that has preceded it?

7.127 The answer is that a member present at a meeting is entitled to vote at any time before the chairman declares the outcome of the voting in a final way. Thus, where a requisition is demanded after a show of hands (and, as indicated above, it must be demanded immediately (see 7.113)), a decision has not yet been made and there is nothing to stop a member who was not present at the show of hands from voting on the requisition or to prevent a member who voted one way at the show of hands changing his mind and voting differently. Just when a vote has finally been settled is a question of fact, which must rest with the chairman. These rules are also subject to any particular requirements imposed by standing orders. Some authorities have adopted a standing order that provides that members must be in the council chamber 'when the question is put' in order to be able to vote. Putting the question means asking for those in favour of a motion, and it would not be in order, under such a standing order, for a member to arrive in the chamber after that point had been reached and expect his vote to be counted. See the discussion at 11.38 on when a committee decision has been finalised.

Voting under misapprehension

7.128 It is not good practice to allow a member to alter his vote after he has cast it. Except, therefore, where a member changed his mind before the final declaration by the chairman of the outcome of the vote (see above), a member who has voted under a misapprehension ought not to be allowed subsequently to alter his vote.

7.129 Voting in meetings, particularly in large meetings, can be difficult to manage and is one of those activities where there is room for error. To have a vote challenged can be embarrassing and confusing and whoever is in charge of the counting, be it chairman or clerk, needs to get it right first time and ensure that members know exactly what it is they are voting on, and when the voting for or against is called. A moment or two devoted to this is time well spent and could avoid possible allegations of illegality later on. A good chairman will also insist that all members are in their seats when formal votes are counted. This not only ensures that a check can be kept on who votes, but also avoids the problem of members entering the chamber and voting after the question has been put if standing orders preclude this (see 7.126).

Preservation of order

Chairman's powers and duties

7.130 The chairman of a meeting is entitled to call upon any disorderly person, whether councillor or stranger, to behave properly. If that person continues to misbehave then, if the person is a stranger (i.e. a member of the public or, conceivably, an officer) he should be asked to withdraw from the meeting; and if he refuses the chairman may direct his removal by such force as may be reasonably necessary for the disorderly person's expulsion. If the person is a councillor he should be asked to withdraw voluntarily; and if he refuses, the chairman's most practical course is to suspend or adjourn the meeting temporarily (see 7.82). The distinction is important because a stranger is present by licence on what are private premises (and this is the case even though there is a statutory right for the public to have access to local authority meetings), whereas a councillor is present by right of his office and cannot be excluded from attending. See *Marshall* v. *Tinnelly* (1937), as to ejection of a disorderly councillor from the meeting of an urban district council.

7.131 Where there is unruly behaviour by several persons, whether councillors or strangers or both, so that the continued transaction of business is impracticable, the chairman may (and in practice ought to) suspend the meeting temporarily until order can be restored: suspend is a more appropriate term than adjourn in such circumstances, although the terms are interchangeable. Thus, in *John* v. *Rees* (1969), Megarry J said this (and the learned judge's views merit quoting at length now that, regrettably, violent disorder at council meetings has become common):

'The first duty of the chairman of a meeting is to keep order if he can. If there is disorder his duty, I think, is to make earnest and sustained efforts to restore order, and for this purpose to summon to his aid any officers or others whose assistance is available. If all his efforts are in vain, he should endeavour to put into operation whatever provisions for adjournment there are in the rules, as by obtaining a resolution to adjourn. If this proves impossible, he should exercise his inherent power to adjourn the meeting for a short time, such as 15 minutes, taking due steps to ensure so far as possible that all present know of this adjournment. If instead of mere disorder there is violence, I think that he should take similar steps, save that the greater the violence the less prolonged should be his efforts to restore order before adjourning. In my judgment, he has not merely a power but a duty to adjourn in this way, in the interests of those who fear for their safety. I am not suggesting that there is a power and a duty to adjourn if the violence consists of no more than a few technical assaults and batteries. Mere pushing and jostling is one thing; it is another when people are put in fear, where there is heavy punching, or the knives are out, so that blood may flow, and there are prospects, or more, of grievous bodily harm. In the latter case the sooner the chairman adjourns the meeting the better. At meetings, as elsewhere, the Queen's Peace must be kept.

If then, the chairman has this inherent power and duty, what limitations, if any, are there upon its exercise? First, I think that the power and duty must be exercised bona fide for the purpose of forwarding and facilitating the meeting, and not for the purpose of interruption or procrastination. Second, I think that the adjournment must be for no longer than the necessities appear to dictate. If the adjournment is merely for such period as the chairman considers to be reasonably necessary for the restoration of order, it would be within his "power and his duty"; a longer adjournment would not. One must remember that to attend a meeting may for some mean travelling far and giving up much leisure. An adjournment to another day when a mere 15 minutes might suffice to restore order may well impose an unjustifiable burden on many; for they must either once more travel far and give up their leisure, or else remain away and lose their chance to speak and vote at the meeting.'

Disorderly conduct by members

7.132 Standing orders will usually set out a procedure seeking first to stop the individual member from engaging in disorderly conduct, and if he does not stop when requested by the chairman, for the temporary suspension of the meeting. The draft core standing order in this respect produced by the working party (see 2.3) was in these terms:

'00–1 If the person presiding is of the opinion that a member has misconducted, or is misconducting, himself/herself by persistently disregarding the ruling of the chair, or by behaving irregularly, improperly or offensively, or by wilfully obstructing the business of the council, he/she may notify the meeting of that opinion, and may take any of the following courses, either separately or in sequence:
   a) he/she may direct the member to refrain from speaking during all, or part, of the remainder of the meeting;
   b) he/she may direct the member to withdraw from all, or part, of the remainder of the meeting;
   c) he/she may order the member to be removed from the meeting; (d) he/she may adjourn the meeting for fifteen minutes or such period as shall seem expedient to him/her.

Variation
Substitute for subparagraphs (a) to (c):
   a) he/she may move that the member named be not further heard; this motion shall not require to be seconded, but shall be put and decided without comment; if it is carried, the member named shall not speak further at that meeting;
   b) he/she may move that the member named shall leave the meeting; this motion

7. Conduct

shall not require to be seconded but shall be put and decided without comment; if it is carried, the member named shall forthwith leave the meeting:

c) he/she may adjourn the meeting for fifteen minutes or such period as shall seem expedient to him/her.

2 If a member of the public interrupts proceedings at any meeting, the person presiding shall warn him/her. If he/she continues the interruption, the person presiding shall order him/her to leave the room where the meeting is being held. If he/she does not leave, the person presiding shall order him/her to be removed. If a member of the public persistently creates a disturbance, the person presiding may adjourn the meeting for fifteen minutes or such period as shall seem expedient to him/her.

3 In the event of general disturbance in any part of the room where any meeting is being held which is open to the public, the person presiding shall order that part to be cleared and may adjourn the meeting for fifteen minutes or such period as shall seem expedient to him/her.

4 The powers conferred by this standing order are in addition to any other powers which the person presiding may lawfully exercise.'

7.133 The terms of this standing order would not preclude the chairman himself from calling the offending councillor to order because of the chairman's common law duty to preserve order (see 7.131); but the chairman would be wise – because of the member's statutory right to be present in the council chamber – not to ask the councillor to leave, even temporarily, without positive assurance that it is the wish of the meeting. There is no power (as in the case of parliament) to suspend a member. The power of the House of Commons to expel a Member of Parliament derives from the ancient usages of parliament. The Speaker is nowadays armed by standing orders with precisely defined powers. The Commons can, if so minded, expel an MP for any reason whatsoever, even though in so doing it effectively disenfranchises the electors who voted the member into office. This extreme power is rarely exercised in full measure. What is more usual is for a Member of Parliament, having been named by the Speaker for, say, gross disorderly conduct, to be suspended under the Commons standing order no.25 for five sitting days of the House including the day of suspension, and then to be escorted from the precincts of the House by the sergeant at arms using such force as may be necessary. It is interesting that the old local authority model standing order no.12 does not provide for a councillor's removal by force. See *R. v. St Mary's, Lambeth* (1832), as to the adjournment of a meeting by the chairman of his own volition when general uproar arose.

7.134 The Nolan Committee was concerned about the absence of sanctions available against members who flout standing orders or otherwise fall short of acceptable behaviour in meetings. As a result of this concern, it recommended that the standards committee deal with such matters, i.e. should have power to recommend disciplinary action against members including the power to suspend councillors from meetings for up to three months. The current position is that the standards committee of a local authority can only deal with such matters if they are the subject of complaints to the Standards Board for England, and as such are referred back to the authority.

Council meetings

Disorderly conduct by the public

7.135 Disorderly conduct by an individual other than a councillor is best dealt with if practicable by his removal after he has been given the opportunity, and refuses, of leaving quietly of his own accord. If the disorder is committed by a number of persons, the suspension of the sitting is preferable either to give the offending persons the opportunity of behaving properly or to facilitate their removal from the meeting. No more force should be used than is reasonably necessary for the purpose of securing the offenders' removal (see *Hawkins* v. *Muff* (1911)). If unnecessary violence is used in ejecting a person, damages may be awarded against the chairman (but only if the chairman personally authorised the removal beforehand (*Doyle* v. *Falconer* (1866)) or subsequently ratified the ejection (*Lucas* v. *Mason* (1875)). If public disorder is likely, then it may be wise to request that the police attend the meeting to ensure that no public order offences are committed, or to exclude the public (see 3.25).

7.136 If a person expelled by order of the chairman resists his removal and lays hand on the chairman or other person who is removing him, it is an unjustifiable assault amounting to a breach of the peace. Such resistance would justify his being given or taken into custody. But mere disorderly conduct short of a breach of the peace, though it may justify ejection, would not justify a person's being given into custody: see *Wooding* v. *Oxley* (1839).

7.137 Old model standing order no. 13 is to the following effect:

> 'If a member of the public interrupts the proceedings at any meeting the mayor/ chairman shall warn him. If he continues the interruption the mayor/chairman shall order his removal from the council chamber. In case of general disturbance in any part of the chamber open to the public the mayor/chairman shall order that part to be cleared.'

A standing order on these lines could now, of course, be applied to proceedings at meetings. Widdicombe felt it was important that there should be this express duty: on a chairman to bring disturbance to a halt because of 'suspicion of connivance by the chair' in disorder at council meetings.

Anticipation of disorder

7.138 It appears that a local authority could properly on reasonable grounds anticipate the probability of disorder and so exclude the public in advance. In *R.* v. *Brent Health Authority ex parte Francis and Another* (1985), it was held that it was lawful for a body to which at that time the PB(AM)A 1960 applied to exclude members of the public from attending a meeting in view of the likelihood that members of the public would disrupt proceedings. Forbes J. said:

> 'Exclusion did not only have the meaning of excluding people already at a meeting but also . . . of preventing people coming at all.'

7. Conduct

Mass demonstrations

7.139 Mass lobbying of councillors attending council meetings and the presence of large numbers of demonstrators in the public gallery are ever-present possibilities that need to be anticipated and appropriately regulated so as to permit orderly and effective representations without disruption of council proceedings and breach of public order. It will rarely be practicable to accommodate all those who may wish to enter the council chamber (and there is no obligation on the local authority to go beyond making reasonable provision in this respect (see 3.17)), but much can be done to avoid trouble and misunderstandings if simple precautionary measures are taken in advance, for example:

- When the presence of large numbers of demonstrators is expected, invite the organisers to attend beforehand for a discussion as to how best to meet their reasonable and lawful wishes.
- Offer to provide assembly points for demonstrators outside the town or county hall or council offices, an opportunity for their leaders to meet the chairman or leader of the council before the meeting begins, and the reservation of an agreed number of seats in the public gallery for representatives of the demonstrators. It may be thought desirable to publicise the likelihood of an abnormal attendance and explain that the general public will be admitted up to the limit of accommodation on a 'first come first served' basis.
- Review security measures to prevent unauthorised access to the council's offices and restrict entry to the public gallery by one door only.
- Alert the police and enlist their help and co-operation: see next paragraph.
- Consult the fire officer on means of escape and maximum numbers that can safely be admitted to the meeting place.
- Consider relaying the proceedings so that a larger number can listen.

Powers of the police

7.140 The police have no power to enter upon council premises, except by leave of the council or its officers, unless they have reason to believe that a breach of the peace is being committed or they have reasonable grounds for believing that an offence is imminent or likely to be committed (*Thomas* v. *Sawkins* (1935)). It is a wise precaution therefore for the local authority to ask police constables to be present when disorder is anticipated.

7.141 Where the police are so employed they should not be called upon to intervene unless there is a breach of the peace or a breach is imminent. The chairman should ask any disorderly person to leave and if this proves ineffectual the chairman should direct the council's own employees to eject the offending person in the first place and only if he violently resists would the police be justified in intervening. The police, indeed, must intervene if there is breach of the peace and may arrest without warrant anyone they believe responsible for such breach.

Duration of council meeting

7.142 Unless standing orders provide to the contrary or the members at a meeting decide otherwise proceedings must continue until all business on the agenda has been dealt with. However, many authorities provide by standing orders for a break in proceedings after a specified period of time, particularly as most meetings of the full council are held in the evening:

'There shall be a first adjournment as soon as is convenient at the discretion of the mayor after one and a half hours for 20 minutes; and thereafter provided the business lasts so long when one hour has elapsed as soon as is convenient and at the discretion of the mayor thereafter there shall be a second adjournment of 15 minutes. In the event that the council meeting continues beyond the second adjournment further adjournment shall be at the discretion of the meeting whose views shall be taken on a show of hands without discussion.

A meeting of the council shall (unless then otherwise determined by show of hands of a proposal by any member) adjourn at 12 midnight and the matter then under discussion and all other business yet to be considered shall be adjourned to a further meeting of the council at a date to be fixed or to the next ordinary meeting of the council.'

7.143 One of the draft core standing orders suggested by the working party (see 2.4) in this connection was to this effect:

'00–1 At a time when:
    a) a period of not less than [two hours] has elapsed since the commencement of a meeting of the council; or
    b) where an item of business is to be considered as opposition priority business, that business has been considered for not less than [half an hour], whichever is later, a member of the council may move, without comment, that the meeting shall end at a time to be specified in the motion.
  2 The person presiding may refuse to accept the motion if a similar motion has been rejected earlier in the same meeting.
  3 If the motion is accepted, it shall be seconded and put without comment.
  4 If the motion is passed, when the time specified in it arrives,
    a) no further points of order shall be raised except by the person presiding;
    b) the person presiding shall then interrupt the discussion of the question then before the meeting;
    c) unless the mover of the motion then under discussion seeks leave to withdraw that motion, the person presiding shall allow him/her to reply to the debate for not more than [five] minutes;
    d) unless the motion then under discussion is withdrawn, the person presiding shall put, without further discussion, all the questions necessary to dispose of that motion;

7. Conduct

e) unless the person appointed to preside in any committee (or a person on his/her behalf) indicates a wish to the contrary, the person presiding shall put, without discussion, all the questions necessary to complete consideration of any reports of that committee which are before the meeting;

f) the person presiding shall call each member who has given notice both of a motion to be moved at that meeting and of a motion that the first motion be considered without prior reference to a committee, to move both motions without comment, shall permit any motions so moved to be seconded without comment, and shall forthwith put both motions to the vote;

g) finally, the person presiding shall close the meeting.'

Transaction of special business

Honorary aldermen and freemen

7.144 A principal council may, by resolution passed by not less than two-thirds of the members voting thereon at a meeting of the council specially convened for the purpose with notice of the object,[23] (no other business can be transacted at such a meeting, but the specially convened meeting could either precede or follow an annual or ordinary or extraordinary meeting of the council), confer the title of honorary alderman on persons who have, in the opinion of the council, rendered eminent services to the council as past members of that council but who are not then councillors of the council.

7.145 An honorary alderman may attend and take part in such civic ceremonies as the council may from time to time decide but, as such, has no right:

- to attend meetings of the council, cabinet or a committee other than as a member of the public (including a joint committee upon which the council is represented); or
- to receive any of the allowances or other payments to which councillors are entitled.

7.146 Section 249 LGA1972 provides that a London Borough, City, borough or royal borough:

> '...may spend such reasonable sum as it thinks fit for the purpose of presenting an address or a casket containing an address to a person upon whom it has conferred the title.'

7.147 It may also, by resolution passed by not less than two-thirds of the members voting thereon at a meeting of the council specially convened for the purpose with notice of the object, admit to be honorary freemen of the city, borough or royal borough, persons of distinction and persons who have, in the council's opinion, rendered eminent services to the city, borough or royal borough, but the admission of a person to be an honorary freeman does not confer on him the rights granted to be an honorary aldermen. The council may spend such reasonable sum as it thinks fit for the same purposes as in the case of an honorary alderman.

7.148 In most cases the proposal to confer the title of honorary alderman or to admit a person to be an honorary freeman will be submitted to the specially convened meeting of the council as a recommendation from the cabinet. Appropriate recommendations would be that:

'1 In pursuance of s.249 of the Local Government Act 1972 . . . be admitted as an honorary alderman /freeman of the . . . in recognition of [the eminent services which s/he has rendered to . . .] [his/her distinguished . . .] [and that his/her name be enrolled on the freemen's roll].

2 That the common seal of the council be affixed to the [enrolment of . . . on the said freemen's roll and to the certificate to be presented to him/ her on his/ her admission as an honorary freeman of . . .] [certificate conferring upon . . . the title of honorary alderman].

3 That an estimated expenditure of . . . be approved for purposes associated therewith and that the leader be authorised to agree any consequential matters.'

Promoting or opposing a bill in parliament

7.149 A local authority, other than a parish or community council, if satisfied that it is expedient so to do, may promote a local or personal bill in parliament; and any local authority – again, if satisfied that it is expedient so to do – may oppose any local or personal bill. In either case, however, it may only do so in accordance with the procedure laid down.

7.150 This procedure requires that a resolution of the council to promote or oppose a bill shall be:

- passed by a majority of the whole number of the members of the authority at a meeting of the authority held after the requisite notice of the meeting and of its purpose has been given by advertisement in one or more local newspapers circulating in the area of the authority, such notice being given in addition to the ordinary notice required to be given for the convening of a meeting of the authority; and

- in the case of the promotion of a bill, confirmed by a like majority at a further meeting convened in accordance with the paragraph above and held as soon as may be after the expiration of 14 days after the bill has been deposited in parliament and, if the resolution is not confirmed, the local authority shall take all necessary steps to withdraw the bill.

For this purpose, the requisite notice is 30 clear days' notice in the case of promotion of a bill and 10 clear days' notice in the case of opposition to a bill.

7. Conduct

7.151 This procedure thus overrules that by which questions before the local authority are ordinarily decided, i.e. by a majority of the members merely present and voting at a meeting, and, further, requires additional notice. Exceptionally, too, in the case of the promotion of a bill there has to be a confirmatory resolution at a further meeting convened after special additional notice. The terms of the statute imply (though they do not expressly state) that the meeting must be specially convened and exclusively for the purpose. Any doubt there may be in this respect could be overcome by arranging for such a meeting to be held immediately before an ordinary meeting of the council.

Political organisation of council business

Acknowledgement in standing orders

7.152 It is increasingly the practice, apart from the statutory provisions providing for political balance in the membership of committees, etc., for authorities to acknowledge the existence and the role of party politics in the provision made in standing orders. There is much to commend this: for example, the chief executive will ordinarily turn to the leader of the council, i.e. the leader of the majority political group on the council (nowadays often chairman of the policy and resources committee) rather than as in the past to the chairman of the council or the mayor when wishing in circumstances of urgency to take the council's collective view of a matter; and, as circumstances may dictate, consult also the leader of the opposition group. The major parties invariably appoint whips for the organisation of group business, and certain nominal duties associated with the membership of the council may well devolve upon them: settling, for example, the seating arrangements in the council chamber.

7.153 With the development of hung or balanced councils, where no one party has overall control, has come the practice of consulting spokespersons of all the main parties. This practice is part of the list of conventions for dealing with political arrangements adopted by authorities, such as hung councils, with little if any experience of such political curiosities. Where spokespersons of several parties are involved in consultations between meetings it is often the case that no action can be taken by officers unless there is unanimity between the politicians.

Party group business

7.154 There is, it is submitted, council territory into which party political organisation should not encroach. Standing orders may properly be drawn up to require the party groups to notify certain information to the council officially, to place nominal duties of a political nature upon the party whips, and such like. However, standing orders must not, for example, by recognising decisions taken in party groups, override the formal decision-making procedure prescribed by law as that would be ultra vires. As regards party balance in committee membership (see 9.53).

181

Council meetings

Standing orders

7.155 The following examples are from the old standing orders of the London Borough of Hammersmith and Fulham. As regards the leader of the council and the leader of the opposition standing orders might provide that:

'Two members of the council selected from time to time, one as leader by the members forming the party in office on the council, and one by those forming the largest party in opposition on the council respectively shall be known as the leader of the council and the leader of the opposition respectively. The leaders may have such deputies as may from time to time be appointed. All the names when so appointed shall be notified to the chief executive for report to the council.

The leader of the council shall be entitled to reply to questions asked by members at meetings of the council upon matters of policy or the general business of the council including such matters as have not been considered by a committee and in any event may act as a spokesman for the council whenever appropriate.

The expression "whenever appropriate" no doubt implies matters of policy, particularly if controversial: formal statements on behalf of the local authority would remain the responsibility of the chairman of the council or mayor.'

7.156 With regard to whips, standing orders might provide that:

'Two members of the council elected from time to time as whips by the members forming the party in office on the council and by those forming the largest party in opposition on the council respectively shall be known as the chief whip and opposition whip respectively.

The whips shall, as far as possible, jointly and in consultation with the chief executive, consider as necessary the despatch of the business at meetings of the council and its committees and the appointment to membership of committees and other bodies.

The party in office on the council may appoint junior whips.'

It should be noted particularly that the whips are charged with the task of considering but obviously not deciding matters of council business. The decisions remain properly to be made by the council, albeit on the recommendation of the whips. The use of a party whip is, however, considered incompatible with the overview and scrutiny process (see 7.154).

7.157 Certain other consequential matters may need to be included in standing orders, e.g. in the standing order dealing with the order of business at the annual meeting, the following item:

> 'To receive a report as to the appointment of leader of the council and leader of the opposition, chief whip and opposition whip, and their deputies as necessary';

and perhaps one to this effect elsewhere:

> 'The seating positions of members in the council chamber shall be such as may be agreed from time to time by the chief whip and opposition whip.'

Notes

1 See Local Authorities (Standing Orders) Regulations 1993, Sch.2, para.2.
2 Para.41 is amended by the LG&HA 1989, Sch.11, para.30.
3 LGA 1972, ss.4(3), 8 (Sch.2, para.3(3)), 23(3).
4 Ibid., s.4(2), 8 (Sch.2, para.3(2)), 15(3), 23(2).
5 Ibid., ss.2(1), 14(1), 8 (Sch.2, para.1), 21(1), 33(1).
6 Ibid., ss.3(2), 15(4), 22(2), which provide that the chairman shall continue in office until his successor becomes entitled to act as chairman; and Sch.12, paras.5(1), 11(1), 27(1), which provide that the chairman, if present, shall preside.
7 Ibid., s.5(1).
8 Ibid., ss.15(6), 34(6).
9 Ibid., ss.5(2), 15(7), 34(7). Strictly interpreted this provision might seem to deny a vice-chairman, unless he resigns first, the opportunity of being elected as chairman in the event of a vacancy in the office of chairman before the next annual meeting!
10 Ibid., ss.5(2), 15(8), 34(8), and Sch.2, para.4(2).
11 Ibid., ss.5(3), 15(9), 34(9), and Sch.2, para.4(3).
12 Ibid., Sch.12, para.5(1).
13 Ibid., Sch.12, paras.11(1), 27(1).
14 Ibid., Sch.12, paras.11(2), 27(2).
15 Ibid., Sch.12, paras.11(3), 27(3).
16 Ibid., Sch.12, para.49(1).
17 Ibid. Sch.12, paras.13(1), 29(1).
18 Ibid. Sch.12, paras.13(2), 29(2) and see 7.102.
19 Ibid., Sch.12, paras.34(2), 18(2). It is expressly provided that each elector eligible to attend may give one vote and no more on any question, whether at a meeting or at a poll consequent thereon: paras.18(1), 34(1).
20 Local Authorities (Standing Orders) Regulations 1993, Sch.2, para.l.
21 The single transferable vote system has long been used in Northern Ireland. In the Electoral Law (Northern Ireland) Order 1972 it is defined thus: '"Transferable vote" means a vote: (a) capable of being given so as to indicate the voter's preference for the candidates in order; and (b) capable of being transferred to the next choice when the vote is not required to give a prior choice the necessary quota of votes or when, owing to the

deficiency in the number of votes given for a prior choice, that choice is eliminated from the list of candidates.'

22 In July 1975 in the House of Commons three MPs cast their vote twice, i.e. both for and against a motion in an attempt, unsuccessfully as it happened, and not seriously it was said, to achieve a quorum on the record and so enable a resolution to be passed to which it was known the majority was not opposed. The ruse was discovered and the Whips concerned had to apologise.

23 Notice would need to be given in accordance with LGA 1972, Sch.12, para.4(2), apart from the specific obligation in this case.

Chapter 8
Council minutes

General considerations

Introduction

8.1 This chapter is concerned with the law and practice relating to the keeping of local authority minutes of proceedings and their authentication, and the obligation to make them available for public inspection. Many of the statutory provisions apply also to minutes of committees and subcommittees, and to executive meetings; where there are differences these will be referred to later in Chapter 12. Also considered here is the form that council minutes take, almost invariably differing from that adopted for committee and subcommittee minutes. For reasons that defy logical explanation, the formality of meetings of the full council is generally reflected in a corresponding formality of style in minuting the proceedings.

What are minutes?

8.2 Minutes, in the sense commonly understood, are brief notes of the proceedings at a meeting that in particular record the decisions made. There is, however, no statutory definition of minutes and at common law there is, no obligation that a permanent or any written record of matters transacted at a meeting should be kept. Clearly it is expedient and convenient, apart from any legal requirement, that minutes should be kept in some permanent form. However, if the record is to have greater weight than mere recollection, the minutes must be made within a reasonable time after the meeting to which they relate (*Toms v. Cinema Trust* (1915)). Even where, as in the case of local authority minutes, the law requires that minutes shall be kept, the minute book may be written up from rough notes taken at the time of the meeting (*Re Jennings* (1851)).

8.3 There is justification for the view that minutes can mean two things: the narrative record of all business transacted at a meeting, and a copy of the resolutions passed by those present. The law permits evidence to explain the narrative, e.g. to show reasons for a decision and the basis upon which it was taken;[1] but not to explain a resolution, and there is a view that resolutions must be framed so as to be self-explanatory, and wholly intelligible without reference to any other document or evidence. In *Re Fireproof Doors Ltd* (1916), evidence was held to be admissible to show that a resolution that was not recorded had in fact been passed.

The minute book

Keeping the minutes

8.4 The law requires that the minutes of proceedings of council and committee (and subcommittee) meetings, when drawn up, shall be 'entered in a book kept for that purpose'. This requirement,[2] formerly enacted in the LGA 1933 and earlier legislation, was rigidly construed, so that it was the practice of many local authorities at one time to insist that the minutes were written up by hand in the numbered pages of a bound book; later that they were entered in such a book either by typing direct on the pages (by means of a special typewriter, probably no longer manufactured, called a book-writer) or by pasting in to the book sheets of paper on which the minutes had been typed. Then later still, before the law was changed, authorities began to defy the strict letter of the law and kept their minutes temporarily in a loose-leaf system until there was a sufficient sheets to warrant binding.

Loose-leaf minutes

8.5 Minutes may now lawfully be 'recorded on loose leaves consecutively numbered, provided each sheet is initialled by the person who signs the minutes to which the leaves relate.' This initialling must be done at the time the minutes are signed.

Preservation in perpetuity

8.6 Minutes must be kept in perpetuity. For this reason they must be prepared on durable paper and, if kept initially in loose-leaf form, bound up ultimately for in order to preserve them. The arrangements should be made the specific responsibility of an identified officer and systematically planned in advance, i.e. it should be decided how frequently the loose leaves are to be bound together (because this will determine the consecutive numbering of pages and the make-up of the index) and whether documents incorporated by reference (see 12.13) are to be bound in the minute book itself as appendices or preserved separately and, if separately, in what manner.

Safe custody

8.7 The safe custody of minutes is important, and it is the responsibility of each principal council:

> '. . . to give directions as to the documents of any council and to make proper arrangements with respect to any documents which belong to or are in the custody of the council or any of its officers.[3] Minutes must be kept under lock and key and ordinarily in fire-resistant safes (although not so inaccessibly stored away as not to be readily available for purposes of inspection): and these precautions are especially needed in the case of minutes kept in a loose-leaf system pending binding.'

8. Council minutes

Form

General

8.8 Council minutes can take whatever form is preferred by the individual authority or relevant officer concerned. There are certain general principles governing the drafting of minutes that should be observed (and these are set out later in Chapter 12 in regard to committee minutes), but the principles are flexible and what matters primarily is that the minutes record clearly and concisely all decisions taken at the meeting and of the other proceedings as is necessary to give reasons to the decision-making. To quote one example only of the wide variation in practice: some authorities meticulously minute all questions asked and the replies given at question time in the council chamber, but most authorities do not.

General style

8.9 As indicated above (see 8.1), council minutes traditionally reflect the formality of council proceedings and are generally different in style to committee minutes. Resolutions can be recorded showing the names of the proposer and seconder, e.g.:

'Moved [or proposed] by Councillor Jones. Seconded by Councillor Smith, and Resolved: That the report of the Cabinet . . . be approved and adopted by the Council.'

Or, as an alternative style:

'It was moved by Councillor Jones and seconded by Councillor Robinson that the report of the Cabinet be approved and adopted by the Council.

An amendment was moved by Councillor Smith and seconded by Councillor Brown that the following words be added to the motion: "except that para.A (Corporate Plan) be referred back to the Cabinet for reconsideration".

After debate the amendment was voted upon and declared not carried, 15 members voting "for" and 25 "against".

A further amendment was moved by Councillor White and seconded by Councillor Black that the following words be added to the motion: 'except that para.A (Corporate Plan) be approved in principle only and that the Cabinet be instructed to report further on the detailed implementation of the Corporate Plan'.

After debate the amendment was voted upon and declared carried by 25 votes to 15.

It was RESOLVED that the report of the Cabinet dated . . . be approved and adopted as amended.'

Or, where the local authority has adopted the practice of using a motion to receive Cabinet reports, i.e. the procedural motion to bring a report before the council for consideration (see 7.42) the style reflecting this could be to the effect, e.g:

'00 Report of the Cabinet

Moved (or proposed) by Councillor Jones, Seconded by Councillor Robinson; and Resolved: That the report of the Cabinet of . . . be received. Amendment Moved (or proposed) by Councillor Smith, Seconded by Councillor Brown: That para.A (Corporate Plan) be referred back to the Cabinet for reconsideration.

After debate,

Amendment put to the vote and declared not carried. Further amendment Moved (or proposed) by Councillor White, Seconded by Councillor Black: That para.A (Corporate Plan) be approved in principle only and that the Cabinet be instructed to report further on the detailed implementation of the corporate plan.

After debate,

Amendment put to the vote and declared carried.

Resolved: That the report of the Cabinet of . . . be approved and adopted as amended.'

8.10 There could be almost endless variations in this style. However, there are some basic principles to be followed in all minuting, particularly the formal minuting of meetings of the full council, and the recording of key decisions of the executives. The final resolution should be clear and ideally capable of being understood without extensive cross-referencing because the more this is necessary the greater the chance of some future researcher being misled or confused, and the more pieces of paper and research that has to be carried out if a public request is made for a copy. Where a number of amendments have been carried relating to the same motion it is helpful to set out in full the final substantive motion, e.g. as in the example in 8.9. Also, it is important that there is consistency within each authority so as to avoid the use of different phrases meaning the same thing, i.e. there should be an agreed standardisation of layout and commonly occurring phrases and terms to avoid any ambiguity. **8.11** There are occasions, i.e. whenever there is a division or a request for a recorded vote, when the names of members present must be recorded to show how each voted – for or against – or abstained from voting. No particular form of minute is required, so long as the manner in which each member voted or abstained from voting is clearly recorded.

Minuting committee reports

8.12 Each local authority has its own practice in the way in which cabinet reports

8. Council minutes

submitted to the full council are incorporated in the council minutes and the debate recorded. Some authorities reprint in council minutes the whole of the text of each cabinet report; others incorporate the reports by reference; a minority adopt in addition some expedient way of using the council agenda as a reference document for day-to-day use (see 8.22).

8.13 The practice most widely adopted appears to be for cabinet reports to be incorporated by reference. For example, the adoption of a cabinet report will be minuted in this manner (and the report itself will have to be sought elsewhere by those who do not have access to the signed minutes):

'Moved by Councillor Jones, Seconded by Councillor Robinson; and Resolved: That the report of the Policy Committee of . . . (set out [specify where]) be approved and adopted.'

Generally the particular report will be identifiable by reference to the council meeting agenda. Where the recommendation in a report is amended or there is debate to be recorded the minuting will be as indicated above in 8.10.

8.14 An example of another kind of practice is where each cabinet report is reprinted within the council minutes.

Minuting question time

8.15 Some local authorities minute verbatim the questions that are asked at council meetings (see 7.41 et seq.), and the answers provided by cabinet members. Where this practice is adopted then both question and answer should be recorded. Some authorities merely record the question with a note to the effect that the portfolio holder/cabinet member replied without specifying the terms of the answer.

Indexing

8.16 What is said later in Chapter 12 about indexing committee minutes applies substantially to the indexing of council minutes.

Authorising the common seal

General considerations

8.17 Because the use of the local authority's common seal on a deed binds the authority (and provides unimpeachable authenticity to any other document to which it is affixed[4]), the seal must be kept in safe custody and used only in pursuance of a resolution of the council or cabinet, or an officer to whom the council has delegated its power in that respect. The old model standing orders deal with both matters.

Safe custody

8.18 The old model standing order provided that the common seal of the council would be kept in a safe place in the custody of the town clerk/clerk of the council and would be secured by two different locks, the keys of which shall be kept respectively by the mayor/chairman and the town clerk/clerk of the council (provided that the mayor/chairman may entrust his key temporarily to another member of the council, and the town clerk/clerk of the council may entrust his key temporarily to any deputy appointed by the council).

In practice now, it is more likely that the common seal will only have one lock on it, if any, and that the keys are kept by officers.

Sealing of documents

8.19 Old model standing order no. 24 is to this effect:

> '1 The common seal of the council shall not be affixed to any document unless the sealing has been authorised by a resolution of the council or of a committee to which the council have delegated their powers in this behalf, but a resolution of the council (or of a committee where that committee has the power) authorising the acceptance of any tender, the purchase, sale, letting, or taking of any property, the issue of any stock, the presentation of any petition, memorial, or address, the making of any rate or contract, or the doing of any other thing, shall be a sufficient authority for sealing any document necessary to give effect to the resolution.
> 2 The seal shall be attested by the following persons present at the sealing, viz., mayor or deputy mayor/chairman or vice-chairman of the council or other member of the council, and the town clerk/clerk or deputy town clerk/ deputy clerk of the council, and an entry of every sealing of a document shall be made and consecutively numbered in a book kept for the purpose and shall be signed by a person who has attested the seal.'

8.20 In practice, it is now more likely that the solicitor to the council has the authority to affix and attest the common seal, together with the chief executive and other chief officers. Those authorities that still provide that the mayor or chairman will attest the seal may find practical difficulties in getting documents sealed on a regular basis.

Date of sealing operative date of document

8.21 A resolution to make, for example, a compulsory purchase order that must be sealed does not itself 'make' the order: the resolution is no more than an expression of intention or instruction to those who have the duty of affixing the seal. A local authority can, subject to exceptions not here relevant, act only by seal for certain purposes, e.g. a compulsory purchase order is not 'made' until sealed (see 1.51).

8. Council minutes

Council minutes as reference documents

8.22 Where the council minutes set out in full the cabinet reports before the full council, this single document (the minutes for a particular meeting) can be referred to in the confident knowledge that the minutes are wholly self-contained. Where, as in the majority of cases, the cabinet reports are not reprinted direct into the minutes, a reader must necessarily look at two documents: the council minutes and, the cabinet reports referred to; and although this may not be an onerous task it is often not difficult to misread or misunderstand the reasons for a decision in the council minutes.

Authentication of minutes

Confirmation

8.23 Council minutes, when written up, and entered in the minute book, are submitted for confirmation to the next succeeding meeting. This means that minutes of the full council, whether of an annual or extraordinary meeting, are properly submitted at the next meeting of the council whatever its character, i.e. the minutes of, say, an annual meeting do not have to wait for confirmation until the next annual meeting.

8.24 There is a mandatory standing order as regards the minutes of an extraordinary meeting to this effect:

> 'Where in relation to any meeting of the full council the next such meeting is a meeting called under paragraph 3 (extraordinary meetings) of Schedule 12 to the Local Government Act 1972, the next following meeting of the authority (being a meeting called otherwise than under that paragraph) shall be treated as a suitable meeting for the purposes of paragraphs 41(1) and (2) (signing of minutes) of that schedule.'

8.25 The term confirmation is misleading. Minutes do not require confirmation in the ordinary sense of that word: the decisions taken at a meeting are of immediate effect (but see 1.51 as to decisions of the executive) and do not depend upon their first being written up and subsequently approved and signed at the next succeeding meeting. The minutes are merely a record of what has already actually taken place but their confirmation – in the manner referred to below – has important legal consequences.

8.26 The act of confirmation does not require the minutes to be read nor need a copy have been circulated beforehand to members. Minutes of the previous council meeting are nevertheless often circulated with the summons and agenda. If the unsigned minutes are circulated it makes it difficult for any person to challenge their accuracy after confirmation. If they are not circulated the minute book should be kept available for inspection by any member who may wish to check the minutes before agreeing to their confirmation and, in any case, the minute book should be laid on the table for, say, half an hour before commencement of the meeting at which the minutes are to be confirmed.

8.27 The only question that can properly arise on the confirmation of minutes is that of their accuracy. Old model standing order no. 9(2), for example, provides that:

> 'No discussion shall take place upon the minutes, except upon their accuracy, and any question of their accuracy shall be raised by motion. If no such question is raised, or if it is raised then as soon as it has been disposed of, the mayor/chairman shall sign the minutes.'

The occasion is not one for a resumption of debate on items recorded in the minutes (see *Mawley* v. *Barber* (1803) and *R.* v. *Mayor of York* (1853)), nor, strictly, should the minutes be used as the basis for reporting subsequent action. The inclusion on an agenda of an item to the effect: '00. Matters arising on the minutes', is bad practice and of doubtful legality.[5] If any item dealt with at a previous meeting needs to be discussed further a separate item should appear on the agenda.

8.28 Old model standing order no.9 provides that:

> 'The mayor/chairman shall put the question that the minutes of the council held on the . . . day of . . . be approved as a correct record.'

This is a convenient arrangement. The motion to confirm the minutes of the previous meeting can be moved and seconded by members who were not present at that meeting although it is preferable that those who were not present should abstain from voting and comment on the motion. Ordinarily, of course, there will be no formal motion: the chairman, whether or not acting in pursuance of a standing order on the lines of old model standing order no.9, will merely ask whether he may sign the minutes as a correct record and will proceed to place his signature in the minute book upon murmurs of assent. Where, however, a member does vote in favour of the signing of the minutes he votes not for the decisions recorded but only for the accuracy of the record and he does not incur any liability or responsibility for the proceedings at such a meeting if he was not present at such meeting (*Re Lands Allotment Co.* (1894)).

8.29 The chairman who signs the minutes does so in pursuance of the requirement that he must do so and he need not have been present at the meeting of which the minutes are a record. If, however, for any reason, e.g. that the chairman suspects an inaccuracy in the minutes but has no support for this contention, and refuses to sign the minutes, the proper course is to record the circumstances by a minute to this effect:

8. Council minutes

'00 Minutes
The minutes of the meeting of . . . were confirmed as a correct record of the proceedings at that meeting but the chairman refused to sign them on the grounds that he believed them to be inaccurate in the following particular . . . but his view was not upheld by the council/ committee /subcommittee.'

Evidence without further proof

8.30 Minutes that have been drawn up and entered in the minute book and signed at the same or next following meeting by the person presiding, i.e. at the meeting at which confirmation takes place, are prima facie good evidence of the proceedings: the law prescribes that any minute purporting to be so signed 'shall be received in evidence without further proof'.[6] It is a common law rule that where minutes have been properly kept they shall be admissible as evidence. The effect of the provisions in the LGA 1972 Sch.12 para.41(1) and LGA 2000 s.22 is that the minutes are inadmissible unless signed. Furthermore, until the contrary is proved, under LGA 1972 Sch.12 para.41(3), the meeting is deemed to have been duly convened and held and all the members present are deemed to have been duly qualified. There is no corresponding provision for meetings of the executive.

8.31 Under the LG (Miscellaneous Provisions) Act 1976 s.41 a document that purports to be a copy of: (i) a resolution, order or report of a local authority or its committee or subcommittees; or (ii) the minutes thereof, and bears a certificate purporting to be signed by the proper officer or someone authorised by the proper officer or the council and stating that the resolution was passed or the order or report was made by the Council (or its committees or subcommittees), is evidence in any proceedings of the matters stated in the certificate and of the terms of the resolution, order, report or minute in question.

The Secretary of State under LGA 2000 s.22 made regulations to modify s.41 LG(MP) Act 1976. The Local Authorities (Executive and Alternative Arrangements) (Modifications of Enactments and Other Provisions) (England) Order 2001) SI 2001/ 2237 brought in similar provisions to the above for executive decisions, but these only refer to copies of decisions made, and the certificate can only be made by the proper officer or another authorised by him, or someone authorised under the LGA 2000.

The effect of the above is that if an officer of the local authority goes into a witness box in court and produces the relevant certified minutes, there is no need to prove that the minutes were actually signed at the meeting or that the signature on them is actually the signature of the person presiding.[7] These provisions do not, however, mean that a signed minute is unchallengeable proof of the events recorded in the minutes. It is open to anyone who wishes to do so, for good reason, to try to prove in court that the minutes are not a true record of what took place at the meeting. But the onus of proof to the contrary is on the person challenging the signed minute.[8]

8.32 The case of *R. v. South Somerset District Council ex parte DJB (Group) Ltd* (1989) shows that the court will not lightly set aside properly authenticated minutes. The company had contended that the minutes of the council's policy and resources committee did not reflect what had actually happened at a meeting and that either the item of business in which it, the company, was interested was not really discussed or the discussion was merely by way of simply rubber-stamping an earlier decision taken between officers and the committee chairman without applying any, or any proper, thought to the item. The court refused to accept that there was anything irregular about the minutes. Saville J said:

> 'The allegations in respect of these minutes are of an extremely serious nature. They necessarily involve the assertion that those responsible for drawing them up and those who support them as an accurate account of what transpired have deliberately set out to adopt a course of dishonest conduct designed to deceive those who read the minutes without full notice or knowledge of what in fact transpired.'

The judge went on to refer to a minute of the next meeting of the committee recording that the minutes of the previous meeting had been approved as a correct record and signed by the chairman. The challenge to the authenticity of the minute, said the judge, necessarily involves the proposition that those present at this later meeting and who had been present at the earlier meeting (and there was a considerable number) were themselves either in the conspiracy to produce wholly inaccurate minutes for the purpose of deception or, at the lowest, had wholly failed in their duty to satisfy themselves that the minutes were an accurate record.

South Somerset is of interest for another reason. In the course of the judgment, the court commented on the principle that observations made by individual councillors in debate cannot be accepted necessarily as the grounds on which the collective decision was taken (see 12.33).

Alteration of minutes

8.33 Once the minutes have been confirmed they must not be altered in any circumstances whatsoever.[9] However, if when a meeting is being asked to confirm the minutes of the preceding meeting and it is agreed – either on a member's representation or that of the chairman – that there is an inaccuracy that needs to be corrected, it is advisable for the fact to be duly noted in the minute recording the signing of the minutes, e.g.:

> 'Resolved: That the minutes of the meeting of . . . were approved and signed by the chairman subject to correction of . . .'

If an inaccuracy is discovered after the minutes have been signed then, again, the inaccuracy should be corrected by resolution, e.g.:

8. Council minutes

'Resolved: That the minutes of the meeting on . . ., approved and signed by the chairman at the meeting on . . . be amended in the following respect to correct an inaccuracy subsequently discovered..

The particular minute challenged and agreed to be inaccurate should never be altered although a pencilled note could properly be made against the disputed minute by the proper officer indicating its subsequent correction.

Inspection of minutes

Statutory provisions

8.34 The public right of inspection of council minutes depends on the type of local authority and the date of the council meeting. Prior to the coming into force of the LG(AI)A 1985 on 1st April 1986, the minutes of the proceedings of every local authority full Council meetings were required to be open to inspection by any local government elector for the area and any such elector was entitled to take a copy or extract from the minutes. That is still the position as regards the minutes of parish and community councils. Now, by virtue of the 1985 Act, the minutes of the council meetings of principal councils are open to inspection by the public generally, but strictly for a period of six years, beginning with the date of the meeting. The position is substantially the same as regards the committee and subcommittee minutes of principal councils

The minutes of the executive are also open to inspection by the public generally, under the regulations made under the Local Government Act 2000 (s.22). SI 2000/3272 (Local Authorities (Executive Arrangements) (Access to Information) (England) Regulations 2000) reg.5 provides that the minutes of an executive decision shall be made available for inspection by members of the public as soon as is reasonably practicable, at the offices of the local authority. Unlike the provisions under the LGA 1972, there is no time limit specified.

Who may inspect

8.35 The simplification of the law by extending the right of inspection of council minutes of principal councils to the public and not just electors alone has eliminated some of the problems that had arisen in the past over who may in fact exercise the right to inspect. Nevertheless, as regards the council minutes of a local authority meeting held prior to 1st April 1986 (and still as regards those of parish and community councils and a parish meeting), the right of inspection vests strictly only in electors, although the right can be exercised through an agent: see *R. v. Gloucestershire County Council* (1936). However, see Chapter 3 for the provisions on Freedom of Information.

8.36 A member of every local authority has always possessed, as a councillor, a common law right to production of documents, including council minutes, which he needs to see to carry out his council duties, but not for any other purpose (see *R.* v. *Wimbledon UDC* (1897) and *Stevens* v. *Berwick-upon-Tweed Corporation* (1835)), although as there is now a public right of inspection the motive of the person inspecting must now be immaterial.

8.37 Strictly speaking, the officer who has custody of the minutes of a parish or community council or parish or community meeting ought to check upon a persons credentials before making the minute book available for inspection. This may rarely be done in practice either because the council or the meeting makes its minutes freely available (e.g. by depositing copies in public libraries in the area) or because it decides that anyone may inspect as a matter of policy.

What may be inspected

8.38 The distinction between council minutes and committee and subcommittee and executive minutes is, for the purposes of inspection, no longer as important as it was prior to the LG(AI)A 1985 because, at least in the case of principal councils, all must equally be available for public inspection. In the case, however, of the minutes of parish and community councils and of all other council minutes of meetings prior to 1st April 1986, the minutes that must be open to inspection by electors include the minutes of a committee if submitted to the council for approval (*Williams* v. *Manchester Corporation* (1897)).[10] Such committee minutes are inseparable from the council minutes because, it has been held, 'one could not understand the approval without seeing the recommendations'.

8.39 The law provides that after meetings of the full council, or committees and subcommittees, the following documents must be open to public inspection at the offices of the council until the expiration of a period of six years beginning with the date of the meeting:[11]

- the minutes, or a copy of the minutes,[12] of the meeting excluding so much of the minutes of proceedings during which the meeting was not open to the public as discloses exempt information;
- where applicable, a summary of the whole or part of the proceedings;
- a copy of the agenda for the meeting;[13] and
- a copy of so much of any report for the meeting as relates to any item during which the meeting was open to the public.

The summary must be prepared by the proper officer where, as a result of excluding exempt minutes, the document open to inspection does not provide the public 'with a reasonably fair and coherent report' of the whole or part of the proceedings without disclosing any exempt information.

However, in relation to reports made under s.8 of the Audit Commission Act 1998, Part VA of the 1972 Act has effect in relation to the report as if s.100C(1)(d) of that Act (public access to copies of reports for six years after meeting) were not limited to so much of the report as relates to an item during which the meeting was open to the public.

8. Council minutes

Background papers

8.40 In addition, if and so long as copies of the whole or part of a report for a meeting of a principal council are required to be open to inspection by members of the public there must be open to inspection at the council's offices for up to four years afterwards beginning with the date of the meeting:

- copies of a list,[14] compiled by the proper officer, of the background papers for the report or the part of the report; and
- at least one copy of each of the documents included in that list. However, there is no obligation to include any document that discloses exempt information or 'any document that, if open to inspection, would disclose confidential information in breach of the obligation of confidence. A member of the public cannot demand the instant production of the papers: it will be sufficient to produce them on request at a suitable time and place (see 8.44); a clause in the original bill enabling the public to have immediate and largely unrestricted access was modified.

8.41 Background papers are defined as those documents relating to the subject matter of the report:

- disclose any facts or matters on which, in the opinion of the proper officer, the report or an important part of the report is based;
- have, in his opinion, been relied on to a material extent in preparing the report;[15]

but do not include any published works.[16]

8.42 There are several questions that arise as a result of the above. Why, for example, was six years fixed as the period for inspection of minutes, agenda and reports when, at least in the case of council minutes, a local authority would ordinarily allow inspection virtually in perpetuity? Does it mean that inspection could be refused to a member of the public who wished to see minutes and other supporting papers more than six years old? Why the difference between the six years for minutes, agenda and reports and four years only for background papers? It may be that s.9 of the Limitation Act 1980 was in mind when a claim must be brought within six years. One kind of document likely to be caught by these provisions is a draft report, e.g. one prepared by officers and changed by the portfolio holder, with perhaps even recommendations altered. Such a report would almost certainly be caught by the statutory provisions, making it open to public inspection. Officers should be aware of this and consider destroying drafts once a final version has been settled.

8.43 Committee clerks' notes taken at a meeting, and on which the minutes are subsequently drafted, do not fall within the documents that must be made available for inspection; they are clearly not minutes, nor are they background papers. It is, however, good practice in any case (see 12.53), to destroy notes taken at a meeting as soon as the relevant minutes have been approved and signed. Otherwise they are of course subject to the provisions of the FOIA.

Council meetings

When minutes may be inspected

8.44 Documents, including minutes, open to public inspection, must be made available at all reasonable hours and:

- in the case of background papers, upon payment of such reasonable fee as may be required for the facility; and
- in any other case, i.e. including minutes, without payment.

Where a document is open to inspection then any person may, subject to what is said below as to copyright:

- make copies of or extracts from the document; or
- require the person having custody of the document to supply a photocopy of or extracts from the document; upon payment of such reasonable fee as may be required for the facility.

Copyright

8.45 There is, however, protection for copyright. Nothing above requires or authorises the doing of anything that infringes the copyright in any work except that, where the owner of the copyright is a principal council, the above does not constitute an infringement of copyright. This means that, although members of the public may inspect copyright documents they must not be allowed to copy them; for example, deposited plans and drawings for planning and building regulations approval may not be copied without the author's consent, but the application forms and the usual sort of site plan could be. Consent to reproduce written material can be implied from the circumstances and a number of authorities have a standard form of reply to the senders of plans, etc., covered by copyright indicating that where there is an obligation to disclose it will be assumed that a waiver from copyright protection has been given. It is arguable, however, how far this would protect an authority against an action for breach of copyright. There might certainly be problems if the communication or plan had been annotated in a way that rebutted any implied consent to waiver, e.g. by marking the plan 'Confidential'.

Obstruction of the right to inspect

8.46 Anyone having custody of the documents of a principal council required to be open to public inspection, who without reasonable excuse:

- intentionally obstructs anyone exercising the right of inspection or of making a copy of or extracts from the document; or
- refuses to furnish copies to any person entitled to obtain them,

is liable on summary conviction to a fine not exceeding level 1 on the standard scale. The absence of the person having custody of the documents is no excuse for the failure to produce the documents for inspection: see *R.* v. *Andover RDC* (1913), where it was

198

8. Council minutes

said that when the clerk to a council goes away some person with authority should be left available to produce the minute book to anyone entitled to see it.

8.47 In the case of parish and community councils and parish meetings, obstruction of the right of inspection and of making a copy of or extract from documents required to be open to inspection by electors renders the person with custody of the documents liable on summary conviction to a fine not exceeding Level 1. The right to take copies is not a right to be furnished with copies (see *Russell-Walker* v. *Gimblett* (1985)).

Notes

1 Evidence was allowed to explain minutes, as distinct from resolutions, in *Westminster Corporation* v. *London and North Western Rail Co.* (1905), where a chairman of the works committee was allowed to prove that the primary object of a committee in providing certain conveniences was for sanitary purposes and not as an underground passage from one side of a street to the other, that being the point of substance in the case and one on which the recorded resolution was silent; and in *Clanricarde (Marquess)* v. *Congested Dis-tricts Board for Ireland* (1914), where the resolution was definitely ambiguous, even if – as was disputed – it amounted to a resolution at all.
2 In *Hearts of Oak Assurance Co. Ltd.* v. *James Flower & Sons* (1935), it was held that, under similar provision in the Companies Act 1929, a number of loose leaves fastened together in two covers in such a way that anyone could take a leaf out and substitute another was not 'a book' within the meaning of that Act.
3 In practice, responsibility for the safe custody of council documents will be placed upon the proper officer (LGA 1972, s.270(3)).
4 Certain documents require by law the affixing of the common seal of the authority, e.g. by-laws for good rule and government: LGA 1972, s.236(3), which however, in the case of by-laws made by a parish or community council not having a seal, permits the authentication by the hands and seals of two members of the council.
5 LGA 1972, s.100(B)(4).
6 It is a common law rule that where minutes have been properly kept they shall be admissible as evidence The effect of the provisions in the LGA 1972, Sch.12, para.41(1)(2), is that the minutes are inadmissible unless signed as prescribed.
7 Under the LG(MP)A 1976, s.41, a document which (a) purports to be a copy of (i) a resolution, order or report of a local authority or precursor of a local authority, or a committee or sub-committee thereof, *or* (ii) the minutes of the proceedings at a meeting of a local authority or precursor of a local authority or a committee or sub-committee thereof, *and* (b) bears a certificate purporting to be signed by the proper officer or some-one authorised on that behalf by himself or the authority and stating that the resolution was passed or the order or report was made by the authority or precursor or committee or sub-committee thereof on a date specified in accordance with para.41 of Sch.12 to the LGA 1972 or the corresponding earlier provisions, is evidence in any proceedings of the matters stated in the certificate and of the terms of the resolution, order, report or minute in question.
8 See *Re Indian Zoedone Co.* (1884). In this case the chairman made an entry in the minute book that a resolution had been confirmed and the court declined, in the absence of evidence that votes were improperly disallowed, to question the decision of the chairman.
9 *Re Cawley & Co.* (1889). In this case the directors at a board meeting passed a resolution making a call on shares, but omitted to state the date of payment. After the minutes had been signed the secretary repaired the omission by adding a date. Esher MR said: 'I trust I shall never again see or hear of the secretary of a company, whether under superior direction or otherwise, altering minutes of meetings, either by striking out anything or adding anything'.
10 Even though in s.228(1) of the LGA 1972, as originally enacted, the term *local authority*

minutes, rather than *council* minutes, was used, the minutes of a committee exercising delegated powers were not open to inspection notwithstanding that the decisions of the committee had in all respects the force and validity of decisions of the local authority itself: *Wilson* v. *Evans* (1962).

11 LGA 1972, s.100C, added by LG(AI)A 1985.

12 It may be convenient ordinarily to make a copy available so as to make it easier not to disclose excluded minutes.

13 Except for the statutory requirement to preserve a copy of the agenda it would be common practice, as in the past, to dispose of the agenda because it has no practical or legal significance after a meeting. Presumably the obligation to preserve the agenda or a copy of it for inspection is to enable a member of the public to check that an item of business was or was not transacted and if it was that the item was duly minuted. See 12.19.

14 The fact that a list must be prepared with copies of the documents on the list means that, conveniently, the originals can be retained in the appropriate files.

15 LGA 1972, s.100D(5). It is probable that the proper officer need not list, or otherwise disclose, papers which have been looked at and rejected as not relevant to the issue reported upon.

16 There is no definition of published works, but presumably the term would cover publications of HMSO and therefore most Government departmental circulars.

Part 3
Committee Practice

Chapter 9

The committee system

Introduction

9.1 As indicated earlier in Chapter 1, the framework of decision-making for the majority of principal councils (county/metropolitan/unitary/district) has undergone drastic changes in recent years with the introduction of the executive/scrutiny split. Notwithstanding the fact that the executive models have their own specific legal regime, the essential elements of the traditional committee system are still very much alive in terms of practice and procedure in the executive, overview and scrutiny, and the regulatory committees.

What is a committee?

Importance of definition

9.2 There is no statutory definition of a committee for purposes of local government, nor of a subcommittee for that matter. Yet it can be important to be able to say what is a committee or subcommittee and what is not. For example, committee and sub-committee meetings, and meetings of an authority's executive under the LGA 2000 when it is considering certain matters (see 3.4), are required to be open to the public, which is not the case of meetings that are not meetings of committees or sub-committees (see 9.3).

9.3 According to the *Concise Oxford Dictionary*, a committee is 'a body of persons appointed for a special function by, and normally out of, a normally larger body'; and in *Chambers Twentieth Century Dictionary* it is defined as 'a portion selected from a more numerous body, or the whole body, to which some special business is committed'. But these definitions are not satisfactory for local government purposes, although it is interesting that they imply a plurality of persons (see 9.4). There are groupings of councillors that might seem to satisfy the dictionary definitions of a committee but which are not local authority committees in a statutory or even common law sense. A working party composed both of councillors and officers is not a committee or a subcommittee because the inclusion of officers within its constitution takes it out of the definition of a committee or subcommittee (see 9.6). It cannot have functions delegated to it and does not need to reach decisions on the basis of a majority of those present and voting. For somewhat similar reasons, so-called committees for consultative purposes (e.g. a joint staff committee or a committee for health and safety purposes) are not local authority committees; and there are within local government committees of a special character that fall outside the generality of committees within the terms of the LGA 1972 (see Chapter 13).

Plurality of membership

9.4 Although delegation to an elected mayor or individual councillor on the executive is authorised under the LGA 2000, for general local government purposes a committee or subcommittee must comprise a plurality of persons. There cannot be a committee (or a subcommittee) consisting only of one person, any more than there could conceivably be a meeting of one person alone (see 1.9). In *R*. v. *Secretary of State for the Environment ex parte Hillingdon London Borough Council* (1986), referred to earlier in connection with the practice of committee chairman's action (see 4.81), the local authority had argued unsuccessfully that it could delegate functions to a committee chairman if it had constituted that single councillor as a committee of one person. The court would have none of it. Having dismissed the argument that there could be delegation to an individual councillor under s.101 of the LGA 1972, Woolf J went on to rule that there could not be a committee of one member alone:

'The 1972 Act . . . must, in my view, be taken to use the word "committee" in the sense that that word is now used [i.e. in ordinary parlance] and if this approach to the interpretation of the section [i.e. s.101] is correct, then the only permissible interpretation is one which involves rejecting the concept of a committee of one . . . had it been the intention that the terms "committee" and "subcommittee" in s.101(1) should include a committee or subcommittee of one, it is considered that this would expressly have been provided for.'

9.5 It is indeed clear that the LGA 1972 supports plurality of membership in, for example, Sch.12, para.39, where it lays down the cardinal principle that all questions coming before the local authority are to be decided by a majority of members present and voting. It would be impossible, of course, to secure a majority in a committee of one. What has been said earlier (see 1.9. and *R*. v. *Swansea City Council ex parte Elitstone Ltd* (1993)) about the minimum number of persons who may constitute a meeting for local government purposes applies equally to the minimum number of persons who may constitute a committee or subcommittee. Accordingly, although the LGA 2000 allows delegation to an individual councillor in specific executive arrangements, the basic 1972 Act position still applies in all other instances of decision-making.

Definition for local government purposes

9.6 It is possible, by collecting together the several references to committees in the relevant statutes, to build up a definition of a committee or subcommittee for purposes of local government. In this way, it can be said that a local authority committee or subcommittee is a body that the council in the case of a committee, or a committee in the case of a the subcommittee, has formally constituted by resolution to act as a unit forming part of the hierarchy of legal power, and:

- has functions of the local authority referred or delegated to it (LGA 1972, s.101);
- has a fixed and not a fluctuating membership (LGA 1972, s.102(2);
- may include persons who are not councillors (s.102(3) and LG&HA 1989, s.13);
- has its proceedings regulated by the local authority's standing orders and/or Sch.12 of the 1972 Act;
- must admit the public and the press to all or part of its meetings;
- cannot wholly comprise or include paid officers of the council;[1]
- must comprise at least two and preferably three members (on the basis that there can be no fewer number to constitute a meeting: see 1.8);
- has a limited term of office and prescribed area of authority (LGA 1972, s.102(2));
- can, in the case of a committee, delegate its functions to a subcommittee (which it alone can appoint) or, equally with a subcommittee, to an officer unless the terms of its appointment forbid it (LGA 1972, s.101);
- must reach decisions by a majority of members present and voting in prescribed manner (LGA 1972, Sch.12, para.39);
- must keep formal minutes of its proceedings in prescribed manner (LGA 1972, Sch.12, para.41);
- will ordinarily be required to report its decisions direct to the council in the case of a committee and to a committee in the case of a subcommittee and not through any intermediary (as standing orders will generally provide); and
- may exclude from participation in the business of its meetings any person, including councillors (save for the exercise of their common law right to be present on the basis of a 'need to know': see 4.6), who is not among the number of members of the committee appointed by the council, or in the case of a subcommittee, appointed by the committee.

9.7 There are, however, committees that fall outside this definition and are not therefore local authority committees under the LGA 1972. There are, for example, consultative committees set up by local authorities comprised of equal numbers of council and trade union or other employee representatives whose decisions must be reached by a majority vote of those on each side; and committees of a special category altogether: school admission appeal committees of local education authorities (see 13.68) whose powers and functions are conferred direct by statute and whose decisions are binding on the local authority.

Committee structure

General principles

9.8 Committees are not just separate groupings of councillors each operating in isolation and independently of one another: committees can have no greater powers than those conferred on them by the council and cannot themselves amend their terms of reference or shelve the business committed to them, and can never dissolve themselves. Committees are part of a unified system and have long been an integral feature of the internal organisation of local authorities in this country. The committee system, it has been said, is engrained in English life and democratic control of local government services would, in the past, have been thought impracticable without it. In addition, the law has obliged local authorities from earliest times to set up particular committees for the discharge of specific functions. The committee in English local government exists to administer, a function that a committee is peculiarly unsuited to perform. Yet this is what, traditionally, the local authority committee has attempted to do: and, against the balance of probability, has performed passably well. It has been the task of committees to administer a number of related services by exercising oversight of the chief officer and department responsible for the executive work, to contribute to policy by making recommendations to the full council for the development of existing and new services, and under delegated authority to make such decisions as may need to be made for the implementation of policy. The close alignment between committees and departments has been largely responsible for the fragmentation of internal machinery and the lack of unity in a local authority in the past. Some committees have performed a co-ordinating role – the finance and the establishment committees particularly – and, before the emergence of the concept of corporate management and the setting up of policy committees, these often succeeded in achieving an integrated approach to the authority's functions.

9.9 Because local authority committees must reach decisions in accordance with the cardinal principle referred to earlier, i.e. by a majority of members present and voting (see Chapter 1), there is no scope for minority reports from councillors who may disagree with the majority view. Their objection can be expressed only by voting against a proposition in committee and in the full assembly; and any member who feels particularly strongly about the issue can have his vote recorded in the minutes.

Flexibility

9.10 An important feature of the traditional committee system as an instrument of administration is its flexibility. New committees can be set up permanently or temporarily as need dictates. Existing committees whose tasks have been completed can be dissolved. Committees whose duties have diminished or lost their former importance may be amalgamated with others. There can, in short, be continual arrangement and rearrangement in this way to meet altered circumstances. Standing committees can be increased or reduced in membership to meet changes in the interests to be represented and the subcommittee organisation can be adjusted accordingly. Special ad hoc committees can be set up to examine and report upon particular matters of topical concern or special importance. Joint committees may be set up to deal with matters which concern more than one committee or to deliberate or act upon matters of common interest to two or more local authorities. The elasticity of the committee system can be stretched, indeed, to the extreme without the necessity of altering, amending or adapting the parent body. This is true, of course, of the committee system of any association but it is of paramount importance to the modern local authority, which has to resolve into a workable, manageable whole a complexity of related and sometimes unrelated functions, many of a highly specialised nature and all possessing individual technicalities. It is no exaggeration to

9. The committee system

say that the resilience of the committee system in local government has largely enabled local authorities to absorb more and more tasks, though not always very successfully.

9.11 There are necessarily physical limitations to this flexibility. The size of membership of the authority and to a less extent its resources in revenue and manpower are limiting factors, not of the quality of flexibility but of the stretch of elasticity. Unless there is a limit to the number of committees set up there will not only be disintegration but also too heavy a call on members' time, and too burdensome a responsibility for imaginative or sustained good work and for the creation of that quasi-specialisation that inevitably emerges from committee experience. For the present it need only be pointed out that the flexibility of the system can be misused either by deploying available resources beyond a certain point or, less common, by not making sufficient use of it. The problems of secretarial work closely bound up with all this will be considered later.

Durability of the system

9.12 In recent years particularly, the disadvantages of the committee system have been thought to outweigh the advantages. In its consultation paper *Modernising Local Government: In Touch with the People*, the government considered the traditional committee structure of local government to be 'inefficient and opaque'. Accordingly, to increase the efficiency, transparency and accountability of local authorities, the LGA 2000 introduced new executive arrangements (see 1.62 et seq.). Nevertheless, notwithstanding the particular procedural rules relating to meetings of the executive, the tripartite split of the executive/scrutiny/regulatory bodies set out in the LGA 2000 still offers recognisable variants of the committee system and emphasises its flexibility and durability.

Legal basis

9.13 It needs to be said at this juncture that at common law and by statute the power of a local authority to appoint committees to discharge its functions is well recognised. There are wide powers in the LGA 1972 enabling an authority to appoint committees (recognising, too, that the authority is compelled for certain functions to appoint specific committees) and to refer and to delegate functions to them.

9.14 The courts have placed considerable credence on the effectiveness of committees, even where powers have not been expressly delegated. Thus it has been held that action taken by an officer on the direction of a committee before the committee's act was confirmed by the council effectively ratified the officer's action. In *Firth* v. *Staines* (1897), a health committee had directed a sanitary inspector to serve notice on an owner to abate a nuisance and after the failure of the owner to comply with it laid an information against him and a summons was issued. After the issue of the summons, the committee's acts were confirmed. The court held, applying the principles of the doctrine of ratification, that the acts of the committee became valid as from the time when they were done. In *Firth* v. *Staines*, however, the committee had had specific authority to act subject to subsequent ratification by the vestry: an unusual arrangement. Where there is express delegation there is, of course, no requirement upon the council to confirm or ratify or approve what has been done under delegated powers. Thus an act of the committee in such circumstances is the act of the local authority and what the committee does binds the council.

9.15 It is thus evident that a local authority's committee system is regulated by law, structure and procedure. It must be framed to meet the authority's objectives: the system is not an end in itself but an administrative instrument through which the authority can effectively, efficiently, lawfully and democratically discharge its several functions.

Structural considerations

9.16 The committee system (including the executive arrangements under the LGA 2000) must be so arranged that it contributes to the effective and efficient management of the local authority's affairs. It must ensure that ultimate direction and control lie with councillors; it must enable them to review progress and the performance of the services provided for the community; and it must assist in the identification of the authority's objectives and the formulation of plans to achieve those objectives.

9.17 If it is to meet these criteria, there should be no more standing committees (including overview and scrutiny committees) than are necessary, the membership of the committees should be small, their terms of reference should be clearly specified, and their relationship to the rest of the decision-making structure clearly defined. Each committee should be concerned with matters that can only be dealt with at member level, i.e. there should ordinarily be no involvement in matters of day-to-day administration that can properly be left in the hands of officers.

Co-ordination

9.18 Maud[2] considered the absence of any kind of managing body within the organisation as one of the fundamental weaknesses of the committee system in English local government. Maud recognised that committees had been accepted axiomatically as 'practically essential as a means of conducting business' where executive authority is 'entrusted to a large body'; and he saw the committee system as 'a contrivance for decentralising the various functions of the council and for creating a number of microcosms of it to meet problems as they arise; it is not a means of establishing responsibilities of individual members or groups of members.'

9.19 This 'disunity in the whole' persuaded Maud to draw up the outline of a management structure based on the following principles:

- effective and efficient management under the direction and control of the members;
- clear leadership and responsibility among both members and officers;
- an organisation that presents to the public an intelligible system of government; and
- responsiveness to the needs of the public.

9. The committee system

Maud felt that the existing committee system made it difficult to identify major issues and to isolate them from routine matters. It considered it necessary to establish more clearly the functions and responsibility of members and officers. To remedy these defects, Maud recommended the establishment of a management board, an idea that had little support at the time although it prepared the way for Bains's policy committee and the same reasoning led to the executive arrangements set out in the LGA 2000.

9.20 Not only is it necessary to co-ordinate executive functions, but it is also necessary to co-ordinate the exercise of the overview and scrutiny function, particularly where those committees are cross-cutting and cover a number of service areas and departmental responsibilities. To that end, a number of authorities have formed an Overview and Scrutiny Management Board to co-ordinate the work programmes and activities of the overview and scrutiny committees and often the membership of that board is made up of the chairs of those committees.

Types of committees

Broad classification

9.21 There are several ways of classifying committees. The broadest classification is between committees with power only to consider and report upon matters within their terms of reference and those with delegated powers to make the final decision on all or some of the matters within their terms of reference. A committee's terms of reference are its remit: they specify, precisely or broadly (preferably always the former), the matters with which the committee is concerned; and they may go further and specify the delegated powers of the committee on matters within the terms of reference. It is crucial that the council is clear exactly what powers it wishes to delegate and that the members of the committee are clear exactly what they have the power to decide. So far as the remit of a committee is concerned, it can be formed to deal with specific programme areas, or can cover more than one service or programme area. The advice at para. 3.21 of Chapter 3 of *Local Government Act 2000: Guidance to English Local Authorities* in relation to overview and scrutiny committees is that:

'Overview and scrutiny committees should take a cross-cutting rather than a narrow service-based view of the conduct of the local authority's business and therefore the aim should be for local authorities to have, at any given point in time, a relatively small number of such committees.'

Statutory and discretionary committees

9.22 Committees may be statutory or discretionary, i.e. there are committees that a local authority is compelled to set up by express statutory enactment, and others that it is not bound to set up but may do so if it wishes. Committees set up year after year are often referred to as standing committees.

Committee practice

Statutory committees

9.23 There are a number of statutory committees that must be established by a local authority, such as a Standards Committee and a Licensing Committee. For those authorities operating executive arrangements, it is also a statutory requirement under s.21 of the LGA 2000 to appoint one or more overview and scrutiny committees. Other statutory committees have become fewer in number over the years. The requirement to set up an education committee was removed by the Education Act 1993, and the Police and Magistrates' Courts Act 1994, Sch.9 saw the end of the local authority police committees. So far as a Social Services Committee is concerned, s.102 of the LGA 2000 provides that an authority operating executive arrangements is no longer required to have a social services committee to discharge social services functions as these will be the responsibility of the executive.

9.24 The LGA 1972, s.101(8), provides that any enactment (except those relating to the statutory committees listed in s.101(9)) that contains provisions empowering or requiring local authorities singly, or in collaboration with other authorities, to establish committees, including joint committees, for any purpose, or enabling a minister to make an instrument to such effect, shall, to the extent that it makes such provision, cease to have effect. This blanket provision means that any statutory provision (other than, as just indicated, the statutory committees continued in operation by the 1972 Act) in force prior to the coming into effect of the 1972 Act need not be followed.

Overview and scrutiny committee

9.25 As stated earlier, it is a statutory requirement for those authorities operating executive arrangements to appoint one or more overview and scrutiny committees. These committees should be cross-cutting and few in number. So far as membership of those committees is concerned, it may include anyone who is not a member of the local authority but they are not entitled to vote, with the exception of church and parent governor representatives on the committee dealing with education matters who are allowed to vote on those issues.

9.26 The LGA 2000 specifically provides in s.21(11) that an overview and scrutiny committee is to be treated as a committee or subcommittee of a principal council for the purposes of the LGA 1972 and it is to be politically balanced. As said in para. 1.70, the LGA 2000 gives overview and scrutiny committees a very specific remit to review or scrutinise decisions taken by the executive or any other part of the council, and make reports to the council or to the executive. They can also report on any matters that affect the authority's area or its inhabitants. Their role includes developing and reviewing policy and holding the executive to account. The committee may require executive members and officers to attend before it to answer questions and may also invite other people to attend meetings. Members and officers have a statutory duty to comply with the requirement to attend and answer questions. Interestingly, s.21(4) of the LGA 2000 prohibits an overview and scrutiny committee from discharging any functions other than those set out in s.21 of the LGA 2000.

9. The committee system

9.27 The key question is how the committee is to discharge its functions. A number of councils have produced a scrutiny 'tool kit' setting out how overview and scrutiny committees will operate. The Guidance issued by the Secretary of State makes it clear that overview and scrutiny committees should consider different approaches and formats for their meetings and it gives a number of examples of good practice, including holding time limited inquiries; have 'new style meetings' outside the town hall; and co-opt from a wide range of community and voluntary groups. An example of a new style meeting by one local authority was to set up a stall in Mothercare during a review of maternity services, which enabled the committee to benefit from the firsthand accounts of new mothers and fathers.

9.28 The new overview and scrutiny committees are still evolving, and do give a tremendous opportunity for councillors to develop and review policy, and contribute to the decision-making process by that means. In addition, they allow the executive to be held to account in a more formal way. The Centre for Public Scrutiny carried out a survey in 2004 into the operation of overview and scrutiny in local authorities. On average, an authority has four scrutiny committees supported by 1.2 full time equivalent (fte) dedicated scrutiny officers, rising to 2.9fte among county and single tier authorities. So far as the perception of overview and scrutiny is concerned, the survey indicated that whilst only 11 per cent gave scrutiny parity of esteem with the executive, 69 per cent of responses stated that scrutiny is valued by the organisation and 89 per cent agreed that scrutiny adds value to the council.

Discretionary committees

9.29 The law confers upon local authorities a general power[3] to appoint a committee (or a joint committee in the case of two or more authorities) for purposes of discharging any of their functions (except functions for which a statutory committee must be established), and to appoint area committees for the purpose of discharging functions delegated by the executive. Even without this express statutory power a local authority could conceivably set up any number of discretionary (non-statutory, or permissive) committees so long as the committees' functions were deliberative and not executive, i.e. limited to considering and reporting. However, without the express statutory power that exists, the authority would not be able to delegate to any such committee because of the maxim delegatus non potest delegare (see 9.74).

9.30 This general enabling but not unrestricted power extends to permit expressly any such discretionary committee to appoint one or more subcommittees and the authority or authorities or, in the case of a subcommittee, the appointing committee to fix the number of members, their term of office and the area (if restricted) within which the committee (or subcommittees) is (or are) to operate (LGA 1972, s.102(2)).

9.31 The restrictions upon this general enabling power are that:

- in the case of a committee for regulating and controlling the finance of the authority, the members must be members of the appointing authority or authorities or, in the case of a subcommittee, of the authority or authorities of which it is a subcommittee (see 9.36);

- in the case of other committees the members may include co-opted, i.e. non-voting persons; and
- in the case of any committee, every member who at the time of his appointment to the committee was a member of the appointing authority or one of the appointing authorities ceases to be a member of the committee when he ceases to be a member of the appointing authority or one of them.

Advisory committees

9.32 A power, first conferred by the LGA 1972, s.102(4), enables an authority either by itself or jointly with another or other authorities to appoint a committee to advise the appointing authority or authorities or executive on any matter relating to the discharge of their functions. An advisory committee may comprise members or non-members[4] of the authority or authorities, appointed for whatever term may be determined; and the committee may appoint one or more subcommittees to advise the committee. The consultative committees that authorities set up for certain personnel functions are not advisory committees under s.102(4).

Special committees

9.33 A special committee is one appointed for a short-term purpose, e.g. to deal with a specific matter that does not fall within the terms of reference of any standing committee or that otherwise is considered to merit particular attention by a committee of members, perhaps selected for their knowledge or experience. Sometimes such a committee is referred to as an ad hoc committee, for obvious reasons. The late J. H. Warren considered that a committee 'regularly appointed from time to time for recurring purposes' should be regarded as a special committee.[5]

9.34 An example of such a special committee is the selection committee appointed to recommend the personnel for standing committees, and often invested with the duty of revising standing orders and the terms of reference to standing committees.

9.35 However, if an authority's standing orders provide for the appointment of a selection committee, or a committee of this kind is in practice regularly appointed year after year, there is justification for considering it a standing committee, even though, as may be the case, the committee is constituted somewhat differently from other standing committees. A second example from Warren is, perhaps, a better one, i.e. a committee appointed by some local authorities to consider the choice of mayor.

Finance committee

9.36 Any committee set up specifically for purposes of regulating and controlling the finance of the local authority or of its area or charged with that responsibility as part of other functions must be composed solely of councillors (LGA 1972, s.102(3)). A number of authorities have formed audit committees to help ensure that the council's financial systems are systematically appraised, obtain assurance that the prevention and detection of fraud and corruption are promoted, and give confidence that the findings of internal and external audit reports are properly considered, implemented and monitored. In authorities with executive arrangements, this has often been either a subcommittee of the executive, or a function of overview and scrutiny. Increasingly, however, authorities are being encouraged to appoint an audit committee as a full committee of the Council, independent of the executive and scrutiny functions and indeed this is a specific recommendation of the CIPFA/SOLACE publication *Delivering Good Governance in Local Government* which was published in 2007.

Committees of parish meetings

9.37 A parish meeting in a parish where there is no separate parish council may set up a committee of local government electors for the parish to discharge any of the functions of the parish meeting. Express power to do this, conferred by the LGA 1972, s.108, was no doubt thought necessary because a parish meeting is not a local authority and therefore the general powers enabling local authorities to set up committees do not apply. Apart from the statutory provision there would appear to be no reason why a parish meeting should not set up a committee of electors for purposes of considering any matter of concern to the parish and reporting back to the parish meeting. Most of the statutory provisions relating to local authority committees apply also to the committees of a parish meeting (s.99).

Committees of community meetings

9.38 There is no express statutory power conferred upon a community meeting to establish a committee of local government electors for the community.

Joint committees

9.39 There are two kinds of joint committee:

- those set up by a single local authority to consider a matter which falls within the terms of reference of two or more standing committees; and
- those set up by two or more local authorities or by a combination of one or more local authorities and another body or bodies for purposes in respect of which they are jointly interested.

The first of these is dealt with below (see 9.40); the other, which is of the character of a committee for a special purpose, is examined in Chapter 13. The term 'joint committee' is also commonly used for committees of council and employee representatives but these are of an entirely different character.

9.40 A joint committee set up by a local authority will be established under its general enabling power to appoint a committee for any purpose it thinks fit. Therefore its membership, term of office, terms of reference and so on can all be determined by the council at its discretion.

Constitution of committees

Membership

9.41 A local authority has discretion over whom it appoints to serve on its committees subject, however, to prescription in respect of statutory committees (see 9.3) and, generally, to the statutory requirements as to political balance (see 9.42). Membership of committees may, with some exceptions, comprise both councillors on the one hand and non-councillors on the other who are ordinarily co-opted members, although the term non-voting members is now more usually employed in relation to co-option, even though (see 4.60) some co-opted members enjoy voting rights. According to *R. v. Brent London Borough Council ex parte Gladbaum* (1989), only the council itself has the power of appointment to and removal of members from a committee. It is a power that cannot be delegated, a decision that sits uneasily with the power over appointments to committees by political groups (see 9.53). So far as membership of any committee of the executive in those authorities operating executive arrangements is concerned, the statutory Guidance makes it clear that only members of the executive itself can be members of any committee of the executive (see Chapter 4 of the Guidance).

Appointment

9.42 Members are selected for committee membership at the council's annual meeting or as soon as practicable thereafter: indeed, there is a statutory requirement substantially to that effect where the local authority is divided into political groups and political balance is to be provided for in the membership of committees (see 9.53). This means that it is desirable to settle in advance of the council's annual meeting, so far as possible, the names of councillors who are to be nominated as members of the various committees. Formerly this was done in an informal manner, with councillors meeting collectively in private or in party groups. Just how the nominations emerged depended on local practice, but it is now common for the process to be formally co-ordinated by the political leadership of each group where the members are divided into political groups.

9.43 Each local authority will still have its own arrangements, but it may be appropriate here to set out the relevant draft standing order among those initially proposed (see 2.4) as part of a set of core standing orders to be prescribed under the LG&HA 1989, Pt.l:

> '*Appointment of committees and subcommittees*
> 00–1 Subject to sections 101 and 102 of the 1972 Act ... at their annual meeting [after each ordinary election of councillors],ᴬ the council:
>   a) shall resolve what committees shall be appointed, and what shall be the terms of reference of each of those committees, and of how many voting members each committee shall consist;
>   b) may resolve that non-voting members, assessors and advisers shall also be appointed to any such committee;

9. The committee system

c) if they resolve to make appointments under sub-paragraph (b), shall specify what number of appointments are to be made and what functions in relation to the committee each person so appointed may exercise; and

d) may resolve what limitations shall be placed on the powers of any such committee to arrange for the discharge by a subcommittee of any functions which they may discharge.

Variation:

Authorities other than county councils may omit reference to the Police Act 1964; authorities with no coastline may omit reference to the Sea Fisheries Act 1966; authorities whose area does not include part of a national park other than the Peak District or Lake District may omit reference to schedule 17 of the 1972 Act; and non-metropolitan district councils may omit reference to the enactments other than sections 101 and 102 of the 1972 Act.

2 The council may at any time amend resolutions under the previous paragraph.

3 Every committee set up under this standing order, and every subcommittee set up by such a committee, shall continue to discharge the functions committed to them until the council or committee, as the case may be, resolve otherwise.

4 Subject to section 102(5) of the 1972 Act (councillor not re-elected to cease to be a member of a committee) and paragraph (7), every person appointed as a voting member of such a committee or subcommittee and every person appointed to exercise other functions in relation to a committee shall continue as such until the appointment is terminated by the authority.

5 Whenever
   a) the council is required to review the allocation of seats on committees between political groups; or
   b) the council resolves to carry out such a review; or
   c) a committee is required to review the allocation of seats on a subcommittee between political groups; or
   d) a committee resolves to carry out such a review,
   the proper officer shall submit a report to the council or committee (as the case may be), showing what allocation of seats would, in his/her opinion, best meet the requirements of section 15(4) of the 1989 Act.

6 In the light of such a report, the council or committee, as the case may be, shall determine the allocation of seats to political groups.

7 Whenever an appointment of a voting member of a committee or subcommittee fails to be made in accordance with the wishes of a political group to whom the seat has been allocated, and whenever such an appointment fails to be terminated in accordance with such wishes, then the proper officer shall make or terminate the appointment accordingly.

Variation:

In place of the words "then the proper officer shall make or terminate the appointment accordingly" may be substituted:
"then, where membership of a committee is concerned, the [Policy and Resources Committee] or their subcommittee appointed to deal with urgent matters and, where membership of a subcommittee is concerned, the committee which

215

appointed them, or their subcommittee appointed to deal with urgent matters, shall make or terminate the appointment accordingly' or 'then the council or the committee, as the case may be, at a meeting at which the wishes of the political group are expressed, or at the next meeting after those wishes are expressed, shall make or terminate the appointment accordingly".[B]

8 Subject to any resolutions by the council under this standing order, every committee may appoint subcommittees for such purposes as they think fit, and may make arrangements for a subcommittee to discharge any of the functions of the authority which the committee may discharge.

9 The chairman and vice-chairman of the council, and the leader of the council (if any), may attend and speak [and move and second motions] (but may not vote) at a meeting of a committee or subcommittee of which they are not voting members.

10 The persons appointed to preside at the meetings of a committee and his/her deputy, may attend and speak [and move or second motions] at a meeting of any subcommittee appointed by that committee, but may not vote unless appointed as a voting member.

11 A member of the council who is not otherwise entitled to attend and speak at a committee or subcommittee shall be entitled to do so (but not to vote) at a meeting of the committee or subcommittee:

a) during the consideration of any motion of which notice has been given which he/she has moved or seconded at a meeting of the council and which has been referred to that committee or subcommittee; or

b) with the agreement of the person presiding at the meeting of the committee or subcommittee.

Variation:
Add:

"(c) during the consideration of any matter which affects his/her ward/electoral division differently from all other wards/electoral divisions."

Notes:
A The draft standing order had these two footnotes appended, i.e.

1. Authorities which are elected by thirds (metropolitan district councils and some non-metropolitan district councils) may prefer to review committee arrangements every year. They should delete the passage in square brackets. Councils which are elected in whole council elections may prefer to set up arrangements for the whole of an electoral period: they should include the passage in square brackets.

2. Section 102(1) of the 1972 Act provides that members of subcommittees are appointed by a committee. However, a council which wishes to appoint the members of subcommittees directly may do so by resolving themselves into a committee of the whole council and as such appointing all the subcommittees.

B The draft standing order had these two footnotes appended, i.e.

1. The effect of the 1989 Act is that, where a seat is allocated to a political group, the decision on which member of the council is to fill that seat rests with that political group.

9. The committee system

2. A member of the council has rights at common law (whether or not this standing order is adopted) to attend, but not speak or vote, at meetings of any committee or subcommittee where the acquisition of information in this way is necessary for his work as a councillor.'

Political balance

9.44 The requirements as to political proportionality in the membership of committees, embodied in the LG&HA 1989, have their origin in the recommendations of the Widdicombe report. The committee felt that the discretion enabling a local authority to appoint whoever it liked to its committees should be conditional upon there being an appropriate political balance in membership. It is now a statutory requirement[6] that where a relevant authority has a membership divided into different political groups (and members are to be treated as so divided when there is at least one political group in existence constituted as prescribed) then, unless there is a decision to the contrary taken with no members voting against, it must ensure that appointments to fill seats on:

- an ordinary committee or subcommittee of the authority;
- an advisory committee and any subcommittee appointed by an advisory committee; and
- a number of prescribed bodies[7] where at least three seats have to be filled by the relevant authority,

are allocated in the same proportion as that in which the council as a whole is divided. There is in that case a duty to review the representation of political groups and to determine the allocation of seats to be filled to 'the different political groups into which the members of the authority are divided' and in so doing ensure, as far as reasonably practicable, to make decisions that conform with prescribed principles. These principles are:

- that not all the seats are allocated to the same political group;
- that a political group with an overall council majority gets a majority of seats allocated;
- subject to (a) and (b) that the total number of seats each political group has on all ordinary committees is in proportion to that group's share of the total council elected membership; and
- subject to (a) and (c) that each political group has the same proportion of seats as it holds on the council as a whole.

Any seats that are or may be filled by people who are not elected members must be taken into account in calculating a majority of all the seats, though not for any other purpose; and an advisory committee seat 'shall not be treated as one which may be so filled unless the authority have determined that it must be so filled'. These principles apply to a relevant authority's representation on outside bodies where at least three of the appointments fail to be made by the authority.

9.45 Once the allocation of seats has been decided upon, there is a duty to give effect to the allocation by making appointments thereto in accordance with the wishes of the political groups. The detailed rules, somewhat complex, are prescribed by regulations.[8] The main purport, however, is as follows. It is for the council formally to resolve, i.e. to comply with the *Gladbaum* dictum,[9] members that are to be appointed to serve on committees in accordance with group wishes. Technically, it might be legal to allow this to be done by a committee since no discretion is involved, but the initial appointment should be made by the council itself to be on the safe side! The wishes of a properly constituted political group for this purpose are taken to be those expressed to the proper officer either orally or in writing by the leader or other representative of the group or in a written statement signed by the majority of the members of the group and, if different wishes of a group are expressed, the proper officer must accept that expressed in the written statement by a majority of the members. To help each group to express its wishes the proper officer is required to notify the leader or other representative of each group of the allocation of the seats to the group or the vacancy in the allocations. If a group fails to express its wishes within a period of three weeks of being notified of the allocation or vacancy, the council may make such appointment as it thinks fit. Any defect in the procedure of a technical or inadvertent nature will not invalidate the proceedings but, obviously, one that renders ineffective the duty imposed will not be excused.

9.46 The foregoing statutory requirements mean that, where the rules as to political proportionality apply, there can be no more one-party committees or subcommittees, but, of course, policies may still be formulated on a single party basis – in a working party that falls outside the definition of a committee (see 9.3) or outside the formal decision-making structure of the authority (see 5.29) – for translation through the legal hierarchy of committees. Where a relevant authority or any other local authority has decided not to adopt the prescribed political balance arrangements for its committee, it can still appoint committees of one, i.e. the majority, party only: see *R. v. Rushmoor Borough Council ex parte Crawford* (1981); *R. v. Newham London Borough Council ex parte Haggerty* (1986).

Revocation of committee membership

9.47 It is clear that a local authority is entitled to put an end to a councillor's membership of a committee at any time. It can do this either by dissolving the committee altogether or by terminating the membership of an individual councillor, i.e. even before the expiration of the term for which he had been appointed. This general concept can be traced back to *Manton* v. *Brighton Corporation* (1951), where it was held that as the council had power to revoke the authority of a committee as a whole it also had power to revoke the authority of a single member before the end of his prescribed period of office. This assertion needs now to be regarded as subject generally to rationality (on the Wednesbury principle (see 1.43)), to the political proportionality regulations (see 9.44) and to compliance with standing orders (see *R. v. Rushmoor Borough Council ex parte Crawford* (1981)) provided any relevant standing order is itself reasonable (see *R. v. Newham London Borough Council ex parte*

9. The committee system

Haggerty (1986) where the local authority was held entitled to formulate criteria as to who should be appointed to its committee subject to rationality).

9.48 There have been cases where the court has had to consider the legality of specific reasons for the removal of a councillor from a committee, but these do not run counter to what has been said in 9.47. A local authority cannot properly deprive a councillor from committee membership purely as a punishment for doing what the councillor is lawfully entitled to do: e.g. if the purpose was to fetter the exercise of discretion: see *R. v. Greenwich London Borough Council ex parte Lovelace* (1990)). In the circumstances of today, however, a local authority can properly remove councillors from committee membership who obstruct the council's policy and replace them. The distinction here is a fine one. In *Lovelace*, above, Neill LJ said:

'It seems to me . . . that at the present day, when local government is organised on party lines, some additional constraints [on committees] resulting from the existence of a party line or strategy on particular issues are inevitable. Penalties by way of punishment must clearly be avoided or any action which is vindictive or malicious. But a political party is entitled to take steps to ensure its cohesion and I can see nothing intrinsically wrong in a decision to change a party's representation on a committee or subcommittee so as to advance the policies which the party considers desirable. In this sense "group discipline" does not connote punishment but an attempt to keep the party group together.'

9.49 The requirements for fairly suspending councillors from committee membership were also examined in *R. v. Portsmouth City Council ex parte Gregory* (1990), which concerned a recommendation to suspend that was beyond a specially appointed subcommittee's powers. There is nothing in the rules governing political balance or committees (see 9.44) to prevent a political group – clearly the majority group in the circumstances just referred to – from changing its representation on a committee.

9.50 These principles relating to the removal of a member from a committee have now to be interpreted in the light of the proportionality regulations, which effectively give the power of appointment, and, by implication, the power of removal to the political groups (see 9.45). It appears that if a particular political group were to insist on one of its members remaining on a committee the council itself could not require that member's removal, even if a significant majority of the council wished this to happen. This also has the effect of reducing the impact, if not in these particular circumstances negating altogether, the decision in *R. v. Brent London Borough Council ex parte Gladbaum* (see 9.41).

Ex-officio members

9.51 Ex-officio members of a committee are those councillors, such as a council chairman or vice-chairman, whose appointment to a committee or subcommittee is by virtue of the office held and not by their selection as individuals. Unless the council determines otherwise, ex-officio members are full members of the committee, able to speak and vote. There appears to be no reason, however, why a local authority should not, if so minded, restrict the right of ex-officio members to that of mere attendance at committees and subcommittees, i.e. with no voting rights; and the view has been expressed that it would equally be in order for the authority to permit an ex-officio member to propose or second a motion but not to vote. Whatever the local arrangement it should, of course, be regulated by formal standing orders and, indeed, this was envisaged in the draft of the proposed core standing orders.

9.52 Ordinarily, the chairman of a committee, and the vice-chairman if there is one, will be ex-officio a member of each of the committee's subcommittees. Old model standing order no. 33 is to this effect:

'1 Every committee appointed by the council may appoint subcommittees for purposes to be specified by the committee.

2 The chairman [and the vice-chairman, if any] of the committee shall be [an] ex-officio member[s] of every subcommittee appointed by that committee, unless [he signifies to the committee that he does] [they signify to the committee that they do] not wish to serve.'

Substitute members

9.53 Many local authorities nowadays operate what has become known as a substitute system, which provides for the attendance at a committee or subcommittee meeting of a substitute member whenever a regularly appointed member cannot be present. It is a practice now more common with the advent of the political proportionality rules (see 9.44), and clearly there is much to be said in preserving the political balance of committees when one or more of its ordinary members are unable to attend a particular meeting. It avoids decisions being taken that are not the wish of the majority of the council and ones likely to be overturned at a higher level or a subsequent meeting. The problem is particularly acute in authorities where the political majority is small or where there is no overall majority. The development of the substitute system is the practical expression of the way in which the needs of parties have usurped the role and responsibilities of individual councillors as committee members.

9.54 There have been conflicting views in the past as to the legality of substitution and some councils that have accepted its legality have from time to time doubted its desirability. There are at least two opinions from leading counsel in support of the legality of such a system and many lingering doubts seem now to have been overridden.

9.55 The main issues now appear to be how to achieve a sensible and workable arrangement that ensures that the membership of every committee is known at any given time and that the right people are present and participating in each meeting. This is generally achieved in one of two ways: either by allowing the mechanics of appointing to a committee to be carried out by an officer on the instructions of the groups concerned or by nominating a prescribed list of substitute members for each

9. The committee system

committee. Either method would seem to be lawful but there are advantages and disadvantages attached to each.

9.56 Leaving matters to an officer (usually the chief executive or secretary) has the advantage of flexibility but needs to be sanctioned by a specific resolution of the council. One way to handle this is to ensure that at each annual meeting a resolution is passed authorising the officer chosen to make changes in the standing appointments to committee and subcommittees on the instructions of the political groups. This ensures that the power to appoint remains with the groups as required by the Local Government (Committees and Political Groups) Regulations 1990, but the administrative action is carried out by the officer concerned. Councils that follow this practice usually specify a time prior to the meetings when nominations have to be made. This should be at least the day before the meeting and preferably longer to allow time for papers to be sent to the substitute with adequate time for them to be read. Technically, this procedure operates as a formal change to the membership of the committee and lasts for as long as is determined by the instructing group. The disadvantages of this method is that it operates against the principle of fixed membership of a committee and encourages last-minute changes, with members being appointed who have no prior knowledge of the work of the committee concerned but who just happen to be available. It is not unknown for some members to be elevated to the status of 'professional substitutes' for no better reason than their lack of regular employment.

9.57 The alternative method, and one that is perhaps to be preferred, is for the council to appoint substitute members itself for each committee and subcommittee. Thus the members will be named and appointed usually at the same time as the regular committee membership is decided at the annual meeting of the council. This method has the advantage of certainty in that the substitute membership is well publicised in advance so that the members concerned can build up some knowledge and expertise in the subject area of their particular committee, but it is not always liked by the political groups because of the lack of flexibility. It does, however, measure up more closely to the principles of committee appointment laid down in the *Gladbaum* case (see 9.41). It also enables the council to maintain an accurate register of committee and subcommittee membership as required by the LGA 1972, s.100G. Where the council is not divided into political groups, this is the only way that substitution can be properly authorised.

9.58 Whichever procedure is used, it is important that it is clearly understood by the members and accurately applied to avoid confusion, embarrassment or even possible illegality. The period covered by the substitution must be clearly set out and so, too, must the position, if the original member and the substitute both turn up at the same meeting (see 9.59). Certainty of membership is vital to the successful operation of any substitute system and only another formal change can revoke the original change. Ideally the practical arrangements should be set out in standing orders.

9.59 If a substitute member is present at a meeting at which the member whom he is replacing turns up during the course of proceedings, the original member should be required to withdraw from further participation in the business. A substitute member attending a meeting speaks and votes in his own capacity: he does not, as it were, relinquish his own personal responsibilities or take on the mantle of the other member. The substitute is personally under the same obligations as any other councillor to disclose an interest in any contract or other matter before the committee or subcommittee and must refrain from speaking or voting if disqualified on that account.

9.60 So far as executive arrangements are concerned, an executive is not able to have a formal substitute or deputy members who are not themselves members of the executive. Also, the executive has no powers to co-opt other councillors or anyone else on to the executive. In practice, councillors from other party groups are invited to cabinet meetings but are unable to vote.

Non-members of a committee

9.61 As to the attendance of non-members of a committee at a meeting of a committee: see Chapter 5.

Size

9.62 The number of members on a committee or subcommittee is a matter to be decided by the local authority or, in the case of a joint committee, the authorities that set it up (LGA 1972, s.102). Several considerations affect the size of membership. One, of course, is to provide for a requisite political balance. In any case, just as there must be a plurality of persons present to constitute a meeting, so too must there be a plurality of persons to constitute a committee or subcommittee .In any case as there is no power to delegate functions to an individual council member there could hardly be said to be the power to delegate to a committee of one member. There is also a limit to the size of a committee because a committee that consists of all members of the council (or perhaps more than that if co-opted members were brought in) cannot by definition be a committee of the parent body (see 9.6). Nevertheless, for procedural purposes, it was once common practice for local authorities to go into committee (see 9.65) to evade the need to conduct business of the full assembly in public, or to constitute a finance and general purposes committee of all members of the council for much the same purpose.

9.63 There are grounds for the view that a local authority committee ought not to comprise fewer than three persons. It cannot comprise one member alone for the reason just given, nor is it desirable that it should comprise two only because the power of the person presiding to give a second or casting vote would mean that the committee could become a dictatorship of the chairman.[10] It could be argued also that even a committee of three members gives considerable power to the chairman in so far as he can cast an original vote or a casting vote if the other two are divided in their views, so as to decide any matter in his favour. These are, possibly, theoretical objections: an authority that constitutes a committee of two or three members must be presumed to know what it is doing (and, in any case, the potential danger is not very real even if the committee is entrusted with executive powers because of the authority's freedom to dissolve the committee at any time); and, of course, it is a convention that a committee chairman should not be too freely disposed to exercise his second or casting vote (see 7.120).

9. The committee system

9.64 Taking account of the foregoing and of the advantages of a small rather than a large committee, an optimum size could be four or five members including the chairman, preferably an odd number so as to eliminate the possibility of too frequent an equality of votes. A small committee is more likely to reach a decision speedily and is less costly to convene; but it may not be fairly representative of political or other opinion or of electoral wards or divisions.

Can there be a committee of the full council?

9.65 If, as indicated above (see 9.4), there is a minimum number of members that may validly constitute a committee or subcommittee, can there be a maximum number? Or, put another way, can there be a committee of the whole membership of the local authority? As a matter of historical fact, before local authorities were compelled to throw open their committees to the public, councils sometimes resolved to go into committee so as to exclude the public and press. No one challenged their right to do so. However, there is now no need for the expedient of going into committee, at least to exclude the public, because such a move would be purposeless.

9.66 There seems, nevertheless, no lawful reason why a local authority should still not decide to go into committee if it wishes, or otherwise set up a committee composed of all members of the council. After all the House of Lords and the House of Commons each resolves itself into a committee of the whole house on occasions (each is itself 'in a less formal guise', says Erskine May[11]) and there is no reason why a local authority cannot do the same, despite the cogency of a contrary view that what purports to be a committee of the whole council cannot by definition be a committee of the parent body. In any case there is no longer today the former justification of the whole assembly going into committee to avoid the obligation to admit the press and public to a meeting: a committee of the whole council cannot evade the obligation to meet in public. Further, that the terms of the 1972 Act, looked at as a whole, presuppose that a committee will comprise fewer members than the whole council membership, and that in the case of delegation of functions to a committee, which the law permits, it would be nonsense to contemplate the delegating body delegating functions to itself, albeit in another guise. Further still, the statutory arrangements for the discharge of functions by committees can be likened to the relation of principal (the council) and agent (the committees), and for the council to appoint itself as agent for itself is nonsensical.

9.67 What if the local authority does set up a committee of the whole membership? It must mean that the formalities required to be observed in the case of council meetings need not be followed, e.g. the chairman of the council does not automatically take the chair (indeed, it would be inappropriate for him to do so) and a committee chairman would need to be elected; and, further, non-voting persons from outside the council's membership could be co-opted.

Terms of reference

Definition

9.68 A committee's terms of reference, its remit, specify the functions with which the committee is charged and define the limits of its authority. Precision is important in framing terms of reference so as to avoid doubt about the scope of a committee's tasks. If the terms are narrowly drawn the committee's powers and duties may be unduly restrictive; if widely drawn there is risk that the terms may overlap those of another committee or committees.

9.69 Terms of reference should be collectively all-embracing and mutually exclusive. By this is meant that the terms of reference of all committees should cover the whole of the council's area of operations, but should be so drawn that one set of terms does not overlap another. However skilfully the terms are drafted it is impossible to foresee every eventuality and thus most authorities provide for the terms of reference of an appropriate committee, e.g. one of the overview and scrutiny committees, to include responsibility for:

> 'Any matter not delegated or referred to or coming under the cognisance of any other overview and scrutiny committee.'

Form

9.70 It is common practice but not essential for terms of reference to be framed in imperative words, e.g.:

> 'To exercise the functions of the council relating to . . .'

or:

> 'To consider and make recommendations to the council upon . . .'

Only a little less favoured is the more ponderously phrased:

> 'There shall be referred to the committee all the powers and duties of the council in relation to . . .'

Delegation to committees

General power to delegate

9.71 Every local authority has power to delegate, within limitations,[12] any of its functions (other than functions with respect to levying or issuing a precept for a rate[13]), including any functions it may be discharging on behalf of another local authority, to a committee or subcommittee (or, indeed, to an officer).

9.72 The LGA 1972 does not use the term delegate as did the LGA 1933. It provides that 'a local authority may arrange for the discharge of any of their functions' and this difference in wording is necessary no doubt because of the wider power now available enabling an authority to arrange for the discharge of functions by any other local authority (LGA 1972, s.101). This could not properly be described as delegation because delegation implies the existence of a principal and a subordinate, whereas the use of another local authority in this way is a matter between a principal and an agent.

Specific power to delegate

9.73 Specific power is conferred upon local authorities required to set up statutory committees to delegate functions to the statutory committee. Subject to the precise executive model adopted, the LGA 2000 allows delegation of executive functions to a committee of the executive. The statutory Guidance makes it clear that the membership of that committee can only include members of the executive (see Chapter 4 of the Guidance).

9.74 Without express statutory power to do so, a local authority would be unable to delegate its decision-making powers because of the common law maxim delegatus non potest delegare. Parliament entrusts functions to local authorities as such, not directly to their committees and subcommittees or officers, and any delegatee entrusted with a task cannot lawfully pass that task on to another without the concurrence of the delegator. Indeed, the earliest of the modern local authorities were expressly denied the power to delegate: s.22(2) of the Municipal Corporation Act 1882 read as follows (although, of course, the concluding words were not italicised in the official text):

> 'The council may from time to time appoint out of their own body such and so many committees, either of a general or special nature and consisting of such number of persons as they think fit for any purposes which, in the opinion of the council, would be better regulated and managed by means of such committees; but *the acts of every such committee shall be submitted to the council for their approval.*'

9.75 County councils when set up under the LGA 1888 were, however, wholly relieved of this disability. Section 82(2) of the 1888 Act provided:

> 'Every committee shall report its proceedings to the council by whom it was appointed, but to the extent to which the council so direct, the acts and proceedings of the committee shall not be required by the provisions of the Municipal Corporations Act 1882, to be submitted to the council for their approval.'

Effect of delegation

9.76 A local authority does not denude itself of its responsibility by delegating functions to committees: this was so decided in *Huth* v. *Clarke* (1890), but now, in any case, the LGA 1972 expressly provides in s.101(4) that:

> 'Any arrangement made by a local authority . . . for the discharge of any functions by a committee, subcommittee (officer or local authority) shall not prevent the authority or committee by whom the arrangements are made from exercising those functions.'

This means two things: first, that the local authority remains responsible (and this, of course, is so of any principal who delegates because it is authority that is delegated and not responsibility) and the committee when it acts does so for and in the name of the local authority; second, that the council can continue to perform the functions that it has delegated.

9.77 In *Goddard* v. *Minister of Housing and Local Government* (1958), the plaintiff challenged the validity of a compulsory purchase order made by a committee under delegated powers and put forward two contentions: one was that the council itself had never applied its mind to the issue, for the resolutions of the council's committees were merely 'rubber-stamped', whereas the council was obliged by statute to 'satisfy' itself. The court held that the council, acting through its committee, was satisfied.

9.78 The principle that an authority can continue to exercise the functions it has delegated could in practice lead to difficulties and possible confusion. Thus the council must take care not to act in a matter known to be receiving a committee's attention under delegated powers or at least not to act without close consultation with the committee. If it wishes to do so it ought first to withdraw the delegated powers from the committee in respect of the particular matter on which it proposes to act itself. What it cannot properly do is to purport to put an end to delegated powers retrospectively so as to invalidate what a committee has done already in exercise of those powers where third-party interests are affected: see *Battelley* v. *Finsbury Borough Council* (1958).

9.79 Some authorities have an arrangement whereby delegated decisions can be converted into recommendations requiring confirmation. This has become known as referencing up and is discussed later (see 11.42).

Method of delegation

9.80 There are two ways in which the terms of delegation can be expressed. An authority can either:

- list the particular matters that a committee is empowered to do without reference to the full assembly; or
- bestow upon each committee the power to take executive action on everything within its respective terms of reference except those matters specifically excluded.

The former is usual where the scope of a committee's delegated power is intended to be limited to a few specific functions and the other where delegation is extensive: the latter is to be preferred because it is easier to put down in writing and interpret in practice and the exclusions highlight the important questions that the full council needs to settle itself.

Handling urgent business

Regulation by standing order

9.81 Every authority makes arrangements to enable urgent business to be dealt with when the matter cannot wait until the next meeting of the appropriate committee. A draft core standing order in this respect was proposed by the standing orders working party (see 2.4) to this effect:

> '00–1 Unless the council have by resolution made other arrangements for that purpose, every committee shall make arrangements for the discharge, in urgent circumstances, of the functions of the authority which the committee may discharge, by appointing either:
> a) a subcommittee of not fewer than three voting members of the committee; or
> b) an officer of the council to discharge those functions.
> 2) Before acting under such arrangements:
> a) any officer so appointed shall consult, so far as practicable, such representatives of the political groups to which seats on the committee have been allocated as those political groups shall designate.
> b) any such subcommittee or officer shall record the urgent circumstances which make it necessary for action to be taken before a meeting of the committee can be arranged.
> 3) Where action is taken under any such arrangement, a report of that action, including a note of the circumstances which made it necessary, shall be laid before the next meeting of the committee.'

9.82 Arrangements for handling urgent business at committee or subcommittee meetings are now governed by statute (see 6.23), which requires the chairman's approval before an urgent item can be considered and for the reason for the urgency to be recorded in the minutes. In practice this has often resulted in the former agenda item of 'Urgent business' being replaced by 'Any business the chairman regards as urgent' or to similar effect, although many councils do not include the item at all in the view that it encourages members to raise items. The reasons given by the chairman for accepting urgent business should be legitimate ones: political expediency or forgetfulness on the part of reporting officers do not accord with the spirit of the legislation.

9.83 So far as those authorities operating executive arrangements are concerned, an urgent decision that is contrary to the policy framework may be taken by the executive if the chair of the relevant overview and scrutiny committee agrees that the decision may reasonably be regarded as urgent in the circumstances. Otherwise, the matter must be referred to the full council for decision. Where a key decision needs to be made in relation to a matter not in the Forward Plan there will need to be five clear days' notice thereof given to the relevant overview and scrutiny committee and the public before the decision is taken. If the matter is urgent and cannot wait for five clear days notice to be given, the agreement of the chair of the relevant overview and scrutiny committee is needed to enable the decision to be made otherwise it will have to wait for the expiry of the five clear days' notice.

Subcommittees

Power to appoint

9.84 A discretionary committee appointed by a local authority individually or by two or more authorities under the LGA 1972 may by that same Act appoint 'one or more subcommittees (s.102(1), (4))', and so, too, may the statutory social services committees (Sch.1, para.10) each constituted as the committee concerned may determine (see 9.94).

9.85 The decision in R. v. *Brent London Borough Council ex parte Gladbaum* (1989) (see 9.41) gave added force to the ordinarily accepted principle that subcommittee membership should not be decided by the full assembly. Because of the difficulty that could arise in practice, particularly for councils that prefer to settle all their committee and subcommittee structure at the annual council meeting, an appropriate legislative amendment negating the effect of *Gladbaum* was inserted into the LG&HA 1989, but has never been brought into force, probably because the effect would have been to remove subcommittees from the political balance rules, since a subcommittee so appointed would not be an 'ordinary' subcommittee. One practical way of avoiding the problems of appointing subcommittees direct by the full council would be for the parent committee at its first meeting to confirm the membership of its subcommittees.

Constitution

9.86 A committee may determine the number of members of each of its subcommittees, the term of office and the area (if restricted) within which the subcommittee is to exercise its authority;[14] and the subcommittees may include non-voting persons. Most of the statutory provisions relating to committees are applicable also to subcommittees (as to the manner in which decisions shall be made, the casting vote of a chairman, the recording of names of members present, the keeping and signing of minutes, the applicability of standing orders, and the validity of proceedings despite defects in its constitution or in the election or qualification of members).

Delegation to subcommittees

9.87 A local authority has a general power in respect of discretionary committees to delegate any of its functions (except with respect to levying, or issuing a precept for, a rate) to a subcommittee direct; and a discretionary committee may, unless the authority otherwise directs, itself delegate any of its functions to its subcommittees; and, in turn, a subcommittee may unless otherwise directed delegate any of its functions to an officer. No longer is a committee bound by the maxim delegatus non potest delegare in delegating to subcommittees as was formerly the case.

9.88 Where an authority has made arrangements for another authority to discharge the functions of the former then, subject to the terms of the arrangements, that other authority may delegate in the same way as an authority in respect of its own functions.

9.89 For reasons explained earlier it is not permissible for a committee to constitute one member as a subcommittee, any more than it is permissible for an authority to constitute a committee of one.

Advantages and disadvantages of subcommittees

9.90 Subcommittees should not be set up unless such a course is unavoidable. Professor K. C. Wheare has said:[15]

'Difficulties are avoided, decisions postponed, discussion shortened or prevented by the use of subcommittees. And the process of referring matters to smaller and smaller bodies seems at times to have no limits – subcommittees have their sections, sections their subsections; there are panels and working parties and informal groups and drafting sectors and segments. There is a sort of law of gravity in committee work by which things are referred farther and farther back and down. Along with this tendency there goes the tendency for each small group to feel a sense of its own importance and to conspire against the body to which it is nominally subordinate.'

9.91 Subcommittees can, however, assist positively in advancing the work of a committee: a smaller group of council members can often more effectively examine a matter requiring detailed consideration, or more efficiently and effectively constitute a staff selection board or panel; and there is the advantage that a small number of members can be called together more easily than the membership of a full committee. Subcommittees should never be set up, as Professor Wheare implies, to postpone an unpalatable decision or as a device to shelve an item of business. Ideally, a committee should decide at the outset of its term of office whether there is need for any standing subcommittees and to accept as a near immutable principle that it shall not set up any ad hoc subcommittee during the council year. If the disadvantages of subcommittees are recognised there is less risk of appointing them needlessly or of misusing those that are unavoidable.

9.92 Nevertheless, it is preferable for a local authority to allow a committee with substantial responsibilities to appoint subcommittees for each identifiably different part of its totality of functions rather than for the authority to divide the responsibilities between two or more committees. It is sometimes thought to be nonsensical to amalgamate, say, two committees and then for the combined committee to appoint two subcommittees. It is, however, demonstrably easier for a committee to coordinate and control the work of two subcommittees than for the full assembly to co-ordinate and control an additional committee.

Working parties

Devolution of decision-making

9.93 A development of the devolution of decision-making from the council in full assembly (which has become increasingly a forum for the discussion and determination of significant policy issues) has been a markedly increased use of small groups of council members or officers or both to make decisions on non-policy questions or to help in policy formulation. Bains favoured the setting up of such working groups, without the constraints of formal subcommittees, in order to provide members with the opportunity to identify themselves with areas of activity in which they have a particular interest and to provide officers with an immediate point of reference for the opinion of elected members.

9.94 Working parties elsewhere are usually of a more conventional character, each set up by and required to report back to the committee that established it. In many cases there is a standing order regulating their constitution and proceedings: one such is to this effect:

'a) Any committee or subcommittee may, within its powers, set up a working party of members and officers for the detailed study of any matter referred to it but such working party shall report to the body from which it was formed and shall not have power to exercise on behalf of the council any authority nor to incur expenditure without prior authority of the committee or relevant subcommittee, nor to issue instructions to any officer likely, in the opinion of the officer or chief executive, to incur expense or to use excessive time without prior authority of the committee or relevant subcommittee. The meeting of any such working party shall be convened and minuted by the director of operations and the terms of reference of such a working party shall include a definition of the objects of the working party, the manner and times at which it shall report back and shall require it to define matters of policy.

b) A working party may set up from among its members a study group or groups which shall be similarly convened and minuted for the purpose of detailed work and such study group or groups shall report back to the working party.

c) The chairman and vice-chairman of a working party or study group shall be appointed by the body establishing the working party or study group, but in their absence at a meeting the party or group as the case may be shall appoint a member then present to act as chairman, and a chairman shall have a second or casting vote as necessary.'

When a working party is not a committee

9.95 The question of whether or not a working party could exist within a local authority outside the committee system was raised by the provisions of the LG(AI)A 1985. Proponents of the Act maintained that any gathering of members dealing with council business must be either a committee or a subcommittee and the public access and notice provisions must therefore apply in all cases. The issue became clearer with the case of *R. v. Eden District Council ex parte Moffat* (1989), where the court at first instance and the Court of Appeal both accepted that the concept of a working party was acceptable in law. The facts on which this case was brought related to events that occurred before the 1985 Act but the principles remain valid. The conclusion reached by Webster J was that there was no reason why a local authority should not create a working party 'to have a think about the best way of doing things'. The body of members at the centre of the dispute was a working party, said the judge, and Eden District Council's standing orders, which allowed access by members to committees and subcommittees, could not be invoked by a councillor who wanted to attend a particular meeting of a working party. The working party in this case also contained officer representation that was regarded as evidence of the intention by the council to establish an informal body.

9.96 The importance of the intention of the council was emphasised again in *R. v. Warwickshire District Council ex parte Bailey* (1991). This case involved a working party established to consider the reorganisation of secondary education in the county and to make recommendations as it thought fit. Public access to the meetings was denied and opponents of the working party's proposals maintained that the meetings were unlawful. The court took the view, however, that the critical factor was the manifest intention of the council so long as there was nothing inherently unlawful behind that intention: the council had quite properly intended the body to be a working party and therefore that was what it was.

9.97 A local authority often seeks to set up working parties or panels as a way of considering matters in private, i.e. without the need to give public notice and so be able to exclude the public and press without the formality of giving adequate reasons. The position appears to be that it is permissible to set up a working party provided the council makes clear its intention to follow that course and there is no conferment of delegated powers. Simply calling a body a working party or a panel may not be good enough, particularly if there is any suggestion or likelihood of executive action being

Committee practice

taken because decision-making is clearly an exercise of the functions of the council which, under the LGA 1972, s.101, can only be carried out by a committee or subcommittee (or officer): any attempt to do so through a working party is inherently unlawful and fails the test in Bailey's case.

Notes

1 LGA 1972, s.80.
2 Maud Report, vol. 1, paras.93-96.
3 LGA 1972, s.102(1).
4 Non-members in this case are voting members: LG&HA 1989, s.13(4).
5 J. H. Warren, *The English Local Government System*.
6 LG&HA 1989, s.15 and Sch.l, and the Local Government (Committees and Political Groups) Regulations 1990. The Local Government (Committees and Political Groups) Regulations 1998 exclude from the voting regulations a number of joint committees exercising specific functions.
7 These bodies are prescribed by LG&HA 1989, Sch.1, para.2, and include a fire authority, a waste disposal authority, a joint authority, any successor to residuary bodies, the Broads Authority, the National Park Planning Boards, a local fisheries committee, a superannuation committee, a National Parks Committee, a board or committee appointed under a local Act and a joint committee appointed under the 1972 Act, s.102(1)(b).
8 Local Government (Committees and Political Groups) Regulations 1990 as amended.
9 See the decision in *R. v. Brent London Borough Council ex parte Gladbaum* (1989) that only the council in full assembly can appoint members to its committees. There is a view, however, that the political proportionality provisions of the LG&HA 1989 must be regarded as having overruled Gladbaum where political groups effectively make appointments to committees. In the circumstances it may be thought prudent, to secure nominal compliance with the ordinarily accepted practice that only a parent body can constitute its own committees, for the full council's formal endorsement, (albeit it that it has no discretion) to be sought to the names of members put forward by the political groups.
10 See nevertheless *R. v. Swansea City Council ex parte Elitestone Ltd* (1993), where it was held that a local authority committee of two members was lawful.
11 Erskine May's *Parliamentary Practice*, 20th edition.
12 LGA 1972, s.101. The limitations are those contained within the 1972 Act (e.g. the election of chairman of a principal council must be conducted by the full assembly) or by any statute passed subsequently. Among other business that cannot be delegated are, e.g. consideration of a s.114 report by the chief financial officer under the LGA 1988, s.115(4), consideration of a s.4 report by the head of the paid service under the LG&HA 1989, s.4(5), consideration of a s.5 report by the monitoring officer under the 1989 Act, s.5(5).
13 Ibid, s.101(6). The former reference to borrowing in this section was removed by the LG&HA 1989, s.45(5). But see now the exclusion from delegation of the determination of an overall borrowing limit under s.45(4).
14 LGA 1972, s.102(2).
15 *Government by Committee* (1955), p. 194.

Chapter 10
Work before meetings

General considerations

Timetable of meetings

10.1 Most local authorities fix their timetable of meetings for a period of one year in advance (at or about the time of the annual council meeting), compiled as a rule by an updating of the programme for the previous year. There is much to commend this widely adopted practice: councillors and officers can enter the dates in their diaries before other commitments arise and it sets the pattern for the organisation and transaction of council business at member level.

10.2 Considerations to be borne in mind in drawing up the timetable include:

- There should be no greater frequency of meetings than the volume of business demands: not all committees need meet in each cycle while some may need to meet more than once.
- The actual dates of meetings should be related to the dates of council meetings, particularly where recommendations may need to be submitted to the full council.
- The order of meetings within the cycle should be related to the character of business: committees that regularly or periodically have to consider the recommendations of other committees must meet at the end of the cycle but in sufficient time before the council meeting to enable reports to be prepared and incorporated within the council agenda. In the case of executive meetings, this is not so crucial as the executive tends to meet on a more regular basis than committees.
- Administrative considerations must not be overlooked: time needs to be allowed for the drafting of items and members briefing, and the final preparation and despatch of the summons and agenda, ensuring that the five clear days are observed.

Indeed, the timetable of meetings can form the basis of a committee programme for administrative purposes, showing the various deadlines that committee clerks will need to observe, including, for example, the last date for the receipt of items for an agenda (see 10.21).

10.3 In particular cases it may not be practicable to prepare a programme for a committee or cabinet (because, for example, of an irregular and unpredictable flow of business). Even then, however, it is desirable at each meeting to fix the date and time of the next meeting (which can be cancelled if need be) rather than wait until there is enough business to warrant calling another meeting.

10.4 A prearranged timetable of meetings does not obviate the necessity of giving separate notice of each meeting at the requisite time: indeed, notification of a committee or cabinet meeting merely by means of the circulation annually of a timetable is unlikely to be held to be proper notice because at common law a summons must be served upon members with an agenda of the business to be transacted. Many authorities prepare a weekly bulletin of meetings, which is circulated for the information of members generally and this serves not only as a reminder to members of particular committee or cabinet meetings in advance of the summons and agenda, but as notification to members who may wish to attend committees or the cabinet if they are not members.

Time of meeting

10.5 The time at which committee meetings are held must be related to the convenience and availability of members. Generally, county councils arrange committee meetings during the day (at the time of Maud, the large majority before 2pm and the remainder in the afternoon), not because the members of county authorities are composed largely of retired people or others of independent means, as often they are, but because of the distance many have to travel and the consequent difficulty of returning home after a late evening meeting. Some other principal councils may be influenced by similar considerations: the former rural district councils used to favour daytime meetings (according to Maud, about evenly divided between morning and afternoon meetings). Most district councils opt in the main for evening meetings: again, according to Maud twice as many larger councils arranged their committee meetings in the evening as in the morning; urban districts and the smaller non-county boroughs had comparatively few daytime meetings and even in the larger non-county boroughs only about a third of the committee meetings were held during the day; and of all the committees in London boroughs only one authority regularly had meetings during the day. It may be that the pattern of timing is being materially affected now by the payments available to members.

Standing orders

10.6 The standing orders working party (see 2.4) included with its draft core standing orders one relating generally to the meetings of committees and subcommittees to this effect:

'00–1 The council may fix the date, time and place of ordinary meetings of communities and subcommittees.

2 If the council do not fix the date, time, or place of an ordinary meeting of a subcommittee, then the committee which appointed them may do so.

3 If the date, time, or place of an ordinary meeting of a committee or subcommittee has not been fixed by the council or the committee (as the case may be), then that

committee or subcommittee shall fix those details of the meeting which have not otherwise been fixed: provided that:

   a) for the first ordinary meeting of any committee or subcommittee, the chairman of the council or, if a person has been appointed to preside in a committee, that person may fix any details which have not otherwise been fixed.

   b) for any other meeting of a committee or subcommittee, the chairman of the council or the person appointed to preside in that committee or subcommittee, after consultation (as far as practicable) with such persons as appear to him/her to be representative of the political groups to which have been allocated seats on the committee or subcommittee, or may cancel a meeting of the committee or subcommittee, or may change any of the details of place, date or time already fixed for the meeting.

4 The person appointed to preside at meetings of a committee or subcommittee, his/her deputy, or the chairman of the council may call a special meeting of the committee or subcommittee at any time.

5 If:

   a) a requisition for a special meeting of a committee or subcommittee, signed by at least two, or one quarter of the total number, of the voting members of a committee or subcommittee, whichever is greater, has been presented to the person appointed to preside at their meetings, and

   b) either he/she has refused to call a meeting or, without him/her so refusing, no special meeting has been called within seven days of the presentation of the requisition,

then any two, or one quarter of the number, of the members of the committee or subcommittee, whichever is greater, may forthwith call a special meeting of the committee or subcommittee.

6 If any person or persons decides to call a special meeting of a committee or subcommittee, he/she shall forthwith give notice that he/she has done so to the proper officer and shall specify the business proposed to be transacted, who shall forthwith give notice to all members of the committee or subcommittee and all persons entitled to receive their papers.

7 Any requisition under paragraph (5) may be presented by being left for the person with the proper officer.'

Convening committee meetings

Notice, summons and agenda

10.7 There is now less difference than formerly between the legal requirements as to the notice and summons in the case of committees and subcommittees, and those of the full council. Public notice of the meeting of every committee and subcommittee of a principal council must be given and the agenda and accompanying reports (excluding any reports or parts of reports for items of business during which the meeting is likely to be closed to the public) made available for public inspection at least five days before a meeting or, if the meeting is convened at shorter notice, then as soon as it is convened. This also applies to meetings of the cabinet. Business not specified on the agenda may not be considered unless the chairman agrees that it is urgent, and in the case of key decisions to be made at meetings of the executive, if approval of the chairman of the relevant overview and scrutiny committee has been obtained; see 9.83. In short, all that has been said earlier (see Chapter 6) about the giving of public notice of a council meeting and its agenda and the making available of agenda papers and reports applies equally to committees and subcommittees of principal councils.

10.8 However, in the case of the meetings of committees and subcommittees of parish and community councils the rules governing the summons and agenda will be those set out in the standing orders of the council concerned or, where standing orders are silent, then as prescribed by common law.

10.9 There is no common form of summons or agenda for a committee or subcommittee meeting. Many authorities omit any formal words of summons, i.e. an agenda is despatched to those entitled to attend headed merely with the name of the committee or subcommittee and the date, time and place of meeting.

10.10 The agenda may also need to be sent to certain councillors other than those appointed to the committee or subcommittee according to local practice, e.g. to ward members with an interest in certain of the items on the agenda or to councillors claiming a 'need to know' (see 4.11) or to substitute members where such an arrangement exists (see 9.59). Regulation 17 of SI 2000/3272 provides that any document that contains material relating to any business to be transacted at a public meeting shall be available for inspection by any member of the local authority. In practice, most authorities make agendas for all meetings available for members to view in the members' room, and some authorities send copies of cabinet agendas to all members.

If a councillor is wrongly summoned because, for example, his surname is the same as another member entitled to be present, that person cannot claim a right to be present. If, nevertheless, the wrong councillor does attend a meeting that he is not entitled to attend and actually votes, his vote is invalid: see 7.108. It is, of course, good practice for the clerk to check that the correct members are in attendance to ensure that this does not happen. Errors in service of the summons do not affect the validity of proceedings.

Regulation by standing orders

10.11 Not many authorities will think it necessary to regulate the convening or agenda of committee meetings, but the working party on standing orders (see 2.4) nevertheless drafted this possible core standing order:

'00–1 At least [five] clear days before every meeting of a committee or subcommittee, or as soon as the meeting is called, whichever is later, the proper officer shall send to every voting member and to every other person entitled to receive the papers of the committee or subcommittee a copy of the agenda for the meeting.

2) The agenda shall include:

a) all items of business which have been, or are deemed to have been, referred to the committee or subcommittee by the council or by another committee or subcommittee, as the case may be;

b) all reports submitted to the committee or subcommittee by the head of the paid service or any chief officer;

c) any item of business directed to be included by the person appointed to preside at the meetings of the committee or subcommittee; and

d) any other item of business of which the requisite notice has been given to the proper officer by a member of the committee or subcommittee (whether voting or not); provided that no member (other than the person appointed to preside at meetings of the committee or subcommittee) may give notice of more than one item of business for any one meeting.

3 The requisite notice is [five] clear days notice in writing before the date fixed for the meeting of the committee or subcommittee.

4 Subject to any directions given by the person appointed to preside at the meetings of the committee or subcommittee, the items of business shall be arranged in such order as the proper officer thinks will best ensure the effective despatch of business.'

Notice of meetings one after the other

10.12 It is not unusual, particularly in the case of smaller authorities, for committee meetings to follow one another on the same day or evening; each to begin upon the conclusion of another. Because a notice must be clear, explicit and unconditional, it is never satisfactory for a committee (or any other body for that matter) to be convened to meet at an indeterminate time 'immediately upon the rising' of an earlier committee: even though it may be felt to be justified in circumstances where the two committees comprise the same membership. For certainty an estimate of the likely starting time should be made and the summons can then clearly state, e.g. that the meeting will commence:

'... at 7 p.m. or upon the rising of the ... committee, whichever is the later.'

Notice to officers and others

10.13 Officers must also be notified of meetings where they are expected to be present, especially, of course, where an officer not usually in attendance (or, indeed, an outside adviser) is being invited to attend for a particular item of business. Such an officer, or other person, may well need to be briefed in certain respects before the actual meeting (see 10.51).

Who may convene

10.14 The proper officer will normally convene committee meetings in accordance with the prearranged timetable and, in consultation with the committee chairman, convene special meetings as circumstances may warrant. There is no provision in law, as in the case of council meetings, for members to requisition a meeting of a committee or the executive, but old model standing order no. 32 is to the following effect:

> 'The chairman of a committee or the mayor/chairman of the council may call a special meeting of the committee at any time. A special meeting shall also be called on the requisition of a quarter of the whole number of the committee, delivered in writing to the town clerk/clerk of the council but in no case shall less than [three] members requisition a special meeting. The summons to the special meeting shall set out the business to be considered thereat, and no business other than set out in the summons shall be considered at that meeting.'

10.15 If there is no standing order to this effect and a number of members demand a special meeting, the committee or executive chairman should agree to one being convened. If he is not prepared to agree, the chief executive would no doubt advise him to do so if the number of members asking was substantial; and if the number comprised the majority of members the chief executive, or proper officer in practice, might well feel obliged to convene a meeting irrespective of the wishes of the committee or executive chairman. If neither committee or cabinet chairman nor chief executive will act, the members could always, of course, make use of their power to call a special council meeting to deal with the situation (see 1.20).

Committee agenda

General principles

10.16 The purpose of a committee agenda (indistinguishable from a council meeting agenda or, indeed, any other agenda) is:

- to provide advance notification of the business to be transacted at a particular meeting; and
- to facilitate the transaction of business at the meeting itself.

The document may have practical purposes in addition (it may often provide the basis for the minutes of the meeting and, indeed, is sometimes written in a form that will aid the subsequent preparation of the minutes), but an agenda's objective must always be to advance the purposes for which the committee has been set up and to do so in an efficient manner. It should be regarded as a document framed to secure or at least encourage decision-making and it can only do this effectively if councillors understand what is being put before them. It should not ordinarily be used merely to inform; and the items placed before the committee should be those that unavoidably demand the committee's consideration. Maud critically observed in its report[1] that it saw the growth of business adding to the agenda of committees and squeezing out major issues that need time for consideration, with the result that members are misled into a

10. Work before meetings

belief that they are controlling and directing the authority when often they are only deliberating on things that are unimportant and making decisions on matters that do not merit their attention. This comment is hopefully less valid now due to the cabinet system, under which members should be controlling the direction of the authority. Item 'for noting' should therefore be limited to those that are strictly necessary, to ensure that members can focus on strategic issues and are not bogged down with triviality.

Agenda setting

10.17 The build-up of cabinet and committee agendas is virtually a continuous process: as soon as one meeting has been held material starts accumulating for the next. It is the committee clerk's responsibility to maintain a list of items awaiting consideration. How this list is kept is a matter of personal inclination or office regulation: it may consist of a card index, a number of sheets of paper, a file of documents (but, for obvious reasons, it is preferable not to retain papers that ought to be filed away elsewhere), or merely a tray or drawer into which is placed a note of items for committee. The material for the draft agenda will come to the committee clerk from various sources; it will comprise:

- items that the committee clerk himself will have 'noted':
  a) matters deferred or retained from previous meetings;
  b) periodically recurring items or reports: it is common practice for the committee clerk to look back at the committee agenda for the corresponding meeting in the previous council year to ensure that matters of annual incidence are not overlooked;
  c) references from other committees, the council, or other bodies.
- other items:
  a) arising out of correspondence, including departmental circulars, etc.;
  b) initiated by other officers;
  c) that individual councillors may ask to be included;
- Forward Plan (cabinet only)
  a) Those items that are set out in the forward plan to bring forward to cabinet.

The extent to which councillors are permitted to call for items to be placed before the executive or committees depends upon the practice of individual local authorities. However, it would seem reasonable to take the view that cabinet or committee membership confers some rights in relation to the committee's agenda and officers might be on difficult ground in refusing to accept an item so long as the matter concerned is within the terms of reference. It would, of course, remain open to the cabinet or committee to refuse to discuss the matter. The position would conceivably be different where the member concerned does not serve on the cabinet or committee since he has the option of raising the issue by way of notice of motion at a council meeting. It is useful for there to be a working arrangement or provision in standing orders' permitting, for example, individual councillors to initiate agenda items only after consultation with the committee chairman or leader of the council.

Committee practice

Control of agenda

10.18 It will be evident that whoever prepares an agenda has a significant, even possibly decisive, influence on the business conducted at the meeting. It has to be accepted that items are nowadays more likely than in the past to be initiated by the leader at the request of the majority group or group spokesperson where no majority group exists. Practice is still developing in this respect and varies substantially between authorities. Widdicombe refers in one of its research volumes to practice in highly politicised local authorities whereby committee chairmen exercise considerable influence over agenda setting. A chairman may demand the right to add items of his own (which generally reflect pressure from his party group) or to postpone, occasionally delete, items that officers intended to include, possibly ask for a change in the order of items and in extreme instances seek to bring about changes in the content of officers' reports.

10.19 Where there is pressure from councillors for an agenda item to be delayed or amended solely for political purposes the issue can be more contentious. If delay involves no legal problems or perceived disadvantage to third parties, then there would be no objection. The inclination of officers will always be, of course, to meet the legitimate wishes of councillors. However, where the delay is inspired by motives of political advantage (Widdicombe's research, for example, discloses instances of the avoidance of 'bad news' prior to a local election) or the item in dispute is one that the officer concerned has, or believes he has, a duty to report at that particular time then there can be a problem. In such a delicate circumstance the chief executive should be brought into discussion with the leader of the council and, with the backing of the monitoring officer where appropriate (see 4.48), an acceptable solution can hopefully be arrived at. Similar difficulties can arise where members demand that the terms of an agenda item (likely to be an officer's report) should be altered. Again it is probable that a compromise can be reached. Officers are nowadays likely always to prepare material for the executive or committees in such a way as to acknowledge the political goals of the majority group and this clearly requires skills of political sensitivity and of drafting. What is important, however, is that officers must insist on their own right to have their own professional or technical viewpoint known, recorded and not significantly amended by members in its published form.

10.20 Problems of the foregoing sort are far from common, but that they do happen at all is indicative of tensions in councillor-officer relations that can develop over the control of committee agenda. Closely linked is the parallel issue of the authorship of committee reports. Instances of members writing their own reports are not unknown, and it is becoming more common for members to present reports on matters within their own portfolio; and although this represents a departure from past practice it does not seem to present a problem, provided that officers have an opportunity of making their professional input, either in writing or orally, on the subject matter of a councillor's report. If all else fails, there is no reason why separate reports should not be prepared, e.g. by the chairman and the service chief officer.

10. Work before meetings

Drafting the agenda

10.21 At an early stage, preferably at a prescribed date prior to the committee meeting (see 10.2), the committee clerk will prepare the agenda in draft. In some authorities this may be circulated to all officers concerned so that they may see what is already on the draft and add matters that they themselves wish the cabinet or committee to know about or decide upon. Where this is the practice, the draft should state the date by which the draft must be returned to the committee clerk together with any additional items, and this date must be rigidly adhered to if the agenda is to be finalised and despatched on time.

10.22 Because an agenda is often compiled of material submitted from several sources some editing will be necessary on the part of the committee clerk, if the final document is not to lack uniformity of style and layout. Many problems can be reduced or avoided if the prescribed deadline for receipt of agenda items is enforced and, of great importance, if there are prescribed rules and guidelines regulating the manner in which material is to be prepared.

10.23 It should be accepted that the agenda is the responsibility of the proper officer and that he is the final arbiter of what goes on the agenda and in what form. An officer should be consulted if an item he has originated is held back, substantially amended or wholly rewritten.

Agenda planning meetings

10.24 In some authorities an agenda planning meeting is held at which all officers concerned in the work of a particular committee meet together, discuss items on the draft agenda, and decide mutually whether a matter is to be submitted as drafted, modified, or left over for a future meeting.

Consultation with chairman

10.25 It is comparatively uncommon for the committee chairman to be consulted on the draft agenda in detail. Such a course might be justified in certain circumstances, e.g. where an item of political sensitivity or major importance is concerned or where a particular member has asked for a matter to be brought before the committee (see also 10.19). A committee chairman will, however, expect to be briefed before the meeting and a cabinet briefing will normally involve all members of the cabinet (see 10.48).

What should be included

10.26 Local practice must determine what kind of items are included on the agenda. As a general guide, however, it may be said that a matter should be placed before the executive or a committee only if:
- it is within their terms of reference;
- it cannot be dealt with at officer level either because it:
  a) raises an issue of policy or principle of major importance not already decided; or

b) demands a decision beyond an officer's delegated authority; or

c) is politically contentious;

- it will eventually require a resolution of the full council, e.g. to meet the requirements of the law or of standing orders; and
- the committee/cabinet has itself requested the information.

10.27 It should be a principle in the conduct of local authority business that everything that needs a decision should be decided at the lowest level at which it may competently be taken. Unfortunately, it frequently happens in local government that decision-making is pushed upwards unnecessarily and councillors are called on to decide matters that could be dealt with at officer level. Of course, there may be occasions when an officer decides that it might be politic to bring before the cabinet/committee a matter on which he has delegated authority. The fact that an officer can be called to account is safeguard enough as a rule against arbitrary decisions at officer level.

10.28 Among matters that do not justify inclusion on a committee agenda are reports that action has been duly taken in pursuance of the committee's instructions (though the committee may be expected to want to know if an officer has been unable to execute a decision!), and information items (e.g. statistical material or trivia – staff movements, resignations, etc.) that do not call for action. As to whether action taken by committee chairmen should be reported, either for information or confirmation, see Chapter 5.

10.29 Items that should be included for noting on the agenda are those where an officer has taken a key decision under his delegated authority, or where a cabinet member has taken an executive decision. Also, exemptions from standing orders relating to contracts should be included under items for noting.

Form

10.30 A committee/cabinet agenda normally consists of a fully documented paper where all relevant information on each item of business is provided on the agenda itself or incorporated in appendices attached to the main document.

Clearly the amount of material produced for members can vary considerably, more often, it seems, because of the practice of the authority rather than the weight or significance of the issue to be decided. Maud reported:

'Behind . . . quite startling variations in the quantity of paper circulated lies a wide divergence of practice in the amount of written information submitted to subcommittees and committees and also in the methods of referring information and recommendations from subcommittees to committees and from committees to council. These differences in practice may in some places arise merely from a persistent adherence, for one reason or another, to different long-established traditions. On the other hand, they may well reflect elsewhere completely different philosophies.'

10. Work before meetings

Some officers feel that the amount of written material should be kept to a minimum so that members can concentrate on a few major issues, but there are others who believe with equal conviction that it is their duty to provide members with the fullest and most detailed information possible so that they can make their own decisions as to what they feel to be significant, rather than having the selection determined for them.

The requirements introduced as a consequence of the LG(AI)A 1985 (see particularly Chapter 3) may have encouraged the submission by officers of more detailed reports than formerly. Certainly oral reporting is no longer permissible unless related to an item already on the agenda or can be justified under the urgency provisions. An item on an agenda that merely states that a report will be made orally is out of order if it gives no indication whatsoever of the subject matter or purport of the report to be made. There is no reason, however, why an officer cannot update orally at a meeting a report that has been properly circulated in advance, although it may be advisable for the likelihood of an updating to be referred to on the agenda and if significant new material is introduced for the chairman to agree to take the update as an urgent item (see 9.82).

10.31 Apart from variations in the amount of paper produced, there are also differences of a more fundamental character. Some authorities incorporate a formal summons as part of the agenda paper; others do not. Some make it a practice to set out the names of all members of the committee at the top of the first page or at the bottom of the formal summons; other authorities restrict this to the first meeting of a new committee.

Order of business

10.32 It is usual for the order of items to be standardised. Certain business must necessarily be dealt with first, e.g. the election of a chairman where this is called for, and confirmation of minutes; and if a deputation is to be received or a presentation made these are matters conveniently dealt with soon after the commencement of proceedings so that persons concerned can be given a definite time to attend. Some authorities prefer to deal with relatively routine or non-controversial matters first and more important business afterwards. In some authorities the agenda is divided into two parts: first, items requiring decisions or special discussion including whether it is to be dealt with in private or not; then items submitted for information/noting. Sometimes the order is so arranged that officers are not required to sit through business that does not concern them. It is good practice to group associated matters together so that members do not find themselves dealing with a jumble of important items of policy and trivial detail. Maud's observations suggest that the amount of attention given to a particular item can often be affected by its position on the agenda and that the order of agenda items is a matter that would repay careful consideration.

10.33 Procedural items are now generally included at the beginning of an agenda. Many local authorities include an item early in the agenda to enable members to declare personal and prejudicial interests or enable the chairman to indicate the existence of urgent business he is prepared to allow later on. This has the advantage, not only of discouraging the submission of so-called urgent items, during the meeting but also of giving notice to any members of the public or press present that one or more items not specified on the agenda are to be discussed later.

First meeting of new committees

10.34 When an entirely new committee is set up or a standing committee is newly constituted with several new members it may be considered desirable:

- to include on the agenda a statement of the names of the members, the committee's terms of reference and, possibly, a resume of the committee's functions; and
- to despatch with the agenda all documents in current use relating to the work of the committee that could provide useful background or essential information for members.

Care should be taken in the selection so as to avoid including documents that soon become out of date: for example, it is questionable whether the members of a staffing committee should be given copies of national schemes of conditions of service because of the cost and difficulty of updating them as changes occur.

Papers for special committees

10.35 It is obvious, no doubt, that when a special committee is set up to inquire into or investigate a particular matter or to consider a specific problem, the first meeting may need to be devoted to certain preliminaries: defining the area of inquiry, ascertaining the basic facts, planning a programme of work and so on. It will usually be helpful if a paper is circulated with the agenda for the first meeting setting out the terms of reference, reciting the circumstances in which the committee came into being and providing as much factual information as can be gathered that is relevant to the task before the members.

Individual agenda items

10.36 Every cabinet agenda item has at least four principal parts:

- the heading;
- the question to be decided, succinctly expressed;
- the relevant facts, including – according to circumstances – a note of the authority's legal powers, of its policy on the subject matter or related topics, and of the financial considerations involved; and
- the options open and the consequences of pursuing each alternative posed.

It may also have a fifth:

- an indication of the particular course recommended, and reasons for the recommendation.

10. Work before meetings

Reports to committees in most local authorities follow the same format, other than for quasijudicial committees (planning and licensing).

10.37 This same order should be followed in officers' reports to cabinet/committee; and it is of crucial importance that councillors are given all the relevant information in order that they may make an informed judgment and reasoned decision. In *R. v. Isle of Wight County Council ex parte O'Keefe* (1991), it was held that a decision of the local authority to make a modification order granting a public right of way should be reached only after a proper consideration of all the evidence and the legal problems involved: the court quashed the decision that had been taken because the officers had failed to present the evidence fully in that they did not include in their report necessary qualifications of the strength of witnesses' evidence on the public user of the path concerned, nor did they include a proper assessment of the submissions of the owner of the land. In an earlier case, *R. v. Rochdale Metropolitan Borough Council ex parte Cromer Ring Mill Ltd* (1982), the law was inaccurately summarised in an officer's report and the court found that the committee had taken into account an irrelevant consideration and its decision was bad.

10.38 Competence in drafting will determine the brevity with which each item is covered. It is not, however, enough merely to use words economically. A sense of proportion is also necessary. Routine matters of minor importance, if they must be submitted for committee consideration, can often be dealt with in a single line. There can be severe condensation in appropriate circumstances: certain knowledge, for example, can be assumed on the part of councillors, and details that members can easily look up for themselves in past minutes, standing orders or other regulations need not necessarily be set out in full. Only local practice and sensible judgment can provide a guide. The order of material within an item can rarely be changed, however, without sacrifice of clarity and logical exposition: the question to be decided; the facts; the courses open and the consequences; and, often, a recommendation.

Routine items

10.39 Routine or regularly recurring items should be standardised in the minimum number of words consistent with clarity. For example, the item that deals with the submission of minutes of the previous meeting for confirmation could be dealt with in one line:

> 'MINUTES. Confirmation of minutes of . . . June, 20...'

though better expressed as, e.g.:

> 'MINUTES
> To confirm the minutes of the meeting of ... June, 20...'

Although councillors can be expected to know the purpose of the item, a reminder in express words could nevertheless be desirable.

There are several similar items that can be set out in summary fashion on the agenda: the election of a chairman and vice-chairman (never the appointment, unless, of course, the item has been placed on the agenda for the chief executive to report formally that the full council has appointed the committee chairman); the appointment of representatives of the council to serve on other bodies; the submission of a subcommittee's report; and so on.

10.40 Apart from routine items as above (where the intention is self-evident), care should be taken to indicate clearly what action is expected of the committee. Briefly expressed items can be introduced in the style: To consider, To decide, To receive. A common error, however, where agenda items are prefixed by the word 'To' is to employ it carelessly and incorrectly:

> 'TOWN CENTRE REDEVELOPMENT To report that . . .'

when what was intended was:

> 'TOWN CENTRE REDEVELOPMENT Chief Executive to report that . . .'

It is good practice to indicate who is in fact reporting particular items.

Item or appendix?

10.41 It is not always easy in practice to determine whether particular business is better presented as an item on the agenda or in an accompanying document. Importance can be a matter of opinion and practice varies, in any case, as to the form of an agenda. Length may be more relevant. An item that can be dealt with in less than a page of type is generally more conveniently included on the main agenda, while one that extends beyond, say, a page in length is probably better dealt with as an appendix. In the majority of cases a committee agenda will contain items of varying length.

Appendices

10.42 The attachment of papers to the agenda as appendices has the advantage of providing separate documents that can easily be incorporated in the subsequent minutes. It also helps speedy preparation of the agenda because the typing or printing work can be distributed among a number of officers; and it invariably makes for a tidier, more easily understood agenda paper.

10.43 Appendices should be identified by letter or number, i.e. either as APPENDIX A or APPENDIX 1, whichever may be preferred, and it assists members in referring to several appendices if the documents are reproduced on different coloured paper, if finances allow. Thus, for example, an item would appear on the agenda paper to this effect:

> '00 REORGANISATION OF FINANCE DEPARTMENT
> Report of Working Party APPENDIX A
> (Yellow)'

and the document itself would be identified by this reference at the top right-hand corner of the first page (on yellow paper):

> APPENDIX A
> (see agenda item 00)

10.44 Sometimes it may be necessary for documents to be attached to appendices. These need to be distinguished from the appendices by, for example, referring to them as ENCLOSURE or STATEMENT or ANNEXE, according to choice, and if appendices are lettered A, B, C and so on, these further attachments can conveniently be numbered 1, 2, 3, etc., or, perhaps, I, II, III, etc. Whatever is favoured, it should be standardised throughout the authority.

Any other business

10.45 It was once common practice for committee agenda to conclude with an item 'Any other business'. Since the coming into force of the LG(AI)A 1985, the practice has properly been discontinued because an item of business may not be considered at a meeting of a principal council unless requisite advance notice has been given (see 6.22). The same applies for cabinet agendas (see 10.36). Some authorities include as a matter of routine a final agenda item for committee meetings 'Any other business which the chairman considers to be urgent' to cover the possibility of urgent business arising. See 10.33 about the desirability of there being an early agenda item to enable notice to be given of urgent business later in the meeting.

Despatch of papers

Need for efficient arrangements

10.46 There must be an efficient arrangement for the issue of notices and despatch of papers to ensure:

- that appropriate notice is given to the press and public;
- that the summons and agenda are in the hands of members by the time prescribed by standing orders; and

- that officers required to be present and any persons invited to attend on the particular occasion are appropriately notified and advised; and that the papers are complete in every particular and that no one entitled to receive them is omitted from the despatch.

This is secured by:

- strict compliance with a checklist of members' names, press representatives and officers' names;
- double-checking that no one has been omitted either by:
  a) writing the names of addressees on the front sheet of the agenda paper and then, after separately selecting the appropriate preaddressed envelopes, putting the papers in the envelopes; or
  b) one officer calling out the names of the addressees and another putting the agenda papers in previously selected preaddressed envelopes;
- ideally (but practicable only in the smaller authorities in compact areas) arranging for personal delivery;
- recording the despatch in a book kept for the purpose.

A prescribed procedure and a record kept help to emphasise the importance of the despatch: failure to serve the summons and agenda correctly could affect the validity of the meeting: see 6.20.

Pre-committee/cabinet briefings

General considerations

10.47 The amount of briefing a committee chairman or cabinet members may require before a meeting depends upon the type of meeting and the experience and/or knowledge of the members. It is usual, and desirable, for the chairman or cabinet to discuss beforehand with the appropriate officers the items on the agenda.

10.48 There are arguably objections to the pre-committee briefing on the grounds that the chairman and officers could agree tactics to steamroller the committee into agreeing a particular course of action. This should not be the purpose. There is nothing wrong in the officer making clear to the chairman what is in his mind and his own preferences or recommendations, but there should be no conspiracy between chairman and officers to force a particular decision upon the committee. If the chairman gains the advantage of knowing what is in the mind of the officers then the officers, for their part, become aware of the chairman's feelings. His views on a matter may well reflect the political opinion of the majority group and this, in turn, will alert the officers to the possible need to treat a matter with sensitivity and discretion.

It is equally important that cabinet briefings are not used as an opportunity for members to ask questions and decide the outcome, as this could make the meeting itself seem like a rubber-stamping exercise. As with committee briefings, they should be used as an opportunity for officers and members to receive each other's views and for issues to be clarified.

10. Work before meetings

10.49 It is for the individual chairman to determine whether there should be a briefing, what form it should take and what officers should be present. In some cases the chairman may prefer to read through the agenda and discuss with the officers concerned those items on which he has queries or needs further information; perhaps a telephone discussion may be sufficient. Other chairmen may think it sufficient to rely on the relevant officer contacting him if circumstances merit a briefing. But, as Maud pointed out:[2]

> 'Whether committee briefing takes place incidentally or on a specific occasion, there is no doubt that in many instances the initiative rests entirely with the officer, who has already prepared (and in some cases already circulated) the agenda and reports.'

Maud contains several paragraphs on the pros and cons of committee briefing; and Widdicombe produced evidence to show that pre-committee briefing was universal.

Committee clerk should be present

10.50 It is essential for the committee clerk to be present at any pre-committee briefing. Sometimes he is not, and this seems to make his task unnecessarily difficult.

Officers and invitees

10.51 It may also be necessary, primarily in relation to procedure, to brief any 'outsider' who has been invited to attend a particular committee meeting: an officer, for example, who is required to be present to speak on an item of business but has never before attended a committee meeting; or an independent adviser who has been invited to attend; or, of course, a deputation who will feel more comfortable if properly briefed beforehand as to what to expect when entering the room, where to sit, how to conduct themselves and so on. It is easy for officers continuously associated with committee work to forget that, for an officer who rarely attends a committee meeting, it can be a discomforting experience to be asked to attend and speak at a meeting at short notice. It can also be a daunting experience for members of the public who may never have attended a local authority meeting before and may be confused by the way in which many meetings are conducted. A preliminary explanatory few words are always appreciated.

Final preparations for meeting

Availability of accommodation

10.52 Before committee papers are finally despatched to council members and others, the committee clerk should check, even though the dates of meetings and accommodation have been prearranged, that:

- a suitable committee room is available with reasonable seating for the public, and table and seating for the press;
- waiting room accommodation is conveniently situated for invitees to the meeting;
- no other committee or subcommittee with common membership has been subsequently arranged for the same time;
- nothing, such as noisy repair work in adjoining accommodation, is likely to interfere with the meeting.

Then, on the day of the meeting, the clerk should inspect the room beforehand to ensure that:

- tables are appropriately arranged[3] and there are sufficient chairs;
- the room is properly equipped, i.e. with notepaper, blotting paper, pen and ink (for the chairman to sign the minutes), water carafes and tumblers of fresh water, and with facilities for displaying maps, etc., or other visual aids;
- heating, ventilation and lighting are functioning;
- tea or coffee will be served at the requisite time;
- emergency evacuation procedure is understood; and
- that the meeting is shown on the notice board in the foyer or entrance hall of the building concerned and that visitors will be escorted to the meeting or waiting room.

10.53 This last point is more important where the committee/cabinet is meeting in an unfamiliar venue, in which case a map of the venue might usefully be sent with the notice showing, e.g. a convenient route of access and car parks available.

What should be taken to the meeting

10.54 The documents needed at a meeting will depend upon the type of committee and the character of business: for a staffing committee; for example, it would be prudent to have ready to hand a copy of the authority's authorised staff establishment, up-to-date handbooks on national conditions of service, staffing regulations, procedure agreements and so on. All papers should be assembled beforehand and, ideally, compared with a standard checklist of items so that nothing is overlooked. Care must be taken to anticipate what may be required: e.g. if a plan is to be referred to, it should be displayed prominently before members begin to assemble and it should be of a scale clearly visible from every seat. Sometimes it may be desirable to draft out alternative versions of likely resolutions.

10.55 The items likely to be on a checklist include:

- minutes of the previous meeting for signature after confirmation;
- current minute book;
- attendance book;
- spare copies of the agenda (now a statutory obligation: see 3.9) and other circulated papers;

10. Work before meetings

- committee clerk's notebook and spare pencils;
- standing orders and any rules or regulations (including earlier policy decisions) governing matters within the particular committee's terms of reference;
- current constitution of the committee: the list of members (and substitute members if any) of the committee and any associated subcommittees, its terms of reference, timetable of future meetings, etc.;
- Forward Plan, schemes, plans, bylaws, files and other papers relating to the business to be transacted, assembled in agenda order, with particular documents flagged for easy reference; and
- standard reference books, yearbook, relevant statutes, etc.

Notes

1 Maud Report, vol.1, para.128. This was written, of course, before performance management became fashionable and the corporate performance assessment (CPA) came into being.
2 Maud Report, vol. 5, para.145.
3 'A long table, and a square table, or seats about the walls, seem things of form, but are things of substance; for a long table, a few at the upper end in effect sway all the business; but in the other form, there is more use of the counsellors' opinions that sit lower': Sir Francis Bacon, *Of Counsel*.

Chapter 11
Work at meetings

Introduction

Business must proceed

11.1 It is good practice and administratively convenient to adopt the principle that business must proceed as planned once a committee meeting has been convened, provided there is no overriding reason why it should not. The general rule is that a meeting that has been properly convened cannot be postponed (see 6.37), although in practice this is often done; but there can be failure to make a meeting, i.e. where, for example, a quorum is not present when the meeting should begin (see 6.38). It is also a general rule that the proceedings of any meeting are invalid if the meeting has not been properly constituted (see 1.33). Strictly speaking, the chair of a committee should satisfy himself that these requirements are fulfilled before the committee proceeds to business (see 7.33). In practice, the chair assumes that due formalities have been met unless he is advised to the contrary or it is self-evident that, for example, there is no quorum. It is submitted that this principle should be extended so that there shall be a presumption, until the contrary is shown to be the case, that a committee has been validly convened and is properly constituted and that the meeting can properly proceed with the transaction of business. The business to be transacted can only lawfully be that of which notice has been given on the agenda (see 6.21) unless:

- the chair accepts it as urgent; or
- whether written or presented orally it merely updates an item already on the agenda without introducing wholly new matter: an agenda item report to be laid on the table is strictly no longer permissible unless it comes under one or other of these headings.

Record of attendance

Attendance of members

11.2 The law provides that the names of council and co-opted members present at a local authority meeting must be recorded. In the case of many parish councils, this is done by providing an attendance book for signature by those present: the book can be passed round at the meeting (in which case the committee clerk in attendance must be alert to ensure that the book is placed in front of latecomers) or, preferably in the

11. Work at meetings

case of large committees, placed at the entrance to the committee room so that those attending can sign before they enter the meeting.

11.3 The attendance book can be an ordinary hard-covered book of ruled pages in which the committee clerk writes as necessary the name of the committee and date of meeting at the top of the page on which members are required to sign. Or, preferably, it can be a prepared two-column loose-leaf sheet headed with the name of the committee and date of meeting, with the names of members typed in the left-hand column; each member is expected to sign on the appropriate line in the right-hand column. This helps in the case of illegible signatures and in determining quickly in the case of large committees who is present and who is absent.

11.4 The usual method for principal councils, however, is for the committee clerk to have a list of the membership of the committee in the book used to take the notes of the meeting, and the committee clerk then puts a tick alongside the names of those members who attend the meeting. The importance of an accurate record of attendance lies in the fact that this will be prima facie evidence for purposes of determining disqualification in the event of failure to attend for a consecutive period of six months (see 4.94) and may be used for other purposes: e.g. in checking council members' subsistence claims. Councillors may wish to avail themselves of the record for political purposes, or for evidence that they were not at a meeting at which unlawful expenditure had been approved (see 4.46).

11.5 Where an attendance book is still kept, standing orders will usually place upon members an obligation to sign it. The old model standing order no. 17 states:

'Every member of the council attending a meeting of the council, or of any of its committees of which he is a member, shall sign his name in the attendance book or sheet provided for that purpose. [And every member attending some other meeting, conference or inspection on approved duty shall sign his name in the register kept for that purpose.]'

The committee clerk would be wise, however, to keep his own check on members' attendance by, for example, ticking against the list of members of the committee as each one enters.

11.6 Councillors who attend a meeting of a committee of which they are not members in exercise of a right conferred upon them by standing orders or of their common law 'need to know' will not ordinarily be credited with an attendance (nor may they take part in the proceedings unless expressly permitted to do so). A standing order governing the attendance of non-committee members might be to this effect:

Any member of the council may be present during a meeting of any committee or subcommittee but unless he be a member of that committee or subcommittee shall not (except with the permission of the chairman) take part in the proceedings thereof, neither shall he be entitled to sign the register of attendance nor to have his attendance reckoned for any purpose of these standing orders.

11.7 On the other hand, a non-committee member present at a meeting by express invitation ought to be credited with an attendance. Standing orders should state specifically the rights of council members in this respect. Old model standing order no. 37 is to this effect:

> 'A member of the council who has moved a motion which has been referred to any committee or subcommittee shall have notice of the meeting of the committee or subcommittee at which it is proposed to consider the motion. He shall have the right to attend the meeting and if he attends shall have an opportunity of explaining the motion.'

It would not be necessary for the council member concerned to move the motion afresh at the committee meeting – indeed, as a non-member of the committee he could not properly do so.

Return of attendances

11.8 It is usual for a return of members' attendances to be prepared as soon as practicable after the end of the council year for circulation to members and the press and for the guidance of the selection committee in determining committee membership for the ensuing year.

Election of committee chairman

Election procedure

11.9 So far as those authorities with leader and cabinet executive arrangements are concerned, it is for the council to appoint the leader of the executive, who chairs the executive meetings. In general, however, it is for the local authority to decide whether committee chairmen shall be appointed by the full council or elected by the committee itself, assuming it wishes to appoint a chairman (see 1.9), but in either case the term of office is normally for the ensuing year. The standing orders working party (see 2.4) produced this draft core standing order in terms obviously influenced by widespread practice ensuring that committee chairmen are nominees, or at least appointed with the consent of the majority party:

'00–1 The council may appoint, from among the voting members, a person to preside at the meetings of a committee or subcommittee, and a person to preside in the absence of the first person.

2 If any appointment possible under the previous paragraph is not made, a committee may appoint, from among the voting members, a person to preside at the meetings of any subcommittee appointed by them, or a person to preside in the absence of the first person, as the case may be.

3 If any appointment possible under the previous two paragraphs is not made, the

committee or subcommittee at their first meeting after the annual meeting of the council shall, from among their voting members, appoint a person to preside at their meetings, and may, in the same way, appoint a person to preside in the absence of the first person.

4 If the persons appointed under the previous paragraphs of this standing order are absent, a meeting of a committee or subcommittee shall appoint, from among the voting members present, a person to preside at that meeting.

5 If it is necessary for the committee or subcommittee to appoint a person to preside, the proper officer shall call on a member of the committee or subcommittee to move that a voting member of the committee or subcommittee shall take the chair.

6 If discussion arises, the proper officer shall exercise the powers of the person presiding to regulate that discussion, and to maintain order at the meeting.

7 The motion, and any amendments, shall be put to the meeting in accordance with standing order 00(5) (voting on appointments).'

No special formalities are called for in the electoral process. Some local authorities formerly provided in standing orders for the election to be conducted by ballot and for members to nominate in advance of the meeting persons for the chairmanship and vice-chairmanship. Where committee chairmen are not appointed by the council it is sometimes the practice for the chairman of the council or mayor to attend the first meetings of committees to preside over the election of chairman and vice-chairman (see 11.10).

Who presides at the election?

11.10 A person cannot preside at his own election (see 7.21) and therefore it is necessary for someone other than the prospective chairman to preside at the outset of the meeting. This may be prescribed by standing orders but it is more likely to be a matter of local practice. Thus the mayor/chairman of the council may attend the initial meeting of all committees each year expressly for the purpose of presiding over the election of a committee chairman. In the absence of the chairman or mayor the committee may appoint a chairman pro tem (the outgoing chairman or the senior member present) and the senior officer present could quite properly ask for nominations for the temporary chairman, or, indeed, for a permanent chairman, particularly since it is now accepted that the appointment of a chairman is not an essential prerequisite for a valid meeting (see 11.14). Where the council appoints the committee chairman he assumes the chair of the committee from the outset.

Eligibility for committee chairmanship

11.11 Some local authorities place restrictions on the eligibility of council and co-opted members (see 4.55, 11.12) for the chairmanship of committees. So, for example, see the two standing orders below adopted by a former county council:

> 'The chairman of the council shall not be appointed as the chairman of any committee of the council except of the selection committee or of any committee specially appointed from time to time.

No member of the council shall be chairman of more than one committee at the same time, nor shall any chairman of a committee act as vice-chairman of another committee at the same time:

> Provided that this standing order shall not (a) apply to any committee specially appointed or (b) be deemed to prevent the chairman of a standing committee from being vice-chairman of the Law and Parliamentary Committee so long as he is a member of either House of Parliament.'

11.12 A co-opted member who possesses voting rights could be elected as a committee chairman. There are, however, some disadvantages in this. A co-opted member chairman has not the political responsibility of a councillor chairman and this could be regarded as a reason for not choosing a co-opted member for that office. In practice, a committee chairman has responsibilities going far beyond his duty to preside at meetings of his committee. Further, unless standing orders specifically allow it, a co-opted member would not be able to present his committee's report or minutes at the full council meeting and pilot through or defend the committee's proposals or answer questions on his committee's work; but a vice-chairman could, of course, perform these tasks on his behalf at the council meeting.

Vice-chairman

11.13 There is much to commend the election of a vice-chairman of a committee because there can then be no doubt who should act in the chairman's absence. It eliminates the need for a separate election of an acting chairman whenever the chairman is absent from a meeting (because the vice-chairman automatically takes the chair in the absence of the chairman at a committee meeting) and it provides training for prospective chairmen.

There should always be a chairman

11.14 There is persuasive modern authority for the principle that a meeting, other than a council meeting, can lawfully proceed without someone in the chair (see 4.79). However, it is undesirable for a committee to proceed without a chairman and thus the members should ordinarily seek to elect one. In the event of there being no nominations or an equality of votes, the meeting should pass a resolution to the effect that it wishes to proceed without a chairman. If a temporary chairman is elected and if, later, the chairman or vice-chairman arrives it is usual, but not essential (as in the case of a meeting of the full council where the chairman or mayor, if present, must preside (see 7.27)) – for the acting chairman to relinquish the chair in favour of the chairman or vice-chairman as the case may be. He will not do this immediately as a rule, but will wait until the conclusion of the item or business under discussion at the time.

Chairman has casting vote

11.15 The chairman or vice-chairman or whoever else may be presiding at a committee or subcommittee meeting has a second or casting vote (LGA 1972, Sch.12, para.39(2)).

Quorum

None prescribed by statute

11.16 No quorum is prescribed by statute in the case of committee meetings, but the local authority has power to prescribe one by standing orders. If it does not do so the committee may determine its quorum.

11.17 The relevant core standing order drafted by the working party on standing orders (2.3) was to this effect:

> '00–1 No business shall be transacted at any meeting of a committee or subcommittee unless at least one quarter of the whole number of voting members of the committee or subcommittee, as the case may be, are present: provided that in no case shall any business be transacted unless at least two voting members are present.
>
> 2 The provisions of standing order 0 shall apply to a meeting of a committee or subcommittee at which a quorum is not present as they would apply if it were a meeting of the council.'

Absence of quorum

11.18 On the principle put forward earlier (see 11.1) that committee business should proceed rather than not, that the objective always should be to transact business rather than delay it, then the following courses might usefully be pursued when at the time fixed for the commencement of a meeting there is no quorum present:

- If it is known for certain or there is reasonable cause to believe that additional members will be present later, the members present could proceed to discuss the business on the agenda on the understanding that, as soon as a quorum is present, the business already transacted will be affirmed by those then present and so legitimise what has been done.
- If a committee has power merely to consider and report there seems no reason why business should not proceed, provided it is made clear at the time of report to

the parent body (the full council in the case of a committee; the committee in the case of a subcommittee) that any recommendations put forward are those of the members concerned and not of the fully constituted committee or subcommittee: the decision of the parent body if it chooses to adopt the recommendations thereby endorses and so validates what has been done.

- If a committee has delegated power then, somewhat similarly, the members present could, notwithstanding the absence of a quorum, proceed to discuss business on the agenda and, instead of taking executive decisions, put forward recommendations for consideration on the same basis as outlined above.

As suggested above, the temporary absence of a quorum should be ignored unless the attention of the chairman and, therefore, the committee is drawn to it expressly.

Confirmation of minutes of previous meeting

General

11.19 What has been said about confirmation at a council meeting of the minutes of the council's previous meeting applies for the most part in respect of confirmation of minutes at a committee or subcommittee meeting. The agenda should provide for this item to be taken as first business (except where there is need to elect a chairman) and the only matters that may properly be raised on the confirmation of minutes are questions as to their accuracy. It is no bad thing to cover this specifically in a standing order:

> 'No motion or discussion shall be allowed upon the confirmation of minutes, except as to their accuracy, and any questions upon this point shall be determined by a majority of the members of the committee present when the matter in question was decided.'

Although it is not unreasonable to expect only those members present at the meeting concerned to vote on the confirmation of the minutes, it may be that a standing order in these terms is invalid because it seeks to infringe a statutory rule that all questions coming before a local authority shall be decided by a majority of those present and voting (LGA 1972, Sch.12, para.39).

11.20 Whereas minutes of a council meeting are usually printed and circulated to council members, practice varies as to whether minutes of a committee meeting should be circulated to committee members (other than where the committee minutes have been submitted in their entirety to the council, a practice that is falling into disuse (see 12.41)). If not then some other arrangement may be thought desirable in order that members may be satisfied as to the accuracy of the minutes before agreeing to their confirmation. In some councils it is the practice to obtain the chairman's approval to the draft committee minutes and to lay the minutes on the table before the commencement of a meeting, so that members who wish may have the opportunity of inspecting them. A standing order to the following effect is useful:

> 'At every committee meeting the minutes of the previous meeting shall be taken as read, but shall be read, either in part, or in their entirety, before signature, if a majority of members of the committee then present so require.'

The practice of obtaining a chairman's approval to draft minutes, though widely adopted, is a questionable procedure because the responsibility for minuting a correct record lies with the committee clerk and in the event of disagreement it is his view that should ordinarily prevail. Clearly there may be advantage in ascertaining whether or not a particular minute will be accepted as a correct record, but if practice is to do this by consulting the chairman the arrangement should be clearly laid down.

Minutes must be of previous meeting

11.21 The law requires that minutes must be confirmed at the same or next following meeting. This was so also under the LGA 1933, Sch.3, para.3(1) of Part V, but there was a useful amendment made by the LoGA 1963, Sch.4, para.44 (not, unfortunately, carried forward into the 1972 Act) that permitted the minutes of committee meetings (but not of council meetings) to be lawfully confirmed at any subsequent meeting, i.e. not necessarily the same or next meeting.

11.22 A mandatory standing order, prescribed in the Local Authorities (Standing Orders) Regulations 1993 provides that the minutes of an extraordinary meeting of the council may be signed at the next ordinary meeting (see 8.23).

Matters arising

11.23 One of the potential problems arising out of the confirmation of minutes is the temptation for members to raise issues apart from simply confirming the minutes as a correct record. At its worst this can lead to an attempt to change a decision taken at the previous meeting and any such discussion should be ruled out of order by the chairman. Some authorities are known to provide an item on the agenda 'Matters arising from the minutes' to allow, for example, members to be advised of the current position of items discussed at the previous meeting. However, this is not regarded as good practice and, unless the subject to be raised is related to a matter specifically referred to in the agenda, may infringe the statutory restriction that only business specified in the notice can be dealt with (LGA 1972, s.100B, added by LG(AI)A 1985).

Recording the proceedings

Introduction

11.24 Because of the informality of committee proceedings, where discussion is discursive and not always directed towards a specific proposition before the meeting, considerable skill is demanded of the committee clerk whose task it is to grasp the collective sense of the committee (see 11.25) and to record the decision that emerges out of the debate. Only very rarely will the chairman ask for a proposition to be moved: it is far more usual for him to say at a particular stage of the proceedings, 'We're agreed then', or words to that effect, and move on to the next business, in confident expectation that the committee clerk will get down on paper a form of words that will fairly reflect the views of the majority. It is this that distinguishes proceedings in committee from proceedings of the full council and makes greater demands upon the competence of the committee clerk.

Sense-taking

11.25 A committee clerk is unlikely to be able to crystallise at any particular point the emergent view of the committee collectively if he is engrossed in extensive note-taking, even less so if he is making a scrupulously accurate short-hand record of all that is being said. It is of little value to the chairman if he turns to the committee clerk for recapitulation of the committee's views to be told that the only guidance available is a verbatim note of what was said by the last speaker. Admittedly it is the chairman's responsibility to 'hold the thread of the discussion, summing it up at intervals if necessary', but not all chairmen do so. The late Lord Normanbrook, who was secretary to the Cabinet until 1962, is reported to have said:

'I used to take the Cabinet notes in longhand, just with an old-fashioned fountain pen. I rarely wanted to get down what was said, except perhaps when they were trying to formulate the wording of an announcement and various people had different versions. What I was trying to get was the sense of a Cabinet meeting.'

This is precisely what the effective committee clerk should strive to do: to capture the sense of the meeting. It is all too easy sometimes for a committee clerk to allow his knowledge of what a committee chairman was briefed to say or a chief officer intended to say – but in fact failed to say explicitly – to influence his view of the consensus reached at a meeting. This is less likely, admittedly, at a committee meeting but can happen when, for example, a committee chairman may be meeting representatives of an outside body. It is a common fault, a serious one, which must be guarded against.

Note-taking

11.26 Just how best to take notes at a committee meeting is very much a matter of personal preference. Some local authorities insist that the committee clerk keeps his notes in a book (which is often preserved: see 12.54), sometimes requiring the agenda to be pasted on to the left-hand pages and the notes recorded on ruled pages opposite; others leave the decision to the committee clerk who may be content merely to make manuscript notes in the margin of the agenda paper. In general terms, the clerk must note down each possible decision as it begins to emerge and then cross it through as the discussion swerves to some other proposition. Apart from keeping track of the discussion the committee clerk should carefully record:

- specific motions with the names of the mover and any seconder and, necessarily, any amendments similarly;[1]
- the name of any individual member who expressly asks that his dissent be recorded: see (4.47);
- the names of members who vote for and against a motion and of those who abstain upon a requisition for the voting to be recorded (see 7.115);
- any incidental happening, e.g. a member's declaration of interest; the chairman's vacation of the chair for a specific item; a temporary adjournment; and so on.

11.27 If there is doubt in a committee clerk's mind about a decision he should ask for clarification immediately, from the chairman, i.e. before the committee proceeds to the next business. This is vitally important because it is useless, after the conclusion of a meeting, to canvass opinion as to what the decision on a particular item of business might have been:[2] apart from dereliction of duty (because the recording of decisions is the committee clerk's responsibility) there is unlikely to be unanimity of opinion among those whose views are sought! If a competent committee clerk does not understand the committee's decision it may safely be assumed that no one else does either. On the other hand, if the sense of the meeting is abundantly clear to the members, neither the chairman nor the majority on the committee will thank the committee clerk in seeking clarification for providing an opportunity for discussion to be reopened on a matter already decided.

11.28 A somewhat different approach in note-taking is necessary if a committee is considering a long-term matter in the course of a series of meetings. Here the committee clerk will not be concerned in minuting the proceedings but in collecting material from which to frame the committee's ultimate report, in delving for facts, in submitting papers on particular aspects of its terms of reference, and so on.

Voting

Ordinary mode

11.29 The law does not prescribe the method of voting at committee or sub-committee meetings but ordinarily it is by show of hands. A draft core standing order (see 2.4), not so far made obligatory (but see 7.102) was to this effect:

'00–1 Except where a requisition is made under the next paragraph, the method of voting at meetings of the council, committee and subcommittees shall be by show of hands.

2 If a requisition is made by the specified number of members, the voting on any question shall be recorded so as to show whether each member present gave his vote for or against that question or abstained from voting.

3 The specified number of members is:

  a) one-fifth of the members entitled to vote at the meeting; or
  b) where the council is divided into political groups, in the case of a meeting of the council, such number as is equal to the number of members of the second largest political group and, in the case of a meeting of a committee or sub-committee, the number of seats on that body allocated to the second largest political group among the members of the council, whichever is the less.

[*Variation:* a smaller number than that specified may be adopted]

4 If a vote is taken by show of hands, any member who is present when the vote was taken may require that his/her vote or abstention shall be recorded in the minutes by notifying forthwith the proper officer of his wish.

5 Where a vote is required on a motion to appoint or elect a member of the council to a position to be filled by the authority, and there are two or more members nominated for that position, the names of all those nominated shall be put to the meeting in alphabetical order of surname. Those entitled to vote shall each vote for only one person. If there is not a majority of those voting in favour of one person, the name of the person having the least number of votes shall be struck off the list and a fresh vote shall be taken, and so on until a majority of votes is given in favour of one person.'

As to entitlement to vote (see 11.33) and on the recording of votes, including a mandatory standing order in this respect: see 7.105.

Counting a vote

11.30 In practice the chairman will call for a show of hands only if unsure of the collective sense of the meeting. When a show of hands is asked for it is a wise precaution for the committee clerk to count the raised hands both for and against and to count aloud as he points to each member so that members can check the voting if they wish. It is, however, for the chairman to declare the decision and thus the committee clerk, after counting, should pause after voicing the total numbers and, even when the decision is obvious, leave it to the chairman to say whether the motion or amendment is carried or lost. Thus the sequence should be:

- Chairman: Those in favour?
- Committee clerk: One, two, three, four, five: five, Mr Chairman.
- Chairman: Those against?
- Committee clerk: One, two, three: three, Mr Chairman.
- Chairman: The motion is carried.

11.31 The importance of this procedure is underlined where there is an equality of votes and the chairman must decide whether to use his second or casting vote (see 11.37):

- Chairman: Those in favour?
- Committee clerk: One, two, three, four, five: five, Mr Chairman.

- Chairman: Those against?
- Committee clerk: One, two, three, four, five: five, Mr Chairman.
- Chairman: (after, no doubt, momentary hesitation): The motion isn't carried; or, I shall use my casting vote: the motion is carried.

11.32 Ensuring that a clear resolution is passed is even more important where, for example, a formal decision is needed to exclude the press and public on account of the likely disclosure of exempt information (see 3.8). This can be facilitated where there is printed on the agenda itself the terms of the necessary motion to be moved so that all the chairman, or any other member, has to do is to move 'That the press and public be excluded as explained on the agenda'. Even when this is done a clear decision has to be taken and minuted. Failure to do so could result in the kind of argument that erupted in North Wales in 1981 where Clwyd County Council's economic development subcommittee failed to ensure than an unequivocal decision to exclude was taken and found it necessary to repeat the meeting before matters could proceed. During subsequent court proceedings Nolan J took the view that it was enough for a chairman 'to take the sense of the meeting' but this must be done 'in a clear and unambiguous way' and minuted accordingly: *R. v. Clwyd County Council ex parte Delyn Borough Council* (1987).

Eligibility to vote

11.33 Not all members present at a committee meeting are necessarily entitled to vote. There may be members present who are not members of the committee, who are attending by invitation or under a claim of a 'need to know' (see 4.11), or under the provisions of a standing order that permits non-members to be present at any committee but does not allow them to take part in the discussion, except by leave of the committee, or to vote. If a councillor under a disability persists in voting his vote is likely to be void (see 7.109); and where a committee or subcommittee is acting in a quasijudicial capacity a vote cast by a member having an interest in the subject matter is likely to render the committee's or subcommittee's decision as contrary to natural justice on account of bias and therefore void (see *R. v. London County Council* (1982), *R. v. Hendon RDC ex parte Chorley* (1993). As to conflict of interest of councillors with local authority employee and/or trade union associations: see 13.23. It is often difficult for the chairman in a large committee to recognise whether those voting are all in fact entitled to vote. The committee clerk ought to draw attention to any vote by someone not entitled to vote but, of course, the difficulty may be no less for him. The chairman might well be advised to remind the assembled gathering that only members of the committee may vote, particularly if the vote is on a crucial matter. Difficulties of this kind can be overcome by requiring non-members to occupy seats apart from the committee members.

Voting rights of non-members

11.34 As indicated earlier (see 4.11), persons present at a committee meeting who are not appointed members of the committee do not possess a right to vote. That, at least, is the position ordinarily. Some local authorities, however, in carefully regulated circumstances, permit a councillor to be present with full voting powers when substituting for an appointed councillor who is absent from the particular meeting (see 9.53). There is also the exceptional position in some authorities where, usually in the case of a planning committee, the authority confers a right on any member of the council, whether or not appointed to the committee, to attend and speak and vote on any matter concerning the area which the councillor represents. Strictly, this practice contravenes the principle that a committee must have a fixed and not a fluctuating membership (see 9.6); and it obviously poses practical problems. It makes difficulties for the chairman. How can he know on each item of business whether the individual councillor is entitled to vote or not? The onus of playing fair may well rest upon the individual councillor under standing orders, but it could be that a councillor might unwittingly vote on an item in which he may not be concerned as the representative of a ward or electoral division.[3] And how should the quorum be calculated? The answer would appear to be by reference to the number of appointed members. But the fact that these questions arise surely casts doubt on the wisdom if not the propriety of such a practice: indeed its legality is open to question.

11.35 Suppose a councillor is summoned to a committee meeting in error (e.g. because of a confusion over similar surnames) and that councillor attends and actually votes and the voting error is not detected at the time? What is the position? First, the proceedings are not invalidated solely on that account, nor can the constitution of the meeting be easily challenged subsequently because of the presumption that after the minutes have been confirmed the meeting was properly constituted. But a vote that is an invalid vote is no vote at all and if such a vote was critical, e.g. if a proposition was carried by one vote, then the decision is open to challenge: see *Nell* v. *Longbottom* (1894), in which it was held that an invalid vote could not be regarded as having been cast (and see 7.106).

Co-opted and non-voting members

11.36 While in general co-opted members on a committee must be treated as non-voting members under the LG&HA 1989, s.13, there are exceptions to this rule by virtue of s.13(4) (see 4.55). Also, s.53(8) of the LGA 2000 specifically provides that a member of a standards committee who is not a member of that authority is entitled to vote at meetings of the committee.

Chairman's second or casting vote

11.37 The statutory power of a chairman of any local authority meeting, including that of a committee or subcommittee, to give a second or casting vote has already been discussed (see 7.120). Some authorities, no doubt to avoid uncertainty, provide specifically in standing orders for a second or casting vote by the person presiding:

'In the case of an equality of votes at a meeting of any committee or subcommittee the chairman presiding thereat shall have a second or a casting vote.'

11. Work at meetings

Reversal or variation of decision at same meeting

11.38 The ordinary rule is that when a meeting has resolved upon a certain issue the resolution cannot at the same meeting be extinguished or changed by a second resolution purporting to rescind or reverse or vary the first. The rule should be observed inflexibly in the case of council meetings. If specific procedure is made for the rescission of resolutions the prescribed procedure must be stringently observed or the purported rescission will be ineffective: *R.* v. *Tralee UDC* (1913).

11.39 The view could be taken, however, that (subject necessarily to standing orders) in the case of committee deliberations, where procedure is informal and a strict order of debate is rarely observed or needs to be, the conclusions or decisions of the committee are not settled until the chairman declares the sitting at an end. Much depends upon the character of the committee and the business being transacted. In the case of a committee appointed for a specific or one very general purpose (as in the case of a committee of inquiry), the discussion may range over the whole terms of reference and such conclusions as may emerge during the course of the discussion are purely tentative ones that are not finally settled until the concluding stages of the proceedings. In such cases, there seems nothing to prevent the committee from changing its mind several times.

11.40 However, this view could hardly be sustained in the case of the ordinary local authority committee sitting to consider an agenda with quite separate items of business. It would not be logical to regard the committee meeting as sitting in continuous session to deal with the business en bloc because in fact each item of business discussed and not deferred is settled there and then by a decision expressly stated or implied. Nevertheless, the wishes of committee members are paramount and, provided that the members present when the business was first dealt with are still present and no others have come into the room and no executive action has been taken on the resolution by a zealous officer, i.e. the circumstances are precisely as they were at the time when the original decision was taken, it would not seem unlawful for the chairman to permit the matter to be reopened.

11.41 Where exceptionally an earlier decision is reversed or varied later the minutes should record only the second resolution as being the properly considered decision of the committee. Where, however, it is the practice to prepare minutes to reflect precisely the order of business and the movement of members in and out of the committee, the minutes would misrepresent the proceedings if the first resolution was not recorded. The dilemma then is that the minutes themselves would record if not an irregularity at least a departure from conventional procedure, which might provide evidence upon which the validity of the second resolution could be challenged. This may be thought further justification for the generally accepted view that a question once settled cannot properly be reopened at the same meeting.

Reference-up of committee decisions

Regulation by standing orders

11.42 A proposed mandatory core standing order put forward by the standing orders working party (see 2.4) envisaged that there might be circumstances where a sizeable number of members of a committee or subcommittee with delegated powers felt it desirable to 'refer-up' a particular question for consideration at either council or committee level as the case may be. The standing order, which commanded little support among local authorities for no doubt obvious reasons, was framed in these terms:

'00–1   This standing order applies where arrangements have been made for the discharge of a function of the authority by a committee or subcommittee, and the operation of such arrangements is referred to in it as "the use of delegated powers".

2   Where a question on the use of delegated powers has been put to the vote at any meeting of a committee or subcommittee, and not fewer than one-fifth of the voting members present at the meeting, immediately after the question has been put to the vote, ask that the provisions of this standing order should be applied, the committee or subcommittee shall submit a report on the use of the delegated powers for consideration by the council or the committee which appointed the subcommittee, as the case may be, at their next meeting.

3   Where, on the consideration by a committee of a report of a subcommittee under the preceding paragraph, not fewer than one-fifth of the voting members of the committee present at the meeting ask that the provisions of this standing order should be applied, the committee shall submit a report on the decision to the council at its next meeting.

4   Subject to paragraph 5, when a question on the use of delegated powers is put to the vote at a meeting of the committee or subcommittee and not fewer than two fifths of the voting members present at the meeting, immediately after the question has been put to the vote, ask that the provisions of this standing order should be applied, the decision shall be of no effect, but shall be treated as a recommendation to the council or the committee which appointed the sub-committee, as the case may be.

Variation:
A proportion smaller than one-fifth or two-fifths may be substituted for those figures.

5   Paragraph 4 shall not apply to any question which arises on an item of business:
   a)   where the committee or subcommittee has, under an obligation arising from the nature of the business to be transacted, heard representations from persons other than members of the council and those appointed by the authority to discharge a function in connection with the committee or sub-committee; or
   b)   which concerns the appointment, discipline or dismissal of a member of the authority's staff.'

Some local authorities have experience of operating a referencing-up procedure and most confirm that it has the effect of slowing down business and result in repeated debate. The inclusion of this proposed core standing order was at the insistence of Government representatives on the working party who saw it as a way of protecting minority interests but it is unlikely that it will be made mandatory.

Duration of committee meetings

Setting a time limit

11.43 Although it is not uncommon for standing orders to set a limit upon the duration of council meetings (or at least set a time at which members must decide whether or not to continue the sitting: see 7.142) it is rare for committee meetings to be so regulated. Nevertheless, there is much to be said for limiting the duration of committee sittings because long meetings are not conducive to good decision-making: members excuse themselves and leave if the meeting is long drawn out, the attention of others wavers as time goes by and concentration on business becomes difficult as members grow tired and possibly hungry, too. Some committee chairs (and a chairman's competence is usually critical) will set themselves or agree with members a target time for completion of business: there is widespread agreement that the efficiency of any meeting dwindles after an hour and a half.

11.44 The morning is no doubt the ideal time for business (though few meetings seem to take place then) and at least the need for lunch provides automatically for a break in proceedings if not for the termination of the meeting. Afternoon meetings suffer the disadvantage of there not being a natural break and evening meetings (common particularly among district councils) suffer every possible disadvantage: they tend to go on far too long and often after members and officers have already worked for a full day beforehand. The only virtues of evening meetings are that members of the public are usually more able to attend them and working members do not need time off from their employment to attend.

Conclusion of meeting

'That concludes the business'

11.45 The chairman should always end the meeting by saying expressly, 'That concludes the business of the meeting' or words to like effect. There can then be no doubt that the meeting has terminated and less likelihood that continuing discussion between members after the end of official business may be misinterpreted as part of the meeting.

Noting the time

11.46 The time at which the chairman declares the meeting at an end should be recorded as evidence of the period of attendance for purposes of members' allowances (see 4.26) and for similar purposes in the case of officers entitled either to overtime payment of honoraria for planned overtime or subsistence allowances.

Collection and disposal of committee papers

11.47 It should be the committee clerk's responsibility to gather up committee papers left behind by members and officers after the meeting. This is particularly important in the case of papers relating to business conducted while proceedings were not open to the public and press; and in the case of very confidential papers the committee clerk will be expected to dispose of them by shredding.

Notes

1 Not to be recorded necessarily in committee minutes but to jog the memory if the chairman suddenly asks 'Was the motion formally proposed [or seconded]?'
2 Or, for that matter, for the committee clerk to decide himself what he believes was decided, on the analogy of the following, variously attributed, as the task of the Cabinet secretary:
    'And so while the great ones repair to their dinner,
    The secretary stays, getting thinner and thinner,
    Racking his brains to record and report
    What he thinks they will think that they ought to have thought!'
3 Decisions of a committee not properly constituted are nevertheless deemed valid by the LGA 1972, Sch.12, para.44(2).

Chapter 12
Work after meetings

Introduction

12.1 At the conclusion of a meeting the clerk should do the following things, the order of priority and urgency depending upon circumstances:

- draft the minutes of the meeting;
- prepare a report for submission to the full council, where the practice locally is to submit reports instead of full minutes to the council (see 12.40);
- advise other officers of any matter referred to another committee;
- notify other officers by the preparation and circulation of an action sheet of actions which fall to them, following the meeting;
- implement the decisions of the committee/cabinet that fall to the committee clerk to carry out personally;
- record in a diary or bring forward system any matters that need to be followed up or reported to a later meeting of the committee;
- record each decision in the appropriate correspondence file; and
- update the index to the committee's proceedings in the minute book.

Matters requiring immediate action

Action sheets

12.2 In some authorities the committee clerk prepares, as soon as practicable after each meeting, a brief summary of proceedings or action sheet (the description varies according to the purpose). The aim is to provide an immediately available guide to the decisions made and, in some instances, details of the officer expected to take executive action. It is for the committee clerk to decide whether the minutes should be drafted prior to this.

12.3 An example of an action sheet is set out below:

'Boston Borough Council
Overview and Scrutiny Committee: 10 June 2007
Decision/Action Sheet

Agenda Item No	*Subject*	*Decision*	*For action by*
1	Minutes: Meeting of 10 May, 2007 . . .	Confirmed	–
2	Apologies	Clrs. Brown, Smith, and Robinson. Best wishes to be sent to Cllr. Brown for speedy return to health.	Chief Executive
3	Membership of Housing Association: appointment of council representative	Cllr. Jones to be nominated	Head of Legal Services
4	Housing estate, Southfield Road: naming.	To be named Robinson Retreat.	Head of Housing'

In some cases there is a fifth section that gives a target date by which executive action is expected to be taken. Items subject to council approval need to be clearly indicated.

References to other committees/cabinet

12.4 Where cabinet follows in quick succession to other committees there is always the possibility of a reference failing to reach the cabinet in time if the committee clerk is slow in providing the necessary information to the other officers concerned. Often the probability of a reference from a committee to cabinet can be foreseen, and in that event it is prudent to include an appropriate item on the agenda of the cabinet.

12.5 References from committee to cabinet are of three types:

- those on which the views of another committee are sought before the cabinet resumes or completes its consideration of the matter concerned;
- those that, as a matter of routine, stand referred to other committees, e.g. staffing matters to a personnel committee or constitutional matters to a standards committee, before consideration by the cabinet or the full council; and
- those that involve matters of policy or important principle that must be placed before full council.

As to 'references-up': see 11.42.

12. Work after meetings

12.6 Unnecessary references between committees and cabinet can be avoided by careful arrangement of business. The general principle should be to place an item only before the committee that has the power to make a decision or frame a recommendation, unless cabinet requests the committee to provide comments.

Urgent executive action

12.7 Next, after references to other committees/cabinet, attention should be given to matters of urgency where failure to take immediate action could frustrate the committee's intention or otherwise prejudice the council's interests. These include:

- items of business on which the committee has expressly instructed that executive action should be taken as a matter of urgency; and
- anticipatory action on recommendations to another committee or the full council where delay could nullify the eventual decision.

A committee clerk should be alert to the need to take action to secure due performance of his committee's instructions, e.g. if a committee is proposing to nominate an officer to attend a study course and the nomination requires the approval or affirmation of another committee, the committee clerk should make a provisional booking without commitment if there is likelihood otherwise that the course will be fully booked before a final decision can be taken. Where immediate action is called for on matters not within the committee's delegated powers the leader or chairman of the council may need to be consulted.

Minutes or reports?

12.8 If minutes are used as the means of reporting the cabinet's proceedings to the full Council, the preparation of these will be a matter of priority for the committee clerk after conclusion of the cabinet meeting: the minutes will need to be drafted, approved by the officers concerned, submitted for the chairman's agreement and printed for inclusion in the council meeting agenda. If, on the other hand, the authority has adopted the report system, it will be the committee clerk's responsibility to prepare the report first and the minutes subsequently: the report will similarly need to be drafted, approved and printed. These differing methods of reporting upwards are discussed later (see 12.40).

Preparation of minutes

Objectives

12.9 The minutes of a meeting cannot be successfully written up without a clear understanding of the purposes that the minutes are to serve. These include the need:

- to establish an accurate record of the decisions taken;
- to comply with legal requirements; and, where minutes are used as the vehicle to bring proposals before the full council, the need also:

- to ensure that the record is sufficiently self-explanatory to enable the council to make a decision in full possession of the relevant facts; and
- to provide adequate information about the authority's business for press and public.

12.10 In practice it is difficult, if not impossible, to meet satisfactorily these several and sometimes conflicting objectives. The obligation upon local authorities to keep minutes of proceedings could be met by brief notes, as the law does not prescribe the form in which minutes shall be written up: but the authority may need to substantiate its actions by production of the minutes authorising the action taken, and the minutes must be drawn up in terms that will satisfy legal requirements. However, although the law imposes constraints, administrative and public relations needs provide scope for skilful and imaginative drafting.

12.11 As a result of the cabinet system, there is no longer a need to prepare two documents: the actual minutes in which are recorded the whole of the committee's proceedings; and a report that, in wholly different style, sets out only those items of business that must be submitted to the full council for information or approval. Only those matters requiring the approval of full council now need to be submitted. The advantages and disadvantages of the report system and the several ways in which it is operated in practice are referred to later (see 12.40).

Drafting minutes

12.12 There is no right or wrong way of preparing minutes: the form adopted by any particular local authority is a matter of individual choice or local custom. The obligation to keep minutes does not mean that the minutes must be written up during the course of the meeting. This could be done,[1] but is not likely to be practicable as the committee clerk needs to be paying attention to the proceedings. It is usual and perfectly permissible for the minutes to be transcribed from rough notes taken at the meeting: see *Re Jennings* (1851).

In course of time a number of cardinal principles of good practice have become widely accepted. Thus, for example, a minute should be:

- brief, i.e. precise and concise, recording exactly what was done and no more;
- self-contained, i.e. complete in itself and intelligible without reference to other documents (but see below); and
- decisive, i.e. there must be no ambiguity or doubt as to the intention; and thus clarity is an indispensable part of the accuracy of the record.

12.13 Minutes can be kept brief by being selective: a minute is not a verbatim record but a summary of the proceedings that includes only the essence of the discussion – not always that – and the decision. It is rarely necessary to reproduce, however summarily, what a particular speaker said; but helpful, as a rule, to pick up the main threads of the discussion that led to the conclusion: indeed there is danger in recording individual contributions since all members are likely to want the same treatment. To be self-contained does not mean that a minute cannot properly refer to supporting material, e.g. an officer's report incorporated as an appendix, a plan, deed or other significant document that cannot physically be made part of the minute book. But a minute must not rely on extraneous material for its understanding or interpretation; the actual resolution should always be understandable on its own. Some authorities now choose to sound-record their meetings, which means that the committee clerk has an accurate record from which to transcribe the minutes.

12.14 Minutes collectively should be complete in the sense that they include at least a brief reference to every item of business dealt with, so that it may safely be assumed that any matter not mentioned was not discussed at the meeting.

Skill in draftsmanship

12.15 Good drafting comes generally from practical experience; what is necessary is workmanlike competence. Though conformity with a pattern may help in producing good work (see, e.g. the next following paragraphs on form), this alone will not produce the clarity and precision necessary in good drafting. Constant attention to the construction of sentences is necessary. All adjectives must be eliminated. The simplest word rather than the unusual must be used, the active rather than the passive style, positive rather than negative construction. Every word must contribute something material to the meaning of the minute: the article 'the', for example, can almost always be omitted before dates and in many other instances, and there is always something additional to learn. With increased skill in drafting comes an appreciation of layout, and then importance begins to be attached to the visual appearance on paper, to the proper balance between the long and the short paragraphs.

Form

Minutes individually and collectively

12.16 In considering the structure of minutes there needs to be examined both the form of the individual minute covering a particular item of business (which, as already indicated, must be complete and self- contained: see 12.13), and that of the set of minutes that collectively relates to the proceedings of a meeting as a whole.

Set of minutes

12.17 Each set of minutes, i.e. the minutes that collectively relate to a particular meeting, will ordinarily follow a prescribed pattern. It will first identify the committee/cabinet concerned and the date of the meeting and also, possibly, the time of commencement and the place of meeting, e.g.:

> 'MINUTES of a meeting of the OVERVIEW AND SCRUTINY COMMITTEE held at the Blanktown Town Hall on Monday, 1st May, 200..., at ...pm.'

Committee practice

There will usually be recorded[2] after this the names of council members and, if any, co-opted members present, distinguishing between the two as a rule, with the chairman's name appearing first and the names of the others in alphabetical order, e.g.:

'Present: Councillor John Smith (Chairman); Councillors Jones, Robinson, Smith T. J., and White; and Messrs. Black, Brown, and Gray.'

12.18 If someone other than the chairman is presiding that member's name will still appear first but followed with an appropriate description (in the chair), or (presiding), according to local practice. Whether or not members' initials are included is, again, a matter of custom. Some authorities prefer to list the names of all members of the committee and to indicate attendance by an asterisk. It is not good practice to include the names of officers who are in attendance because the officers are not part of the membership of the committee. However, some authorities do record officers who attend working groups or other meetings, and if so it should be clearly marked that these are officers attending, to avoid confusion.

12.19 The minutes should be prepared to reflect the order in which business was transacted. This is also a logical order because it is often convenient to record, for example, a change in chairmanship, e.g.:

'Councillor John Brown relinquished the chair at this point and Councillor Jack Smith assumed it.'

or some other happening, e.g.:

'Councillor White declared a personal and prejudicial interest in the next succeeding item of business and, left the meeting before the commencement of discussion.'

These items could not very well be inserted in the minutes unless the minutes followed the actual sequence of business. Some authorities follow the order of the agenda; but in doing so you should incorporate the agenda paper in the minute book in order to shorten the text of minutes by cross-referencing to material in the agenda. This is not necessarily good practice, even if convenient, as:

- the agenda has no legal significance, though it must be kept open for public inspection (see 8.39) and a meeting can refuse to discuss or receive an item on the agenda; and
- it may encourage the drafting of resolutions that are understandable only when read with the agenda.

12. Work after meetings

Individual minutes

12.20 Section 22(3) of the Local Government Act 2000 provides that a written record must be kept of prescribed decisions made at cabinet meetings. An individual minute of the cabinet should consist of a heading and a preamble or narrative (if required) Under reg. 3 of SI 2000/3272, it must also contain:

- a record of the decision, together with the reasons for the decision;
- details of any alternative options considered and rejected by the cabinet at the meeting at which the decision was made; and
- a record of any conflict of interest in relation to the matter decided that is declared by any member of the cabinet, together with a note of any dispensation granted by the authorities' standards committee,

and must be numbered distinctively.

12.21 There should, be a uniform style adopted throughout the authority. For example, using in some instances:

'The committee decided to . . .'

and at other times:

'Resolved: That . . .'

This may cause a reader to believe there is significance in a difference that is no more than an inconsistency.

Heading

12.22 A minute heading or title should be brief and explanatory of the subject matter; once settled it should be retained unaltered to facilitate indexing, at least in its main wording, for all subsequent minutes on the same subject. There is advantage in referring immediately after the heading to previous minutes or the last minute on the same subject.

12.23 It is not always easy, however, to determine the wording of the heading. Take, for example, the following:

'908. Flooding: Riverside Area (see Minute 866)
The Borough Engineer reported on the flooding which had occurred in . . .'

It is a matter of judgment in relation to the particular circumstances whether the heading might more appropriately be reversed so that it becomes:

> '908. Riverside Area: Flooding (see Minute 866).'

If the subject of flooding is a continuing problem before the committee, then this might fairly be chosen as the main part of the heading. If, on the other hand, the committee has a special interest in the Riverside Area it is preferable that this should form the main part. In either case, despite the merit of brevity, a heading of one or the other alone would not be satisfactory; if flooding is used by itself it implies that flooding in general is the subject matter of the minute; and if Riverside Area is used alone the heading could mean anything.

12.24 A common error is to use a wholly inappropriate heading. An example is using an Act of Parliament as the heading to a minute that is not in any way concerned with the statute as such:

> '418. Food Safety Act 1990
> The Head of Legal Services reported that at xxchester Court on 1st January 20..., the firm of . . . had been fined for ...'

12.25 There is some justification for the view that a heading is not really part of a minute and should, if it appears at all, be placed in the margin of the minute book as a head note in this fashion:

> 'Flooding: 908.   The Borough Engineer reported
> Riverside   on the flooding that had
> Area (see Preamble   occurred in . . . Minute 866)'

12.26 A preamble or narrative should be included only if it serves a purpose, i.e. it contains the reasons for the decision and details of alternatives considered. It may be appropriate to indicate the officer who brought a particular matter before the committee/cabinet, but if the officer's act is no more than procedural there is no need to recite it. An example of an entirely superfluous preamble is:

> '123 Local Government Association: Annual Conference, 20...
>
> The Chief Executive submitted an invitation to the Council to appoint delegates to the 20... annual conference of the Local Government Association to be held at Brighton from . . . to . . .
>
> Resolved: That Councillors Smith, Brown and Robinson be appointed as the Council's delegates to attend the 20... annual conference of the Local Government Association to be held at Brighton from . . . to . . .'

12. Work after meetings

If, however, the officer is making a recommendation or tendering advice there is merit in including a reference to the recommendation or advice so submitted, e.g.: 'The Chief Executive advised the Committee that...'; and, vitally important, that the advice should be minuted if an officer provides advice which he considers it his duty to give and the committee/cabinet chooses to disregard it:

> 'The Borough Solicitor advised the committee that in his view there was no legal authority for the expenditure which the committee wished to incur...'

There are particular circumstances, of course, where the law requires the calling of a special meeting to consider a report of the monitoring officer or the chief finance officer advising the local authority of the risk or certainty of legal or financial impropriety (see 13.17).

12.27 The preamble can properly be used to record in narrative form the tenor of the discussion on the particular item of business but in an impersonal way, i.e. not attributing views to individual members. The main advantages of this form are that it makes for brevity. A point raised by one speaker will often be taken up and developed by others; in an impersonal minute the secretary need record it only in its final form. The impersonal style tends to avert suggestions for amendment of the minute, for members naturally look with special care at paragraphs that attribute statements to them personally, and tend to ask for additions and modifications that are not strictly necessary for the purpose of a minute. This can be done, for example, in this way, not necessarily following the order in which the points were made:

> 'The following points were raised in discussion: (a) ...;(b) ...; and (c) ...'

or, where there was broad agreement on the points raised:

> 'The committee had regard to/took account of the following points made in the course of discussion: (a) ...; (b) ...; and (c) ...'

What must be avoided – at all costs! – is this form:

> 'Mr A. said . . .; Mr B. replied . . .; and Mr C. then pointed out that . . .'

Such a discursive description in conversational style obscures the thread of discussion and leaves the minute-writer open to charges that he has misinterpreted what Mr A. or Mr B. said or unfairly summarised their contribution.

12.28 It is doubtful whether there is merit in recording that discussion preceded the decision without indicating the gist of it, e.g.:

> 'After discussion [it was] Resolved: That . . .'

Admittedly it conveys to a reader that at least the committee did not merely accept unquestioningly the advice of a chief officer or rubberstamp a recommendation of a subcommittee, but it does little else. The presumption must be that councillors considered the question before them. In many instances, where the course of action is clear cut, the chairman is likely to have said, as the particular item on the agenda was reached, 'Agreed?' and the members, in effect, replied 'Yes', and the meeting passed to the next item of business.

12.29 It is not usual to record in the preamble the procedural steps through which the members reached their decision. Thus, for example, the names of proposers and seconders of motions, whether passed or not, are not normally recorded; nor, ordinarily, is any record kept – as already indicated – of the contribution of particular members to the discussion.

Unsupported statements

12.30 Care needs to be taken, in drafting a preamble that goes to some length, not to include independent sentences that represent statements unidentified as to their source. This is permissible in a committee report because of the presumption that all that is included represents the collective view of the committee unless otherwise indicated. In the case of a minute this is not so. For example, a narrative may begin in this way: 'The Chief Executive explained that . . .' and continue at length. When, however, the Chief Executive's reported statement goes on to a new point it is never sufficient just to begin a new paragraph but, in order to avoid an unsupported statement, i.e. one not clearly attributable to anyone in particular, it is necessary to write either 'The Chief Executive went on to say . . .' or 'The Chief Executive further reported that . . .' or words to that effect.

Reasons for decisions

12.31 This may be an appropriate point at which to examine the question whether the reasons for a decision of the council or one of its committees or subcommittees should be minuted as well as the resolution itself. There are some instances where the authority is bound to provide reasons for its decisions (executive decisions), and in the case of the rejection of a planning application, for example, and in such circumstances these reasons must be minuted. In all cases, if an authority can show the reasons why it reached a particular decision, the authority's act can be expected to have greater credibility in the minds of those affected by the decision. On the other hand, this provides evidence for those who may wish to dispute the decision to show that the decision was an unreasonable one in the light of the considerations that influenced the authority in reaching it. Nevertheless, it would seem a good principle that an authority should always be prepared to justify its action by giving a reason, unless there are overriding considerations to suggest it should not do so. It seems that in the absence of a recorded decision the courts may take the view that the authority had no reason for the decision taken: in *R. v. Penwith District Council* (unreported but see *Local Government Chronicle*, 1st May 1987, pp.14–15) the court quashed the local authority's decision on the ground that as no reason had been given for it – a refusal to permit street trading – it had to be assumed that it had no good reason for reaching the conclusion it had reached. The desirability of giving reasons is the greater where the interests of third parties are involved: see *R. v. Lambeth London Borough Council ex parte Walters* (1993) and *R. v. Bristol City Council ex parte Bailey* (1994). In the former, a decision on a housing tenancy allocation was held to be unlawful because no reasons were given, whereas in the latter the giving of reasons was not required because the hearing was in public. *Halsbury's Laws* considers that the rationale is that:

> '. . . the obligation to provide a reasoned decision will exist when general considerations of procedural fairness require it, and factors such as the need for reasons to give substance to a right of appeal; to explain an otherwise aberrant outcome; to demonstrate that issues had been properly addressed; the nature of the interest affected by the decision and the extent to which the interest is affected by the decision; the need to promote transparency in the decision-making process; whether the duty would impose an undue burden on the decision maker or otherwise frustrate the purpose to be achieved by the decision maker; and the extent to which the judgments made were capable of being reasoned, or whether they were simply matters of academic or other evaluation. This list is not exhaustive. What is relevant will depend on the particular context concerned. The outcome of the application of this principle will differ from case to case depending on the circumstances; this simply reflects the fact that the weight to be attached to similar considerations will vary from context to context.'

12.32 It may be that in particular circumstances it would be against the council's interests (and, therefore, it may be presumed, against the public interest) for a reason to be disclosed; or it may be that the reason is far from certain: the fact that a decision has been reached even unanimously does not necessarily mean that all those who voted were similarly motivated or influenced by the same considerations. In *R. v. London County Council ex parte London and Provincial Electrical Theatres Ltd* (1915), Pickford LJ said, at pp. 490 and 866:

> 'With regard to the speeches of the members. . . I should imagine that probably hardly any decision of a body like the London County Council . . . could stand if every statement which a member made in debate were to be taken as a ground of the decision. I should think that there were probably few debates in which

someone does not suggest as a ground for decision something which is not a proper ground; and to say that, because somebody in debate has put forward an improper ground, the decision ought to be set aside as being founded on that particular ground is wrong.'

Taylor J expressed himself thus in *R. v. City of Swansea ex parte Quietlynn Limited* (1986), reported in Lexis:

'If every observation made by a councillor in all frankness in the course of debate were to be regarded as some bar to his voting or an indication that he had, in the end, taken into account an irrelevant consideration, it is hard to see how local government could continue to function. One would either have people clamming up and avoiding saying those things which they felt it right to say, lest they later heard other views which persuaded them that what they had said ought to be discounted, or one would have an obligation on a councillor to abstain from voting or even to leave the committee whenever he had it pointed out to him that something he had said was outside the statutory criteria in that particular context.'

Two things emerge from the above. One is that the contribution of individual councillors to a debate should never be minuted: something already advised (see 12.27). The other is that wherever possible councillors should be asked to agree on the terms of the reason for their collective decision; and if a reason is not voiced then an officer should not record his own interpretation of the grounds on which the authority or committee or subcommittee was influenced collectively.

12.33 Where there is no possibility of misinterpreting a committee's conclusions properly drawn or inferred from the facts before them that led finally to the decision, the following can be used:

'The committee [concluded] [took the view] [were of the opinion] that . . . and [accordingly] [for that reason] [on those grounds]
Resolved: That . . .'

Or, less positively:

'The committee [inclined to the view] [felt the balance of advantage suggested] [considered it prudent] that . . . and [accordingly] [for that reason] [on those grounds]
Resolved: That . . . Decisions'

12. Work after meetings

12.34 The decision should ordinarily be set out at the end of the individual minute in the form of a resolution. If, however, the minute falls naturally into different sections the resolutions may properly be interspersed appropriately at the end of each section rather than brought together at the end. In every case each resolution should commence with the word That, preferably indented from the margin of the text, and preceded in capital letters or underlined or in heavy type or some other distinctive manner by the word RESOLVED.

12.35 There are rules ordinarily to be observed in framing resolutions apart, of course, from what has been said about clarity and brevity:

- The introductory phrase RESOLVED: That governs all that follows. Thus it is correct to write:

  'RESOLVED: That the Head of Human Resources be authorised:
  i) to make all appointments of clerical and administrative staff within the council's authorised establishment;
  ii) to sign on behalf of the council contracts of employment in respect of such appointments; and be required to submit periodically to the cabinet a list of all such appointments made.'

  but not:

  'RESOLVED: That the Head of Human Resources be authorised:
  i) to make all appointments of clerical and administrative staff within the council's authorised establishment;
  ii) that he be authorised to sign on behalf of the council contracts of employment in respect of such appointments; and a list of all such appointments be submitted to the cabinet periodically.'

- Because a resolution should be self-contained it is bad practice to employ such phrases as:

  'RESOLVED: accordingly.'

  or:

  'RESOLVED: That the matter be dealt with accordingly.'; or where the decision cannot be fathomed without reference to an accompanying report:
  'RESOLVED: That the recommendations in the report of the Director of Corporate Services (a copy of which marked A is attached to these minutes) be approved.'; or, though with less objection, to make use of the heading:
  'Clerical and administrative staff
  RESOLVED: That the Head of Human Resources be empowered to make all appointments of this character within the council's authorised establishment.'

- Resolutions can be numbered serially (at least through each set of minutes) as an additional safeguard against tampering with the minute book by deletion:

  'RESOLVED: 1. That . . .'

12.36 There are also matters of individual style. For example, the resolutions of, a working party without delegated powers may be preceded by either:

> 'RESOLVED TO RECOMMEND: That . . .'

or

> 'RECOMMENDED: That . . .'

or

> 'RESOLVED: That the council be recommended to . . .'

or, preferably, because the resolution can then be identifiable as the council's resolution without alteration of the words:

> 'RESOLVED: That it be recommended to the council that . . .'

And there is advantage often in clearly indicating which officer is to take executive action:

> 'RESOLVED: That . . . and that the Chief Executive be authorised to take all such steps as she considers necessary to comply with the Council's resolution . . .'

Some authorities favour the style: 'RESOLVED UNANIMOUSLY . . .' on particular occasions of formality or when desirous of indicating to a recipient of the authority's sympathy or congratulations that the council is patently 'at one'. On the other hand, the use of 'Resolved unanimously' might imply some lesser value of resolutions not so distinguished.

Procedural considerations

12.37 Where full minutes are submitted, it is desirable that the attention of the council in the case of committee minutes, and the attention of the committee in the case of subcommittee minutes, is directed to matters of significance. Where there is no delegation of powers this may be sufficiently evident by the use of heavy type to denote recommendations, but there are other methods, e.g. by sidelining recommendations in the margin or (a practice not to recommended because it increases the volume of paper) by extracting and listing together separately all recommendations for the parent body's consideration. Even in the case of reports, as distinct from minutes, recommendations should be clearly distinguished from the main text.

12.38 Some local authorities divide each set of minutes (or reports) into two parts to distinguish between matters dealt with by the committee under its powers and those that are referred respectively. Whether there is virtue in such an arrangement is a matter of opinion, but it can facilitate proceedings at the council meeting.

Reporting upwards

Minutes or reports

12.39 The minutes of the cabinet can be used to report the cabinet's proceedings to the full Council. Similarly a subcommittee's minutes can be the mechanism by which the subcommittee reports to its parent committee. The view is taken by some local authorities that this is an efficient and economical arrangement: minutes must be prepared in any case as a matter of administrative and legal necessity and it is unnecessary and time-consuming for another, different, document to be produced either to advise the parent body of action taken in pursuance of delegated powers or to bring before it matters upon which the parent body alone can make the final decision. Other authorities prefer the report system as the method of bringing before the parent body the proceedings of the cabinet or subcommittees, as the case may be, for purposes of information or consideration. As to the advantages and disadvantages of the report system: see 12.42.

12.40 Minutes record, in the past tense, the business actually transacted at a particular meeting: very often an individual minute (as distinct from a resolution) may be intelligible only by reference to preceding minutes on the same subject matter and they must, in the case of cabinet, recite the reasons which influenced the meeting in reaching its decision or the alternative courses of action considered and rejected. A report, on the other hand, normally written in the present tense, need not limit itself to matters actually dealt with at a particular meeting: it can deal with an issue comprehensively, covering proceedings at several past meetings, and so present to the parent body a full account in readable, intelligible form. The style, too, is different: e.g. 'The cabinet has considered . . .', or 'We have considered . . . and now recommend'.

Challenge to cabinet minutes at full council

12.41 It can happen, where a local authority submits cabinet minutes rather than reports to the full council, that the minutes will be before the council in advance of their confirmation by the cabinet. What, then, should happen if a councillor questions the accuracy of a cabinet minute and the question of accuracy is critical either to the council's understanding of what has been decided or could affect what is proposed? The minute, even if its inaccuracy is evident to the full council, cannot properly be corrected because that can only be done by the cabinet when the minutes come before it for confirmation. The correct procedure would be for the member who is challenging the accuracy of the minute to move its reference back to the cabinet. If the motion is approved it will be for the cabinet to consider the objection when it comes to confirm the minutes at the next meeting. In practice it seems unlikely that such a motion would be approved: after all, the minutes will have been drawn up by the officers and probably approved by the leader; and the leader is likely to oppose the reference back and will conceivably be supported by cabinet members present at the council meeting. If, of course, the report system is adopted a procedural problem of this kind cannot arise (see 12.43). It would be perfectly proper for the full council to debate a motion seeking to refer back a paragraph in the report or to amend a recommendation contained in it.

Advantages and disadvantages of the report system

12.42 The comparative advantages and disadvantages of the contrasting systems may seem self-evident: they have, in any case, been thoroughly discussed elsewhere. If business dealt with by a subcommittee is considerable, and as presumably it does not involve questions of major policy, there may seem little advantage in submitting the full minutes of proceedings to the parent body. However, in the case of the cabinet it could be argued that the preparation of a report to full council in addition to the minutes is unnecessary, particularly as all members of overview and scrutiny committees have access to cabinet reports. However, members often prefer to receive a full report with the council agenda, and clearly it would be impracticable to leave it to be decided in each instance whether the full council should sometimes be advised by minutes and sometimes by report. There must be one system laid down and properly regulated to ensure that the full council receives essential information whether advised by a report or by minutes. It is the content rather than form that matters in this respect. In an inquiry into certain irregularities in the ARP services of Newcastle-upon-Tyne during World War II, Sir Roland Burrows QC, suggested that the submission of a committee report rather than the full minutes to the city council was partly the reason why the council had failed to detect what was going on. On the other hand, a minute can be equally inadequate: see *R. v. Brent London Borough Council ex parte Gunning* (1985) (and 12.45) where the decision of a local education authority was held to be ultra vires largely because the authority had not been provided with sufficient information in a committee minute on which to reach a decision).

12.43 Criticism from individual council members that the report system denies them full knowledge of the council's activities stems from the belief that a comprehensive knowledge is necessary for proper performance of their duties as councillors. Most people would think this a mistaken view. Council members should, however, be able to obtain the information they want easily if it is information to which they are entitled.

12.44 Local authorities that adopt the report system may think it prudent to have arrangements to confirm any other committee decisions that require confirmation but that have not been included in the reports – either by accident or design! The standing orders of Leicestershire County Council include the following:

12. Work after meetings

> '1 A member may give notice in writing to the chief executive at any time not later than 10am on the day before a meeting of the council that he objects to any decision of a committee or subcommittee which requires the confirmation of the council.
>
> 2 The chairman of the council shall propose the confirmation of all decisions of committees or subcommittees which require the confirmation of the council and which were taken at every meeting by a committee or subcommittee held not later than the Thursday before the meeting of the council except:
>   a) any decision which has been objected to under paragraph (1) of this standing order;
>   b) any decision with regard to any matter still under consideration;
>   c) any decision which is to be the subject of a special report to the council.'

Provision is then made for individual motions to be moved by members objecting to any committee or subcommittee decision under the standing order. This procedure not only formally confirms all decisions that are not covered by individual reports but also allows members to challenge and debate them if they so wish.

Statutory committee reports to council

12.45 Cases that have come before the courts in relation to committee reports to the full assembly have done so because of a statutory obligation on the local authority to consider a report from the relevant committee before exercising obligatory functions (referred to briefly: see e.g. 9.32). This is now the position in only one instance: the social services committee. In R. v. *Kirklees Metropolitan Borough Council ex parte Molloy* (1987), on a judicial review of the education committee's decision to close a school, it was held that the decision must be quashed because the authority had not had before it 'a proper report' of the education committee. Mann J recognised that it was not easy to say what exactly was a report but quoted from the judgment of Forbes J in R. v. *Liverpool City Council ex parte Professional Association of Teachers* (1984):

> 'There is argument about what a report consists of . . . [in my view] a committee should either make some recommendation or should at least, if not making a recommendation, set out the arguments for and against a particular course of action. Otherwise I cannot see how . . . the authority are to inform themselves adequately of the views of the . . . committee before performing . . . their functions . . .'

Of R. v. *Brent London Borough Council ex parte Gunning and Others* (1986), Mann J said in *Kirklees*:

'. . . a report must in my view involve an evaluation. It must be an account of the issues involved in a decision . . . A bland recommendation does not in my judgment satisfy the requirements of statute. An evaluation is essential. . .'

Although the foregoing cases concern reports from the education committee, the principles apply equally to the social services committee, i.e. of the need of there being a proper evaluation of the courses of action proposed is one that clearly should be followed as a precept in all instances of committee reports to the full council and, of course, of subcommittee reports to a parent committee.

12.46 It seems that the courts would regard the requirement upon a local authority to 'consider a report' as satisfied even if the authority had to take account of a document incorporated in the committee's minutes by reference. In *Nichol and Others* v. *Gateshead Metropolitan Borough Council* (1988) it was held that the council had properly considered a report of its education committee when it had before it a minute of the committee that indicated that the committee had followed a recommendation in a report of the director of education, a copy of which had been sent to every member of the council, and had adopted one of the options put forward in the officer's report. It may be thought, nevertheless, that this is not good practice: the incorporation of documents in minutes by reference ought to be restricted to instances where the document cannot physically be included (see 12.13).

Hybrid systems

12.47 Some authorities attempt, with varying degrees of success, to combine the advantages of the report system with the advantages of submitting full minutes to the parent body. Thus an authority will submit to the full assembly 'only certain sections of the minutes', the choice being made administratively, sometimes on the basis that only non-delegated business will be reported selectively or by the committee itself. Where the practice of submitting full minutes means the minutes on confidential matters must be drawn in general terms, only certain unreported minutes will be written up solely for recording in the committee minute book.

Methods of reproduction

12.48 Some local authorities cling to traditional methods of reproducing the council meeting agenda. Apart from the substantial cost involved this brings problems in finalising and printing committee reports in time for incorporation with the agenda. Word processors have revolutionised the preparation of council and committee papers, but the heavy peak load of work in the committee cycle often taxes the authority's resources.

12.49 A discussion of the economics of differing methods of reproduction would be beyond the scope of this book. The efficient organisation of committee work involves necessarily careful regard to the demands made upon the authority's administrative machinery. Some years ago the (now disbanded) Royal Institute of Public Administration produced a pamphlet on *Local Authorities Minutes and Reports*. It is now rather dated but the following steps recommended in seeking a solution to this problem still have some relevance:

'a) Lower the height of the peak by reducing as far as possible the amount of text to be reproduced;

b) Seek to spread this peak over the maximum possible period, perhaps by some rearrangement of the committee cycle;

c) See how far existing resources of staff and machines can be pooled for this particular operation without causing undue dislocation of normal work;

d) Assess the amount of overtime that might be forthcoming each month from typing and non-typing staff to make internal reproduction practicable;

e) Determine what additional staff and machines would be required to bridge any gap that may still remain between the desirable and the practicable;

f) Investigate the cost and speed of service to be obtained from firms that undertake duplication commercially and might be employed to supplement the council's own resources.'

Other work involved

Implementation of decisions

12.50 It is ordinarily the committee clerk's responsibility to see that committee decisions are implemented either by ensuring that the appropriate officer is advised of the action to be taken or by himself performing certain of the executive work. Reference has already been made to the importance of taking urgent executive action immediately after a committee meeting and to the practice of some authorities in circulating an action sheet (see 12.2 and Chapter 7). On many items, however, action will need to be delayed until the committee's recommendation has been accepted by the council or, prudently, until the minute has been written up.

12.51 Practice varies widely in this respect. In some cases a memorandum is circulated to chief officers indicating the action that is expected of them; in others it is well established that officers will automatically take action on the minutes as soon as they are promulgated and on the basis, say, of any action sheet already circulated. This latter is probably the ideal situation, provided the committee clerk chases those items that may be required.

12.52 It is not usual for the committee clerk to go to the length of satisfying himself that a particular chief officer has done what is expected of him. Most officers do not appear to think that the arrangements for ensuring that action is taken on council and committee minutes constitute a problem.

Destruction of committee clerk's notes

12.53 Once the minutes have been confirmed the committee clerk's notes should be destroyed. The reason for this is that there should be no other record, however informal, that might cast doubt upon the correctness of the official record. If the notes are known to be retained (and many authorities do seem to favour keeping them) there is always the likelihood that they may be required to be produced, whether under the Freedom of Information Act 2000 or otherwise. If the notes constitute a verbatim shorthand record (which is unlikely) there should, of course, be no possibility of their contradicting the minutes. Indeed, it could be argued that the notes are of value in supporting the minutes if challenged, but otherwise rough notes are capable of misinterpretation and could in that event be capable of proving the opposite!

12.54 Though some authorities favour retention of the committee clerk's note, opinion generally is divided on the issue. The benefit of retention might be thought to be demonstrated in *R. v. Hereford and Worcester County Council ex parte Wellington Parish Council* (1995), which concerned a gypsy site and questions of possible bias on the part of members of the county planning committee. The committee clerk gave evidence on affidavit and produced his notebook to show the way in which the meeting had proceeded and the contributions made by individual members. Despite the usefulness of the notebook in this case, destruction after confirmation of the minutes still seems the safest course.

Indexing

12.55 Minute books must be indexed, for self-evident reasons. Unless it is possible to trace the minute on a particular matter the decision, at least as a record, might as well not exist. Indeed, there is much to commend the practice of recording separately, possibly bound up as an addendum to standing orders, a copy of minutes on matters of policy or important principle that are of continuing effect.

12.56 The indexing should be carried out in a systematic manner in accordance with prescribed guidelines formulated by each local authority to meet particular needs and entrusted to someone with knowledge and understanding of the subject matter and the purposes for which the index is likely to be used. There are many minutes that do not merit indexing: the record of apologies for absence (if, indeed, these are minuted at all); the confirmation of minutes; matters of purely procedural or transitional interest. Where full committee minutes are submitted to the council there seems no advantage in duplicating in the index to the council minute book the individual items in committee minutes that are more appropriately indexed in the minute books of the respective committees.

12.57 It is usual to bind up sets of minutes in volumes covering a year or half-year (perhaps multiples of a year for committees that seldom meet) according to the amount of business transacted. Each minute book should have an index relating exclusively to the minutes it contains. The easiest way to build up an index is on a loose card system that can then be transcribed for incorporation in the binding. The task is facilitated if each minute has a standardised heading and explanatory subheading (see 12.22). The impact of new technology on minute storage and retrieval is likely to be considerable and advantage should be taken of the facilities available.

Minute numbering

12.58 Each minute should be numbered consecutively. This facilitates indexing, reference and cross-reference from one minute to another, and makes more difficult

12. Work after meetings

any tampering with the minute book, i.e. it is impossible for a new page to be fraudulently substituted or a particular minute omitted altogether (although, of course, a spurious minute could be written in to replace the authentic one). In any case each page of a minute book should be initialled by the person who signs the particular set of minutes to which the pages relate.

12.59 It is a matter of individual choice or local practice whether the numbering is recommenced for each set of minutes, i.e. the minutes relating to a particular meeting, or is continued throughout, say, the council year (of advantage if the minutes are bound annually). There is simplicity in beginning with 1 again for each set of minutes though cross-referencing is necessarily lengthier (assuming cross-referencing is favoured), as indeed it is if there is renumbering for each year. It means, for example, that the reference to a previous minute on the same subject will need to be 'See minute no.10 of 1st May 19...' or 'See minute no. 00 of 197-l7-' instead of merely 'See minute no.1,000'. On the other hand, the reference to date may facilitate retrieval of the particular minute required.

Inspection of committee minutes

12.60 Since 1st April 1986 the minutes of committees (including cabinet) and subcommittees of principal councils have been open to public inspection on the same terms and subject to the same limitations as in the case of council minutes (see 8.39-8.40). Prior to that date only the minutes of the education committee were open to inspection and only by local Government electors. The minutes of other committees and subcommittees were (and, strictly speaking, still are) only open to inspection so far as they were laid before the council meeting for approval. The minutes of committees and subcommittees of parish and community councils are still not required to be open for inspection. Where an embargo continues it is nevertheless open to the local authority to allow inspection at its discretion. Councillors have always possessed a common law right to inspect committee and subcommittee minutes so far as it may reasonably be necessary to enable them to carry out their council duties (see 8.36-8.37). What has been said earlier about the times when council minutes may be inspected applies also to committee and subcommittee minutes (see 8.44) as it does regarding obstruction of the right of inspection (see 8.46-8.47).

Notes

1   Indeed, the terms of the LGA 1972, Sch.12, para.41, that minutes shall be signed *at the same* or next ensuing meeting envisages that this might be done.
2   The names of members present at a meeting must be recorded, though not necessarily in the minutes: LGA 1972, Sch.12, para.40.

Part 4
Miscellaneous Meetings

Chapter 13

Meetings for special purposes

Introduction

13.1 This chapter deals with a number of committees and panels and similar groups whose meetings or the particular business to be transacted call for special treatment. There can be no exhaustive list of these because many local authorities have set up special committees and the like for purposes that arise out of peculiarly local circumstances, but the examples selected are thought to cover the more important of those of concern to the majority of the authorities.

13.2 In several of these cases the rules governing meetings are not substantially different from those applicable to conventional local authority committees but certain of them, either in their constitution or their functions or in the procedure that they must follow, differ significantly. Also covered in this chapter are election meetings and some quasimeetings, such as public inquiries, etc., with which local authorities are concerned indirectly.

Joint committees

Power to appoint

13.3 Among the several arrangements that local authorities may make for the discharge of their functions is that which provides for two or more authorities to discharge functions jointly so long as it is not a function that the law requires to be discharged by a specified committee (LGA 1972, s.101(5)). For purposes of discharging a function jointly the authorities may appoint a joint committee. The number of members of the joint committee, their term of office (which must not extend beyond their term of office with the appointing authority) and the area within which the joint committee shall exercise its authority must be fixed by the appointing authorities; the membership may include persons who are not members of the appointing authorities (so long as they are not disqualified for membership).

Executive and advisory powers

13.4 Two or more authorities, in discharging any of their functions through a joint committee, may delegate executive powers to the joint committee, other than the function with respect to levying or issuing a precept for a rate. There is separate statutory power (although the terms are substantially the same) enabling two or more authorities to join in appointing a joint committee 'to advise the appointing authorities on any matter relating to the discharge of their functions'.

Expenses

13.5 The expenses incurred by a joint committee of two or more authorities, whether appointed under the LGA 1972 or any other enactment,[1] are to be defrayed by those authorities in such proportions as they may agree or in case of disagreement as may be determined:

- in any case in which those authorities are the councils of parishes or communities or groups of parishes or communities situated in the same district, by the district council; and
- in any other case, by a single arbitrator agreed on by the appointing authorities or, in default of agreement, by the Secretary of State (LGA 1972, s.103).

Standing orders

13.6 Standing orders regarding a joint committee of two or more local authorities (irrespective of the statute under which the joint committee is appointed) may be made by those authorities, dealing with the quorum, proceedings and place of meeting of the joint committee (including any subcommittees); but, subject to any such standing orders, the quorum, proceedings and place of meeting can be such as the joint committee itself may determine.

Committees meeting jointly

13.7 There is another kind of joint committee or, more accurately, a coming together within the local authority of two committees of their own volition to discuss a matter in which they have a common interest. Such an arrangement is a purely informal one and, if procedural and other problems are to be avoided, the arrangement should be such that one committee has invited to its meeting the members of the other for an informal discussion. There can then be no dispute as to who takes the chair or how a vote should be taken because the 'attending' councillors would have no vote.

Joint boards

Distinguishable from joint committees

13.8 A joint board or, as it is sometimes called, a joint authority, is fundamentally different from a joint committee. There is no general power permitting the establishment of joint boards, but specific power is contained in a number of statutes and in each case the rules as to its constitution are prescribed.

Joint boards

13.9 A joint board is a corporate body, created by order of a minister, requiring in many cases the approval of parliament: it has perpetual succession, a common seal and it can hold land. Unlike a joint committee, a joint board cannot be dissolved by agreement; it has independent financial powers, including the power to borrow money, and obtains its revenue from constituent authorities by means of precepts.

13.10 The order or other instrument creating the joint board will ordinarily prescribe its constitution and the rules governing meetings procedure. As to the unique position of local authority members on a joint planning board (and other joint boards where members hold statutory office) see Chapter 5, and as to the new statutory joint authorities, see 14.12.

Statutory meetings to consider officers' reports

General

13.11 There are two circumstances in particular where a relevant local authority (see 1.6) has a statutory duty to hold a meeting of the whole council to consider a report from an officer: a report from the monitoring officer under s.5 of the LG&HA 1989, or from the chief finance officer under s.114 of the LGFA 1988. Pending the meeting the council must not proceed with implementation of the proposal or decision or whatever course may be intended: the subject matter is, in effect, frozen until the meeting. Because, as will be evident below, the duty cast upon the officers is analogous, there needs to be in practice a close working relationship between all the officers concerned. To help in determining an acceptable procedure, a working party bringing together the main local government officer bodies initially produced a guidance note to assist in the provision of sound legal and financial advice to councillors.

Monitoring officer's report

13.12 The duties of the monitoring officer (see 4.49) include reporting to the authority on any proposal decision or omission by the council or a committee or subcommittee or a joint committee on which the authority is represented or by an officer of the authority that has or is likely to contravene the law or lead to maladministration (LG&HA 1989, s.5). Where the council operates executive arrangements, then the monitoring officer must report to the executive in relation to any such proposals, decisions or omissions of the executive itself. No duty to report on any maladministration arises unless the Local Government Ombudsman has conducted an investigation in relation to the proposal, decision or omission concerned.

13.13 It is the monitoring officer's duty, during preparation of his report, to consult with the head of the paid service and the chief finance officer (who has somewhat analogous duties (see 13.14)); and as soon as practicable after its preparation to arrange for a copy of it to be sent to each member of the authority or, where what is being challenged is the concern of a subcommittee, to members of the parent committee as well as the subcommittee. The duty is to be discharged by the monitoring officer personally and immediately, i.e. the report's circulation is not to await the summoning of the meeting by the proper officer.

Miscellaneous meetings

Chief finance officer's report

13.14 The duties of the local authority in regard to a report from the monitoring officer are without prejudice to the analogous duties under s.114 of the Local Government Finance Act 1988,[2] which fall on the officer designated by the authority for that purpose who will be the chief financial officer under s.151 of the 1972 Act. The chief finance officer is required to report in similar manner to the council (or the executive if in relation to any function of the executive) whenever the authority, a committee or joint committee or an officer has made or is about to make a decision that involves or would involve illegal expenditure or likely to cause loss to the authority or is about to enter an illegal item or account;[3] or where it appears to him that expenditure in a financial year is likely to exceed the resources, including sums borrowed, available to meet that expenditure.[4] The chief finance officer is required to consult the head of the paid service and the monitoring officer in preparing his report in the case of likely illegality or loss of expenditure[5] but in the other case, i.e. where the issue is one of financial judgment, there is no such obligation to consult.

The meeting

13.15 The aforesaid duties cast upon the monitoring officer and the chief finance officer have been indicated in broad terms because our concern here is primarily with the meeting, which in the circumstances the council is required to hold to consider any report so made. The meeting must be held within the specified period of 21 days after the report has been circulated to councillors.[6] It need not necessarily be a special meeting held solely for the purpose of considering the report: the report could quite properly be considered at an ordinary meeting of the council if one is due to be held within the prescribed period although – a matter for local decision – it might be thought desirable in view of the importance of the circumstance to convene a special meeting for the purpose to take place immediately before the ordinary meeting. The meeting must be of the council: the duty cannot be delegated.[7] There is no detailed statutory prescription governing the convening of the meeting or the conduct of the business: what is important, of course, is that the business to be transacted, i.e. to consider the relevant report, is clearly indicated on the agenda (and a copy of the report must be circulated with the summons and agenda if it has not been sent to councillors already as will have been so in most instances), accompanied by a statement, if not set out in the report, of the consequences of failing to take requisite action. What needs to be done can be expected to be spelled out by the chief finance officer where expenditure is likely to exceed resources but in the other cases, i.e. whether the report is made by the chief finance officer or the monitoring officer, the meeting is likely to have before it a report from the chief executive of the courses open to the council to achieve lawfully and properly whatever it may be that has been aborted. In such a report by the chief finance officer there is an express duty on the proper officer, i.e. the officer who has been assigned responsibility for the task, to notify the authority's auditor of the date, time and place of the meeting; and if the auditor is not satisfied that the authority's decision at the meeting overcomes the problems identified in the report, he may proceed to take further action in his own right.

13. Meetings for special purposes

13.16 Subject to the provisions of the Freedom of Information Act 2000, there is no obligation to make any report by the monitoring officer or the chief finance officer available for public inspection. The necessary meeting to consider the report will, of course, be open to the press and public and subject to the rules of exclusion in regard to confidential information and exempt information (see 3.8) the report should be made available to the press and public.

Judicial and quasi-judicial business

General considerations

13.17 There are occasions when a meeting is required to conduct business that is judicial or quasi-judicial in character: invariably a meeting of a committee or sub-committee or the like because the full assembly could not effectively exercise such a role. Examples include: the grant of licences where there is scope for or the need to exercise discretion (as opposed to instances where a licence issues automatically given the fulfilment of specified conditions); the exercise of powers that affect the interests of individuals whether or not they have a right to be heard and the hearing of appeals by the authority's employees against disciplinary measures (see *Ridge v. Baldwin* (1964) and 13.43). In all such cases the committee or subcommittee must observe the principles of natural justice. In most instances where a committee or subcommittee is exercising a judicial or quasijudicial function it can properly meet in private because the subject matter will be exempt information.

13.18 It is a cardinal principle that not only must justice be done but also it must manifestly be seen to be done. There is, therefore, a responsibility on councillors when acting in a judicial or quasijudicial capacity (and officers, too, if present on such an occasion) to conduct proceedings in such a way that parties appearing before them have no reason to suspect bias or be encouraged to challenge the proceedings on some grounds of impropriety.[8] Apart from the above, it is important that members of the committee or subcommittee should be present in the committee room at the outset of the meeting and remain there until a decision has been reached. It would be wholly improper for a councillor to participate in reaching the decision if he had not heard all the evidence; and it would be most unlikely that a councillor, who is not a properly appointed member of the body concerned, could establish a 'need to know' to allow him to attend a quasi-judicial hearing.

The Human Rights Act 1998

13.19 The importation into English law of the European Convention on Human Rights by the Human Rights Act 1998 has particular relevance in relation to a local authority's decision-making process. Under the 1998 Act, it is unlawful for a public authority to act in a way that is incompatible with a Convention right unless, as the result of one or more provisions of primary legislation, the authority could not have acted differently.

Miscellaneous meetings

Article 6 (1) of the Convention (Right to a Fair Trial) stipulates that:

'In the determination of his civil rights and obligations or of any criminal charge against him, everyone is entitled to a fair and public hearing within a reasonable time by an independent and impartial tribunal established by law. Judgment shall be pronounced publicly but the press and public may be excluded from all or part of the trial in the interest of morals, public order or national security in a democratic society, where the interests of juveniles or the protection of the private life of the parties so require, or to the extent strictly necessary in the opinion of the court in special circumstances where publicity would prejudice the interests of justice.'

Any hearing held by a local authority must comply with Article 6 and the rules of procedure should ensure that is the case subject to exceptions. This may include the right of effective access to a court and adequate disclosure of relevant evidence. At the end of the hearing, committee members should normally retire on their own to consider their decision. It will rarely be the case that it will be necessary for an officer to accompany them, as any legal or procedural advice should normally be given in the presence of all those involved.

13.20 In addition, Article 8 of the Convention (Right to Respect for Private and Family Life) states that:

'Everyone has the right to respect for his private and family life, his home and his correspondence, and there shall be no interference by a public authority with the exercise of this right except such as is in accordance with the law and is necessary in a democratic society in the interests of national security, public safety or the economic well-being of the country, for the prevention of disorder or crime, for the protection of health or morals, or for the protection of the rights and freedoms of others.'

In essence, therefore, the relevant committee must ensure that any interference with such rights is proportionate, when reaching their decision.

A useful booklet entitled *Acting on Rights: A Guide to the Human Rights Act 1998* has been produced by the Local Government Association and deals with these issues.

Natural justice

13.21 Where in the exercise of a discretion by a local authority the rights and interests of an individual are affected, the authority, through a committee in practice, is under a duty to exercise its discretion fairly and without whim or bias. Lord Esher, in *R. v. West Vestry of St. Pancras* (1890), said:

298

'. . . they must fairly consider the application and exercise their discretion on it fairly, and not take into account any reason for their discretion which is not a legal one. If people who have to exercise a public duty by exercising their discretion take into account matters which the courts consider not to be proper for the guidance of their discretion, then in the eyes of the law they have not exercised their discretion.'

An authority, or indeed any body of persons, that has a duty in law to determine questions affecting the rights of subjects must act judicially and this means in general terms (because a dissertation on the relevant law is beyond the scope of this book) that it must comply with the principles of natural justice.

13.22 These principles, as evident from decisions of the courts, are that the local authority must reach its decision fairly, without bias and in good faith, and must give a reasonable opportunity to the parties concerned to put their case, though not necessarily in person or by representative, and it may not act as a judge in its own cause. If the statute under which the authority is purporting to act lays down a procedure then that procedure must be followed; but otherwise it is not necessary for the procedure of a court of law to be followed (*R. v. Electricity Commissioners* (1924): any procedure that does not offend the principles of natural justice may be employed. The courts can review a decision made in a judicial or quasijudicial capacity if there is an error in law disclosed on the face of the record (*Local Government Board* v. *Arlidge* (1915)), except where the statute concerned provides that an order made it may not be questioned in legal proceedings. In several instances a statute gives a right of appeal to a person aggrieved by a decision of a local authority, either to a minister or to a court of law.

Staff consultative committees

General principles

13.23 Two important general principles govern committees of this character: one is that their function is advisory (such a committee can have no executive power to commit the employing authority); and the other, in conformity with the practice of all collective bargaining, is that decisions can only be reached upon the affirmative vote of a majority on each side voting separately.[9]

13.24 However, if the process of consultation is to have the confidence of the employees, the employing authority should take care to ensure that its representatives are knowledgeable and can speak with authority and in expectation that when they join with the other side in commending a course of action to the local authority it is likely that the proposal will be accepted. Somewhat similarly the employees side should be truly representative of the workforce for whom they purport to speak. Such a committee's deliberations must take place in an atmosphere conducive to free and meaningful discussion. Thus it is usual for the chairman to be chosen in turn from each side, and when an employer's side representative is serving as chairman the other side should select a vice chairman and vice versa.

Miscellaneous meetings

13.25 Although the aim should be to embrace within the scope of each consultative committee as many categories of employee as practicable it was usual in the past – because of their differing interests and conditions of service – for there to be separate committees covering officers and manual workers respectively, often termed a joint staff committee for the former and a joint works committee for the latter.

Conflict of interest in staff negotiations

13.26 Local authorities are required[10] to secure that, so far as practicable, their interests in negotiations that govern local authority terms and conditions of employment are not represented, directly or indirectly, by persons who are both members of an authority and in such employment, i.e. with another local authority, or by persons who are both members of an authority and an official or employee of a trade union whose membership includes people in local authority employment. The term *negotiations* is not defined but needs to be distinguished from *consultation*. If a staff consultative committee does enter into negotiations, the local authority must ensure that its choice of employer side representatives does not contravene the law. It might also be wise for employing authority members selected to hear disciplinary appeals (see 13.44) not to be councillors with an interest in staff negotiations even though an appeals tribunal could hardly be said to be concerned with negotiations.

Model constitutions

13.27 The constitution and rules of procedure of consultative committees vary considerably in detail and are always settled by agreement between the employing authority and employee representatives.

Clerking the committees

13.28 The committee's constitution will provide for the appointment of either a single secretary to clerk the committee's proceedings or joint secretaries, i.e. one appointed by each side, whose respective responsibility is to frame the matters to be placed on the agenda and to take appropriate action on decisions. Where there are joint secretaries it is usual, nevertheless, for the employer's side secretary to take charge of the dispatch of agenda, preparation of draft minutes, and servicing the committee generally.

13.29 Where there is only one secretary of the committee that officer, even if a council officer (and especially if the authority's personnel officer), should regard himself as the servant of the committee collectively. If the personnel officer is secretary, he must in acting in that capacity be at pains to be impartial, to facilitate the process of consultation and, so far as he may deem it advisable to intervene in discussion, should do so in a conciliatory role; and in drafting the minutes (which must be approved by both sides) must see to it that the arguments put forward by each side are fairly summarised. The secretary-cum-personnel officer will ordinarily advise the employer's side either in writing beforehand or at a pre-committee briefing (it is usual for each side to meet separately before the meeting of the full consultative committee);

but it may be necessary for him to express an employer viewpoint during the course of proceedings and in that event he must make it clear that he is then speaking as the personnel officer. The combined task obviously calls for diplomacy and skill.

Safety committees

13.30 The Health and Safety at Work, etc. Act 1974 (H&SWA 1974) makes it the duty of every employer – and that includes, of course, every local authority – to ensure, so far as reasonably practicable, the health, safety and welfare at work of all its employees (s.2 (1)). The employer has a duty to consult safety representatives, i.e. representatives of the employees,[11] with a view to the making and maintenance of arrangements enabling the employer and the employees to co-operate effectively in promoting and developing measures for this purpose and may be required by the safety representatives or may itself so elect to establish a safety committee or committees to keep health, safety and welfare measures under review.

13.31 The Safety Representatives and Safety Committees Regulations 1977 provide that an employer must establish a safety committee within three months of being requested in writing to do so by at least two safety representatives who made the request and with representatives of recognised trade unions whose members work in any workplace in respect of which the committee is to function; and is required to post a notice stating the composition of the committee and the workplace or workplaces covered by it in a place where the notice may be easily read by employees. The Health and Safety Commission has produced guidance notes that provide advice on the objectives and functions of safety committees, their membership and conduct. The notes suggest, for example, that each safety committee ought to have a separate identity, i.e. it ought not to form part of an existing consultative committee for more general purposes, and that it is more likely to prove effective if related to a single establishment rather than a collection of geographically distinct places, although it is recognised that there may be a place for a safety committee at higher level in large organisations. The constitution, rules and procedure of the committees should be settled by joint consultation between management and trade unions (see 13.26).

13.32 A safety committee will be advisory in character and will function in much the same way as other consultative committees, i.e. decisions will be made by majority vote on either side and the decisions will be recommendations, ordinarily to the staffing committee.

Staff selection panels

General considerations

13.33 Many local authorities incorporate in their standing orders a number of staffing regulations although the regulations do not as a rule govern meetings for the interview and appointment of staff and associated personnel matters. Most have in the past been directed primarily at the prohibition of canvassing councillors by applicants for employment. The selection of staff on the basis predominantly of an interview has long been the traditional way in which local authorities have made their selection of prospective staff, often by over-large appointments panels comprised not infrequently in the past by councillors with little if any training in staff selection techniques. This process has been the subject of much criticism, which led to the Local Authorities (Standing Orders) (England) Regulations 2001. These regulations require the appointment, dismissal or disciplining of all staff below deputy chief officer level (apart from political assistants) to be the responsibility of the Head of Paid Service, or an officer nominated by him.

13.34 So far as the appointment of chief officers is concerned, the Local Authorities (Standing Orders) Regulations 1993 stipulate that:

'1 Where the authority propose to appoint a chief officer and it is not proposed that the appointment be made exclusively from among their existing officers, they shall:

   a) draw up a statement specifying:

      i) the duties of the officer concerned, and

      ii) any qualifications or qualities to be sought in the person to be appointed;

   b) make arrangements for the post to be advertised in such a way as is likely to bring it to the attention of persons who are qualified to apply for it; and

   c) make arrangements for a copy of the statement mentioned in paragraph (a) to be sent to any person on request.

2–1 Where a post has been advertised as provided in standing order 1(b), the authority shall:

   a) interview all qualified applicants for the post, or

   b) select a shortlist of such qualified applicants and interview those included on the shortlist.

  2 Where no qualified person has applied, the authority shall make further arrangements for advertisement in accordance with standing order 1(b).

3 Every appointment of a chief officer shall be made by the authority. The regulations, in Pt.II of Sch.1, provide for these authorised variations:

  1 The standing orders may provide that:

   a) the steps taken under standing order 1 or 2 above may be taken by a committee, subcommittee or chief officer of the authority;

   b) any chief officer may be appointed by a committee or subcommittee of the authority, or a relevant joint committee.

  2 The standing orders may provide that where the duties of a chief officer include the discharge of functions of two or more local authorities in pursuance of section 101(5) of the Local Government Act 1972:

   a) the steps taken under standing order 1 or 2 above may be taken by a joint committee of those authorities, a subcommittee of that committee or a chief officer of any of the authorities concerned; and (b) any chief officer may be appointed by such a joint committee, a subcommittee of that committee or a committee or subcommittee of any of those authorities.

  3 There may be excluded from the application of standing orders 1 to 3:

   a) any appointment of a non-statutory chief officer (within the meaning of section 2(7)(a) or (b) of that Act), and

   b) any appointment in pursuance of section 9 (assistants for political groups) of the Act.'

13. Meetings for special purposes

All local authority staff are now required to be appointed solely on 'merit' (LG&HA 1989, s.7).

Summons and agenda

13.35 The summons and agenda for a selection panel, constituted as a sub-committee and governed by the rules as to political proportionality (see 9.53), will comprise in every case:

- notification of date, time and place of the meeting;
- an indication of the panel's terms of reference and powers, e.g. to this effect if the panel possesses delegated power: 'to interview selected candidates and make an appointment to the post of . . .' or to this effect if not possessing such power: 'to interview selected candidates and to recommend an appointment to the post of . . .'; and
- such documents as may be thought appropriate to enable the members to study in advance: the job description of the post; the job specification[12] of the kind of candidate sought; and a copy of the applications and/or a summary of them.

13.36 The candidates will obviously need to be invited to attend for the interview before the selection panel. They should be given advance notice (indeed, there is much to commend the practice of thinking out the programme sufficiently far ahead to enable candidates to be advised of the probable date of interview when they first apply for an application form and particulars of the post), asked to come at staggered times and told how best to get to the town or county hall or offices concerned. A comfortable waiting room should be available for them when they arrive.

Purpose of selection interview

13.37 It would be an oversimplification to say that the object of the selection interview is to select and appoint a candidate to the job concerned. The interview, in any case, is only part of the total selection process. There is likely in practice depending upon the seniority of the job to have been some form of aptitude test, nowadays of some sophistication, and a preliminary interview of candidates at officer level to determine a shortlist. There are enquiries to be made beforehand and formalities to be dealt with subsequently before the contract of employment is finalised: the taking up of references, medical clearance and so on. Nevertheless, the interview is in most cases the critical stage in the process and will usually result in the selection of a favoured candidate.

13.38 The purposes of the interview may be summarised:

- to give each candidate information about the job (although ideally most of the information required should have been provided by the written particulars of the appointment);
- to obtain or check the basic facts about the shortlisted candidates;
- to permit observation of the candidates' outward appearance and manner;

- to test by oral question and answer the candidates' capabilities as relevant to the job;
- to enable an assessment to be made of the personality of the candidates, using this term in the most general sense to include both intelligence and personal qualities; and
- to influence the favoured candidate towards accepting the job if the panel wishes him to take it.

The ultimate choice of candidate ought to be a matter of mutual agreement between members of the interviewing panel. There is risk of making an unsatisfactory decision where the choice is decided on a formal vote. If the panel is a sizable one (as, regrettably, is still the case in some authorities, especially for chief officer appointments), a candidate chosen on the basis of having secured most votes may have been selected as a minority choice if the majority of interviewers have spread their votes among other candidates. If there is voting it may be preferable to proceed on the basis of old model standing order no.16.

Conduct of the interview

13.39 It is impossible here to deal comprehensively with the considerations to be borne in mind in conducting an interview for the selection of staff.
Essentially, of course:

- the right rapport must be established between interviewers and interviewee, something more easily secured in the informality of a one-to-one conversation but difficult sometimes in the case of a panel. It is the chairman's responsibility to seek the candidate's co-operation, reduce the tension that must exist in such a situation, and ensure that the interview is conducted courteously and efficiently;
- the candidate should be greeted cordially, told the names of the interviewers (if these are not displayed on nameplates in front of them), treated with utmost consideration during questioning, and given an opportunity at the end of asking questions and of adding anything he may wish in support of his candidature; and
- throughout the chairman must be firm and see that neither he nor any of the panel are being put in the position of interviewee. He should ensure that council members (and officers) give full attention to the business in hand, that nothing occurs that may disconcert the candidate or put him at a disadvantage. He should not be required to sit facing the light so that members of the panel are mere faceless silhouettes against a window, nor at the far end of a long table so that he has difficulty in hearing questions from the distance. At best the interview is an artificial situation in which, as a rule, neither interviewers nor candidates behave as they would in other circumstances. There must, of course, be no telephone or other interruptions, nor – quite unpardonable – must tea be served in the middle of an interview. It is no bad thing, however, to break off for refreshments at a convenient time.

The proceedings must be businesslike. Sometimes well-meaning attempts at informality can be disastrous. It is better to sit the candidate on the other side of the table than in an easy chair where he will either perch uncomfortably on the edge or sink into its depths. The best interviews, given the drawbacks, are those conducted in a traditional but wholly friendly and businesslike manner.

13.40 Any member of the selection panel not present throughout the interviews ought not to cast a vote in the decision to select. In *R. v. Birmingham City Council ex parte McKenna* (1992), a selection panel of six members had been properly appointed under the terms of the former E(2)A 1986, ss.35-37 and the Education (School Government) Regulations 1989 to interview and appoint a head teacher. The panel chose to make the selection process a three-stage business: first a meeting to consider the written applications, second to interview the long list of those selected, and third a meeting to interview the shortlisted candidates and make the appointment. An unsuccessful candidate challenged the decision on the grounds that one of the members of the panel did not attend the second meeting although she was present at the third when she had agreed with the unanimous decision (to reduce the long list to a shortlist) taken in her absence at the second meeting. An application for judicial review was subsequently refused (on a number of grounds not connected with the issue we are considering) and in reaching its decision the court decided that the long list interview meeting (when the member was absent) was not an essential step in the appointment process. Though the point may be arguable, it surely seems to imply that if the member had been temporarily absent during the final interviews and had nevertheless voted to appoint the chosen candidate, the decision might well have been successfully challenged.

13.41 It used to be said that there is no restriction on the type of questions that may be put to candidates, save those that relate to religious or political views. That must now be modified. Questions that may imply that the selection could be biased on grounds of sex or race or other types of unlawful discrimination are likely to involve the employing authority appearing before an industrial tribunal if the candidate concerned is not appointed. Alternatively, questions may be put about the social awareness of the candidate that could be interpreted as politically orientated. Clearly the interviewing process needs to be conducted in a way that will detect fitness for the job and to persuade candidates that merit has been the overriding criterion.

13.42 The following is suggested as a checklist on procedure:

- Preliminary discussion: clarify key qualities/competencies being sought; decide systematic approach: time to be devoted to each candidate, when to break for refreshments, apportionment of questioning, etc.; ensure no likelihood of interruptions;
- Receive candidate: introduce panel;
- Check that candidate is a firm applicant and willing to accept the job if offered;
- Invite candidate to:
  a) make any presentation that may have been requested;
  b) give outline of experience, stressing that which he considers relevant; or
  c) say what he does in present post;
- Ask questions of candidate; invite:
  a) panel members to ask questions;
  b) officers to ask questions;
- Ask candidate whether:

a) he wishes to add anything in support of his candidature;
b) he has any questions;

- Thank candidate for attending, ask him to retire and either:
  a) tell him to wait; or
  b) say he will be advised of the panel's decision in due course;
- Consider decision in light of:
  a) written applications; and
  b) impression gained at interview; and
  c) result of any aptitude or other test; and – with reserve –
  d) references; against job specification;
- Call back successful candidate and offer appointment (or, if appropriate, say that a decision will be communicated to him); and
- Tell unsuccessful candidates of decision and thank them for attending.

The panel chairman, should keep a check on time devoted to each candidate and ensure that all areas of necessary investigation are adequately covered by questions.

Staff appeals tribunals

General considerations

13.43 A staffing committee will need to provide an internal appeals machinery to deal with three types of hearing:

- appeals against disciplinary measures;
- appeals against salary grading; and
- unresolved grievances; and to set up a subcommittee, panel or tribunal to deal with each or all three types of case.

The term tribunal has merit because of its judicial connotation. Councillors in reaching a decision in appeal cases are exercising a quasi-judicial role (see 13.17).
 13.44 The membership should be as small as the rules governing political balance permit, the councillors chosen should ideally be ones who enjoy the confidence of both council and employees, and have received the necessary training. They should be empowered to make the final decision so far as the local authority is concerned. There is advantage in establishing a pool of members from which an appeals panel can be selected because of the expertise that is built up by their experience and the greater likelihood of uniformity of approach. The council should take account of the statutory provisions relating to the conflict of interest of councillors involved in staff negotiations (see 13.26), even though membership of an appeals panel may, strictly, not be caught.
13.45 The constitution of the tribunal and the procedure adopted at its meetings will depend to some extent upon local arrangements governing employee appeals. For example, where, as is usual, the power to take disciplinary measures is delegated to chief officers, the appeals tribunal can be appointed by and out of the personnel or staffing committee or personnel subcommittee; but if only the personnel or staffing

committee or subcommittee can dismiss an employee, the tribunal will need to be comprised of members who are not members of the committee or subcommittee that made the original decision, and this makes for anomalous situations. It means that the personnel or staff committee or subcommittee does not have the final say, but that councillors with ordinarily no staffing responsibility are empowered to settle an appeal from a decision of members charged with that responsibility on behalf of the local authority. Much the same dilemma can arise on appeals on salary questions, but in these cases the position can more correctly be regarded as a matter of an appeals tribunal reviewing a decision made by its parent committee or subcommittee in the light of representations of the officer aggrieved. In the case of the dismissal of an employee, there may be a further appeal outside the local authority to an employment tribunal if the employee, having the requisite service, challenges the disallowance of his appeal and alleges unfair dismissal. (See Employment Rights Act 1996, s.94.)

Disciplinary hearings

13.46 The arrangements that local authorities make for the hearing of appeals against disciplinary action are still largely for each authority to determine[13] (other than in the case of disciplinary action against the head of the paid service and other statutory affairs (see 13.54)) although the LG&HA 1989, s.8, enables the Secretary of State to make regulations in respect of all categories of local authority employed staff. An authority's discretion is, however, constrained by considerations of natural justice (see 13.21) and the recommendations in the ACAS code on Disciplinary Practice and Procedures in Employment. Each authority's disciplinary code should define what constitutes disciplinary action – in the case of the head of the paid service a statutory definition applies (see 13.54) – and regulate the manner in which breaches of discipline are to be handled. What is important is that employees should know what constitutes misconduct likely to lead to disciplinary action and the probable consequences of such misconduct. Thus disciplinary action when necessary must be taken:

- in a manner which is fair to the employee concerned;
- in strict accordance with the council's own procedures;
- in conformity with any statutory provisions that apply; and
- in accordance with a procedure that provides a right of appeal against action taken at first instance.

13.47 The notice of the hearing sent to the appeals tribunal with the date, time and place of meeting (the date should have been agreed with the appellant and his trade union or other representative) should be accompanied by a report setting out the facts that led to the disciplinary action taken, the disciplinary action itself, the reasons for it and possibly also an indication of alternative courses open to the tribunal if it wishes to allow the appeal. The tribunal must also be provided with a copy of any representations made by the appellant. The appellant and his representative must be provided with a copy of all the papers made available to members of the tribunal.

Natural justice

13.48 When an appeals tribunal is hearing an appeal against disciplinary action (or against a salary grading claim or seeking to settle a grievance), it is acting, of course, in a quasi-judicial capacity and must observe the principles of natural justice. These principles in relation to judicial and quasi-judicial business in committee have already been discussed (see 13.17), but their application specifically to the conduct of disciplinary proceedings was considered in *Khanum* v. *Mid-Glamorgan Area Health Authority* (1978), in which the Employment Appeal Tribunal said:

> '... in the end how nearly a domestic disciplinary inquiry, a statutory inquiry by a statutory body, a public statutory inquiry, or any other inquiry which has to make decisions, must approach to the full-blown procedure of a court of justice is, no doubt, a matter of degree. But in our judgment as regards the sort of domestic tribunal with which we are concerned in this case [a domestic inquiry and disciplinary hearing by an area health authority] the law is as it was expressed by Harman, J., in *Byrne* v. *Kinematograph Renters Society Ltd* [1958] 1 W.L.R. 762, and approved and applied by the Privy Council to the conduct of a university vice-chancellor's inquiry into cheating in examinations in *Fernando's Case*:
>
> > "What then are the requirements of natural justice in a case of this kind? First, I think that the person accused should know of the nature of the accusation made; secondly, that he should be given an opportunity to state his case; and thirdly, of course, that the tribunal should act in good faith. I do not myself think that there is really anything more."'

There is, perhaps, something more to be added and it is this. Members who take the final decision must have been present throughout the hearing and thus vote on the whole of the evidence: anyone who entered the room after the proceedings began or absented himself for part of the hearing ought not to be allowed to vote (see 13.40).

13.49 It must be obvious that a tribunal cannot be regarded as acting in conditions of complete impartiality because it will always be reviewing a decision already made by the management of which it forms a part. This was well expressed in another EAT case, *Corina* v. *Berkshire County Council* (1979):

> 'It is a fallacy to suppose that in the course of internal grievance or disciplinary procedures you can have a neutral disciplinary or appellate "tribunal" short of an express provision for recourse to outside arbitration through ACAS or otherwise, something which involves its own disadvantages. The people who have to hear and decide on the matter, in internal procedures, are limbs of the employer and so not "impartial" in any true sense. What, as a matter of natural justice you are entitled to, is that they shall come to their decisions honestly.'

13. Meetings for special purposes

Who should represent the parties?

13.50 The officer who is to represent the council at a disciplinary or grievance hearing should, ideally, be the officer who took the initial disciplinary decision against the appellant or heard his grievance at first instance (and this will ordinarily be the chief officer or, conceivably, a senior officer in the department). It ought not to be the personnel officer because, among other reasons, he may well be the appeal tribunal's adviser. The personnel officer must remain impartial until a final decision has been taken on behalf of the employing authority, i.e. after the decision of the tribunal in a disciplinary matter, when he may well represent the local authority before an industrial tribunal. The expression council's representative should thus be interpreted to mean the departmental chief officer or his representative.

13.51 The ACAS Code of Disciplinary Practice and Procedures in Employment says that the employee should be accorded the right to be accompanied by a trade union representative or a fellow employee of his choice; and most local authority codes, likely in every case to have been agreed with employee representatives, will contain similar provisions. However, what if notwithstanding such provisions an employee wishes to be accompanied or represented by a lawyer or a relative? Most authorities would probably not wish to place any restriction on the freedom of the individual to be represented by whoever he wishes. Nevertheless, there is support for the view that a tribunal, which is entitled to regulate its own procedures, could properly refuse to allow legal representation, at least if the applicable code expressly forbids it. Lord Justice Cairns expressed the view in *Enderby Town Football Club Ltd* v. *Football Association Ltd* (1971), p.609, that 'it is open to an organisation to make an absolute rule that a tribunal set up by it is not to hear legal representations'. This view was cited by Lord Justice Orr in *Maynard* v. *Osmond* (1977), which concerned an appeal by a police constable against a decision that he was not entitled to be legally represented in disciplinary proceedings against him under the Police (Disciplinary) Regulations 1965:

'No authority cited to us lends support to the view that the denial either of a right to legal representation or of a discretion to allow it contravenes the rules of natural justice and while we are concerned in this case with regulations made by a minister under statutory powers and not with a domestic tribunal constituted by contract, I am inclined to agree with the view provisionally expressed by Lord Justice Cairns in *Enderby Town Football Club Ltd* v. *Football Association Ltd . . .*'

In this same case, Lord Denning considered that, even if a man was not entitled as of right to be legally represented in disciplinary proceedings, the disciplinary body should have discretion to allow it:

> 'Legal representation should not be forbidden altogether. The tribunal should have discretion so as to permit him to have a lawyer if they think it would assist. They are the masters of their own procedure; and, unless expressly forbidden, should have a discretion to permit it.'

13.52 Despite these differing views the Court of Appeal ruled in the *Maynard* case in favour of allowing a police constable to be legally represented in disciplinary proceedings and thought in principle such a right should be accorded to other individuals in other disciplinary proceedings:

> 'On principle, if a man is charged with a serious offence which may have grave consequences for him, he should be entitled to have a qualified lawyer to defend him. Such has been agreed by the Government of this country when it adhered to the European Convention on Human Rights. But also, by analogy, it should be the same in most cases when he is charged with a disciplinary offence before a disciplinary tribunal, at any rate when the offence is one which may result in his dismissal from the force or other body to which he belongs; or the loss of his livelihood; or, worse still, may ruin his character for ever.'

Subsequently, so far as police affairs are concerned, the Police (Conduct) Regulations 1999 (SI 1999/730) give the right of legal representation where an officer's job or rank is at risk, in relation to officers below the rank of chief superintendent. More senior officers are entitled to legal representation and to be reimbursed their costs.[14]

Procedure

13.53 The following is an example, couched in terms of advice for the chairman, of the procedure which should be followed at the hearing of an appeal against disciplinary action by any local authority employee (but see 13.54 as regards disciplinary action in the case of the head of the paid service) and subject to modification in cases where a disciplinary procedure is specifically prescribed as, e.g., in the case of police officers, fire fighters, teachers, etc. The council's representative (CR) – the departmental chief officer or his representative (see 13.47) – puts his case first and the appellant's representative (AR) puts the case for the appellant (A) afterwards:

- Call in together CR, AR and A;
- Invite CR to put the council's case;
- After each of the CR's witnesses (if any) has given evidence;
- Ask AR whether he (or A) wishes to ask questions of the witness;
  - Ask whether members of the tribunal wish to ask questions of the witness; and
  - Ask CR whether he wishes to re-examine his witness.

13. Meetings for special purposes

- After CR has completed his case:
  - Ask AR whether he has any questions he wishes to put to CR; and
  - Ask whether members of the tribunal wish to ask questions of the CR.
- Invite AR to put A's case.
- If AR calls witnesses then after each has given evidence:
  - Ask CR whether he wishes to ask questions of the witness;
  - Ask whether members of the tribunal wish to ask questions of the witness; and
  - Ask AR whether he wishes to re-examine his witness.
- After AR has completed his case:
  - Ask CR whether he has any questions to put to either AR or A; and
  - Ask whether members of the tribunal wish to ask questions of AR or A.
  - Invite CR to sum up the council's case if he wishes to do so.
  - Invite AR to sum up A's case if he wishes to do so.
  - Ask all parties to withdraw except the tribunal's adviser.
  - Deliberate upon the case.

The tribunal may confirm, amend or reject the original decision and may recall both parties to clear points of uncertainty on the evidence given, but if recall is necessary both parties are to return notwithstanding that only one is concerned with the point giving rise to doubt.

- After a decision has been reached, call back both parties and announce either:
  - the tribunal's decision if it possesses delegated power; or
  - that the decision will be communicated to the parties as soon as possible: in either case the decision must be confirmed in writing.

Disciplinary action against Head of the Paid Service, Monitoring Officer or Chief Finance Officer

13.54 The Local Authorities (Standing Orders) Regulations 1993, as amended by the Local Authorities (Standing Orders) (England) Regulations 2001, prescribe a mandatory standing order that relevant authorities must make regulating the investigation of alleged misconduct on the part of the head of the council's paid service,[15] its monitoring officer or its chief finance officer. The regulations also define disciplinary action in these terms:

> '"Disciplinary action" in relation to a member of staff of a local authority means any action occasioned by alleged misconduct which, if proved, would, according to the usual practice of the authority, be recorded on the member of staff's personal file, and includes any proposal for dismissal of a member of staff for any reason other than redundancy, permanent ill-health or infirmity of mind or body, but does not include failure to renew a contract of employment for a fixed term unless the authority has undertaken to renew such a contract.'

311

Miscellaneous meetings

The regulations provide for the involvement of a designated independent person to be appointed by the authority and remunerated by it, in every case where a complaint of misconduct requires to be investigated against the head of the paid service, monitoring officer or chief finance officer. This independent person – who is to be agreed between the authority and the relevant officer or, in default of such agreement, appointed by the Secretary of State – has these duties to discharge:

> The designated independent person:
> 'a) may direct:
> > i) that the authority terminate any suspension of the relevant officer; or
> > ii) that any such suspension shall continue after the expiry of the period referred to in para. 3 of Sch. 3 (or in provisions to the like effect); or
> > iii) that the terms on which any such suspension has taken place shall be varied in accordance with the direction;
> > iv) that no steps (whether by the authority or any committee, subcommittee or officer acting on behalf of the authority) towards disciplinary action or further disciplinary action against the relevant officer, other than steps taken in the presence, or with the agreement, of the designated independent person, are to be taken before a report is made under subparagraph (d) below;
> b) may inspect any documents relating to the conduct of the relevant officer which are in the possession of the authority, or which the authority has power to authorise him to inspect;
> c) may require any member of staff of the authority to answer questions concerning the conduct of the relevant officer;
> d) must make a report to the authority:
> > i) stating his opinion as to whether (and if so, the extent to which) the evidence he has obtained supports any allegation of misconduct against the relevant officer; and
> > ii) recommending any disciplinary action which appears to him to be appropriate for the authority to take against the relevant officer; and
> e) must no later than the time at which he makes his report under subparagraph (d), send a copy of the report to the relevant officer.'

The regulations provide that no disciplinary action in respect of the head of the paid service, monitoring officer or chief finance officer, other than permitted suspension, i.e. suspension on full pay terminating no later than the expiry of two months beginning on the day on which suspension takes effect, may be taken by an authority other than in accordance with a recommendation in a report made by the independent person.

13.55 The implication of what is said in the foregoing paragraph must be that the employing authority will need to involve the designated independent person in its disciplinary appeals procedure. How it will do so appears to be a matter for the authority (in the light necessarily of any guidance that may be issued by the appropriate national negotiating bodies), but it would appear to be nonsensical for the authority and the independent person each to go over the same ground, assessing whatever evidence there may be against the officer, hearing his response to the allegation and so on.

13. Meetings for special purposes

Standards Committee

13.56 The Nolan Committee proposed that each local authority should establish a standards committee that would command a special position in the council's management structure. It would be composed of senior members and chaired by someone other than the leader of the council with power to examine allegations of misconduct by councillors and to recommend disciplinary action to the full assembly. These powers of recommendation would include proposing the withdrawal by particular councillors from decision-making and the suspension of a member for up to three months.

13.57 As mentioned in Chapter 1, these proposals eventually resulted in the LGA 2000 establishing an ethical framework for local authorities and, at local level, each relevant authority has the obligation to establish a standards committee that has the statutory duty to promote and maintain high standards of conduct by members and co-opted members of the authority; and to assist them in observing the authority's Code of Conduct. The committee need not be politically balanced, and must have at least three people on it. At least two of the committee members must be councillors and at least one member of it must be independent of local government. If there are parish councils in the area covered by the local authority concerned, then there must also be at least one parish councillor on the committee. The Standards Board for England recommends that there be at least two independent people on a standards committee and encourages councils to appoint more than one parish representative. There are current moves to require that at least half of the committee should be independent, and that it is chaired by one of the independent people. This is becoming increasingly the case in practice, in any event. The independent representatives must be approved by a majority of councillors after public advertisement under the procedure set down in the Relevant Authorities (Standards Committee) Regulations 2001.

13.58 So far as meetings of the standards committee is concerned, there is a quorum of at least three, including one independent representative. Also, a parish representative must be present when matters relating to parish councils are being discussed. Members of standards committees should not be whipped or told how to vote, but should consider matters impartially and without regard to party loyalty.

13.59 So far as complaints in relation to the Code of Conduct are concerned, those matters referred to a local level by ethical standards officers are considered by the standards committee of the relevant authority under the Local Authorities (Code of Conduct) (Local Determination) Regulations 2003. Guidance was issued by the Standards Board in November 2004 to monitoring officers and standards committees on how investigations and local determinations should be carried out.

13.60 A hearing by the Standards Committee is subject to time limits set out in the 2003 Regulations referred to (see 13.59) and a hearing should be held within three months of receipt by the monitoring officer of the ethical standards officer's report. In *R (on the application of Dawkins)* v. *Bolsover DC & The Standards Board for England* (2004), non-compliance with the timescales set out in the Regulations was capable of being waived, but the standards committee had to demonstrate a genuine and determined effort to meet the deadline. In that case, the test had not been met. In determining whether a councillor had failed to comply with the requirements of the

Code as regards personal and prejudicial interests, the proper test to be applied by the committee is whether, viewed objectively, the councilor had a personal or prejudicial interest in the matter. In *Victor Scrivens* v. *Ethical Standards Officer* (2003), it was held that the mistaken but reasonable view of the councillor that he had no such interest was irrelevant as the test was an objective one, a subjective test would confer too much latitude on the conduct of a member.

13.61 At the hearing by the standards committee of a complaint, the chairman will introduce those present and explain how the hearing will be run. The suggested procedure will normally consist of three stages. Firstly, the investigating officer will present the case as set out in the investigator's report, and the member complained of will respond. Each may call witnesses as appropriate. The committee will then retire to consider the representations and upon the committee's return the chairman will announce the committee's findings of fact.

13.62 Secondly, based on the facts found, the member will then be invited to give relevant reasons why the committee should not decide that he has failed to follow the Code of Conduct. The committee will then consider any representations from the investigator and the member will then respond. The committee will again retire to consider the representations and upon the committee's return the chairman will announce the committee's decision as to whether or not the member has failed to follow the Code.

13.63 The third stage of the process depends on whether or not there is a finding that there has been a failure to follow the Code. If no breach is found to have taken place, then the committee can move on to consider whether it should make any recommendations to the relevant Council as appropriate with a view to promoting high standards of conduct among members. If there has been a failure to follow the Code, then the committee will consider any representations from the investigator and the member as to whether or not the committee should set a penalty and, if so, what form any penalty should take. The committee will again retire to consider the matter.

13.64 Should a standards committee find that there has been a breach of the Code of Conduct, it can impose one or any combination of the following:

- censure the member;
- restrict the member's access to the premises and resources of the authority for up to three months, ensuring that any restrictions are proportionate to the nature of the breach and do not unduly restrict the member's ability to perform his or her duties as a member;
- order the member to submit a written apology in a form satisfactory to the standards committee;
- order the member to undertake training specified by the standards committee;
- order the member to participate in a conciliation process specified by the standards committee;
- suspend, or partially suspend, the member for up to three months; and/or
- suspend, or partially suspend, the member for up to three months or until such time as the member either submits a written apology that is accepted by the standards committee or the member undertakes any training or conciliation ordered by the standards committee.

13. Meetings for special purposes

13.65 As soon as reasonably practicable after the end of the hearing, the committee shall issue a written decision, including adequate reasons for the decision, and shall publish a summary of the findings and decision in a local newspaper. If the finding of the committee is that the member has not breached the Code, then that member can ask the committee not to publish that finding. Where there has been a finding that the Code has been breached, then the member concerned has the right to apply in writing to the president of the Adjudication Panel for England for permission to appeal against that finding. Such application must be received by the president within 21 days of the members' receipt of the written decision of the committee.

13.66 Whereas complaints under the Code of Conduct have to be referred to the Standards Board, complaints made under a local authority's own internal protocols such as a member/officer protocol could be referred direct to the standards committee, subject to its terms of reference. The statutory procedures and penalties set out above would not apply to such complaints. Instead, the complaint would be dealt with by the committee under its general powers, including those set out in s.111 of the LGA 1972. Those powers were considered by the Court of Appeal in *R. v. Broadland District Council ex parte Lashley* (2001). In that case a chief executive had issued instructions that apart from nominated officers, staff were not to have any dealings with Councillor Lashley and the chief executive also banned that member from entering the council offices other than to attend council meetings. In essence, the court considered such restrictions to be unlawful. The court was inclined to agree with the view, however, that the standards committee could 'name and shame' a councillor and could recommend that a councillor be removed from a particular committee.

Meetings of governing bodies

Introduction

13.67 There is within local government an immense variety of governing bodies. These include, for example, informal groups of council and co-opted members (sometimes local residents also) appointed by a social services committee to visit residential establishments, and the formally constituted boards of governors of schools set up by local education authorities. It would be unprofitable to attempt to refer to each one of the many types of such bodies that exist. Whatever their type, however, it is a matter of good practice and convenience where such matters are not prescribed by law that each should be accorded clearly defined terms of reference, so that even if the precise constitution has not been set down on paper at least there is no uncertainty about the powers and duties of members individually and the body collectively. Preferably, too, each meeting should be minuted even if the note of proceedings is no more than a brief aide-mémoire. Ideally, standing orders or rules of procedure should be drawn up as well.

School governors

13.68 The Education Act 2002 requires that, for every school in which primary and secondary education is provided, there shall be a governing body constituted as a corporate body set up under an instrument made by the local education authority, i.e. the councils of counties, metropolitan districts, unitary authorities, London boroughs and the common council of the City of London. The Education and Inspections Act 2006 has introduced new duties on governing bodies and brought about changes to governors' roles. The constitution of the governing body is related to the type of school, number of registered pupils and the membership is in several categories including, for example, appointees of the local education authority, parent and teacher governors, co-opted persons, and the head teacher ex officio unless he chooses not to be a governor. The detailed regulation of the constitution of governing bodies, their membership and term of office, and functions, is outside the scope of this book. See, however, *R. v. Warwickshire County Council ex parte Dill-Russell* (1991), where it was held that an authority is entitled to remove school governors so that the composition of the body reflects the political make-up of the council. The court said there is no distinction between the power to appoint to preserve political weighting and the power to remove having the same objective. The removal of governors, other than co-opted governors or foundation governors of voluntary schools, can only be carried out by the persons or bodies appointing them and must be in the interests of the school. The power of removal must be exercised in accordance with the School Governance (Constitution) Regulations 2003.

13.69 The meetings and proceedings of governors are dealt with under the School Governance (Procedures) (England) Regulations 2003, which contain provisions relating to the disqualification of persons from membership of governing bodies (for bankruptcy, etc., and criminal convictions, or failure to attend meetings over a period of 12 months); the resignation and removal of governors and the filling of casual vacancies; the election of a chairman and vice-chairman; the tenure of office of governors, and particularly in relation to meetings and proceedings thereat. These again are very detailed regulating the circumstances in which a member of a governing body is required to withdraw from a meeting. Provision is made in the regulations for the delegation of functions by governing bodies and the establishment of committees, and as to the meetings and proceedings of selection panels.

School staff selection panels

13.70 In general, and subject to the provisions of the School Staffing (England) Regulations 2003, the procedure at meetings of a selection panel for the appointment of head teachers and deputy head teachers should follow that described earlier (see 13.33). In particular, it is submitted, a governor ought not to vote in the final choice of candidate if he has not been present when all the candidates were interviewed. If, however, the selection procedure has involved more than one meeting, e.g. one to consider written applications, another to interview a long list of candidates, the absence of a governor from one of the earlier meetings does not necessarily invalidate the decision of the selection panel to make an appointment. This was the case in *R. v. Birmingham City Council ex parte McKenna* (1992) (see 13.40), where the court refused judicial review of a governors' selection panel because despite some irregularities (e.g. there was a failure to appoint a substitute governor to fill a vacancy), the irregularities were of no significance or consequence nor was the absence of a governor from an earlier meeting of the selection panel.

Appeals against school admission decisions

Appeal committees

13.71 There is statutory provision allowing parents of a child to make representations when their expressed preference for a certain school or college is not complied with by the local education authority or the governing body of a voluntary school. An appeal committee must be set up for this purpose, constituted in accordance with Sch.25 of the School Standards and Framework Act 1998. The decision of such a committee is binding on the local education authority and governing body, save that an aggrieved parent may in limited circumstances resort, only on process not decision, to the Secretary of State.

13.72 The appeal committee is not a committee or subcommittee of the local authority. That is clear from several of the statutory provisions that, for example, expressly exclude the application of the provisions of the LGA 1972 relating to local authority committees, and from the fact that the committee is subject to the Tribunals and Inquiries Act 1992 and to the supervision of the Council on Tribunals. The committee is within the jurisdiction of the local government ombudsman (see *R. v. Commissioner for Local Administration ex parte Croydon LBC* (1989)).

13.73 The statutory provisions relating to the constitution of the committee and its proceedings are set out in Sch.21 of the School Standards and Framework Act 1998. An appeal committee must consist of three or five members appointed by the local education authority from categories of people who are eligible as lay members or who have experience of education. There must be at least one member from each category. Certain people are disqualified from membership including any councillor from the local education authority or member of the governing body of the school concerned, and any employee of the local authority other than a teacher (except that any teacher employed at the school concerned is also disqualified).

13.74 The prescribed procedure, applicable to all school admission appeal committees, requires that the committee must give an appellant an opportunity for an oral hearing and to be accompanied by a friend or be represented. The hearing must ordinarily be held in private and the decision made by a simple majority of the members with the chairman permitted to exercise a second or casting vote if necessary. The decision and the grounds on which it was reached must be communicated to the local education authority and to the appellant. There is a school admissions code of practice on the procedure for appeals.

Appeals against pupils' exclusions

13.75 A head teacher – and only a head teacher – may exclude a pupil from school on disciplinary grounds and the specified procedure must be followed, keeping parents, governing body and local education authority informed. There is provision for reinstatement at the direction of the governing body or authority, for appeal against permanent exclusion, and for governing bodies to appeal against an authority's reinstatement direction. Appeals by parents are ordinarily made to a committee constituted under the Education (Pupil Exclusions and Appeals) Regulations 2002.

School organisation proposals

13.76 From 24th May 2007, the Education and Inspections Act 2006 introduced a new system for decision-making in relation to proposals to open, close or alter schools. The Act abolished the School Organisation Committee which had previously made such decisions. Decisions are now made either by the Council (as an Executive Function) or by the Adjudicator depending on the type of proposal. If the decision is made by the Council there is a right of appeal by the Church of England or Roman Catholic Diocese, the Governing Body of non-Community schools and the Learning Skills Council (if the proposal involves children over 16). A more detailed account is outside the scope of this book, but there is a useful DfES website setting out the processes at www.dfes.gov.uk/schoolorg/

Chief Executive's corporate management team

Its character

13.77 It has long been a practice in many authorities for the chief executive (formerly, of course, the clerk or town clerk) to hold regular meetings with his chief officer colleagues. In the past these have varied in character, according to local custom, from mere social gatherings for the exchange of opinion and information largely about the officers' respective areas of involvement, to more purposeful but still informal meetings concerned with high-level co-ordination and the discussion of matters of policy or important principle. These meetings have now been supplanted in most instances by more formal meetings of properly constituted management teams of the kind originally envisaged by the Maud Committee but modelled more specifically on that sketched out by Bains. They are distinguishable from their forerunners by the fact that the management team is usually an integral part of the management process of decision-making and control.

13.78 Maud recommended that the principal officers should work as members of a team of managers and specialist advisers and see that the same approach is adopted by their staff at all levels and it saw the principal officers working together on matters that transcend the purely professional and departmental considerations under the clerk's leadership and producing agreed and co-ordinated recommendations to be put to Maud's management board.

13. Meetings for special purposes

Bains believed that the officers' management team:[16]

> '... should have a corporate identity and a positive role to play in the corporate management of the authority. It is the counterpart, at officer level, of the policy and resources committee. Its members do not attend primarily as representatives of particular departments, though on occasion it will be necessary for them to speak in that capacity; they are there as members of a body created to aid the management of the authority as a whole.'

Bains discussed the role of the management team and its size, the support it would need from interdepartmental working groups and its terms of reference. It thought the team had two broad functions. The first is the long-term strategic function of considering and advising on what policies the council should be adopting to cope with changing needs and circumstances, and the second the overall management co-ordinative and progress-chasing role.

Proceedings and business

13.79 The business of the management team should be transacted with some measure of, but not too much, formality. There should be a prearranged timetable of regular meetings and a notice and agenda circulated on each occasion to those entitled to attend; individual officers should have the opportunity of originating matters for discussion but the agenda should be controlled by the chief executive; minutes should be kept and copies circulated. The distinguishing feature of management team meetings is that business is conducted as a cabinet. The chief executive will occupy the chair as of right and there will ordinarily be no voting (or the team could vote the chief executive out of the chair!). The chief executive will make the decisions either on the basis of a consensus of opinion or on his view of the balance of argument on a particular issue, or may make his own judgment of what needs to be decided after taking account of what is said by his colleagues. Members of the team will usually accept collective responsibility for the advice that in the final resort the chief executive tenders to the council.

13.80 One of the by-products, as it were, of compiling an agenda is that the chief executive can examine it in draft and delete any items he thinks do not warrant the attention of the management team. It is important that meetings of the team should not be cluttered up with matters that can be competently dealt with elsewhere, by chief officers individually or in consultation with others either in company or not with the chief executive. Otherwise the team will fail constantly to perform its corporate role. The mere fact that a proposal of one officer may impinge on the work of others is not itself sufficient justification for bringing the matter to the management team (or almost everything, important or otherwise, that, for example, the treasurer or personnel officer wants to do could be held up for management team consideration). The matter must be of major importance or affect council policy to warrant the

319

formal attention of the team as a whole. The team exists to facilitate the business of the local authority, not to obstruct progress.

13.81 Bains thought it 'difficult to lay down specific terms of reference' for the management team, but the following is a suggested shortlist of the kind of items that would need to come before the team:

- important questions of a corporate character and matters of major importance that cannot properly be dealt with by the individual officer or officers concerned;
- matters referred to the team for consideration from the policy and resources committee (or cabinet);
- policy matters on which collective advice is to be submitted to council or committee;
- formulation of proposals for linking presentation of objectives, programmes and budgets;
- identification and review of objectives and priorities;
- monitoring progress against plans; and
- strategic questions concerning the acquisition, use, motivation, development and levels of manpower resources.

13.82 There can be a problem where a management team has fairly formal meetings and minutes of its proceedings and councillors may express a wish to see the minutes of particular decisions and sometimes even ask for regular access to papers. When such a request is declined – as would ordinarily be the case – the member may seek to rely on his 'need to know' and this raises a difficult question. It is, however, one less likely to arise if the relationship between the management team and councillors has been spelt out and understood from the outset. The management team's deliberations are part of the authority's management arrangements, i.e. the province of officers, rather than part of the authority's decision-making process, which is the remit of members. In most instances it would seem appropriate for the chief executive to advise that members do not need to see the record of his management team's discussions to enable them to carry out their duties as councillors.

There will also be at many authorities regular informal meetings between the management team and leading councillors (either cabinet members or chairs of committee depending on the executive arrangements of the council) which will be the forum for ensuring officers and members of the administration co-ordinate their respective programmes.

Election meetings

Use of local authority premises

13.83 The Representation of the People Act 1983, consolidating previous enactments to like effect, obliges a local authority to permit the use of certain schools and halls for meetings for purposes connected with parliamentary and local government elections.

13. Meetings for special purposes

Parliamentary elections

13.84 A candidate at a parliamentary or European parliamentary election is entitled,[17] for the purpose of holding public meetings in furtherance of his candidature, to the use at reasonable times between the receipt of the writ for the election and the day preceding the day of election, of any room that it is the practice to be let for public meetings and that is maintained wholly or mainly at public expense, and any suitable school room, i.e. at a county school, voluntary school or grant-maintained school situated in the constituency or an adjoining constituency if more reasonably accessible. Local education authorities, district councils and London borough councils must prepare lists of suitable available rooms, which should also include details of the person to whom application for the use of a room should be made. A local authority cannot refuse the use of such premises even if the candidate's views are offensive to many people – see *Webster* v. *Southwark London Borough Council* (1983) – but the police should be contacted if it is believed that the views to be put forward at a meeting are likely to be so extreme that they may cause disruption or offence and a risk to public order. In other respects, a candidate, no matter what his political persuasion, has a relatively unfettered private law right to hire a public meeting room so long as it is for the purpose described in the statute. It must be a public meeting in furtherance of his candidature (see *Ettridge* v. *Morrell* (1986)). Some local authorities provide political parties with questionnaires designed to find out precisely whether the intended meeting is a public meeting within the meaning of the RPA and require production of a valid insurance certificate for public indemnity insurance.

13.85 Where a room is thus used the person by whom or on whose behalf the meeting is convened may be required to pay for expenses incurred in preparing, warming, lighting and cleaning it, in providing attendants for the meeting and restoring the room to its usual condition, and for any damage caused.

13.86 A candidate is required to give reasonable notice if he wishes to take advantage of these rights, but there cannot be any interference with the hours during which a room in school premises is used for educational purposes or with the use of a meeting room either for the purposes of the person maintaining it or under a prior agreement for its letting.

Local government elections

13.87 Similar statutory provisions apply in respect of local government elections.[18] A candidate is entitled to the use of school rooms during the period between the notice of election and the day preceding election day, free of charge, except that expenses incurred by the person having charge of the room and payment for any damage must be made.

Disturbance at election meetings

13.88 Anyone who, at a lawful public meeting held for the foregoing purposes, acts or incites others to act in a disorderly manner for the purpose of preventing the transaction of the business for which the meeting was called is guilty of an illegal practice. This applies to:

- a political meeting held in any constituency between the date of the issue of a writ for the return of a Member of Parliament for the constituency and the date at which a return to the writ is made; and
- a meeting held with reference to a local government election in the electoral area for that election on, or within three weeks before, the day of election.

Public inquiries

Types of inquiry

13.89 There are several occasions when a local authority may become involved in the organisation of a public inquiry. The authority may:

- need to provide appropriate facilities for the holding of:
  - a statutory public inquiry, i.e. one held 'by or on behalf of a Minister';
  - a non-ministerially appointed mandatory inquiry; or
  - a discretionary inquiry which may be appointed by the appropriate Minister; or
- decide itself to set up an inquiry for some purpose relating to one or other of its functions.

The distinctions are important. Those inquiries that qualify as statutory inquiries within the meaning of s.16(1) of the Tribunals and Inquiries Act 1992 fall under the supervision of the Council on Tribunals and are subject to prescribed procedural rules. These include inquiries constituted to inquire into and report upon objections to compulsory purchase orders and inquiries held prior to the determination of appeals against refusal of planning permission. Non-ministerially appointed mandatory inquiries are not subject to this supervision; for example, one conducted by the Boundary Commission (i.e. not held 'by or on behalf of a Minister') into local objections to proposed alterations to constituency boundaries. Discretionary inquiries set up by a Minister include, for example, one into matters connected with the policing of an area.

13.90 In all instances where the local authority is not itself initiating the inquiry the authority will nevertheless be involved often in providing accommodation for the inquiry and the requisite facilities for its conduct, including such administrative duties in connection with it as the minister or an inspector on his behalf may require. In the case of a major inquiry – though necessarily, depending on its character – the authority may need to designate a member of staff as a programme officer to assist the inspector over a wide sphere of tasks including, possibly, the recording of objections and representations received and corresponding with objectors over the clarification of their objections, availability for attending the inquiry, the number of witnesses who will be called and so on. In cases, however, where the local authority decides to

13. Meetings for special purposes

hold an inquiry, public or otherwise, the authority itself has responsibilities that extend much wider because the authority will need to determine the terms of reference and appoint someone or a committee to hold the inquiry (see 13.93).

Procedure

13.91 The procedure at an inquiry will be at the discretion of the inspector or whoever else may have charge of the proceedings. Most statutory inquiries are by their character adversarial because the issue will ordinarily be argued out by supporters of and objectors to a proposed scheme or course of action or whatever it might be.[19]

Practical arrangements

13.92 There is, as it were, no standard layout of a room in which an inquiry is to be held but the room must be adequate for the purpose, easy of access, and reserved for the likely duration of the proceedings. Essential points to be borne in mind include the following:

- Seating and tables must be provided in a convenient arrangement for the participants, e.g. parallel facing table and chairs for supporters and opponents respectively, with the inspector's/chairman's table between them forming a square U is the usually preferred layout, but the size and shape of the room itself will be governing constraints.
- Reasonable facilities should be provided: notepaper, pencils, water carafes and tumblers with fresh water, display boards for maps, etc., and possibly visual aid equipment. Direction signs should be displayed at the entrance to the building indicating the room in which the inquiry is being held, and to car parks, lavatories, etc., but attendants should also be on duty to assist those attending.
- Ample seating must be provided for witnesses and others behind the front tables for the advocates on the respective sides.
- Provision should be made for accommodating members of the public and press with easy access to telephones, etc.

13.93 Where the local authority has set up an inquiry there are important preliminary steps to be taken:

- the terms of reference of the inquiry must be settled;
- a chairman must be appointed and, if desired, a committee or commission to assist him, and the fees or remuneration to be paid must be set;
- the date when the inquiry is to begin must be fixed, as well as the period within which the inquiry's report is to be submitted; and
- evidence should be invited from interested parties by such means as may be appropriate.

Licensing committees

13.94 The Licensing Act 2003 gave responsibility for licensing to local authorities. Section 6 of the Act provides that the licensing authority must establish a committee, which should consist of a least 10 but no more than 15 members. In turn the licensing committee can delegate its functions to a sub-committee that has been established by it, or by an authorised officer of the licensing authority, who would normally be the licensing officer. The licensing committee and consequently the sub-committee does not need to be politically balanced. The sub-committee would usually have three members on it, although it is arguable that the quorum for such meetings could be two, with the chairman having the casting vote. It is good practice to ensure that members of the sub-committee are chosen from the main pool of licensing committee members, in order to ensure that the same members do not hear every case.

13.95 The time and place of the hearing should be arranged by the authority, and the hearing should be held in accordance with Licensing Act 2003 (Hearings) Regulations 2005 (SI 2005/44) reg.5. The authority is under strict time scales within which they must hold a meeting, and under reg.6(3) the authority must give at least five working days' notice before the date of the hearing. In addition, reg.7 sets out the information that must be sent out with the notice of hearing.

13.96 The time limits for holding a hearing differ depending on the type of application that is before the sub-committee, and these are set out in the Hearing Regulations Sch.1.

13.97 The authority may dispense with holding a hearing (reg.9) if all parties agree that a hearing is unnecessary. This will usually be when representations to the application have been withdrawn or when all parties have reached agreement.

13.98 All hearings should take place in public, although an authority may exclude the public where it considers that the public interest in doing so outweighs the public interest in the hearing (reg.124(2)). The conduct of the hearing should be conducted in accordance with the hearing regulations and a decision regarding the application should be made 'forthwith'. A record of the hearing must be taken in a permanent and intelligible form and must be kept for six years from the date of determination or, where an appeal is brought against the determination, the disposal of the appeal (reg.30).

13.99 The regulations provide for notices to be transmitted by electronic means where they are capable of being accessed by the recipient and that person has agreed to this method in advance (reg.34) and they also allow that clerical mistakes may be corrected by the authority (reg.33).

Notes

1 The expenses of the joint planning committee for Greater London, if incurred with the approval of at least two-thirds of the local planning authorities, are to be defrayed by those authorities in such proportions as they may decide or, in default, as the Secretary of State may determine: LGA 1985, s.5(3).
2 LG&HA 1989. s.6, applies to the Common Council of the city of London and successor bodies to residuary bodies, the same requirements as to the other local authorities under the LGFA 1988.
3 LGFA 1988, s.114(2).
4 Ibid., s.114(3).

13. Meetings for special purposes

5 Ibid., s.114(3A)
6 Ibid., s.115.
7 Ibid., s.115(4).
8 If there is a defect in procedure the court will intervene. Thus in *Ex parte Ladbroke Group* (1969), the decision of a committee was quashed where, when considering a contested application for renewal of a licence under the Betting, Gaming and Lotteries Act 1963, the chairman twice announced that he was ready to give a decision before counsel had completed cross-examination and then appeared to reach a decision without consulting the other members of the committee.
9 Although it might be thought that committees of this character could be set up under the provisions of the LGA 1972, s. 102(4), which empower the establishment of committees 'to advise . . . on any matter relating to the discharge' of an authority's function, the obligation to decide questions 'by a majority of the members . . . present and voting thereon (Sch.12, para.39(1), as applied to committees by para.44) would make this impracticable. These committees are not, therefore, committees of the local authority in the ordinary sense: in a way they exist in limbo. The Community Rights Project has argued in the past that there are in practice two meetings taking place simultaneously! Then the provisions on access for the public and press would apply to the councillors' meeting but not to the officers' meeting. This would appear to strain credibility beyond the limit.
10 LG&HA 1989, s.12.
11 These representatives must be appointed by recognised trade unions from among the employees (s.2 and Safety Representatives and Safety Committee Regulations 1977 (see 13.31)).
12 The job description is a statement, in whatever detail circumstances may require, of the content of the job; the duties and responsibilities, its place in the organisation, the salary grade and so on. The job or person specification lists the personal qualities required in the candidate who can be expected to perform the job to the prescribed standard. A statement covering these requirements will have been prepared to meet statutory requirements in the case of chief officer appointments (see 13.38).
13 An interesting point of some significance arose in *Cabaj* v. *Westminster City Council* (1994), where the EAT ruled that the hearing of an employee's appeal against dismissal had been defective because only two of the three members of the council's internal appeals tribunal had been present. The EAT said that the council's standing orders (which prescribed a quorum of two for a subcommittee – and the tribunal was a subcommittee under that) did not overrule the requirements of the council's disciplinary code, which stipulated a membership of three and which formed part of the employee's contract of employment. The Court of Appeal's decision in 1996 accepted that the council had failed to observe its disciplinary code, but said this did not necessarily mean that the dismissal was unfair because that was for an industrial tribunal to decide in relation to all the relevant facts.
14 Police (Conduct) (Senior Officers) Regulations 1999 (SI 1999/731).
15 The head of an authority's paid service is appointed by 'designation' under the LG&HA 1989, s.4(1). The officer is in practice usually the chief executive but not necessarily so. This means that in many instances the appointment of 'head of the paid service' is not part of an officers contract of employment in his substantive post of chief executive or otherwise and this may lead to complications: see further *Knight's Law and Practice of Local Authority Employment*. The monitoring officer is also a designated officer under s.5.
16 Bains Report, para.5.38.
17 RPA 1983, s.95 and the European Parliamentary Election Regulations 2004 (reg.67).
18 RPA 1983 s.97, applied, with modifications, to elections of the European Assembly by the European Assembly Regulations 1984.
19 The Secretary of State is given power to direct inquiries wherever any minister is authorised to make decisions under the LGA 1972 or any other enactment relating to the functions of local authorities: s.250.

Chapter 14
Meetings of other public bodies

Introduction

14.1 There are many bodies, statutory and otherwise, that operate within the sphere of local government, apart from local authorities themselves, either on the fringe of local government or with functions that were at one time the responsibility of local authorities. It seemed appropriate that there should be some brief reference to the meetings procedure of certain of these bodies. In some cases their practices are indistinguishable from those that have long been part of the management process of local government, but in others there are distinctive features. The most important, for purposes of this work, are the police authorities (see 14.6) created under the Police and Magistrates' Courts Act 1994 (but see now the Police Act 1996). These bodies are defined as local authorities and many of the provisions of the LGA 1972 and other relevant legislation apply to them.

14.2 There are also many quasi-official and voluntary bodies in which local authorities have an interest and/or to which they provide grant aid. Among the first category is, for example, the Local Government Association, and the national negotiating bodies regulating the pay and conditions of service of local authority staff. All these bodies substantially follow local authority practice as regards their meetings procedure. Of the others, too numerous to mention, are bodies such as community relations councils, council tenants' liaison committees, neighbourhood councils and so on.

Statutory joint committees

Created out of reorganisation

14.3 As a consequence of the abolition of the Greater London Council and the metropolitan county councils, provision was made in the LGA 1985 for the establishment of joint authorities to administer county-wide a number of former county functions that it was considered could not be discharged effectively and efficiently at borough or district level. In each case the joint authority is a corporate body, similar in most respects to a joint board, except that it owes its existence to an Act of Parliament rather than to a ministerial order, and in general they are treated as local authorities. Their members are subject to the same rules as to disqualification, and the statutory provisions in regard to meetings procedure apply to them, including the obligation to admit the public and press to their meetings.

14.4 The joint authorities established under the LGA 1985 are:

- metropolitan county fire and civil defence authorities;
- London Fire and Civil Defence Authority; and
- metropolitan county passenger transport authorities,

and formerly included metropolitan county police authorities, as to which see now the free-standing police authorities set up in 1995 (see 14.6). There are other similar authorities, e.g. a waste disposal authority established under the LGA 1985, s.10; the Broads Authority; a joint or special planning board constituted for a National Park by order under the 1972 Act, Sch.17, paras.1 or 3 and fire authorities in some shire counties under the LGA 1992.

Membership

14.5 The members of the joint authorities are in most cases the elected members of the constituent borough or district councils nominated to serve on them. The numbers to be appointed are prescribed and subject to alteration by ministerial order, having regard to the number of local government electors in the constituent authorities' areas (LGA 1992 s.29, Sch.10). It is expressly provided – distinguishing a joint authority from a joint board in this respect – that a constituent council may at any time terminate an appointment and appoint another member of the council in his place, but where this power of replacement is exercised the council must give notice one month in advance of the new appointment and of the termination of the previous appointment to the joint authority concerned (ss.29-32). The provisions as to the filling of vacancies follow substantially the usual pattern of such arrangements for joint committees and joint boards. What is unusual, indeed, is that it was the first time that any statute had recognised that politics is a reality in local government, in that each constituent council must, as far as practicable, ensure in making or terminating appointments to joint authorities 'that the balance of parties for the time being prevailing in that council is reflected in the persons who are for the time being members of the [joint] authority and for whose appointment the council is responsible' (s.33). The joint authority is required to give public notice of changes in its membership.

Police authorities

Statutory provisions

14.6 Parts I and II of the Police and Magistrates' Courts Act 1994 (PMCA 1994) set up new police authorities in England and Wales from 1st April 1995. What had previously been, outside the Metropolitan Police area, committees of county councils, combined authorities established under individual schemes or under the LGA 1965 in metropolitan areas became independent authorities with changed membership.[1] The original concept of these new authorities, as largely removed from local control with chairmen appointed by the Home Secretary as proposed by the then Government, was significantly changed during the passage of the Bill through parliament. This was particularly evident in the House of Lords where many fears were expressed at what was seen as centralising control of the police. The resultant police authorities remain controlled by local elected members but with added members (see 14.8). For many purposes the authorities remain classified and defined as local authorities, sharing many of the practices and problems of councils, but there are also significant differences. The relevant provisions of the PMCA 1994 were repealed and incorporated in the Police Act 1996 (PA 1996).

Membership

14.7 Each police authority must consist of 17 members unless the Secretary of State makes an order[2] specifying an odd number greater than 17. Such orders are rare and only Greater Manchester, Thames Valley, Dyfed Powys and Devon and Cornwall have managed to achieve an increase. The basis for success appears to be either the geographical area covered by the authority or the existence within the area of more county and district councils than there are elected member places on the police authority.

14.8 In an authority of 17 members, nine elected councillors are appointed by the relevant councils within the area, three magistrates are appointed by a panel or panels representing the magistrates' courts committee, and five independent members are appointed by the remaining members of the police authority following completion of the prescribed selection procedure.[3]

Appointment of councillors

14.9 The councils entitled to take part in the appointment of elected members to the police authority are counties in shire areas and districts in metropolitan areas. In practice this includes the unitary authorities created by local government reorganisation that are given the designation of county. Where no such unitary council exists, then the county alone is responsible for making all nine appointments. In other cases a joint committee comprising representatives of each relevant authority is given the responsibility. Composition of the joint committee is a matter for agreement between the relevant councils with provision for a decision in default by the Secretary of State. The proceedings of the joint committee and the way in which it reaches decisions are regulated by s.99 of the LGA 1972 which applies Sch.12 of the 1972 Act to meetings and proceedings of local authorities, and police authorities and their committees, including a joint committee. The joint committee itself does not have to be politically balanced as it is not constituted under the LGA 1972. In practice, many joint committees do reflect the political balance of the relevant councils concerned, although a number – particularly covering areas where political control of the council is the same – comprise only one representative from each council, e.g. the leaders.

14.10 A joint committee can appoint whoever it wishes to fill the nine places on the police authority. The only requirements are that those appointed should be members of the relevant councils and that the appointments reflect 'so far as practicable' the balance of the parties prevailing among the members of the council 'taken as a whole'. The joint committee can use whatever criteria it chooses to decide on the appointments, subject to the above constraints. The members appointed are not representatives of the councils of which they are members, they are appointees of the joint committee (or the relevant council where only one exists). This can be difficult to impress on members, particularly at budget time.

14.11 Securing appointments from a joint committee giving the desired party balance can be difficult. The most straightforward process would seem to be to calculate the number of seats each party is entitled to, and then divide the total between the relevant councils on some rational basis, e.g. population or expenditure. This can result in some police authorities being allocated members whose policies are not to their liking. It would appear that they have no rights in the matter; the decision of the joint committee would seem to be unimpeachable except perhaps by application for judicial review should the decision be made wholly on unreasonable grounds. No provision for appeal from a joint committee's decision is allowed for in the PA 1996. Opportunity is given in the Act to change membership from time to time in order to retain the right party balance. In R v. *Joint Committee for the purpose of making appointments to Humberside Police Authority, ex parte East Riding of Yorkshire Council* (2001), Mrs Justice Rafferty in a somewhat controversial judgment considered the issue as to whether the number of independent members on each constituent authority should be taken into account by the joint committee when deciding how many members of each political party should be appointed to the Police Authority. She decided that independent members do not enter into the calculation of the balance of political parties and are, therefore, not entitled to any proportion of seats on the police authority irrespective of the numbers of independent members on the constituent authorities.

14.12 The qualifications and disqualifications attaching to members of police authorities are set out in Sch.2 of the PA 1996. Appointment of elected members is for a maximum of four years but the appointing body – joint committee or relevant council – can determine a lesser period in any particular case. It appears uncertain whether a member appointed for four years can subsequently be removed by his appointing body except that under para.20 of Sch.2, a council or joint committee may remove a member of the police authority within that period for reasons of political balance. One of the guiding principles behind the creation of police authorities was the establishment of an independent body building up its own expertise. The wording of the PA 1996 suggests that subject to qualification, age and political balance an appointment, once made, cannot be revoked.

Appointment of magistrates

14.13 Appointment of the three magistrates is undertaken by a panel of the magistrates courts committee or committees within the police authority area . The length of the appointment is subject to the same rules as for elected members. The only requirement is that they should be serving magistrates within the area: the fact that they might also be elected members of relevant councils does not affect their qualification to be appointed as magistrates, although magistrates are not eligible to be appointed as independent members.

Miscellaneous meetings

Appointment of independent members

14.14 The five independent members are appointed by the elected and magistrate members in accordance with prescribed procedure. Selection panels are established with shortlists drawn and submitted to the Home Secretary. Appointment must be for the full period of four years unless the consent of the Secretary of State has been obtained for a shorter period. Consent has been obtained in at least one case where a vacancy occurred shortly before the expiry of the original four-year term. In another similar case, consent to appoint for a lesser period was refused on the grounds that there was no reason why the terms of office of the independent members needed to expire on the same date. The process by which the elected and magistrate members select the independent members is entirely of their own choosing. Advertising is undertaken nationally by the Home Office with supplementary local advertising as required. Interviewing candidates is optional. The selection panel needs to be reappointed every two years. Among the categories of persons ineligible for appointment as independent members are members of counties, districts, county boroughs (in Wales) and London boroughs within the police authority area as well as magistrates.

Procedure at police authority meetings

14.15 For many legal and administrative purposes police authorities are included within the definition of local authorities. Subject to exceptions referred to later the provisions of the LGA 1972 that govern local authority meetings also govern police authority meetings as well as those of their committees and subcommittees. In particular, ss.94-98 relating to pecuniary interests apply, and although police authorities are included within the remit of the local government ombudsman, police authority members are not covered by the National Code of Local Government Conduct (see 4.3). Elected and independent members are required to complete the statutory register of interests required by s.19 of the LG&HA 1989. No obligation is placed on magistrate members who may, of course, complete the voluntary register under s.96 of the LGA 1972.

Chairman and vice-chairman

14.16 The PA 1996 contains a separate provision requiring the appointment of a chairman. This must be done each year at the annual meeting and is the first business transacted at the meeting. Although there is no statutory limit placed on the length of time a chairman may continue, there is a trend among police authorities for a limit to be voluntarily placed on holding the office. The provisions of the LGA 1972 ensuring that a chairman remains in office until his successor is appointed do not apply to police authorities. Although the attendant problems of chairmen presiding over their own election (see 7.21) does not automatically apply, the question still arises over the mechanics of arranging the appointment at the annual meeting. There is nothing to prevent a chairman being appointed 'until his successor is appointed', but if this is done it would, perhaps, be unwise to allow him, if he were to be the candidate, to take the chair while nominations are sought. In no circumstances should a chairman in that position exercise a casting vote.

14.17 A better practice and the more widely used is to appoint 'until the next annual meeting of the police authority'. This then allows the term of office to run out at the commencement of the next annual meeting, i.e. at the published time of the meeting, so enabling the clerk to ask for nominations and conduct any necessary ballot. There is no provision for a police authority meeting to proceed without a chairman. If the chairman is absent, then the members present are required to appoint another of their number to preside. Should there be a failure to elect a chairman as required, then the next course is to attempt to appoint a chairman for the day to enable the meeting to proceed. A subsequent appointment can then, all being well, be made at the next meeting.

14.18 There is no provision in the PA 1996 for the appointment of a vice-chairman. This appears to have been a deliberate omission rather than an oversight and probably stems from the original government proposals to appoint the chairman of the police authority centrally rather than allow election by the authorities. Many police authorities wished to appoint vice-chairmen for the sensible purpose of having a second person to refer to in case of urgency and have someone to deputise for the chairman as a consultant, as well as to chair meetings. Since s.111 of the LGA 1972 applies to police authorities, there seems no good reason why a member should not be given the title of vice-chairman and whatever powers are necessary to deal with matters usually, but not exclusively, in the absence of the chairman. These powers cannot, of course, extend to taking executive action for the reasons explained earlier (see 4.60). When designating a member as vice-chairman it ought to be recorded that he would preside at meetings in the absence of the chairman. This should be enough to secure compliance with the revised Sch.12 of the LGA 1972.

Voting

14.19 Voting is carried on in the usual way and there is only one particular requirement, i.e. that a decision on the precept level must be carried by a majority of the members of the authority at that time including a majority of the elected members at that time. Any vacancy would be deducted from the number of members in calculating the majorities, but there would need to be more than one vacancy to make any practical difference in an authority with 17 members. A second or casting vote is given to the person presiding at a meeting.

Reports and agenda

14.20 Since s.100 of the LGA 1972 applies to police authorities all the usual rules governing notice of meetings and publicity for agenda and reports have to be complied with. Police authorities are, however, given certain statutory rights and duties with regard to the production of reports and agenda items. A police authority can call for a report on a specific matter from the chief constables and can specify the form of the report. If the chief constable takes the view that disclosure of the information is not in the public interest or does not relate to the discharge of the functions of the police authority, then the matter can stand referred to the Home Office for a decision.

14.21 Annual reports are also required from the chief constable on the policing of the area and the Secretary of State can require an authority to report to him on specified matters relating to the discharge of the authority's functions or the policing of the area.

Officers

14.22 Every police authority is required to appoint a clerk and a chief finance officer. No duties are prescribed for the clerk but these would include the usual responsibilities of summoning and running meetings, ensuring that the decisions of the authority are implemented and advising generally on its functions and the like. The obligation to appoint a chief finance officer is identical with the obligation imposed on local authorities generally.

14.23 There is also a requirement for each police authority to designate one of its officers as monitoring officer with the same duties and responsibilities laid down in the case of local authorities. These include the right to require the police authority to provide the necessary staff, accommodation and other resources to enable him to carry out his duties. The monitoring officer cannot be the chief finance officer and the usual practice is to appoint the clerk.

14.24 All other civilian staff employed by police authorities are under the direction and control of the chief constable, except those agreed as exceptions: the exceptions usually include all the support staff required by the clerk and chief finance officer.

14.25 Particular problems arise over the extent to which police authorities can exercise control over civilian staff for whom they legally act as employer but who are under the direction and control of the chief constable which includes the power to appoint and dismiss (see 14.24). Authorities can find themselves in the position of defending actions for breach of employment law without having any power to influence the events that led up to the action complained about. The only solution would appear to be either an agreement with the chief constable to allow the police authority involvement, e.g. a right to hear appeals over grievances, or to take action against the chief constable in extreme cases. This impasse results from the failure of the Government to clarify the rights and duties of the various parties in the legislation.

Notes

1   PA 1996, s.4, Sch.2.
2   Ibid., Sch.2, para.26.
3   Ibid., Sch.3

Appendices

Appendix 1
Call-in guidance

What is a call-in?

A call-in is simply the referral of a decision made, but not yet implemented, to the Overview & Scrutiny Committee. It is a key way of holding the Cabinet to account. A called-in decision cannot be implemented until it has been considered by the Overview & Scrutiny Committee, which can examine the issue and question the decision-taker on the actions taken.

What can be called-in?

Call-in powers relate to executive (Cabinet) functions. Subject to the exceptions listed below, any decision made by the Cabinet or a *key decision* made by an officer with delegated authority from the Cabinet may be called-in.

What can't be called-in?

The following categories of decision cannot be called-in:

- a decision which is not a key decision, and which has been taken by an officer under delegated powers (*If, in the future, delegation to individual Members of the Cabinet is permitted, this exclusion will also apply to non-key decisions taken by the Leader or a Portfolio Holder under delegated powers*);
- a decision which the decision-taker has certified as urgent (giving reasons) in accordance with the Council's Rules of Procedure;
- a decision relating to a matter which has already been the subject of a call-in during the previous six months;
- *any* decision relating to a non-Cabinet function, whether taken by a Committee or an officer under delegated powers;
- a decision by the Full Council; or
- a decision taken at stage 4 of the call-in procedure (see below).

In particular, it should be noted that the Overview & Scrutiny Committee cannot scrutinise individual decisions made by, or on behalf of, the Regulatory Committees of the Council, e.g. decisions relating to development control, licensing, registration, consents and other permissions. Nor can it scrutinise decisions relating to individual members of staff taken by the Staffing Appeals and Officer Appointments Committees. Furthermore, although they may be key decisions (and included in the Forward Plan), decisions taken by the Cabinet when preparing annual budget or new policy proposals *for submission to the full Council* will not be subject to call-in. In these circumstances, the Full Council is responsible for the final decision and, in any event, the Council's Rules of Procedure require that the Overview & Scrutiny and Policy Development Committees must be consulted by the Cabinet, even if they have been involved earlier in the process anyway.

When can a decision be called-in?

It is important that the call-in process is not abused, nor causes unreasonable delay; the main tool of the Overview & Scrutiny Committee to improve the delivery of policies and services should be detailed reviews, rather than call-ins.

The Overview and Scrutiny Procedure Rules in Part Four of the council's constitution specify formal safeguards for the use of call-in. These include rules about the number of members who must request a call-in and a restriction that prevents any decision on the same matter being called-in on more than one occasion within a six-month period. The constitution also suggests that call-ins should be reserved for exceptional circumstances. Broadly, a decision can be called-in when members:

- believe it may be contrary to the normal requirements for decision-making
- believe it may be contrary to the council's agreed policy framework and/or budget
- need further information from the decision-taker to explain why it was taken.

Call-in checklist

The above rules and criteria can be brought together in the following checklist of questions (or tests) that can be used when a member is considering a call-in. Questions 2–5 can also be used by authors to test draft reports for cabinet.

1 Can the decision actually be called in?	*If the answer to any of questions 1 (a)-(g) is yes, then the decision CANNOT be called-in.*	
	a) Does it relate to a non-executive function?	☐
	b) Was it a non-key decision taken by an officer under delegated powers?	☐
	c) Was it classified as an urgent decision?	☐
	d) Has this issue been called-in in the last six months?	☐
	e) Does the decision relate to an existing call-in (i.e. decisions taken in relation to a reference back)?	☐
	f) Does the decision relate to the formulation of a policy or budget matter that requires full council approval?	☐
	g) Was it a decision taken by full council?	☐

Appendix 1. Call-in guidance

2 Was the decision in accordance with the council's policy framework?

   a) What is the relevant policy or strategy? ☐
   b) Is the decision contrary to that policy? ☐
   c) If yes, how? ☐

3 Was the decision in accordance with the agreed budget or budget procedures?

   a) Is there funding for the proposal in an agreed budget/capital programme? ☐
   b) If no, have the rules for virement and supplementary estimates been observed? ☐

4 Was the decision taken in accordance with the principles of good decision-making (Article 12 of the Constitution)?

   a) Does the decision comply with the council's constitution, i.e.:
      • Articles of Constitution ☐
      • Scheme of Delegation ☐
      • Rules of Procedure ☐
      • Codes and Protocols? ☐
   b) Was the decision reasonable within the common meaning of the word, i.e. rational, based on sound judgment? ☐
   c) Was the decision reasonable within the legal definition of 'reasonableness', i.e. was everything relevant taken into account, and was everything irrelevant disregarded? ☐
   d) Was the decision proportionate, i.e. is the action proportionate to the desired outcome? ☐
   e) Was the decision taken on the basis of due consultation? ☐
   f) Was the decision taken on the basis of professional advice from officers? ☐
   g) Were human rights respected and/or will the decision give rise to any human rights implications, i.e. without discrimination, the right of an individual to:
      • liberty and security; ☐
      • the enjoyment of their property; ☐
      • a fair trial; ☐
      • respect for private and family life; ☐
      • freedom of thought, conscience and religion; ☐
      • freedom of expression; and ☐
      • freedom of assembly and association, etc? ☐
   h) When the decision was taken, was there a presumption in favour of openness? ☐

5 Has the decision been well explained, i.e. do you need more information?

   a) Was it clear what the reasons for the decision were? ☐
   b) Was it clear what the desired outcomes were? ☐
   c) Was it clear what alternative options (if any) were considered? ☐

d) Was it clear why the alternative options were not chosen? ☐

e) Do you need any more information/ clarification? ☐

How does call-in work?

Every decision that is subject to potential call-in cannot be implemented until the end of the call-in period. The call-in period lasts for *five working days* after notice of the decision is published by the Head of Legal and Democratic Services.

Decision notices will normally be published on the Friday of the week in which the decision was taken. This means that the normal call-in period will expire at 5pm on the following Friday (adjusted for bank holidays as appropriate). The call-in procedure itself follows four stages.

Stage 1

A valid call-in request must be submitted in accordance with the current rules in the constitution. The request must say who is making the call-in and to which decision it relates. It must also give brief reasons why the decision is being called in. A pro-forma is available. Requests may also be submitted by electronic mail, fax or telephone. If the call-in is to be submitted by e-mail, only one Member need submit the actual form. However, individual e-mails (or letters) in support of the request must also be submitted by the other Members specified on the request form before the end of the call-in period.

Call-ins submitted by fax or telephone must be followed up in writing with the required number of signatures before the end of the call-in period.

Stage 2

When the officers receive a valid call-in request with respect to a decision, then that decision may not be implemented until that decision has completed the call-in procedure. The officers will refer the call-in to the next available meeting of the Overview & Scrutiny Committee. A special meeting may also be convened if appropriate, e.g. in cases of urgency. Members who have requested the call-in will have the right to address the Committee when it deals with the issue.

Stage 3

The Overview & Scrutiny Committee will consider the called-in decision and decide to take one of the following courses of action (the Overview & Scrutiny Committee's decision should not be adjourned or delayed without an exceptional reason):

• to allow the decision to be implemented without further delay;
• to refer the decision back to the cabinet (irrespective of who the original decision-taker was) together with the observations of the Overview & Scrutiny Committee.

Appendix 1. Call-in guidance

The cabinet will then take the final decision, and that decision may not be called in;

- to request the Cabinet to allow further time for the Overview and Scrutiny Committee to consider the issue and make observations at a later date;
- to seek the advice of the Head of Legal and Democratic Services and/or the Chief Finance Officer as to whether the decision is contrary to, or not wholly in accordance with, the policy framework or the budget and, if applicable, to refer the matter to the full council for a final decision.

Stage 4

Reference back to cabinet

Where the Overview & Scrutiny Committee decides to refer the decision back, the cabinet must reconsider the decision in the light of any observations of the Committee. Where the Overview & Scrutiny Committee has requested more time to consider an issue, the cabinet must have regard to the urgency, and to the Budget and Policy Framework Rules, when deciding whether to implement the decision.

Reference to Head of Legal and Democratic Services and/or Chief Finance Officer

The Overview & Scrutiny Committee may refer any called-in decision to the Head of Legal and Democratic Services (Monitoring Officer) and/or the Chief Finance Officer if it considers it to be contrary to the policy framework or budget. The officer(s) will then submit a report on the matter to the next meeting of the cabinet. A copy of this report will be sent to all members of the council. No action may be taken in respect of the decision or its implementation pending that meeting.

If, in that report, the Head of Legal and Democratic Services (Monitoring Officer) and/or the Chief Finance Officer is of the view that a decision referred to him/her by the Overview & Scrutiny Committee is not a departure from the policy framework or budget, the decision may be implemented immediately. A report to this effect will be submitted to the Overview & Scrutiny Committee for information. If, however, a referred matter is deemed to be a departure from the policy framework or the budget by the Head of Legal and Democratic Services and/or the Chief Finance Officer, the cabinet has two options. Firstly, it may choose to adjust its decision to bring it within the policy framework or budget, in which case it can then be implemented. In these circumstances, the cabinet would submit a report to the next meeting of the Overview & Scrutiny Committee explaining its actions. Secondly, if the cabinet does not wish to adjust its original decision, it must prepare a report for the full council. This report must include the views of the Overview & Scrutiny Committee. No action may be taken in respect of the decision or its implementation until the council has met to consider the matter.

Reference to full Council

Subject to the provisions above, the Overview & Scrutiny Committee may require that any called-in matter *which has been deemed to be (and remains)* contrary to the policy framework or budget is referred to the full Council. The report to the full Council will set out the views of the cabinet and the Overview & Scrutiny Committee and the advice of the Head of Legal and Democratic Services and/or the Chief Finance Officer. The council may:

- decide that the decision is within the existing policy framework and/or budget (in which case it can be implemented); or
- amend the financial regulations or policy concerned to encompass the decision (in which case it can be implemented); or
- agree that the decision is contrary to the policy framework or budget and require the cabinet to reconsider the matter in accordance with the advice of the officer(s).

This document is reproduced with the kind permission of St Edmundsbury Borough Council.

Appendix 2
Model Code of Conduct

Statutory Instrument 2007 No. 1159
The Local Authorities (Model Code of Conduct) Order 2007
The Secretary of State for Communities and Local Government makes the following Order in exercise of the powers conferred by sections 50(1) and (4), 81(2) and (3), and 105(2), (3) and (4) of the Local Government Act 2000.
The Secretary of State has consulted in accordance with section 50(5) of that Act.
The Secretary of State is satisfied that this Order is consistent with the principles for the time being specified in an order under section 49(1) of that Act.

Citation, commencement and application
1–(1) This Order may be cited as the Local Authorities (Model Code of Conduct) Order 2007 and comes into force on 3rd May 2007.
(2) This Order applies–
(a) in relation to police authorities in England and Wales; and
(b) in relation to the following authorities in England—
    (i)   a county council;
    (ii)   a district council;
    (iii) a London borough council;
    (iv) a parish council;
    (v)   the Greater London Authority;
    (vi) the Metropolitan Police Authority;
    (vii) the London Fire and Emergency Planning Authority;
    (viii) the Common Council of the City of London;
    (ix) the Council of the Isles of Scilly;
    (x)   a fire and rescue authority;
    (xi) a joint authority;
    (xii) the Broads Authority; and
    (xiii) a National Park authority,
and in this Order references to "authority" are construed accordingly.

Model Code of Conduct
2–(1) The code set out in the Schedule to this Order ("the Code") has effect as the model code issued by the Secretary of State under section 50 of the Local Government Act 2000 as regards the conduct which is expected of members and co-opted members of an authority.
(2) Subject to paragraphs (3) to (6), every provision of the Code in the Schedule to this Order is mandatory for an authority.

341

(3) Paragraph 6(c) of the Code is not mandatory for police authorities, the Greater London Authority, the Metropolitan Police Authority, the London Fire and Emergency Planning Authority, fire and rescue authorities and joint authorities.

(4) Paragraph 7 of the Code is not mandatory for parish councils.

(5) Subject to sub-paragraph (6)(c) and (d) below, paragraphs 10(2)(c)(i) and (ii), 11 and 12(2) of the Code are mandatory only for county councils, district councils and London borough councils, the Common Council of the City of London and the Council of the Isles of Scilly.

(6) The following provisions of the Code are mandatory only for an authority which is operating executive arrangements–
  (a) in paragraph 1(4), in the definition of "meeting"–
      (i) sub-paragraph (b);
      (ii) in sub-paragraph (c), the words "or its executive's" and ", or area committees";
  (b) paragraphs 9(6), 9(7) and 12(1)(b);
  (c) in paragraph 11(a), the words "your authority's executive or"
  (d) in paragraph 11(b), the word "executive,"; and
  (e) in paragraph 12(2), the words in brackets.

Disapplication of certain statutory provisions

3. The following provisions shall not apply (where they are capable of doing so) to an authority that has adopted a code of conduct or to which such a code applies–
  (a) sections 94 to 98 and 105 to the Local Government Act 1972.
  (b) section 30(3A) of the Local Government Act 1974;
  (c) regulations made or a code issued under sections 19 and 31 of the Local Government and Housing Act 1989.
  (d) paragraphs 9 and 10 of Schedule 7 to the Environment Act 1995; and
  (e) any guidance issued under section 66 of the Greater London Authority Act 1999.

Revocation and savings

4–(1) Subject to paragraphs (2) and (3), the following orders are revoked–
  (a) the Local Authorities (Model Code of Conduct) (England) Order 2001;
  (b) the Parish Councils (Model Code of Conduct) Order 2001;
  (c) the National Park and Broads Authorities (Model Code of Conduct) (England) Order 2001; and
  (d) the Police Authorities (Model Code of Conduct) Order 2001.

(2) The Orders referred to in paragraph (1) continue to have effect for the purposes of and for purposes connected with–
  (a) the investigation of any written allegation under Part 3 of the Local Government Act 2000, where that allegation relates to conduct which took place before the date when, pursuant to section 51 of that Act–
      (i) the authority adopts a code of conduct incorporating the mandatory provisions of the Code in the Schedule to this Order in place of their existing code of conduct;

    (ii)   the authority revises their existing code of conduct to incorporate the mandatory provisions of the Code in the Schedule to this Order; or

    (iii)   the mandatory provisions of the Code in the Schedule to this Order apply to members or co-opted members of the authority under section 51(5)(b) of that Act;

(b)   the adjudication of a matter raised in such an allegation; and

(c)   an appeal against the decision of an interim case tribunal or case tribunal in relation to such an allegation.

(3)   Any order made under section 83 of the Local Government Act 1972 shall have effect for the purpose of prescribing the form of a declaration of acceptance of office in relation to a county council, district council, London borough council and a parish council.

SCHEDULE
THE MODEL CODE OF CONDUCT

PART 1
GENERAL PROVISIONS

Introduction and interpretation

1–(1) This Code applies to **you** as a member of an authority.

(2) You should read this Code together with the general principles prescribed by the Secretary of State.

(3) It is your responsibility to comply with the provisions of this Code.

(4) In this Code–

"meeting" means any meeting of–

(a)   the authority;

(b)   the executive of the authority;

(c)   any of the authority's or its executive's committees, sub-committees, joint committees, joint sub-committees, or area committees;

"member" includes a co-opted member and an appointed member.

(5) In relation to a parish council, references to an authority's monitoring officer and an authority's standards committee shall be read, respectively, as references to the monitoring officer and the standards committee of the district council or unitary county council which has functions in relation to the parish council for which it is responsible under section 55(12) of the Local Government Act 2000.

Scope

2–(1) Subject to sub-paragraphs (2) to (5), you must comply with this Code whenever you–

(a)   conduct the business of your authority (which, in this Code, includes the business of the office to which you are elected or appointed); or

(b)   act, claim to act or give the impression you are acting as a representative of your authority, and references to your official capacity are construed accordingly.

(2) Subject to sub-paragraphs (3) and (4), this Code does not have effect in relation to your conduct other than where it is in your official capacity.

(3) In addition to having effect in relation to conduct in your official capacity, paragraphs 3(2)(c), 5 and 6(a) also have effect, at any other time, where that conduct constitutes a criminal offence for which you have been convicted.

(4) Conduct to which this Code applies (whether that is conduct in your official capacity or conduct mentioned in sub-paragraph (3)) includes a criminal offence for which you are convicted (including an offence you committed before the date you took office, but for which you are convicted after that date).

(5) Where you act as a representative of your authority—

    (a) on another relevant authority, you must, when acting for that other authority, comply with that other authority's code of conduct; or

    (b) on any other body, you must, when acting for that other body, comply with your authority's code of conduct, except and insofar as it conflicts with any other lawful obligations to which that other body may be subject.

General obligations

3–(1) You must treat others with respect.

(2) You must not—

    (a) do anything which may cause your authority to breach any of the equality enactments (as defined in section 33 of the Equality Act 2006);

    (b) bully any person;

    (c) intimidate or attempt to intimidate any person who is or is likely to be—

        (i) a complainant,

        (ii) a witness, or

        (iii) involved in the administration of any investigation or proceedings,

    in relation to an allegation that a member (including yourself) has failed to comply with his or her authority's code of conduct; or

    (d) do anything which compromises or is likely to compromise the impartiality of those who work for, or on behalf of, your authority.

(3) In relation to police authorities and the Metropolitan Police Authority, for the purposes of sub-paragraph (2)(d) those who work for, or on behalf of, an authority are deemed to include a police officer.

4. You must not—

    (a) disclose information given to you in confidence by anyone, or information acquired by you which you believe, or ought reasonably to be aware, is of a confidential nature, except where—

        (i) you have the consent of a person authorised to give it;

        (ii) you are required by law to do so;

        (iii) the disclosure is made to a third party for the purpose of obtaining professional advice provided that the third party agrees not to disclose the information to any other person; or

        (iv) the disclosure is—

            (aa) reasonable and in the public interest; and

      (bb) made in good faith and in compliance with the reasonable requirements of the authority; or

  (b) prevent another person from gaining access to information to which that person is entitled by law.

5. You must not conduct yourself in a manner which could reasonably be regarded as bringing your office or authority into disrepute.

6. You–

  (a) must not use or attempt to use your position as a member improperly to confer on or secure for yourself or any other person, an advantage or disadvantage; and

  (b) must, when using or authorising the use by others of the resources of your authority–

    (i) act in accordance with your authority's reasonable requirements;

    (ii) ensure that such resources are not used improperly for political purposes (including party political purposes); and

  (c) must have regard to any applicable Local Authority Code of Publicity made under the Local Government Act 1986.

7–(1) When reaching decisions on any matter you must have regard to any relevance provided to you by–

  (a) your authority's chief finance officer; or

  (b) your authority's monitoring officer,

where that officer is acting pursuant to his or her statutory duties.

  (2) You must give reasons for all decisions in accordance with any statutory requirements and any reasonable additional requirements imposed by your authority.

Part 2
INTERESTS

Personal interests

8–(1) You have a personal interest in any business of your authority where either–

  (a) it relates to or is likely to affect–

    (i) any body of which you are a member or in a position of general control or management and to which you are appointed or nominated by your authority;

    (ii) any body–

      (aa) exercising functions of a public nature;

      (bb) directed to charitable purposes; or

      (cc) one of whose principal purposes includes the influence of public opinion or policy (including any political party or trade union),

    of which you are a member or in a position of general control or management;

    (iii) any employment or business carried on by you;

    (iv) any person or body who employs or has appointed you;

    (v) any person or body, other than a relevant authority, who has made a payment to you in respect of your election or any expenses incurred by you in carrying out your duties;

(vi) any person or body who has a place of business or land in your authority's area, and in whom you have a beneficial interest in a class of securities of that person or body that exceeds the nominal value of £25,000 or one hundredth of the total issued share capital (whichever is the lower);

(vii) any contract for goods, services or works made between your authority and you or a firm in which you are a partner, a company of which you are a remunerated director, or a person or body of the description specified in paragraph (vi);

(viii) the interests of any person from whom you have received a gift or hospitality with an estimated value of at least £25;

(ix) any land in your authority's area in which you have a beneficial interest;

(x) any land where the landlord is your authority and you are, or a firm in which you are a partner, a company of which you are a remunerated director, or a person or body of the description specified in paragraph (vi) is, the tenant;

(xi) any land in the authority's area for which you have a licence (alone or jointly with others) to occupy for 28 days or longer; or

(c) a decision in relation to that business might reasonably be regarded as affecting your well-being or financial position or the well-being or financial position of a relevant person to a greater extent than the majority of–

(i) (in the case of authorities with electoral divisions or wards) other council tax payers, ratepayers or inhabitants of the electoral division or ward, as the case may be, affected by the decision;

(ii) (in the case of the Greater London Authority) other council tax payers, ratepayers or inhabitants of the Assembly constituency affected by the decision; or

(iii) (in all other cases) other council tax payers, ratepayers or inhabitants of your authority's area.

(2) In sub-paragraph (1)(b), a relevant person is–

(a) a member of your family or any person with whom you have a close association; or

(b) any person or body who employs or has appointed such persons, any firm in which they are a partner, or any company of which they are directors;

(c) any person or body in whom such persons have a beneficial interest in a class of securities exceeding the nominal value of £25,000; or

(d) any body of a type described in sub-paragraph (1)(a)(i) or (ii).

Disclosure of personal interests

9–(1) Subject to sub-paragraphs (2) to (7), where you have a personal interest in any business of your authority and you attend a meeting of your authority at which the business is considered, you must disclose to that meeting the

existence and nature of that interest at the commencement of that consideration, or when the interest becomes apparent.

(2) Where you have a personal interest in any business of your authority which
relates to or is likely to affect a person described in paragraph 8(1)(a)(i) or
8(1)(a)(ii)(aa), you need only disclose to the meeting the existence and nature
of that interest when you address the meeting on that business.

(3) Where you have a personal interest in any business of the authority of the type
mentioned in paragraph 8(1)(a)(viii), you need not disclose the nature or
existence of that interest to the meeting if the interest was registered more
than three years before the date of the meeting.

(4) Sub-paragraph (1) only applies where you are aware or ought reasonably to be
aware of the existence of the personal interest.

(5) Where you have a personal interest but, by virtue of paragraph 14, sensitive
information relating to it is not registered in your authority's register of
members' interests, you must indicate to the meeting that you have a personal
interest, but need not disclose the sensitive information to the meeting.

(6) Subject to paragraph 12(1)(b), where you have a personal interest in any
business of your authority and you have made an executive decision in
relation to that business, you must ensure that any written statement of that
decision records the existence and nature of that interest.

(7) In this paragraph, "executive decision" is to be construed in accordance with
any regulations made by the Secretary of State under section 22 of the Local
Government Act 2000.

Prejudicial interest generally

10–(1) Subject to sub-paragraph (2), where you have a personal interest in any
business of your authority you also have a prejudicial interest in that business
where the interest is one which a member of the public with knowledge of the
relevant facts would reasonably regard as so significant that it is likely to
prejudice your judgement of the public interest.

(2) You do not have a prejudicial interest in any business of the authority where
that business–

(a) does not affect your financial position or the financial position of a person
or body described in paragraph 8;

(b) does not relate to the determining of any approval, consent, licence,
permission or registration in relation to you or any person or body
described in paragraph 8; or

(c) relates to the functions of your authority in respect of–

(i) housing, where you are a tenant of your authority provided that
those functions do not relate particularly to your tenancy or lease;

(ii) school meals or school transport and travelling expenses, where
you are a parent or guardian of a child in full time education, or are
a parent governor of a school, unless it relates particularly to the
school which the child attends;

(iii) statutory sick pay under Part XI of the Social Security Contributions and Benefits Act 1992, where you are in receipt of, or are entitled to the receipt of, such pay;

(iv) an allowance, payment or indemnity given to members;

(v) any ceremonial honour given to members; and

(vi) setting council tax or a precept under the Local Government Finance Act 1992.

Prejudicial interests arising in relation to overview and scrutiny committees

11. You also have a prejudicial interest in any business before an overview and scrutiny committee of your authority (or of a sub-committee of such a committee) where–

(a) that business relates to a decision made (whether implemented or not) or action taken by your authority's executive or another of your authority's committees, sub-committees, joint committees or joint sub-committees; and

(b) at the time the decision was made or action was taken, you were a member of the executive, committee, sub-committee, joint committee or joint sub-committee mentioned in paragraph (a) and you were present when that decision was made or action was taken.

Effect of prejudicial interests on participation

12–(1) Subject to sub-paragraph (2), where you have a prejudicial interest in any business of your authority–

(a) you must withdraw from the room or chamber where a meeting considering the business is being held–

(i) in a case where sub-paragraph (2) applies, immediately after making representations, answering questions or giving evidence;

(ii) in any other case, whenever it becomes apparent that the business is being considered at that meeting;

unless you have obtained a dispensation from your authority's standards committee;

(b) you must not exercise executive functions in relation to that business; and

(c) you must not seek improperly to influence a decision about that business.

(2) Where you have a prejudicial interest in any business of your authority, you may attend a meeting (including a meeting of the overview and scrutiny committee of your authority or of a sub-committee of such a committee) but only for the purpose of making representations, answering questions or giving evidence relating to the business, provided that the public are also allowed to attend the meeting for the same purpose, whether under a statutory right or otherwise.

Appendix 2. Model Code of Conduct

PART 3

REGISTRATION OF MEMBERS' INTERESTS

Registration of members' interests

13–(1) Subject to paragraph 14, you must, within 28 days of–

    (a)   this Code being adopted by or applied to your authority; or

    (b)   your election or appointment to office (where that is later),

register in your authority's register of members' interests (maintained under section 81(1) of the Local Government Act 2000) details of your personal interests where they fall within a category mentioned in paragraph 8(1)(a), by providing written notification to your authority's monitoring officer.

  (2) Subject to paragraph 14, you must, within 28 days of becoming aware of any new personal interest or change to any personal interest registered under paragraph (1), register details of that new personal interest or change by providing written notification to your authority's monitoring officer.

Sensitive information

14–(1) Where you consider that the information relating to any of your personal interests is sensitive information, and your authority's monitoring officer agrees, you need not include that information when registering that interest, or, as the case may be, a change to that interest under paragraph 13.

  (2) You must, within 28 days of becoming aware of any change of circumstances which means that information excluded under paragraph (1) is no longer sensitive information, notify your authority's monitoring officer asking that the information be included in your authority's register of members' interests.

  (3) In this Code, "sensitive information" means information whose availability for inspection by the public creates, or is likely to create, a serious risk that you or a person who lives with you may be subjected to violence or intimidation.

The Local Authorities (Model Code of Conduct) Order 2007 is reproduced under the terms of Crown Copyright Policy Guidance issued by HMSO.

Model Code of Conduct
Guidance for Members 2007

This guide from the Standards Board for England provides an overview of the revised Model Code of Conduct. The Code of Conduct applies to all members and co-opted members of local authorities, and all members are required to sign up to it as part of their declarations of acceptance of office.

The Code of Conduct does not apply to the actions of authorities as a whole, or to the conduct of its officers and employees.

This guide is issued by the Standards Board for England under the *Local Government Act 2000* for elected, co-opted and appointed members of:

- district, unitary, metropolitan, county and London borough councils
- parish and town councils
- English and Welsh police authorities
- fire and rescue authorities (including fire and civil defence authorities)
- the London Fire and Emergency Planning Authority
- passenger transport authorities
- the Broads Authority
- national park authorities
- the Greater London Authority
- the Common Council of the City of London
- the Council of the Isles of Scilly

1 Introduction

Adopting the Model Code of Conduct

Your local authority will have until 1 October 2007 to adopt the Code of Conduct. After this time, members of authorities that have not adopted it will be automatically covered by it. To avoid confusion with the previous Code, the Standards Board for England ('the Standards Board') encourages your local authority to adopt the Code of Conduct at its first opportunity.

It is also important that the Code of Conduct is adopted in its model form, without amendment. This will give certainty to members and the public as to what standards are expected. It will ensure consistency throughout local authorities, avoiding confusion for members on more than one authority and for the public. It will also minimise the legal risk of your authority adopting additional provisions which are unenforceable. However, there is one important exception. The right to make representations, answer questions and give evidence like a member of the public when a member has a prejudicial interest is not a mandatory provision for:

Appendix 3. Model Code of Conduct Guidance for Members 2007

- parish and town councils
- English and Welsh police authorities
- fire and rescue authorities (including fire and civil defence authorities)
- the London Fire and Emergency Planning Authority
- passenger transport authorities
- the Broads Authority
- national park authorities
- the Greater London Authority

Therefore, this right will only apply to the above authorities if paragraph 12(2) of the Code of Conduct is adopted by them. Simply adopting the mandatory provisions will not incorporate this important change.

The ten general principles of public life

The Standards Board recommends that your local authority includes a preamble to the Code that it adopts, which outlines the ten general principles governing the conduct of members of local authorities. These ten general principles are set out in the *Relevant Authorities (General Principles) Order 2001*. They are based on the Seven Principles of Public Life set out by the Committee on Standards in Public Life and appear in full in Table 1.

These principles define the standards that members should uphold, and serve as a reminder of the purpose of the Code of Conduct.

As these principles do not create a statutory obligation for members, the Standards Board cannot accept allegations that they have been breached. However, you should be aware that a failure to act in accordance with these general principles may amount to a breach of the Code of Conduct. For example, by placing yourself in situations where your honesty and integrity may be questioned, your conduct may be "conduct which could reasonably be regarded as bringing a member's office or authority into disrepute" as stated in paragraph 5 of the Code of Conduct.

Deciding when the Code of Conduct applies to you

The Code of Conduct applies to you:
1. Whenever you act in your official capacity, including whenever you conduct the business of your authority or act, claim to act, or give the impression you are acting, in your official capacity or as a representative of your authority.
2. At any time[1], where your behaviour has led to a criminal conviction. However, only paragraphs 3(2)(c), 5 and 6(a) have effect in these circumstances when you are acting in your private capacity. Otherwise, the Code of Conduct does not apply to your private life.

---

[1] Transitional Note: Until such time as there is Parliamentary approval for amendments to section 52 of the *Local Government Act 2000* which reinstates the situation prior to Collins J's decision in *Livingstone* v. *Adjudication Panel for England* 2006, the Code of Conduct does not apply to conduct outside of the performance of your functions as a member. Only if you have engaged in an activity which has a link with the functions of your office will any conduct in your private capacity be covered by the Code of Conduct. If the legislative amendments are passed, the Code of Conduct will also apply to criminal activity which has led to a conviction.

Where you act as a representative of your authority on another relevant authority, you must, when acting for that other authority, comply with their Code of Conduct. You may also act as a representative of your authority on another body, for example as a school governor. When acting for that other body, you must comply with your authority's Code of Conduct, unless it conflicts with lawful obligations of the other body.

Table 1 The ten general principles of public life

Selflessness – members should serve only the public interest and should never improperly confer an advantage or disadvantage on any person.

Honesty and integrity – members should not place themselves in situations where
their honesty and integrity may be questioned, should not behave improperly, and should on all occasions avoid the appearance of such behaviour.

Objectivity – members should make decisions on merit, including when making appointments, awarding contracts, or recommending individuals for rewards or benefits.

Accountability – members should be accountable to the public for their actions and the manner in which they carry out their responsibilities, and should co-operate fully and honestly with any scrutiny appropriate to their particular office.

Openness – members should be as open as possible about their actions and those of their authority, and should be prepared to give reasons for those actions.

Personal judgement – members may take account of the views of others, including their political groups, but should reach their own conclusions on the issues before them and act in accordance with those conclusions.

Respect for others – members should promote equality by not discriminating unlawfully against any person, and by treating people with respect, regardless of their race, age, religion, gender, sexual orientation or disability. They should respect the impartiality and integrity of the authority's statutory officers and its other employees.

Duty to uphold the law – members should uphold the law and, on all occasions, act in accordance with the trust that the public is entitled to place in them.

Stewardship – members should do whatever they are able to do to ensure that their authorities use their resources prudently, and in accordance with the law.

Leadership – members should promote and support these principles by leadership, and by example, and should act in a way that secures or preserves public confidence.

2.General obligations under the Code of Conduct

Treating others with respect

See Paragraph 3(1) of the Code.

You must treat others with respect.

In politics, rival groupings are common, either in formal political parties or more informal alliances. It is expected that each will campaign for their ideas, and they may also seek to discredit the policies and actions of their opponents. Criticism of ideas and opinion is part of democratic debate, and does not in itself amount to bullying or failing to treat someone with respect.

Ideas and policies may be robustly criticised, but individuals should not be subject to unreasonable or excessive personal attack. This particularly applies to dealing with the public and officers. Chairs of meetings are expected to apply the rules of debate and procedure rules or standing orders to prevent abusive or disorderly conduct.

Whilst it is acknowledged that some members of the public can make unreasonable demands on members, members should, as far as possible, treat the public courteously and with consideration. Rude and offensive behaviour lowers the public's expectations and confidence in its elected representatives.

Complying with equality laws

See Paragraph 3(2)(a) of the Code.

You must not do anything which may cause your authority to breach any equality laws.

Equality laws prohibit discrimination on the grounds of sex, race, disability, religion or belief, sexual orientation and age.

The provisions of these laws are complex. In summary, there are four main forms of discrimination:

- Direct discrimination: treating people differently because of their sex, race, disability, religion or belief, sexual orientation or age.
- Indirect discrimination: treatment which does not appear to differentiate between people because of their sex, race, disability, religion or belief, sexual orientation or age, but which disproportionately disadvantages them.
- Harassment: engaging in unwanted conduct on the grounds of sex, race, disability, religion or belief, sexual orientation or age, which violates another person's dignity or creates a hostile, degrading, humiliating or offensive environment.
- Victimisation: treating a person less favourably because they have complained of discrimination, brought proceedings for discrimination, or been involved in complaining about or bringing proceedings for discrimination.

Equality laws also impose positive duties to eliminate unlawful discrimination and harassment and to promote equality. They also impose specific positive duties on certain authorities.

Under equality laws, your authority may be liable for any discriminatory acts which you commit. This will apply when you do something in your official capacity in a discriminatory manner.

You must be careful not to act in a way which may amount to any of the prohibited forms of discrimination, or to do anything which hinders your authority's fulfilment of its positive duties under equality laws. Such conduct may cause your authority to break the law, and you may find yourself subject to a complaint that you have breached this paragraph of the Code of Conduct.

Bullying and intimidation

See Paragraphs 3(2)(b) and 3(2)(c) of the Code.

You must not bully any person including other councillors, council officers or members of the public.

Bullying may be characterised as offensive, intimidating, malicious, insulting or humiliating behaviour. Such behaviour may happen once or be part of a pattern of behaviour directed at a weaker person or person over whom you have some actual or perceived influence. Bullying behaviour attempts to undermine an individual or a group of individuals, is detrimental to their confidence and capability, and may adversely affect their health.

This can be contrasted with the legitimate challenges which a member can make in challenging policy or scrutinizing performance. An example of this would be debates in the chamber about policy, or asking officers to explain the rationale for the professional opinions they have put forward. You are entitled to challenge fellow councillors and officers as to why they hold their views.

It is important that you raise issues about poor performance in the correct way and proper forum. However, if your criticism is a personal attack or of an offensive nature, you are likely to cross the line of what is acceptable behaviour.

You must not intimidate or attempt to intimidate any person who is or is likely to be a complainant, a witness, or involved in the administration of any investigation or proceedings relating to a failure to comply with the Code of Conduct.

However much you may be concerned about allegations that you or a fellow councillor failed to comply with the Code of Conduct, it is always wrong to bully, intimidate or attempt to intimidate any person involved in the investigation or hearing. Even though you may not have breached the Code of Conduct, you will have your say during any independent investigation or hearing, and you should let these processes follow their natural course.

If you intimidate a witness in an investigation about your conduct, for example, you may find yourself subject to another complaint that you breached this paragraph of the Code of Conduct.

Compromising the impartiality of officers of the authority

See Paragraph 3(2)(d) of the Code.

You must not compromise, or attempt to compromise, the impartiality of anyone who works for, or on behalf of, the authority.

You should not approach or pressure anyone who works for, or on behalf of, the authority to carry out their duties in a biased or partisan way. They must be neutral and should not be coerced or persuaded to act in a way that would undermine their neutrality. For example, you should not get officers to help you prepare party political material, or to help you with matters relating to your private business. You should not provide or offer any incentive or reward in return for acting in a particular way or reaching a particular decision.

Although you can robustly question officers in order to understand, for example, their reasons for proposing to act in a particular way, or the content of a report that they have written, you must not try and force them to act differently, change their advice, or alter the content of that report, if doing so would prejudice their professional integrity.

Disclosing confidential information

See Paragraph 4(a) of the Code.

You must not disclose confidential information, or information which you believe to be of a confidential nature, except in any of the following circumstances:

- *You have the consent of the person authorised to give it.*
- *You are required by law to do so.*
- *The disclosure is made to a third party for the purposes of obtaining professional advice (for example, your lawyer or other professional adviser) provided that person agrees not to disclose the information to any other person.*
- *The disclosure is in the public interest. This is only justified in limited circumstances, when all of the following four requirements are met:*
  - *the disclosure must be reasonable*
  - *the disclosure must be in the public interest*
  - *the disclosure must be made in good faith*
  - *the disclosure must be made in compliance with any reasonable requirements of your authority.*

In relation to the disclosure of confidential information in the public interest, the four requirements to be met are outlined in more detail below.

1. The first requirement, that the disclosure must be reasonable, requires you to consider matters such as:
    - Whether you believe that the information disclosed, and any allegation contained in it, is substantially true. If you do not believe this, the disclosure is unlikely to be reasonable.
    - Whether you make the disclosure for personal gain. If you are paid to disclose the information, the disclosure is unlikely to be reasonable.
    - The identity of the person to whom the disclosure is made. It may be reasonable to disclose information to the police or to an appropriate regulator. It is less likely to be reasonable for you to disclose the information to the world at large through the media.

- The extent of the information disclosed. The inclusion of unnecessary detail, and in particular, private matters such as addresses or telephone numbers, is likely to render the disclosure unreasonable.
- The seriousness of the matter. The more serious the matter disclosed, the more likely it is that the disclosure will be reasonable.
- The timing of the disclosure. If the matter to which the disclosure relates has already occurred, and is unlikely to occur again, the disclosure may be less likely to be reasonable than if the matter is continuing, or is likely to reoccur.
- Whether the disclosure involves your authority failing in a duty of confidence owed to another person.

2. The second requirement, that the disclosure must be in the public interest, needs to involve one or more of the following matters or something of comparable seriousness, that has either happened in the past, is currently happening, or is likely to happen in the future:

    (a) A criminal offence is committed.
    (b) Your authority or some other person fails to comply with any legal obligation to which they are subject.
    (c) A miscarriage of justice occurs.
    (d) The health or safety of any individual is in danger.
    (e) The environment is likely to be damaged.
    (f) That information tending to show any matter falling within (a) to (e) is deliberately concealed.

3. The third requirement, that the disclosure is made in good faith, will not be met if you act with an ulterior motive, for example, to achieve a party political advantage or to settle a score with a political opponent.

4. The fourth requirement, that you comply with the reasonable requirements of your authority, means that before making the disclosure you must comply with your authority's policies or protocols on matters such as whistle-blowing and confidential information. You must first raise your concerns through the appropriate channels set out in such policies or protocols.

In summary, to decide whether the disclosure is reasonable and in the public interest, you may need to conduct a balancing exercise weighing up the public interest in maintaining confidentiality against any countervailing public interest favouring disclosure. This will require a careful focus on how confidential the information is, on any potentially harmful consequences of its disclosure, and on any factors which may justify its disclosure despite these potential consequences. In some situations, it is extremely unlikely that a disclosure can be justified in the public interest. These will include where the disclosure amounts to a criminal offence, or where the information disclosed is protected by legal professional privilege.

Preventing access to information

See Paragraph 4(b) of the Code.

You must not prevent anyone getting information that they are entitled to by law.

You must not prevent any person from accessing information which they are entitled to by law. This includes information under the *Freedom of Information Act 2000* or those copies of minutes, agendas, reports and other documents of your authority which they have a right to access. To find out more about what types of information the public can access, contact the Information Commissioner's Office by visiting www.ico.gov.uk or by calling 0845 630 6060.

Disrepute

See Paragraph 5 of the Code.

You must not bring your office or authority into disrepute while acting in your official capacity, or at any time through criminal activity that leads to a criminal conviction.[2]

As a member, your actions and behaviour are subject to greater scrutiny than that of ordinary members of the public. You should be aware that your actions in both your public and private life might have an adverse impact on your office or your authority. Dishonest and deceitful behaviour in your role as a member may bring your authority into disrepute, as may conduct in your private life which results in a criminal conviction, such as dishonest, threatening or violent behaviour.

Using your position improperly

See Paragraph 6(a) of the Code.

You must not use, or attempt to use, your position improperly to the advantage or disadvantage of yourself or anyone else.

You should not use, or attempt to use, your public office either for your or anybody else's personal gain or loss. For example, your behaviour would be improper if you sought to further your own private interests through your position as a member.

In addition to paragraph 6(a), paragraph 12 is also relevant to the proper use of your position. Paragraph 12 supports your role as a community advocate, representing and speaking for the concerns of your community, even where you have a prejudicial interest. This right applies to you at meetings where you have a statutory right to speak or you are provided with the same opportunity to speak as ordinary members of the public would be allowed. If your authority does not allow members of the public to attend the relevant meeting for the purpose of speaking to it, paragraph 12 will not apply to you unless you have a statutory right to speak on the matter.

You must leave the room or chamber immediately after you have made the representations, given your evidence, or answered questions, and make no further attempt to influence the decision. If the meeting decides that you must stop speaking to the meeting, even if you have more to say, you must stop and leave the room. If you

---

[2] Transitional Note: Until such time as there is Parliamentary approval for amendments to section 52 of the *Local Government Act 2000* which reinstates the situation prior to Collins J's decision in *Livingstone v. Adjudication Panel for England* 2006, the Code of Conduct does not apply to conduct outside of the performance of your functions as a member. Only if you have engaged in an activity which has a link with the functions of your office will any conduct in your private capacity be covered by the Code of Conduct. If the legislative amendments are passed, the Code of Conduct will also apply to criminal activity which has led to a conviction.

fail to comply with the meeting's direction or paragraph 12 of the Code of Conduct, you may be found to have improperly influenced the decision.

The authority's resources

See Paragraph 6(b)(i) of the Code.

You must only use or authorise the use of the resources of the authority in accordance with its requirements.

Where your authority provides you with resources (for example telephone, computer and other IT facilities, transport or support from council employees), you must only use these resources or employees for carrying out your local authority business and any other activity which your authority has authorised you to use them for.

You must be familiar with the rules applying to the use of these resources made by your authority. Failure to comply with your authority's rules is likely to amount to a breach of the Code of Conduct.

If you authorise someone (for example a member of your family) to use your authority's resources, you must take care to ensure that this is allowed by your authority's rules.

Using resources for proper purposes only

See Paragraphs 6(b)(ii) and 6(c) of the Code.

You must make sure you use the authority's resources for proper purposes only. It is not appropriate to use, or authorise others to use, the resources for political purposes, including party political purposes. When using the authority's resources, you must have regard, if applicable, to any Local Authority Code of Publicity made under the Local Government Act 1986.

You should never use council resources for purely political purposes, including designing and distributing party political material produced for publicity purposes.

However, your authority may authorise you to use its resources and facilities for political purposes in connection with your authority's business. For example, holding surgeries in your ward and dealing with correspondence from your constituents. In this case, you must be aware of the limitations placed upon such use for these purposes. Using your authority's resources outside of these limitations is likely to amount to a breach of the Code of Conduct.

Considering advice provided to you and giving reasons

See Paragraph 7 of the Code.

(*Please note*: paragraph 7 is not mandatory for parish councils. However, your parish may choose to include an obligation to take account of your clerk's advice in the Code your authority adopts.)

You must have regard to advice from your monitoring officer or chief finance officer where they give it under their statutory duties.

If you seek advice, or advice is offered to you, for example, on whether or not you should register a personal interest, you should have regard to this advice before you make your mind up. Failure to do so may be a breach of the Code of Conduct.

You must give reasons for all decisions in accordance with statutory requirements and any reasonable requirements imposed by your authority. Giving reasons for decisions is particularly important in relation to regulatory decisions and decisions where people's rights are affected.

Where members disagree with officer recommendations in making a decision, members will need to take particular care in giving clear reasons for the decision.

3. Personal and prejudicial interests

Personal interests

Key points:

Two types of personal interest

You have a **personal interest** in any business of your authority where it relates to or is likely to affect:

(a) An interest that you must **register**.

(b) An interest that is not on your register, but where the well-being or financial position of you, members of your family, or people with whom you have a close association, is likely to be affected by the business of your authority more than it would affect the majority of:

- inhabitants of the ward or electoral division affected by the decision (in the case of authorities with electoral divisions or wards)
- inhabitants of the Assembly constituency affected by the decision (in the case of the Greater London Authority)
- inhabitants of the authority's area (in all other cases)

These two categories of personal interests are explained in this section. If you declare a personal interest you can remain in the meeting, speak and vote on the matter, unless your personal interest is also a **prejudicial interest**. What constitutes a prejudicial interest is outlined in the next section.

Effect of having a personal interest in a matter

You must declare that you have a personal interest, and the nature of that interest, before the matter is discussed or as soon as it becomes apparent to you except in limited circumstances. Even if your interest is on the register of interests, you must declare it in the meetings where matters relating to that interest are discussed, unless an exemption applies. When an exemption may be applied is explained opposite.

Appendices

Exemption to the rule on declaring a personal interest to the meeting

An exemption applies where your interest arises solely from your membership of, or position of control or management on:

1. any other body to which you were appointed or nominated by the authority
2. any other body exercising functions of a public nature (for example, another local authority). In these exceptional cases, provided that you do not have a prejudicial interest, you only need to declare your interest if and when you speak on the matter.

Example: if you are attending a council debate on education policy and are also a local education authority appointed governor, you would only need to declare an interest if and when you decided to speak during the debate. If you do not want to speak to the meeting on the decision, you may vote on the matter without making a declaration.

(a) Interests you must register

> Key points:
> All members have to provide a record of their interests in a public register of interests.
> You must tell your monitoring officer in writing (in the case of a parish councillor, perhaps through your clerk) within 28 days of taking office, or within 28 days of any change to your register of interests, of any interests which fall within the categories set out in the Code of Conduct, outlined below.

You need to register your interests so that the public, authority staff and fellow members know which of your interests might give rise to a conflict of interest. The register is a document that can be consulted when (or before) an issue arises, and so allows others to know what interests you have, and whether they might give rise to a possible conflict of interest. The register also protects you. You are responsible for deciding whether or not you should declare an interest in a meeting, but it can be helpful for you to know early on if others think that a potential conflict might arise. It is also important that the public know about any interest that might have to be declared by you or other members, so that decision making is seen by the public as open and honest. This helps to ensure that public confidence in the integrity of local governance is maintained.

As previously mentioned, you must tell your monitoring officer in writing within 28 days of taking office, or within 28 days of any change to your register of interests, of any interests which fall within the categories set out in the Code of Conduct. These categories include:

- Your membership or position of control or management in:
  - any other bodies to which you were appointed or nominated by the authority
  - any bodies **exercising functions of a public nature** (described below), or

directed to charitable purposes, or whose principal purposes include the influence of public opinion or policy, including any political party or trade union

- Your job(s) or business(es).
- The name of your employer or people who have appointed you to work for them.
- The name of any person who has made a payment to you in respect of your election, or expenses you have incurred in carrying out your duties.
- The name of any person, company or other body which has a place of business or land in the authority's area, and in which you have a shareholding of more than £25,000 (nominal value) or have a stake of more than 1/100th of the share capital of the company.
- Any contracts between the authority and yourself, your firm (if you are a partner) or a company (if you are a paid director or if you have a shareholding as described above) including any lease, licence from the authority and any contracts for goods, services or works. Where the contract relates to use of land or a property, the land must be identified on the register.
- Any gift or hospitality over the value of £25 that you receive as a member and the person you believe to be the source of the gift or hospitality.
- Any land and property in the authority's area in which you have a beneficial interest (or a licence to occupy for more than 28 days) including, but not limited to, the land and house you live in and any allotments you own or use.

If you have sensitive employment, which you would like to withhold from the register of interests, please see below for more information.

What is 'a body exercising functions of a public nature'?

The phrase 'a body exercising functions of a public nature' has been subject to broad interpretation by the courts for a variety of different purposes. Although it is not possible to produce a definitive list of such bodies, here are some of the criteria to consider when deciding whether or not a body meets that definition:

- Does that body carry out a public service?
- Is the body taking the place of local or central government in carrying out the function?
- Is the body (including one outsourced in the private sector) exercising a function delegated to it by a public authority?
- Is the function exercised under legislation or according to some statutory power?
- Can the body be judicially reviewed?

Unless you answer 'yes' to one of the above questions, it is unlikely that the body in your case is exercising functions of a public nature.

Examples of bodies included in this definition: regional and local development agencies, other government agencies, other councils, public health bodies, council owned companies exercising public functions, arms'-length management organisations carrying out housing functions on behalf of your authority, school governing bodies. If you need further information or specific advice on this matter, please contact your monitoring officer.

(b) Interests that are not on your register

> Key points:
>   You have a personal interest in a matter if that matter affects the **well-being or financial position** of you, members of your **family**, or people with whom you have a **close association**, more than it would affect the majority of people in the **ward or electoral division** affected by the decision, or in the authority's area or constituency.

You must also look at how any matter would affect your interests or those of members of your family or close associates. This includes:

- your and their jobs and businesses
- your and their employers, firms you or they are a partner of, and companies you or they are a director of
- any person or body who has appointed you, members of your family or close associates, to any position
- corporate bodies in which you or they have a shareholding of more than £25,000 (nominal value)

What does 'affecting well-being or financial position' mean?
The term 'well-being' can be described as a condition of contentedness and happiness. Anything that could affect your quality of life, either positively or negatively, is likely to affect your well-being.

A personal interest can affect you, your family or close personal associates positively and negatively. So if you or they have the potential to gain or lose from a matter under consideration, a personal interest would need to be declared in both situations.

Who is a member of your family or close associate?
A member of your family should be given a very wide meaning. It includes a partner (someone you are married to, your civil partner, or someone you live with in a similar capacity), a parent, a parent-in-law, a son or daughter, a stepson or stepdaughter, the child of a partner, a brother or sister, a brother or sister of your partner, a grandparent, a grandchild, an uncle or aunt, a nephew or niece, and the partners of any of these people.

A person with whom you have a close association is someone that you are in either regular or irregular contact with over a period of time who is more than an acquaintance. It is someone a reasonable member of the public might think you would be prepared to favour or disadvantage when discussing a matter that affects them. It may be a friend, a colleague, a business associate or someone whom you know through general social contacts.

Appendix 3. Model Code of Conduct Guidance for Members 2007

What if I belong to an authority without wards?

If you are a member of an authority that does not have wards, you will need to declare a personal interest whenever you consider a matter in a meeting of your authority if it affects the well-being or financial position of you, your family, or people with whom you have a close association, more than it would affect other people in your authority's area.

What if I am not aware of my personal interest?

Your obligation to disclose a personal interest to a meeting only applies when you are aware of or ought to be aware of the existence of the personal interest. Clearly you cannot be expected to declare something of which you are unaware. It would be impractical to expect you to research into the employment, business interests and other activities of all your close associates and relatives. However, you should not ignore the existence of interests which, from the point of view of a reasonable and objective observer, you should have been aware.

Prejudicial interests

1. What is a prejudicial interest?

Key points:
Your personal interest will also be a **prejudicial interest** in a matter if all of the following conditions are met:

(a) The matter does not fall within one of the **exempt categories** of decisions.
(b) The matter affects **your financial interests** or relates to a **licensing or regulatory matter**.
(c) A member of the public, who knows the relevant facts, would **reasonably think your personal interest is so significant** that it is likely to prejudice your judgement of the public interest.

An explanation of each of these points follows.

(a) Exempt categories of decisions

Paragraph 10(2)(c) of the Code of Conduct states that a member will not have a prejudicial interest if the matter relates to any of the following functions of their authority:

- Housing: if you hold a tenancy or lease with the authority, as long as the matter does not relate to your particular tenancy or lease.
- School meals or school transport and travelling expenses: if you are a parent or guardian of a child in full-time education or you are a parent governor, unless it relates particularly to the school your child attends.
- Statutory sick pay: if you are receiving this, or are entitled to this.

- An allowance, payment or indemnity for members.
- Any ceremonial honour given to members.
- Setting council tax or a precept.

(b) Financial interests and licensing or regulatory matters

You can only have a prejudicial interest in a matter if it falls into one of the following two categories:

(a) The matter affects your financial position or the financial position of any person or body through whom you have a personal interest.

   Examples: an application for grant funding to a body on your register of interests; a contract for services between the authority and that body; or leasing a property to or from a close associate or member of your family. Your financial position can be affected directly or indirectly, favourably or unfavourably, substantially or marginally.

(b) The matter relates to an approval, consent, licence, permission or registration that affects you or any person or body with which you have a personal interest.

   Examples: considering a planning or licensing application made by you or a body on your register of interests; Licensing Act licences; pet shop and dog breeding licensing; petroleum licences; street trading licences; taxi licensing; consent, approval or permission pursuant to a contractual document such as a lease or commercial contract; street collection permit; or lottery registration.

(c) What is so significant that it is likely to prejudice your judgement?

If a reasonable member of the public with knowledge of all the relevant facts would think that your judgement of the public interest might be prejudiced, then you have a prejudicial interest.

You must ask yourself whether a member of the public – if he or she knew all the relevant facts – would think that your personal interest was so significant that it would be likely to prejudice your judgement. In other words, the interest must be perceived as likely to harm or impair your ability to judge the public interest.

The mere existence of local knowledge, or connections within the local community, will not normally be sufficient to meet the test. There must be some factor that might positively harm your ability to judge the public interest objectively. The nature of the matter is also important, including whether a large number of people are equally affected by it or whether you or a smaller group are particularly affected.

Some general principles must be remembered when applying this test. You should clearly act in the public interest and not in the interests of family or close associates. You are a custodian of the public purse and the public interest and your behaviour and decisions should reflect this responsibility.

Example: you would have a prejudicial interest in a planning application proposal if a member of your family lives next to the proposed site. This is because your family member would be likely to be affected by the application to a greater extent than the majority of the inhabitants of the ward affected by the decision (or authority, if your authority does not have wards) and this gives you a personal interest in the issue. The existence of the close family tie means a reasonable member of the public might think that it would prejudice your view of the public interest when considering the planning application. It does not matter whether it actually would or not.

2. What to do when you have a prejudicial interest

Even where you have a prejudicial interest, the Code of Conduct supports your role as a community advocate and enables you in certain circumstances to represent your community and to speak on issues important to them and to you. However, this right is not mandatory for certain types of authorities (including parish councils and police authorities). For such authorities it will only apply if paragraph 12(2) of the code is expressly adopted by your authority and the public are allowed to speak to meetings of your authority. Simply adopting the mandatory provisions will not incorporate this important change.

Key points:

If you have a **prejudicial interest** in a matter being discussed at a meeting, you must declare that you have a prejudicial interest and the nature of that interest as soon as that interest becomes apparent to you. You should then leave the room, **unless members of the public are allowed to make representations, give evidence or answer questions about the matter,** by statutory right or otherwise. If that is the case, you can also attend the meeting for that purpose.

However, you must immediately leave the room once you have finished or when the meeting decides that you have finished (if that is earlier). You cannot remain in the public gallery to observe the vote on the matter. In addition, you must not seek to **improperly influence** a decision in which you have a prejudicial interest. This rule is similar to your general obligation not to use your position as a member improperly to your or someone else's advantage or disadvantage.

Do I have a statutory right to speak to the meeting?

The Code of Conduct does not provide you with a general right to speak to a meeting where you have a prejudicial interest. However, in limited circumstances, legislation may provide you with a right to speak (for example, licensing hearings and standards hearings) which the Code of Conduct recognises. If so, you will be allowed to exercise that right to speak. Your monitoring officer should be able to confirm whether this is relevant to your case.

If I don't have a statutory right, will I be allowed to speak to the meeting?

The Code of Conduct aims to provide members with the same rights as ordinary members of the public to speak on certain matters in meetings, despite having a prejudicial interest. These rights are usually governed by your authority's constitution, procedure rules or standing orders, and may be subject to conditions including time imits or the fact that representations can only be made in writing.

If an ordinary member of the public would be allowed to speak to a meeting about an item, you should be provided with the same opportunity. You will be able to make representations, answer questions or give evidence, even if you have a prejudicial interest in the item. You may not take part in the discussion or observe the vote.

When must I leave the room where the meeting is held?
You must leave immediately after you have made your representations, given evidence or answered questions, and before any debate starts. If the meeting decides that you should finish speaking, despite your intention to say more, you must comply with the meeting's decision. Although members of the public may be allowed to observe the discussion and vote on the matter, you are not allowed to do so and must leave the room immediately. Failure to do so may be viewed as an attempt to **improperly influence** the meeting.

What does improperly influencing a decision mean?
You must not use your position or attempt to use your position improperly to further your own interests in a way that is not open to ordinary members of the public. Clear examples of improper influence would be using coercion, harassment, inducement or pressure to influence a matter. It may also be improper if you refuse to leave the meeting, or continue to speak to a meeting, on a matter in which you have a prejudicial interest, after the meeting has decided that you must stop speaking and leave.

What if the public are not allowed to speak to the meeting on the matter?
If an ordinary member of the public is not allowed to speak on the matter, you cannot do so if you have a prejudicial interest. You must leave the room where the debate is being held and not seek to influence the debate in any way.

This may be the case, for example, where your authority is discussing a confidential matter in closed session or does not have procedure rules or standing orders in place that allow members of the public to speak at a meeting of your authority. Like the public, you are not allowed to participate if you have a prejudicial interest. However, where the public may be allowed to sit in the public gallery to observe the meeting, you ill be required to leave the room during the debate and vote.

If I have a prejudicial interest, how else can I influence the decision?
You can still present your views to the meeting through other means and influence the decision in a way that is not improper. For example, you can:

- Make written representations in your private capacity. The Standards Board recommends that the existence and nature of the interest should be disclosed in such representations. You should not seek preferential consideration for your representations. Such written representations should be addressed to officers rather than other members of the authority.
- Use a professional representative to make, for example, a planning application on your behalf.
- Arrange for another member of your authority to represent the views of your constituents on matters in which you have a prejudicial interest.

3. Dispensations

If I have a prejudicial interest, can I obtain a dispensation to allow me to take part in the meeting?

Key points:

You can apply in writing to your local standards committee for a dispensation on one of the following grounds:

- over 50 per cent of the authority or committee members would be prevented from taking a full part in a meeting because of prejudicial interests
- the political balance at the meeting would be upset[1]

You must apply for a dispensation individually and not as a group or authority. If the standards committee approves your application, it must grant the dispensation in writing and before the meeting is held. If you need a dispensation, you should apply for one as soon as is reasonably possible. Only the standards committee can grant the dispensation and will do so at its discretion. The standards committee will need to balance the public interest in preventing members with prejudicial interests from taking part in decisions, against the public interest in decisions being taken by a reasonably representative group of members of the authority. If failure to grant a dispensation will result in an authority or committee not achieving a quorum, this may well constitute grounds for granting a dispensation.

The Standards Board cannot grant dispensations or advise on whether or not they should be granted. For further advice on dispensations, you should contact your monitoring officer.

4. Special categories of interest

1. Gifts and hospitality

Key points:

You must register any gifts or hospitality **worth £25 or over** that you receive **in connection with your official duties as a member**, and the source of the gift or hospitality.

You must register the gift or hospitality and its source within 28 days of

---

[1] Please note there is currently a problem with the drafting of the Dispensation Regulations. The political balance criterion is linked to an authority being unable to comply with its duty under section 15(4) of the *Local Government and Housing Act 1989*. This duty requires the appointment of committees that reflect the overall political balance of an authority. However, the duty does not arise in relation to individual meetings either of the authority or its committees. For this reason it is difficult to envisage circumstances in which the criterion would be met. Until such time as the appropriate amendments are made to the Regulations it is not likely that dispensations would be granted on the basis of the political balance criterion.

receiving it. Like other interests in your register of interests, you automatically have a **personal interest** in a matter under consideration if it is likely to affect a person who gave you a gift or hospitality that is registered. If that is the case, you must declare the existence and nature of the gift or hospitality, the person who gave it to you, how the business under consideration relates to that person and then decide whether that interest is also a **prejudicial interest**.

Once three years have passed since you registered the gift or hospitality in your register of interests, your obligation to disclose that interest to any relevant meeting ceases.

Is the gift or hospitality connected to my official duties as a member?

You should ask yourself, would I have been given this if I was not on the council? If you are in doubt as to the motive behind a gift or hospitality, we recommend that you register it or speak to your monitoring officer or your parish clerk where appropriate. You do not need to register gifts and hospitality which are not related to your role as a member, such as Christmas gifts from your friends and family, or gifts which you do not accept. However, you should always register a gift or hospitality if it could be perceived as something given to you because of your position or if your authority requires you to.

What if I do not know the value of a gift or hospitality?

The general rule is, if in doubt as to the value of a gift or hospitality, you should register it, as a matter of good practice and in accordance with the principles of openness and accountability in public life. You may have to estimate how much a gift or hospitality is worth. Also, an accumulation of small gifts you receive from the same source over a short period that add up to £25 or over should be registered.

2. Overview and scrutiny committee meetings

Please note: this section will not apply to parish and town councils, English and Welsh police authorities, fire and rescue authorities (including fire and civil defence authorities), the London Fire and Emergency Planning Authority, passenger transport authorities, the Broads Authority, national park authorities and the Greater London Authority.

You have a prejudicial interest in any business before an overview and scrutiny committee or sub-committee meeting where both of the following requirements are met:

- That business relates to a decision made (whether implemented or not) or action taken by your authority's executive or another of your authority's committees, sub-committees, joint committees or joint sub-committees.
- You were a member of that decision making body at that time and you were present at the time the decision was made or action taken.

If the overview and scrutiny committee is checking a decision which you were involved in making you may be called to attend the meeting to give evidence or answer questions on the matter. However, you will not be able to attend the meeting in this manner unless your authority's constitution or standing orders allow members of the public to attend the overview and scrutiny committee for the same purpose. You will, however, be able to attend the meeting to give evidence or answer questions if you are a leader or cabinet member of an authority operating executive arrangements, provided you follow the normal rules for executive members who have personal and prejudicial interests.

3. Executive or cabinet roles

Please note: this section will not apply to parish and town councils, English and Welsh police authorities, fire and rescue authorities (including fire and civil defence authorities), the London Fire and Emergency Planning Authority, passenger transport authorities, the Broads Authority, national park authorities, the Greater London Authority or any other authorities that do not have executive arrangements. If you are a leader or cabinet member of an authority operating executive arrangements, you must follow the normal rules for executive members who have personal and prejudicial interests.

If your interest is personal but not prejudicial, you can advise the executive on the issue and take part in executive discussions and decisions as long as you declare your interest. You can also exercise delegated powers in the matter as long as you record the existence and nature of your personal interest.

If you are an executive member who can take individual decisions, and you have a prejudicial interest in a decision, your authority may make other arrangements as set out in sections 14–16 of the *Local Government Act 2000*. This means that the decision can be taken by an officer, another cabinet member, the full executive, or a committee of the executive.

Although you have a prejudicial interest in a matter, you may be able to make representations, answer questions and give evidence as long as a member of the public would have the same rights, but you are barred from decision-making about that matter individually or in cabinet. You also should not participate in any early consideration of it, or exercise any delegated powers in relation to it. If you have delegated powers in that area, you should refer the consideration and any decisions on the matter to the cabinet to avoid the perception of improper influence.

4. Sensitive information

Key points:

You may be exempt from having to include sensitive information on your register of interests. If your personal interest in a matter under discussion at a meeting is sensitive information, you will need to declare that you have a personal interest but you will not have to give any details

Sensitive information may include your sensitive employment (such as certain scientific research or the Special Forces) or other interests that are likely to create a serious risk of violence or intimidation against you or someone who lives with you.

Appendices

You should provide this information to your monitoring officer and explain your concerns regarding the disclosure of the sensitive information; including why it is likely to create a serious risk that you or a person who lives with you will be subjected to violence or intimidation. You do not need to include this information in your register of interests, if your monitoring officer agrees. Ultimately, you must decide what information to include on your publicly available register of interests.

How to contact us:

The Standards Board for England
Fourth Floor
Griffin House
40 Lever Street
Manchester M1 1BB
www.standardsboard.gov.uk

For enquiries about the Code of Conduct, please contact:
Enquiries line: 0845 078 8181
enquiries@standardsboard.gov.uk

For further copies of this publication, please contact:
publications@standardsboard.gov.uk

Reproduced with the permission of the Standards Board for England.

Appendix 4

How do I register and declare interests, and register gifts and hospitality?

DECLARING INTERESTS FLOWCHART – QUESTIONS TO ASK YOURSELF
(Non-overview and Scrutiny Meetings)

What matters are being discussed at the meeting?

Personal Interest

Does the business relate to or is it likely to affect any of your registered interests? These will include
- persons who employ you, appointed you or paid your election expenses;
- your business, company ownership, contracts or land; or
- gifts or hospitality received (in the previous three years of this Code)

or

Might a decision in relation to that business be reasonably be regarded as affecting, to a greater extent than the majority of other council tax payers, ratepayers or inhabitants of the ward affected by the decision (or the Authority's area as a whole if there is no electoral ward or division that you represent),
- your well-being or financial position; or
- the well-being or financial position of:
  - o a member of your family or any person with whom you have a close association; or
    - any person or body who employs or has appointed such persons, any firm in which they are a partner, or any company of which they are directors;
    - any person or body in whom such persons have a beneficial interest in a class of securities exceeding the nominal value of £25,000;
  - o any body of which you are a member or in a position of general control or management and to which you are appointed or nominated by your authority; or
  - o any body exercising functions of a public nature, directed to charitable purposes or whose principal purposes includes the influence of public opinion or policy (including any political party or trade union) of which you are a member or in a position of general control or management?

Yes — *No*

YOU HAVE A PERSONAL INTEREST
You must disclose the existence and nature of your personal interests as a member of the meeting (subject to certain exemptions [para 9(2)])

You can participate in the meeting and vote (or remain in the room if not a member of the meeting)

Prejudicial Interest

Would a member of the public, with knowledge of the relevant facts, reasonably regard your personal interest to be so significant that it is likely to prejudice your judgement of the public interest? *No*

Yes

- Does the matter affect your financial position or the financial position of any person or body through whom you have a personal interest?
- Does the matter relate to an approval, consent, licence, permission or registration that affects you or any person or body with which you have a personal interest?
- Does the matter not fall within one of the exempt categories of decisions? *No*

Yes

YOU HAVE A PREJUDICIAL INTEREST

Are members of the public allowed to make representations to the meeting, give evidence or answer questions about the matter by statutory right or otherwise?

Yes — *No*

You can attend the meeting for that purpose *[if your parish/town council has adopted that provision]* but IMMEDIATELY after you have finished (or when the meeting decides that you have finished) ...

You must leave the room
You cannot remain in the public gallery to observe the vote on the matter. You must not seek to improperly influence the decision

Appendix 5
Scrutiny checklist – some do's and don'ts

DO
- Remember that scrutiny:
    - Is about learning and being a 'critical friend'; it should be a positive process
    - Is not opposition
    - Should result in improved value and enhanced performance
- Take an overview and keep an eye on the wider picture
- Check performance against local standards and targets and national standards, and compare results with other authorities
- Benchmark performance against local and national performance indicators, using the results to ask more informed questions
- Use panels to get underneath performance information
- Take accout of local needs, priorities and policies
- Be persistent and inquisitive
- Ask effective questions – be constructive not judgmental
- Be open-minded and self-aware – encourage openness and self-criticism in services
- Listen to users and the public, seek the voices that are often not heard, seek the views of others – and balance all of these
- Praise good practice and performance improvement – and seek to spread this throughout the authority
- Provide feedback to those who have been involved in the review and to stakeholders
- Anticipate difficulties in Members challenging colleagues from their own party and officers challenging their colleagues
- Take time to review your own performance

DON'T
- Witch-hunt or use performance review as punishment
- Be party political/partisan
- Blame valid risk taking or stifle initiative or creativity
- Treat scrutiny as an add-on
- Get bogged down in the detail
- Be frightened to ask basic questions
- Tackle too many issues in insufficient depth
- Start without a clear objective and brief
- Underestimate the task
- Lose track of the main purpose of scrutiny
- Lack sensitivity towards other stakeholders
- Succumb to organisational inertia
- Duck facing failure – learn from it and support change and development
- Be driven by data or be paralysed by analysis – keep a strategic overview, and expect officers to provide high level information and analysis to help

This document is reproduced with the kind permission of St Edmundsbury Borough Council.

Index

Index

Index

Index

Index

Index

Index

Index

Index

Index

Index

Index